The Shell Hacker's Guide to X and Motif

The Shell Hacker's Guide to X and Motif

Alan Southerton

John Wiley & Sons, Inc.
NEW YORK / CHICHESTER / BRISBANE / TORONTO / SINGAPORE

This text is printed on acid-free paper.

Published by John Wiley & Sons, Inc.

Library of Congress Cataloging-in-Publication Data

Southerton, Alan

The Shell Hacker's Guide to X and Motif: operating system utilities, X Window System Motif window manager / Alan Southerton

p. cm.

Includes index.

ISBN 0-471-597228 (book). — ISBN 0-471-597236 (book/disk set)

Printed in the United States of America

10 9 8 7 6 5 4 3 2 1

*This book is dedicated to my loving wife,
Cameron, and all the things she has done for me.*

ABOUT THE AUTHOR

Alan Southerton is the Product Reviews Editor of *UNIXWORLD Magazine*, a McGraw-Hill publication. Mr. Southerton has written five other books, including *Modern UNIX*, *Windows 3.0 Programming Prime*r, and *Interleaf Publishing*. Mr. Southerton and his wife, Cameron McLean Wicker, a Boston-area attorney, have two sons, Thomas and William.

CONTENTS

PREFACE

Believe me, I never wanted to get deeply involved in writing what I call the Xmenu software. I should have known better than to even think about taking on a project like Xmenu. I live with the peril of UNIX every day. As someone who covers the UNIX product market—directing others in the way they critically appraise products—I knew my time could be better spent in other endeavors (most of them over the object-oriented rainbow). But I didn't listen to the doubting voice. I forged ahead anyway in my attempt to write a piece of software that would work on different UNIX boxes running the X Window System or X (or whatever you want to call it).*

I had some other parameters, of course. I didn't want to break into C programming to accomplish anything. Early in the book I toyed with the idea, and you'll see a hint of it in Chapter 4, which has a short C program to convert hexadecimal numbers. There's a way to do the same thing in the UNIX shell, however. And this was the ground I wanted to defend, my cause célèbre, my raison d'être, my possible undoing.

Other people in the industry told me I should be using this or that tool. For example, the public domain **tcl** scripting language was mentioned. So was the Visual Korn shell and Metacard, which I wrote extensively about in my fifth computer book, *Modern UNIX*. But I was having none of it. You, the readers, after all, deserve a solution or two using the tools already at your disposal. Meanwhile, my scripts began to proliferate, and my co-workers and associates began to ask if I could port the scripts to their systems.

Why was I so compulsive? Because UNIX, X, and Motif offered users and administrators so much flexibility, but hardly gave them any built-in way to access it. True, systems like the Santa Cruz Operation Inc.'s Open

* The reason I draw attention to how you refer to the X Window System is that some devotees believe you should never call it "X Windows." Other people, many of whom are involved in marketing computer goods, or computer magazine journalism, prefer to call it "X Windows."

Desktop came bundled with a desktop manager, but the users under my observation—and I did feel like a presiding physician sometimes—refused to do anything more with it than drag and drop icons. I think the malady that we all suffered from was having to use too many different operating environments. It was like the common cold of computing and everyone around me was reaching for an over-the-counter medication named Microsoft Windows.

Now I have nothing against desktop managers. In *Modern UNIX*, I delved into the desktop managers and spent untold hours making them sing in different environments. And I guess that's when the seed for the Xmenu software was formed. Even then, I found myself creating scripts and menu items so I wouldn't have to type long commands at the command line. I guess I was stubborn, but sometimes I'd rather do something with a script than take two minutes longer to do it using drag-and-drop acrobatics.

ANTI-MENU MANIACS

For as long as computers have been displaying their data on CRTs, there have been anti-menu maniacs. You especially find them in database environments and electronic publishing shops, two traditional havens for lots of menus. When you do find an anti-menu maniac, look around and see how many of his or her co-workers are merrily being productive.

I personally see the anti-menu maniac's viewpoint—because I have run across labyrinthine menus that were as convoluted as some voice mail systems. But I don't agree with the zeal with which the anti-menu maniacs prosecute their case. After all, even the bitmap button interfaces that adorn some of the most popular software on the market—and I'm not just talking UNIX software—are, in a sense, menus. Given this fact (and given the facts that desktop manager software is still in its infancy and prescient recognition software is struggling at the zygote stage), there is still a place for traditional-looking menus.

It is true that with desktop manager software you can do most of the things that Xmenu does. But you still have to be conversant in UNIX scripting, X resources, possibly window manager menu files, button bindings, and keyboard translations. On top of this, with a desktop manager you have to learn another scripting language, or some form of rules lexicon. So, by all means, learn the inner workings of the desktop manager, but in the meantime you can use Xmenu as your springboard into controlling the modern UNIX desktop. Or, for those of you who don't need to learn much, but just study an approach and structure, then look at Xmenu as a soundingboard.

The consolation prize for anti-menu maniacs when it comes to Xmenu is you don't have to use it if you don't want to. It's like a television set in the livingroom. It's there, but you don't have to turn it on.

Why? Because window managers as a rule, and Motif specifically, don't interfere with other functionality. In the X.desktop desktop manager, for example, you can run the desktop manager and use the mouse to move and copy objects, but you can still access the Motif menus by sliding the mouse to either side of the screen, and clicking there to pop up the menu. Normally, window managers pop up whenever you depress one or more buttons on the background, or root, window. But X.desktop's background window is not the root window; it is a regular everyday window that fills the screen—and manages to glue itself to the root window so no other windows can come between them. In its default configuration, X.desktop limits your access to the root window. If you use X.desktop, you can settle for the limited access, which is along either side of the screen, in a sliver of real estate about 10 pixels wide. You can also modify button binding and translation resources to allow the Motif menus to permit access from the X.desktop background window. Many users prefer to run X.desktop in a smaller window as an adjunct to—instead of a new layer on—the X and Motif environment. All in all, if you use X.desktop or another desktop manager, you should expect it to support Motif, instead of smothering it.

I have to admit that I like the global perspective that menus bring to the desktop. And it is somewhat of a tradition to link menus with the desktop in UNIX. Sun's Sunview windowing system and Interleaf's electronic system began the tradition in the mid-1980s when the UNIX workstations first became popular. In any event, the underlying mechanism for the Motif menus is what is really important. Without the mechanism—whether it comes in the form of menus or bitmap buttons—the window manager forces users into doing things in a narrowly defined way. But what if you don't like that way? I ask myself that question every time I reach for the **f.lower** function on Microsoft Windows. It just ain't there!

THE RIGHT FUNCTIONALITY

The purpose of Xmenu is not to deliver an absolutely perfect set of menu utilities. The intent of Xmenu is educational. Above all, Xmenu represents an approach to controlling the desktop, and the Xmenu software—as it appears throughout the book and on the distribution diskette—is an example of that approach. But this is not an apology. I expect some of you will use the menus. I hope others will consider using them. All in all, they increase productivity at the computer, even for users who prefer to use the command line.

As you read this book and examine the contents of the distribution diskettes, if you have them, think about which routines are appropriate to your site. The Xmenu software is extensive and you may not want to use the entire package all of the time. For example, it is possible to divide the Xmenu menus into separate components. The most natural division is along the lines of the three root menus. The *Resources Menu*, for instance, could be removed from the menu system, but a mechanism was created to allow the user to access it when necessary (see especially Chapters 8 and 10).

The Shell Hacker

Who is the shell hacker? The first image that always comes to my mind is a figure in the shadows, feverishly trying to enter a large, dark building, going through key after key on a very large key chain.

This is not a negative image. The figure in the shadows is entitled to the key chain and definitely has the right to enter the building. It's just that no one is making entry into the building easy. Not even a light has been left on. Many people would give up, try elsewhere. But the figure in the shadows is persistent and curious, and in no way malicious.

All too often, however, the term *hacker* is used to mean a villainous person. The media have skewed the meaning of the word in this direction. Even so, to many UNIX users the term is one of veneration. A hacker is someone who is capable of solving problems; someone who knows a lot about many different things. If there is a personality flaw that UNIX people see in hackers it is that they they have to be intellectually enticed to solve problems. Pure nobility is dwindling. Too many demands have been put on veteran hackers.

It is okay to be a hacker. At times, we all have to be hackers if we want to overcome a computing obstacle. If it makes you feel better—or makes your boss feel better when he or she asks you why you put in a voucher for a shell hacker's book—the correct name for computer villains is *crackers*.

ACKNOWLEDGMENTS

A book with the scope of *The Shell Hacker's Guide to X and Motif* is the stuff of a group effort. And the group that lent assistance to this project is a large one.

The roll includes David Granz, a hybrid Microsoft Windows, UNIX, and X Window System programmer, based in Wenham, Massachusetts; and Edwin Perkins, Jr., an electrical engineering consultant at the Computer Connection at MIT, who provided a true multi-environmental perspective gained from the Rensselaer Polytechnic Institute labs.

Also deserving much thanks are Natalie Engler, Assistant Editor at UNIXWORLD magazine and Emily Dawkins, Research Assistant at Newline Computer Services Inc. (Beverly, Massachusetts), which specializes in X Window System interoperability and Microsoft Windows interoperability consulting. I would also like to thank Diane Cerra, my editor at John Wiley & Sons, and her assistant, Terri Hudson, for their divine patience and high-quality approach to writing and producing computer books. Much thanks also goes to Frank Grazioli, Managing Editor at John Wiley & Sons.

My family also deserves thanks and I would be remiss for not pointing this out. My wife Cameron, sons Thomas and William, my mother Kathleen, and my niece Katie all deserve credit.

I hope *The Shell Hacker's Guide to X and Motif* is many things to many people. I have attempted to render a picture of X and Motif that addresses concerns for power users and administrators using the best windowing environment available, the X Window System.

CHAPTER 1
X Perspective

TALES IN FLEXIBILITY

UNIX has always been a flexible environment for anyone who wanted to take the time to learn how to take advantage of its flexibility. With the X Window System and the Motif window manager, its flexibility is enhanced considerably. Getting UNIX, X, and Motif to cooperate, however, isn't always that easy; it's almost as if the flexibility gets in the way of establishing a functional interface.

Sense can be made of it all: an approach or two—your own method to the madness of limitless options—and you can refine a system using UNIX, X, and Motif so that you benefit from all three environments. And this is important, because all too often UNIX has been decried as an archaic system that should be laid to rest—even though it is perhaps the best operating system available to run a graphical user interface (GUI). On the other hand, a healthy respect for UNIX—and a healthy use of shell scripts, as you'll see in the coming chapters—can optimize your use of the graphical user interface.

And who are you? You are an advanced user, capable of using the shell and not afraid of learning the UNIX commands necessary to write efficient shell scripts—that is, if you don't already know them. And you're also the type of person who wants to provide better interface methods for other users, either because it is part of your job responsibility, or because you want to advance yourself in multiuser, multitasking computing—because that is the direction in which the computer industry is moving. So read this chapter if you want. It talks about basic concepts of UNIX, X, and Motif and also focuses on some user interface issues at large.

X SERVER SUMMARY

Although *client-server computing* is a term that has been around for a long time, it solidified itself in the UNIX community—if not the entire computing community—when Sun Microsystems Inc. started a client-server advertising campaign in the early 1990s.

To some UNIX folk, it seemed absurd that Sun made itself appear as though it had just bought into the paradigm, because there was nothing special about a more powerful system supporting less powerful client systems. In fact, this was what the X Window System was all about—and had been all about since its inception in 1984.

But now, in the 1990s, client-server computing is the most important kind of computing. And when you talk to advocates of client-server computing—many of them from the PC and Apple worlds—they describe it as breaking an application into two pieces: a frontend, which handles the interface and minimal processing chores; and a backend, or engine, which resides on a remote system (probably UNIX) and serves the frontend.

This, of course, is exactly the model of the X Window System, except that it occurs at a systemwide level, not at the application level. But X failed to get its message across in as well-crafted a manner as the Sun commercial. Given its academic origins (and its total lack of a marketing organization until 1993, when the X Industry Association was formed), any message that X had was bound never to get across to the general computing public. What's more, unlike the Sun commercial, X did not lend itself to advertising slogans. Then and now, it is nearly impossible to encapsulate the functionality of X into a 30- or 60-second commercial.

The truth of the matter is that X is client-server computing. There is only one difference that exists between it and computing that relies on one or two powerful machines: The X rendition allows all systems on the network to act as server—and all systems on the network to act as client—while it adheres to the frontend/backend paradigm, even if the server and client happen to reside on the same machine, which is the case if you have a standalone UNIX workstation running X.

Even though it can't be encapsulated, the range and architecture can be succinctly summarized. The following truths are held to be self-evident by experienced X users:

- Only the server interacts with the display, keyboard, and mouse. Driving this is the X Protocol, which is hardware independent, meaning applications (clients) need not concern themselves with hardware details.

- The X server and any client can run on any system on the network, together or separately.

- The X server can manage multiple clients on the same display, but these clients don't have to originate on the same system.

- A client can communicate with multiple servers, meaning that with one command, a single instance of an application can be started on multiple systems.
- A server can manage multiple monitors attached to the same workstation. Including this capability in the windowing system is a boon for developers and users of graphics-intensive applications such as CAD and electronic design software.

It is up to the individual user and site administrator to structure X in a client-server world. How else could Sun advertise itself as a client-server company? Sun relies on the X Window System as much as any other hardware vendor in the UNIX community. Yes, it is true that Sun also had its Network File Systems (NFS) and Network Information Service (NIS) in mind when it released the advertisement. But NFS and NIS environments are likely to be found wherever X is found.

One unpardonable sin built into X is its assumption that users, businesses and marketing people wouldn't mind X changing the meaning of a few words. Okay, you might be able to accept that, but the words happened to be *client* and *server*. Yes, in the X Window System, the server is no longer a robust machine responsible for supporting lesser machines. Instead, it is a piece of software, the X server, similar in importance to the UNIX kernel, but not even necessarily located on the type of servers Sun mentioned in its advertisements. Indeed, the X server can be located on any machine on the network, including X terminals—which to the uninitiated seem more like clients.

Oh well. There's little chance now that someone can change the course of history. No one is going to propose that the X server be renamed the X kernel, not even the X Industry Association, which has to stay on friendly terms with the MIT X Consortium, which still performs all the development work for new versions of X.

So let's take a close look at the X server. On one level, it is the interface to the display hardware, which consists of the monitor, keyboard, and mouse. But it is not a simple interface like a device driver. In a way, it enriches the hardware by adding windows to the basic features it has to offer the application programmer, and ultimately, the end user. As a result, the X workstation—whether it is a UNIX-class workstation, a PC running Desqview/X, a Microsoft Windows X server, or an X terminal—is a hybrid hardware/software device. Figure 1-1 illustrates the relationship between the X server and client applications on a network.

On another level, the X server is like an operating system that governs the display technology. Everything you do in X must pass through the X server. The X server handles whatever it can by itself without passing requests to

Figure 1-1 If each system pictured is a complete X system, with server and client software, how many possible combinations of peer-to-peer access are there? Hint: Each system can run clients off all five systems—and each system can also run the X server off all five systems.

the application—such as mouse movements and requests to resize windows. This reduces a lot of programming overhead, and in a network environment, a lot of network traffic.

From a design viewpoint, the architects of the X server—the personnel at the Massachusetts Institute of Technology, including Robert Scheifler and Jim Gettys, the originators of X—decided to put as little functionality in the server as possible. This was reminiscent of the early philosophy that shaped UNIX and its once-small kernel. As a result, the X server became eminently portable and today finds itself on three major operating systems—VMS, DOS, and many different variants of UNIX.

What are the specific functions of the X server? As noted, the X server handles all keyboard and mouse input as well as all display output. More specifically, here are some of the things the server does:

- Opens, maintains, and closes windows
- Manages fonts and displays text using the fonts
- Manages the background screen (or *root window*)
- Draws monochrome and color bitmaps
- Maintains colormaps, which define colors as pixels
- Draws vector graphics objects, such as lines and circles

- Manages application resources and properties
- Manages network connections and host access

Compared with the many things that occur in a window system, these duties are few in number. In fact, much of the activity that occurs on an X Window System platform is handled by clients. First and foremost among the clients is the window manager, which is responsible for managing the user interface for windows, menus, dialog boxes, icons, and other components.

CLIENT SUMMARY

On the client side of things falls the responsibility for maintaining a given application. In fact, *client* and *application* are virtually synonymous in the X world. This book often refers to clients as *client programs*, which is redundant, but the choice of words ensures that the reader knows exactly what is being said.

Among other things, the client must assume the responsibility for communicating with the X server. It needs to do this to keep the server happy and so it can maintain its own display in its window or windows. Here are some concerns for the client program:

- Redraw the contents of its window.
- Interpret keyboard input.
- Perform application-based processing. For example, a math program would perform calculations.
- Maintain the interface components internal to the client, even though they resemble window manager components.
- Send requests to the X server and monitor and respond to events from the X server.

The concepts of *requests* and *events* are important ones in a GUI-based environment. As a desktop customizer, system administrator, or advanced user, you need not be concerned with the theoretical aspects of these topics. Requests, especially, are subject matter more appropriate for programmers. Events, however, are good to know about when it comes to customizing mouse and keyboard *bindings*. The **xev** client program, which is explained in Chapter 4, is your portal into the world of events.

There is one more client responsibility we haven't mentioned. And it is important to this book:

- Clients are responsible for retrieving and setting resources specified by users. As a result, clients are expected to provide resource statements by which the user can change colors, fonts, and many other items. Many clients also offer command-line switches to modify some, if not many, of their resources.

The main reason resources are so important to the client—and to the X Window System in general—is that they provide users and sites with a standard way to make adjustments for different types of hardware configurations, including systems running X terminals or PC-based X servers under Microsoft Windows, off the same UNIX host. Thus, in order to calibrate a presentable look and feel on each display, resources have to be configured on a per-user basis.

WINDOW MANAGER SUMMARY

The Shell Hacker's Guide to X and Motif, as its name implies, favors the Motif window manager. This is not the result of bias or even personal preference—just the recognition of trends in the UNIX industry. Also, it should be noted here that Motif is the name given to the user interface definition of the window manager, and **mwm** is the the real name of the window manager. To make things easier, however, this book refers to **mwm** as Motif.

In describing window manager generalities here, as well as in presenting scripts and menu routines throughout the rest of the book, it has been kept in mind that other window managers exist. Of these, Sun's OpenWindows is the most notable, and it will continue to have a limited role in the workstation community through the mid-1990s. Another notable window manager is **twm**, which comes standard with X. Other window managers usually originate with public domain contributions. For more information on these, access Netnews and check the **comp.sources.windows** newsgroup.

What are the window manager's responsibilities? Generally, the window manager is responsible for maintaining a consistent look and feel, as well as consistent behavior. It achieves its goals by adding *components* to each window, including menus, buttons, and frames, and by instituting a consistent functionality for these controls. It also provides a detailed set of resources, which let the user modify the appearance and behavior of the components. Additionally, most window managers come with a set of functions—the notable exception has been the first release of UNIXware from Novell Inc.

Listing the actual duties of the window manager as distinct from the duties of the X server is meaningless. The duties of the window manager and X server—to the end user and even the person configuring the system—

overlap too much. For example, Motif provides the interface mechanism to close a window—any of several ways—yet the X server performs the actual closing operation. If the X server and window manager had been conceived as a single software system like the Apple Macintosh graphical user interface, only system programmers would bother to make the distinction here. So the list of chores for the window manager includes some of those of the X server:

- Opens and closes windows
- Provides a resource interface, but does not manage resources and properties like the X server
- Manages the active window status, ensuring that only one window is the main active window
- Maintains the stacking order, or *z-order*, of windows until the user or an application changes it
- Manages the focus policy, which determines how the user makes windows active (roughly, either click-to-type or pointer-based)
- Reduces windows to icons and restores windows from icons
- Manages the icon *parking lot* either by setting icon behavior on the root window or by creating a special window like the Motif icon box
- Manages colormaps and allows the user some method of transferring the colormap to a specified application
- Provides an interface to create button and keyboard bindings
- Provides a programmable interface to create popup menus

This list could be even longer if we considered some emerging features found in public domain window managers and third-party products. For example, the requirement that a window manager provide some interface to the virtual desktop that the X server can support is a good candidate for the list. Conversely, some experts might argue that the window manager is responsible for fewer things than are on the list, and definitely question the requirements that a window manager support button and keyboard bindings and programmable menus.

XMENU SUMMARY

Although the graphical user interface movement has concentrated on providing easier-to-use tools to end users, it has often overlooked the person who is dedicated to the UNIX shell—the shell hacker. It is one of the ironies of the graphical user interface that life at the keyboard is necessarily made easier for inexperienced users, but harder for experienced users.

Many experienced users who try to rely on GUI tools often get frustrated to the point that their productivity diminishes. This is especially true when these users experiment with file navigator programs and desktop managers. In point of fact, the people who create GUI software for the UNIX system—men and women who have learned to use their systems well—balk at making the move to a complete GUI environment.

The basic assumption is that users will never get any better at using computers—so GUI tools don't have to address user-interface performance issues. They just have to work, no matter how slowly. Of course, this is one of the best-kept secrets in the computer market, and as a result, there have been few products aimed at making things easier for professional programmers and proficient users.

Xmenu explores this void, venturing into the graphical as much as the character-mode cobwebs of the shell. It acknowledges the fact that experienced users can type and might want to limit the use of the mouse, including drag and drop techniques. For example, it's a pretty hard pill to swallow if you have to click on a series of icons and execute a menu command when a **mv *.doc** only takes 0.9 seconds at the keyboard. It is even more disconcerting if you do use the GUI method to move a series of icons—representing the files—and later learn that the desktop manager didn't move the files, but rather made symbolic links to the files located in the new directory you created. And so goes the irony of GUIs.

There are many areas in which GUI tools can aid experienced users, however. Whether the tools are menus or full-fledged applications that include buttons, list boxes, and dialog boxes, experienced users should not consider them all bad. So many users are frustrated doing things the GUI way, because they know they could be doing it much faster the old-fashioned shell hacker's way. What is needed is a blending of the two worlds—and the Xmenu menus make an attempt at this.

First of all, the Xmenu menus make extensive use of the old—the commands and utilities UNIX is famous for—to complement the new. The workhorse commands in the more than 120 scripts that accompany the Xmenu menus include **cat**, **cp**, **cut**, **echo**, **egrep**, **grep**, **join**, **mv**, **sed**, and **set** among others. All scripts are programmed for the Bourne shell, which is the UNIX convention, and use the range of script constructs, including **if** statements, and **for** and **while** loops; particularly heavy use is made of **case** statements.

The meeting ground for the old and the new is the Xterm window.* This is where you can write and test your own scripts in a GUI environment. And in many cases, it is Xterm that allows you to execute scripts from a GUI-based mechanism, such as a menu command (although any software that lets you run a subshell would suffice). Additionally, Xterms can serve as your primary input and output mechanism in the GUI world. Experienced scripters should rejoice at this, because there is a future for the databases and other programs you have built over the years. Just let Xterm handle all the input and output for you. And if you have ever done any script programming that involves cursor manipulation, you'll find it even easier in Xterm. In addition to some built-in resource options, Xterm supports escape sequences that allow you to position the cursor using scripts. Xterm also provides the first character-mode terminal interface that is truly portable across different UNIX variants and hardware platforms.

The Xmenu scripts and the different ways of using Xterm yield an extensive menu system that once again blends Xterms and UNIX commands to provide the end user with a GUI interface. For example, the **talk** command is used with an Xterm and provides the familiar user-to-user interface, but the command is invoked from a menu item, not the command line. This is another level of melding the old with the new: it is both the method and product of the Xmenu scripts.

Otherwise, in a nutshell, the Xmenu menu software consists of three main menus, a modified default menu, and several other menus bound to keys. Most of the key-accessible menus are simply submenus in the main menu structure. In some cases, the menu appears identical to its counterpart in the main structure, but other times it has been slightly modified.

Power Hacking

While some might wonder why anyone would want to talk about maximizing their efficiency at using the shell, there's reason to talk about it, even in a GUI world—especially in a GUI world.

The standard UNIX shells, plus any public domain shell you might be familiar with, always concern themselves with making life easier for users who spend long hours at the command line. But speaking of long hours, it usually takes long hours to become skilled enough at the shell before you begin to cash in on its special tools. For example, new C shell users might take to **!!** right away, but it will likely take them days, months, or even years

* In this book, frequently mentioned commands, utilities, and X client programs are capitalized for text purposes. Leading this convention is Xterm, which because of its importance, deserves the respect of a proper noun.

to learn the rest of the symbols that recall previous commands, or parts of commands.

Working in an Xterm, the GUI contribution to the sage art of shell hacking, adds a modern dimension. Here are a few things you should think about doing in Xterms if you are not already doing them:

- Display man pages and use the scrollbar to scroll through previous material.
- Program your PageUp and PageDown keys to page through previous material.
- Use the cut and paste buffer to execute the same command in different Xterms.
- Use the cut and paste buffer to reexecute all or parts of previous commands.
- Display the command history in the C and Korn shells and cut and paste previous commands.
- Cut and paste history items into a file and create shell scripts on-the-fly.
- Program a function key to act as a paste button and paste commands and text.

Not only is this a reason to propagate the use of Xterms at your organization, it is a reason to reevaluate the demise of the character-based way of looking at things. Users may not be as efficient using GUI applications in all cases, especially if many of those users have experience in character-based applications. Maybe this explains why systems such as IBM's AS/400 computers continue to be popular. Maybe a lot of users out there are satisfied with character-based environments, and are, or will be, content with windowing systems that provide a way to work in multiple character-mode sessions at the same time.

The reality, as so often is the case, will likely be a blend of the old and the new, until the new becomes so proficient that it does the old as well as the old did it in the first place. Until then, don't overlook Xterm—which already does a lot of character-based things better than character-based terminals can.

X MISCELLANY

There are many different things—a mix of software products, industry groups, and plain old phenomena—that you need to know about in order to enhance your skills in UNIX and the X Window System. The one sure thing about the UNIX and X environment is that you always can learn something new. The following sections summarize some subjects with which you should be concerned on a regular basis.

Your Operating System

The word *variant* used to have a lot of meaning in the UNIX community and it still does among some people. Succinctly, it refers to a vendor implementation of UNIX. This is as opposed to the official System V release of UNIX as, for many years, determined by AT&T. The irony here is that AT&T never made a popular hardware platform to run UNIX, so some other vendor's variant has always been better loved.

Variant probably started losing its meaning with the serious advent of BSD, the Berkeley Software Distribution from the University of California at Berkeley, distributed into commercial computing in various ways. The most notable way was through Sun's adoption of much of BSD in SunOS. As a result, using *variant* to describe BSD was not quite getting the point across—after all, BSD was built from the ground up as a different incarnation of UNIX. Once again, however, with Sun now having moved to System V, replacing SunOS with Solaris, it is more a matter of variant.

Whatever you call it, realizing there are different UNIXes in the world is necessary for anyone interested in configuring and administering UNIX systems in a heterogeneous environment. For example, while many of the scripts that support the Xmenu menus are totally portable, others are not. When this is the case, a note is made of the fact—sometimes, an alternative command is even included in the script. So, just as you should be aware of different versions of X—if you still have X11R4 running—you should also be aware of different versions, or variants, of UNIX. Table 1-1 presents the major variants you might encounter.

Finally, among some of the versions of UNIX in Table 1-1, there are special PC versions or Intel-based hardware. IBM, which offers the most disparate PC version compared with its workstation version, offers AIX for PCs. Sun, which once came out with a version of SunOS for its 386/i computers, now offers Solaris for 486 and later PCs. And Next, which started its graphical NextStep operating system on Motorola 68030 and 68040 workstations, offers NextStep for advanced PCs. Additionally, there are more than 15 independent vendors offering UNIX for PCs. Of course, this number dwindles from time to time, but just as it does, yet another vendor begins selling a PC version of UNIX.

Table 1-1 Major UNIX Implementations

Product	Influences	Vendor
AIX	BSD, SVR3, OSF/1	IBM
HPUX	SVR3, SVR4	Hewlett-Packard
NextStep	BSD, Mach kernel	Next Computer Inc.
OSF/1	SVR3, BSD, Ultrix	DEC
Solaris	SVR4, SunOS	Sun Microsystems
SunOS	SVR3, BSD	Sun Microsystems
Ultrix	BSD, SVR3	DEC
UNIXware	SVR4	Novell Inc.
V/386	SVR3, XENIX	Santa Cruz Operation

The MIT X Consortium

The Massachusetts Institute of Technology (Cambridge, Mass.) is crucial to the continued development of the X Window System. It decides which new technologies go into X, develops them, and distributes them to the public domain.

With about 100 members, including Digital Equipment Corp., Hewlett-Packard, IBM, and the Santa Cruz Operation, the consortium actually serves as the development arm of the X industry. In fact, before the formation of the X Industry Association (Freemont, Calif.), the X Consortium was the only organization that held any world view regarding X. All the vendors involved—if they weren't also supporting rival window systems—had their own particular brand of X to impart. And every one of them left the letter X out of the name they ultimately chose for their windowing system.

The consortium was founded by the X Window System's principal inventor, Robert W. Scheifler. The consortium's roots are in MIT's Project Athena, which was responsible for the first two versions of X. In 1988, MIT, Apple, AT&T, DEC, HP, and Sun contributed $150,000 each to form the consortium. At about the same time, the OSF and UNIX International formed, and the feud over window managers—OSF/Motif versus Open Look—began to overshadow the consortium's efforts.

The X Consortium differs from the Open Software Foundation (Cambridge, Mass.) because it provides the technology for OSF/Motif. But the two organizations have much in common and have most of the same member vendors. The main difference is that historically Sun refrained from joining the OSF. With the biggest desktop workstation vendor absent, the only place for joint and meaningful decisions was the X Consortium. Today, however, the less formal alliance known as the Cooperative Open Software Environment (COSE) provides a forum for the major vendors to share their technology.

The X Consortium is the best source for finding out what is going to happen to X next. Major revisions in X11R6, which should carry X into the later part of this decade, include a multithreaded X server, a low bandwidth protocol to support 9600 baud modems, enhancements to 2-D graphics and image processing, additional internationalization features, a C++ programming interface based on the Interviews toolkit, hardware synchronization extensions, and a comprehensive set of performance tests.

Going through channels with your system software vendor is one way to get information on X, but email is your best bet. Most of the consortium's affairs are conducted by email. In this sense, the consortium is vastly accessible. In fact, anyone might answer a query that you post to the net: an MIT staff engineer, an engineer from one of the big systems vendors, or just another user like you. If you don't have netnews access, you can get placed on the Consortium's **xpert** mailing list by sending a request to **xpert-request@expo.lcs.mit.edu**; or get on a general announcements mailing list by sending a request to **x-announce-request@expo.lcs.mit.edu**.

You can also get information on X by joining a local chapter of the X User's Group (XUG). You can send email to (**xug@ics.com**) for membership information. XUG has about 16 chapters in the United States as well as chapters in Japan, Israel, and Italy. Other X organizations include: the Bay Area Motif Developers Group (**edmark@isi.com**); the French X User Group (phone: +33 99 54500); the European X User Group (**brwk@doc.-ic.ac.uk**); and the German X User Group (**mcvax!unitdo-!tub!olaf**).

The Open Software Foundation

The express purpose of the Open Software Foundation (OSF) is to provide new systems software technology to its member vendors. It is a private organization—a cartel, so to speak—and has actually come under fire for stifling free market competition. But its philosophical, if not legal, protection from such charges is its mission to deliver industry-standard software to the computer industry.

Nowhere has the OSF been more successful than with Motif. Even against the popularity of the Sun Open Look interface—and in spite of the quest of desktop manager software to displace the importance of the window manager—OSF/Motif has prevailed. Many factors are responsible, not the least of which is the fact that Motif closely resembles Microsoft Windows. In fact, Microsoft Windows and OSF/Motif are actually descended from the same graphical user interface, namely the OS/2 Presentation Manager, in its incarnation during Microsoft's tenure with OS/2.

The Motif window manager is only the runtime component of the OSF's overall Motif environment. For programmers, they make available the Motif toolkit and widget set, which is based on the Xt Intrinsics programming component of the X Window System as shown in Figure 1-2.

In addition to the programming component, Motif supports the User Interface Language (UIL). The language is not so much designed for users to interface with Motif as it is for programmers to interface with Motif's widgets. The UIL language, in simplified terms as compared with function calls with numerous parameters, lets programmers build interfaces in separate files. UIL files are then compiled along with the rest of the code for the programmer.

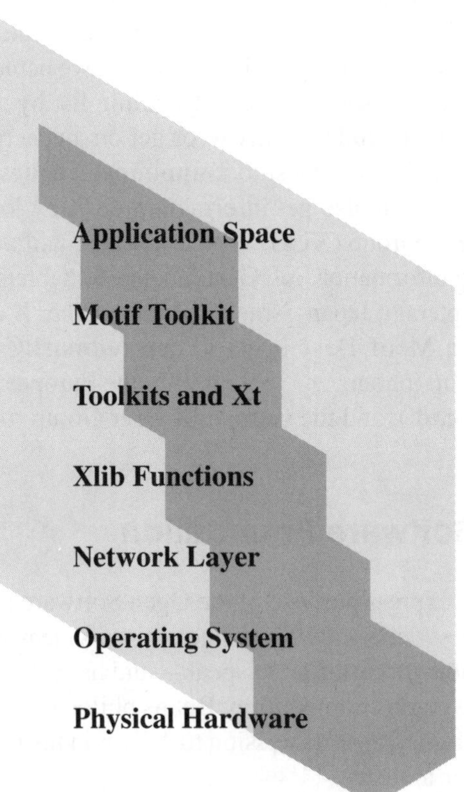

Figure 1-2 Development model for the X Window System and Motif.

The component for compiling UIL code is the Motif Resource Manager (MRM). Neither UIL nor MRM have been as successful as third-party products that offer a complete User Interface Management System (UIMS). The power of UIMS software is that it provides the programmer with GUI tools to build widgets and connect blocks of program logic together, among other things.

The OSF has another responsibility when it comes to Motif. It is charged with being the sole overseer of the Motif Style Guide. This is no small task, and as a result, the OSF operates two certification programs. The first confirms whether a third-party implementation of the Motif window manager conforms with industry standards—the OSF's own standards as well as ones it has adopted from other organizations. Second, the OSF certifies applications and produces an extensive self-test for vendors. In any event, the OSF's extensive distribution of its *OSF/Motif Style Guide* (ISBN —13-640616-5) has played a major role in the success of Motif.

Network Services

Any summary of a modern computing environment would be negligent if it omitted the Network File System (NFS) and the Network Information System (NIS). After Ethernet (the UNIX standard governing the physical layer of the network) and TCP/IP (the UNIX standard for the network and transport layers), NFS and NIS are without rival. Only X itself, with remote display sharing, has even begun to approach the importance of NFS and NIS.

The NFS and NIS contributions to industry-standard computing are the result of development by Sun Microsystems. In large part, they contribute to the stature of UNIX today, and they certainly add a dimension to the X Window System you wouldn't see otherwise. In addition to NFS and NIS, however, **ftp**, **telnet**, and UNIX's own remote commands play an important role in an X Window System network. Combined, the different networking components, UNIX and X, provide a rich network environment.

The beauty of NFS is that end users see any filesystem mounted on the network as a local filesystem. This means you can use standard UNIX commands to access remote data. It also means applications can work seamlessly with files located on other machines; and applications residing on other machines appear to run locally. Further, any system on the network can be an NFS server, an NFS client, or even both at the same time. Usually, NFS filesystems become available as the result of commands executed in startup files, but you can mount and unmount an NFS filesystem from the command line. Major benefits of NFS include the following:

- Automatic reconnection of the server after crash recovery, because of the stateless design of the NFS server
- File location sharing between dissimilar operating systems, including UNIX, DOS, VMS, and the Apple Macintosh
- Access to remote filesystems and centralized storage of data and applications
- Access to remote output devices such as printers and plotters
- Access to other remote devices such as tape drives, CD players, and scanners

End users do not have to copy files when they use NFS. Instead, all users on a system can have access to a single file, on a single exported file system somewhere on the network. This greatly reduces the storage of redundant data and makes the tedious task of revision control bearable.

When it comes to NIS, the benefits are not as numerous as those with NFS, but administrators like it. Without it, users would be more demanding of their administrators. The best thing about NIS from a user's viewpoint is that it distributes the same login and environment information across the network. The net result is no matter what machine you log in at, you will always be allowed access and you will always get the same environment.

NIS has several implications for X environments. Most importantly, NIS logs users into their own home directory, whether or not they have logged in at their own system. This means that, as a desktop customizer or system administrator, you can generally rely on the home directory as a good place to store important resource files. In addition, you can also rely on the user having the same shell environment. Thus, instead of your configuration prism focusing on machines, it focuses on users. Combined with the X Display Manager Protocol (embodied in the **xdm** program from the MIT X Consortium), NIS gives you a first-rate approach to modern network computing.

Not to be forgotten, though, the older networking utilities—**ftp**, **telnet**, and the so-called "r" commands—give you excellent access to the network from the command line. While **ftp** is a file transfer utility, and not as important to X users as **telnet** or the **rsh** command, it is still a vital tool for getting files from systems not connected via NFS. Anyone configuring an X server on Microsoft Windows, for instance, will find it invaluable if NFS has not been set up (which is often the case).

The **telnet** utility, as well as the **rlogin** command, are also vital to network users. From an X perspective, their important feature is the mere fact they let you log into other systems on the network. Once aboard a remote system, you can then execute X client programs and have them display on the system from whence you originally came. Most X client programs have a command line option, called **-display**, to facilitate this. Alternatively, you can set the system's $DISPLAY variable to any X system on which you want to run a remote program.

Of the "r" commands, **rlogin** and **rsh** are among the most important. With **rsh**, which lets you remotely execute a program, you can add remote features to the scripts and menus you build under X and Motif. For example, for slower machines on the network, you might want to offload processing to faster machines. Using the **rsh** command to execute a program on a remote system and display it on the slower, local system is the most straightforward way to do this. (If you merely access the program via NFS, the local machine is still the one that executes the program.)

X on PCs and Apples

For a UNIX person moving into the PC and Apple Macintosh environments, X is a reason for getting to know DOS, Microsoft Windows, and the Macintosh GUI—a bridge into a formerly alien world. The same holds true for users moving from the PC and Apple environments into UNIX, but this is a change in graphical user interfaces, not a change in the way you think about computing in general.

This is quite a difference. The people from the UNIX market who are entering the PC and Apple markets are often technical people whose mission is to make sure the PCs, Macs, and UNIX systems work in harmony. People moving into UNIX are often just making an adjustment—like bank customers have made an adjustment to automated teller machines, and grocery store clerks have learned not to lament the customer who presents them with a VISA card.

Instead of handing over a credit card, PC and Apple users click on a button and get instant access to UNIX and the X Window System. This is definitely a frontier situation—a place for the curious cat to die several deaths—and PC and Apple users can take any of several approaches to the situation:

- Follow a routine course and habitually use the same application or two, without ever venturing into the frontier.
- Use applications on UNIX and X hosts, and begin to take advantage of the server's storage and compute resources.
- Get to like UNIX and X so much that the X server becomes the dominant GUI on the PC or Apple, relegating the local GUI to the status of just another process.

Given the availability of applications in the PC and Apple worlds—and their low cost and general aim of being easy to use—it is likely that a majority of users won't fall into the third camp. And with the presence of Microsoft Windows/NT—an improvement in the PC environment that, if nothing else, provides ground for a more flexible GUI environment—there is reason to believe that PC and Apple systems can maintain a performance pace comparable to UNIX and X, at least in the area of frontend applications.

From an architecture viewpoint, the PC and Apple users' experience with X and Motif can be significantly different from the way users on UNIX workstations see X and Motif. Here are the different ways PC and Apple users can access X and Motif:

- Run a single application from the UNIX system, via the network, and have the local window manager—either Microsoft Windows or Macintosh OS—tend to management issues.
- Run the X root window in a window on the PC or Apple system. This presents the PC and Apple user with the concept of a desktop in a window. Any applications from the UNIX host stay within this window.
- Run the local X server so that it sets up a standard root window on the PC or Apple system. The net effect of this is to reduce Microsoft Windows or MacOS, whichever the case may be, to a windowed process.

The desktop administrator needs to set up an X and Motif environment for PC and Apple users, as much as he or she does for other users. The special needs of PC and Apple users must be considered, however. For one thing, PC and Apple users won't require extensive customizing, but instead need menu options to access specific applications and X clients from their local window manager. Resource management—setting colors, fonts, and other preferences—is still a concern, but good X server software for PCs and Macs should offer a built-in resource-setting mechanism.

X and DOS

Users of X on UNIX workstations should be sympathetic to the plight of Quarterdeck Office Systems, Inc. Trying to institute any software standard in the DOS environment is difficult because of Microsoft Corp.'s prevalence in the market. Yet Quarterdeck has been persistent, and Desqview/X is a component that can be easily introduced into a UNIX and X environment.

For UNIX users, one of the neat things about Desqview/X is you can run DOS programs on your UNIX system. This includes all character-mode programs (even ones that write directly to the DOS hardware) and Microsoft Windows programs. Because Desqview/X uses TCP/IP and NFS—usually if an optional software package for the PC is added—PCs running Desqview/X become, for all intents and purposes, peers of UNIX workstations. Desqview/X, moreover, implements 32-bit multitasking under DOS.

The biggest advantage of Desqview/X to UNIX users is the access it gives them to DOS software. For users with two systems in their office—a UNIX workstation and a DOS PC—Desqview/X provides a way to get rid of the PC: As long as you can access a PC on the network somewhere, you can run DOS programs. Here are a few other interesting features of Desqview/X:

- Run multiple DOS sessions in windows on the PC.
- Run multiple DOS sessions on a UNIX system running X.
- Run Microsoft Windows on a UNIX system running X.
- Run remote applications—DOS or UNIX—on the PC.
- Run the Motif window manager on the PC, or Quarterdeck's own window manager.
- Configure resources, menus, and bindings the same way for the PC as you do for UNIX systems running X.

All in all, Desqview/X is a solid adjunct to a network with both DOS PCs and UNIX workstations. With improvements in PC hardware and device driver software, Desqview/X stands a chance of becoming more than an adjunct. Its a long road, though, and the growing presence of Microsoft Windows/NT shifts much of the PC-to-X connection to the PC X server.

CHAPTER 2
Starting Line

MANY WAYS TO START X

For various reasons, vendors have sought to distinguish themselves at the X starting line. But even given variations in the names of startup files—for example, Sun uses **openwin** and SCO once used **startx**—there are really only two ways:

- **xinit**—executable file that invokes the X server and kills the server upon termination
- **xdm**—a deamon-like process, styled along the lines of the **getty** program, giving users a way to directly log into X

Both methods have their pros and cons among different categories of users. From a business user's viewpoint, **xdm** is preferable because the **xdm** login box is less intimidating than using naked UNIX. From an experienced UNIX user's viewpoint, **xinit** is preferable. For one thing, it gives experienced users more flexibility in starting X through release X11R4. For another thing, **xinit** does not require as much memory as **xdm**.

In X11R5, however, enhancements made to **xdm** leveled the playing field, and you can fully expect that **xdm** will become the predominant approach. In the meantime, the choice between **xdm** and **xinit** is a phenomenon worth noticing:

- The **xdm** method distances the great majority of users from the tools and knowledge they need to support their own environment.
- The **xdm** frontend makes UNIX and X more like Microsoft Windows and Apple Macintosh systems.
- And **xdm** places a premium on administration skills and interface engineering.

If you administer your own system, or many systems at a business or university, you probably don't use **xdm** yourself—although a good interface to **xdm**, such as the one included in Hewlett-Packard's *Visual User Environment* (VUE) rendition of X and Motif, should provide mouse and keyboard accelerator access to the UNIX shell in case you have entered single-user mode.

Besides making it possible for you to access the shell, **xinit** gives you lots of flexibility if you need to have conditional startup procedures. For instance, in a programming environment **xinit** custom startup scripts can provide access to different servers. Businesses and universities may have this same need as they discover that different X servers have different effects on different software applications. And sites using Sun's OpenWindows likely also have the need to switch between window managers.

What issues are there besides managing the connection to X? In a business environment, where systems stability is the goal, there is a minimum demand to vary the startup method. If the environment is less stable—more open, perhaps—there is more of a need. For instance, the business might be running numerous Sun systems capable of running Sun's OpenWindows or a third-party X server with Motif. Sun itself began reselling such products after it joined the Cooperative Open Software Environment (COSE).

For administrators, system integrators, and programmers, or anyone else responsible for maintaining the window environment—in other words, the reader of this book—there is a greater need to formalize startup methods without sacrificing flexibility. The larger the organization, or the closer it is to developing or maintaining X applications software, the more important the need to be able to move between different X servers and different window managers, and different versions of the same window manager.

This chapter describes both **xdm** and **xinit** methods. Perhaps it is biased to cover **xinit** in as much detail as **xdm**, but the bias is not necessarily the author's. The **xinit** method is not only a habit with a lot of people, it gives you the feeling that UNIX is underneath it all.

XDM IS AFOOT

From the user's viewpoint, **xdm** is a login window that appears when you turn on the monitor. The **xdm** program itself is running as a daemon and manages the login box, which is called **xlogin** after the widget that displays the box.

In concept, the **xdm** process is similar to the **getty** and **login** processes that manage user access to UNIX. It is also invoked from the same file as **getty**. On System V and OSF/1 platforms, **xdm** is invoked from **inittab** file.

On BSD and SunOS systems, look for the call to **xdm** in the **rc.local** file. Here is a sample command line from the **inittab** file on an OSF/1 system:

```
xdm:23:respawn:/sbin/sh /sbin/xdm.init \
          respawn > /dev/console 2>&1
```

The **inittab** entry tells the system to execute **xdm** at run levels of **2** and **3**. The third field tells it to ensure that the process is always running, even if you use a **kill -9** on it. The next two fields run the specified processes, in this case the Bourne shell and **xdm.init**, which is a recursive shell script that starts **xdm** and takes **respawn** as an argument:

```
# Just exit if /usr not mounted.

if [ -f "/usr/bin/xdm.init" ]; then
     /sbin/sh /usr/bin/xdm.init $1
else
     exit
fi
```

And if Sun systems use **xdm**—it is not the default startup method under OpenWindows—it is called from the **rc.local** file. The following example assumes **xdm** is installed in the default location:

```
# Just exit if /usr not mounted.

if [ -f /usr/openwin/bin/xdm/xdm ]; then
     /usr/openwin/bin/xdm/xdm
     echo -n "Starting Xdm"
fi
```

Given that **xdm** is both a program that manages the **xlogin** widget and the connection to X, it has several more options than **xinit**. But as the previous example indicates, you don't have to use them. The reason is that all the options, with but one exception, can be specified as resources in the **xdm-config** file. The one exception is the **-config** option, which specifies the **xdm** resource configuration file, which defaults to **xdm-config**, so you don't need to use this option either. The only other exception is the **-xrm** option, which is a common option among X clients. As explained later, it lets you load resources directly from the command line.

Table 2-1 describes the resources you can use in **xdm-config**. The resource name for all table entries is **DisplayManager**. Listed under each entry is the equivalent **xdm** command line option.

Table 2-1 Xdm Configuration Resources

Resource	Flag	Description
daemonMode	-nodaemon	The default value of true ensures that **xdm** runs as a daemon process. Specifying false lets you run **xdm** on a session basis.
debugLevel	-debug	The default value of 0 quits debugging. Specifying a nonzero value prints C-style debugging messages.
errorLog	File-error	Specifies the file for **xdm** error messages and error messages from related scripts.
resources	-resources	Specifies **xdm** resource file, which is usually called **Xresources**, not to be confused with the file that **xrdb** loads.
servers	-server	Specifies the file for X servers that need continuous management by **xdm**. In other words, servers that do not use XDMCP.
requestPort	-udpPort	Port on which XDMCP requests are monitored (default is UDP 177). For use by experienced administrators or programmers debugging the connection.
session	-session	Specifies the name of the startup configuration file once **xdm** is ready to load X. This is an important file for customizers and is described fully in the following pages.

Xdm File Organization

Like many UNIX startup programs, knowing **xdm** is knowing its related files. In what is more than a measure of good taste, the **xdm-config** file provides a built-in roadmap to the **xdm** files.

The **xdm-config** file, as with other **xdm** files, is usually stored in **/usr/lib/X11/xdm**. Here is a version of **xdm-config** that works for both X11R5 and X11R4 (note that $XDMHOME represents **/usr/lib/X11/xdm**):

```
! xdm-config, configuration file
! Called by xdm by default
! $XDMHOME should be /usr/lib/x11/xdm
! Config file locationsDisplayManager.servers:
```

```
$XDMHOME/Xservers
DisplayManager.errorLogFile: $XDMHOME/xdm-errors
DisplayManager.pidFile: $XDMHOME/xdm-pid
DisplayManager*resources: $XDMHOME/Xresources
DisplayManager*startup: $XDMHOME/Xstartup
DisplayManager*reset: $XDMHOME/Xreset
DisplayManager*session: $XDMHOME/Xsession

! Config values for xdm
DisplayManager*daemonMode: False
DisplayManager*userPath: :/usr/bin/X11:/usr/bin:.
DisplayManager*systemPath:\
               :/usr/bin/X11:/usr/bin:/home/bin:.
DisplayManager*systemShell: /bin/sh
DisplayManager.0.authorize: True
DisplayManager*authorize: False
```

You should know about all the **xdm** configuration files, but most important are **Xsession** and **Xresources**. If a file does not exist on the system, yet is still specified in **xdm-config**, the specification is ignored and default values, if necessary, are used. This is often the case for the **Xstartup** file, which is a vestige of X11R3. The **Xservers** file is somewhat of a vestige, too, because XDMCP obviated much of its original purpose of establishing X sessions on X terminals.

The **Xservers** file is still used, however, to get setup information for the local console. Here is an example from DEC OSF/1:

```
:0 secure /usr/bin/X bc
```

The first and second fields are read by **xdm** to determine the screen associated with the local console, as well as the security status. The third and last field, which is also read by **xdm**, executes the name server. (In the example, the **X** server also specifies **bc** to turn on bug compatibility mode.)

Other useful files in **xdm-config** are **xdm-errors**, which obviously stores error messages; **xdm-pid**, which stores the process id for **xdm**, but is only advisable to use when you want to kill all sessions managed by **xdm**; and **Xreset**, which runs a program when **xdm** terminates a given session. Like **Xstartup**, the **Xreset** file is rarely used.

The next two sections describe the important files—**Xsession** and **Xresources**—but as you may have noticed from the **xdm-config** example, **xdm** supports other resources. The complete set of resources is listed in Table 2-2 with brief descriptions.

Table 2-2 Selected Xdm Operational Resources

Resource	Default	Description
accessFile		List of systems with XDMCP access.
authComplain*	true	Disables use of the login window.
authDir	xdm	Default **xdm** directory. X11R5 only.
authFile*		File with server authorization data.
authName*		List of authorization mechanisms.
authorize*	true	Determines if authorization is used.
autoRescan	true	Rereads config files on session exit.
cpp		Specifies C preprocessor for **xrdb**.
daemonMode	true	Runs **xdm** as daemon or one time (**false**).
errorLogFile		File to store **xdm** error messages.
exportList		Environment variables for **xdm** programs.
failsafeClient*	xterm	Runs client if failsafe session is needed.
grabServer	false	Locks server down briefly after login input.
keyFile		Authentication key (usually not supported).
lockPidFile	false	Locks **xdm-pid** to one **xdm** daemon.
openDelay*	5	Seconds between attempts to start X server.
openRepeat*	5	Number of attempts to start the X server.
openTimeout*	30	Seconds waiting for X server to respond.
pidFile		File that contains the **xdm** process id.
pingInterval*	5 min	Ping interval for remote display monitoring.
pingTimeout*	5 min	Wait time after pinging remote displays.
removeDomainname	true	Removes domain from XDMCP systems.
requestPort	177	UDP port for XDMPC requests to **xdm**.
reset*		Root program **xdm** runs after X session.
resetSignal*	SIGHUP	Signal number **xdm** to reset X server.
resources*		Names the **xdm** resources file.
setup*		Root program for **xdm** to modify login.
session*		Names the user's session startup file.
startAttempts*	4	Attempts by **xdm** to start X server.
startup*		Root program for **xdm** to modify startup.
systemPath*		Path used by **xdm** to find programs.
systemShell*	/bin/sh	Shell used by **xdm** during session.
terminateServer*	false	Terminates X server at end of a session.
userAuthDir*	$HOME	Directory to store authorization file.
userPath*		Path for user programs used in X session.

* Indicates resources that should use the full name of the display in the resource statement. For example, **DisplayManager._0.authorize: true** is a full resource statement.

As the footnote to the table indicates, there are two types of **xdm** resources: those that set general characteristics of **xdm**, and others that set the resources associated with a unique display. If you are not concerned with different displays, you don't have to specify the display number in a resource statement. If you do need to display numbers, remember that **xdm** resource statements use the underscore character to represent periods and colons. For example, a resource statement for a system with a display numbered **0** and a screen numbered **1** would look like this:

```
DisplayManager._0_1.authorize: true
```

More information is available on resources in Chapter 3. For now, just note the special way of handling server display and screen numbers. (Incidentally, the **authorize** resource in the example should always be set to true if you want the local X server to have direct access to **xdm**.)

The Login Box

The **xdm** login box is where new users often meet X for the first time. The idea of using a login box, versus executing a command in a UNIX shell, is not new with X. Sun's SunView environment used it and so does Next Next-Step environment. All in all, a GUI-based login box seems to be rapidly becoming a convention.

Most sites find the default login box (see Figure 2-1) acceptable. It usually has two fields for user name and password; two buttons named "Ok" and "Abort" and several keyboard-only functions, including one that acts as an override—provided you have entered your user name and password properly—and puts you in a *failsafe* session, which is simply an Xterm in raw X. In other words, the window manager is not run and a small Xterm comes up. You have no way to move or resize the Xterm, but you can execute other programs from it.

The resources for the login box are defined in the **Xresources** file in the **xdm** suite of files. Of the resources defined here, the keyboard resources, or *translations*, provide the most fertile ground for customizing (see Chapter 9 for a full description of translations). In addition to letting you define key press actions, such as backspace and right cursor movements, you can define the failsafe mechanism in **Xresources**. The **set-session-argument** controls the failsafe mechanism.

As the person responsible for other users' systems, you might also want to offer this capability to **xdm** to advanced users, so they could switch into different, previously configured work sessions. In the next section, as well as the section on the **.xsession** file, the examples build a login box selection mechanism that lets users make any of several choices at startup.

Figure 2-1 A login box from a DEC system.

The Xresources File

The **Xresources** file controls login box resources. The name **Xresources** is arbitrary, but conventional. Recall that you specify the path and name of this file in **xdm-config** using the **DisplayManager*resources** statement. You can specify the resource on a global basis, a display-by-display basis, or a group basis:

```
!Global resource
! $XDMHOME should be /usr/lib/x11/xdm

 DisplayManager*resources: $XDMHOME/Xresources

!Display basis
 DisplayManager*sparky_0*resources: /home/bills/.xdm

!Group basis (by type of X terminal)
 DisplayManager*HPXT*resources: /home/hp/admin/.xdm
```

Where you store the resources for the login box is a site-specific decision. Advanced users might like to have access to the resources so they can customize their login box. A business or organization might say hands off, however. Although the Xresources file is itself harmless, other **xdm** files, such as **Xsetup** and **Xreset** are anything but harmless. Therefore, it might be a wise policy to squirrel away everything to do with **xdm** in **/usr/lib/X11/xdm** and limit access to users.

Authoritarian organizations might even use the login box to issue a stern warning against potential system trespassers. In the following example, a terse warning is presented. Note that true line endings are denoted by **$$**, but you should not include these in your file.

```
!Login box message and appearance resources

!Text of message
 xlogin*Login.greeting: \n\n\nLogin on
                        %hostname%\n\n\n\n\  $$
 This is a secure system and should be treated
            as such. Only authorized    \n\  $$
 personnel should attempt to log in. All
          others are considered to be   \n\  $$
 electronic trespassers and are subject
            to criminal prosecution.    \n   $$

!Additional resources
 xlogin.Login.namePrompt: User Name:\ \
 xlogin.Logint.passwdPrompt: Password:\ \
 xlogin.Login.fail: Typing Error?
 xlogin.Login.borderWidth: 5
 xlogin.Login.foreground:  white
 xlogin.Login.background: forest green
 xlogin.Login.width: 1024
 xlogin.Login.height: 1024
 xlogin.Login.y: 0
 xlogin.Login.x: 0
```

Again, this is a login at an authoritarian organization. So the first thing of importance is to warn trespassers away. You can provide a decent-size message (up to 255 characters), as the example does, and include line returns in the message by ending each line with the **\n** sequence. The second backslash is required to escape the actual line ending in the file on all lines except the last line in the message. The **%hostname%** variable lets you reference the hostname in **xdm** resource statements. The extra spaces at the end of the text lines in the **namePrompt** resource forced the text to justify along the left margin (omit the spaces if you want to center the text).

The remaining statements in the **Xresources** file are not necessary to display the message—nor is the **namePrompt** resource for that matter. By default, the login box sizes itself so that the full message can be displayed. Adjusting the width of the login box with the **xlogin.Login.width** resource lets you better format the output. For example, without adjusting the width of the login box, the authoritarian message would push up against the left and right borders of the box.

Otherwise, the resources create a login box that is the same size as the root window—1024 by 1024 pixels—with forest green as the background color and white as the foreground color. The **xlogin.Login.x** and **xlogin.Login.y** resources set the login box's starting position, which is the upper left-hand corner of the screen, or 0,0. Also, when setting the user name and password resources, you must append one or more spaces to the text string if you want to include whitespace. These statements recognize neither single nor double quotation marks. Finally, the **xlogin.Login.fail** resource specifies a message for the error popup that appears if you make a mistake typing or enter the wrong user name or password.

At a friendlier organization, you might want to put the login box to a more practical use than scaring strangers. Instead of the stern message, you could include a list of items associated with key presses—a menu, after a fashion, of different sessions the user can enter. Here's the code, which includes special key translations to support the menu items:

```
!Systemwide Xresources file for Xdm
 xlogin*Login.greeting: \n\n\nLogin on %hostname%\n\n\n\
 F5 User's Choice F6 Wordprocessing F7 Xterms/Editors\n\
 F8 Database F9 DTP & Graphics F10 Network & Mail
!Additional resources
 xlogin*Login.namePrompt: User Name:\ \
 xlogin*Login.passwdPrompt: Password:\ \
 xlogin*Login.fail: Typing Error?
 xlogin*Login.borderWidth: 5
 xlogin*Login.foreground: white
 xlogin*Login.background: forest green
 xlogin*Login.NameField.translations: #override\n\
 :<Key>F1: activate() next-tab-group()\n\
 :<Key>F2: activate() next-tab-group()\n\
 :<Key>Return: activate() next-tab-group()\n\
 :Ctrl<Key>R: abort-login()\n\
 :Ctrl<Key>u: end-of-line() delete-to-start-of-line()
 xlogin*Login.PasswordField.translations: #override\n\
 :<Key>F1: set-session-argument(failsafe) activate()\n\
 :<Key>F2: set-session-argument(fs) activate()\n\
 :<Key>F5: set-session-argument(F5) activate()\n\
 :<Key>F6: set-session-argument(F6) activate()\n\
 :<Key>F7: set-session-argument(F7) activate()\n\
 :<Key>F8: set-session-argument(F8) activate()\n\
 :<Key>F9: set-session-argument(F9) activate()\n\
 :<Key>F10: set-session-argument(F10) activate()\n\
 :<Key>Return: set-session-argument() activate()\n\
 :Ctrl<Key>C: abort-login()\n\
 :Ctrl<Key>R: restart-session()
```

Other than the translation statements, this set of resources is similar to the previous set. Notice that the login greeting message has been changed: It now lists sessions associated with function keys. The function keys, in turn, define a session argument. The translation function for this is **set-session-argument**. The arguments used in the example, with the exception of the first two, are the function key name itself. The other two arguments define failsafe sessions. The one bound to F1 is conventional. It comes in the default **Xresources** file as shipped by the MIT X Consortium. The **fs** is added here. It allows users to select their own failsafe session.

One other thing you might want to do with login menus: If your site uses more than one window manager, these are definitely good candidates for treatment as early on in the configuration process as possible. It relieves the user of the responsibility of running the window manager, either from the **.xsession** file, or from an Xterm window after X loads. This is desirable for two reasons: you don't have to administer the window manager command statement in each **.xsession** file; and you exert control over the way the window manager is loaded (of which, more later). Here's a simple three-item menu for window managers:

```
xlogin*Login.greeting: Login on %hostname%\n\
F5-Motif    F6-OpenWindows    F7-twm
```

As before, you use the **set-session-argument** to pass the selection to the **Xsession** file. This time, however, instead of using the function key label as the argument, use the executable filename for the window manager. This provides the foundation for you to write a generic routine to execute the window manager as in the following:

```
wm=$1 #set-session-argument
   if [ -f "$wm" ]; then
      $wm &
else
      xterm -ls
      exit
fi
```

In the example, the window manager is loaded in the background, assuming that a client will be run later in the **Xsession** script, or in the user's **.xsession** script. You may have to enforce this point by locking users out of their own **.xsession** file, much like some administrators lock users out of their shell startup files. (Users don't lose any ability to make changes to their environment because—by all rights—the locked file should call a secondary startup script.) The last thing the example does is to load an Xterm if no window manager has been specified. The **-ls** option is used here so a login shell is run in the Xterm. The Xterm is run in the foreground, because it is the only client sitting between the user and a return to the login screen.

In addition to example translations, **xdm** supports several other translations. Most of them define editing key behavior. Some others provide additional functionality, including the X11R5 translation **abort-display**. Thanks to **abort-display**, administrators and other privileged users can drop down into a UNIX shell, called **xdmshell** in some implementations. Table 2-3 lists selected **xdm** translations.

Table 2-3 Selected Xdm Translation Resources

Translation	Description
abort-display	Terminates **xdm** and the X server and starts a UNIX shell such as the special **xdmshell**.
abort-session	Effectively kills and restarts the X server. Sometimes a convenient way to reinitialize X.
allow-all-access	Permits unlimited access to the X server, bypassing the **.Xauthority** file. This can be a severe security hole.
restart-session	Resets the X server. Handy if you need to load new **xdm** resources or refresh the login screen.

Where do the arguments from the translations go? To the **Xsession** script, which either processes them or passes them to the **.xsession** script. Before you get to this point, though, you might want to think about using the **Xsetup** script.

The Xsetup Script

As if there weren't enough startup scripts, X11R5 added **Xsetup** up to the roster. It is far from redundant, however. With the **Xsetup** script you can achieve complete control over the login interface—not that it does anything to the login box, but it does let you run other X clients alongside the login box.

Of course, you really don't want to execute too many clients from **Xsetup**. Why give the user—and any stranger who happened by—free access to an Xterm? Clients you might be interested in running are **xclock** or another clock program, a message-of-the-day program, and any client that harmlessly displays something on the root window.

The overriding concern in client selection is don't run any clients with backdoors into the system. The **xdm** program shuts off keyboard access to the system.

As for displaying images, other chapters describe methods for controlling the root window. In the present context, you might think about implementing the MIT X Consortium **xsetroot** client to load a bitmap on the root window. Alternatively, you could use a public domain program such as **xloadimage** or **xv** to load full-color images. In fact, you could create special image files—for example, GIF or TIFF files—and use them to present menu choices so you don't have to convert the login box's greeting message into a menu. Here is a short example:

```
#!/bin/sh
# Xsetup, xdm script
# Syntax: called by xdm

# Following assumes DisplayManager*systemPath
# has been set in the xdm-config file

  xclock -g +800+50
  xloadimage -root \
             -colors 16 /usr/system/images/login.gif
```

The script runs **xclock** and places it in the upper right-hand corner of the screen. The script then runs **xloadimage** to load an image file called **login.gif**. Only 16 colors, or shades of gray in terms of this reproduction, are used because the image file is basic (see Figure 2-2).

The **Xsetup** program is executed immediately after **xdm** reads the **xdm-config** script. As a result, it inherits the $DISPLAY, $PATH, $SHELL, and $XAUTHORITY environment variables. Other environment variables, including ones set in **.profile**—given that the previous example was a Bourne shell script—are not available to the script because no user session has been run yet. Only the **xdm** session, and the environment variables it has set or collected from the system, are in effect. In addition to the ones mentioned, these include $HOME, $TERM, and $USER.

Overall, the lack of access to environment variables at the system level makes the **xdm** startup method somewhat more tedious to control in that, with **.xinitrc**, all environment variables are inherited from the login shell. The solution is to add needed environment variables and path statements to the **Xsession** file. This doesn't help you with **Xsetup**, but it will take care of most other system environment requirements.

Figure 2-2 Using Xsetup to create an initial desktop.

The Xsession Script

With X running and waiting, and with the login successfully completed, it is time for the **Xsession** script to come into play. Here are the possibilities:

- **Xsession** handles the rest of the startup process, and loads the window manager and one or more clients.
- **Xsession** performs any preliminary systemwide processing and passes control to **.xsession**, which loads clients and the window manager.
- **Xsession** immediately passes control to **.xsession**.

Probably the least advisable method is the last one. If you chose this method, you would have to ensure that all users maintained a minimal number of systemwide defaults, such as the failsafe translation in the login box. And the first method, in which **Xsession** does all the work, prevents users from setting up their own environments—and makes it difficult to later configure a way for users to save their sessions. (The concept of saving a session minimally implies that most, if not all, of the clients in a session can be restored. Even better, and not impractical, would be a mechanism to restore the clients along with any pertinent history.)

The best method is the dual approach. Use **Xsession** to set systemwide defaults and load any clients that you want to appear on everyone's display.

Now you have to ask the question: What client should run as the last foreground process? If you don't run Motif or another window manager as the last process, an advisable approach (see *Starting Motif* later in this chapter), you might consider running the window manager from **Xsession**. Doing so gives you ultimate control over the appearance and behavior of Motif. By using the **-xrm** resource option, you can override any resources the user might set.

As for where you implement the translations for the login menus from the previous two sections, it depends on what is more important: user control or company standards? The following example can be used as a default **Xsession** file.

```
#!/bin/sh
# Xsession script

# System environment variables
  XAPPLRESDIR=/home/resources
  XMENU=/usr/xmenu
  XBIN=/usr/bin/X11
  export $XAPPLRESDIR $XMENU $XBIN

# Initial values
  arg=$1
  startup="$HOME/.xsession"
  resoruces=$HOME/.Xdefaults"

# Redirect output to error file
  exec > $HOME/.xsession-errors 2>&1

# Determine window manager, assuming F3 and F4 are
# menu choices for OpenWindows and twm. Also check
# for failsafe value set to F1.
  case $arg in
     F1) exec xterm -geometry 80x24-0-0 -ls ;;
     F3) wm=$OPENWINHOME/bin/olwm ;;
     F4) wm=$XBIN/twm ;;
      *) wm=/usr/bin/mwm ;;
```

```
  esac

  if [ -f $startup ]; then
     exec $startup $arg
  else
     if [ -f $resources ]; then
        xrdb -load $resources
   fi
# Execute the window manager in background
  $wm &

# Run a startup client. If you kill the startup
# client later, the session terminates.
  exec $XBIN/xterm -C -name console -iconic
```

The first thing **Xsession** does here is check for the failsafe translation. If the user has asked for a failsafe session, **$1** is equal to failsafe. The use of the Bourne shell's bare **test** mechanism lets you test for the existence of **/usr/bin/xterm**, as well as for **$1**. If the tests are successful—that is, if there can be anything successful associated with a failsafe session—an Xterm with slightly larger than normal geometry appears.

Next comes a case statement that tests for the selected window manager. If no window manager has been selected, the case statement defaults to Motif. All three window managers have their focus policies set to similar behavior, thanks to the **-xrm** option. This is a form of enforcement to which your users might object. It is simply used here to show you what you can do.

Finally comes the test for **.xsession**. If it exists and is executable, **Xsession** goes aheads and executes it. Otherwise, an Xterm is started as a foreground process. The Xterm also takes the **-C** option, which ensures that it receives console messages.

One thing the **Xsession** file in the example doesn't do is check whether **.Xdefaults** goes by another name. Among many X users, it is conventional to call it .**Xresources**, instead of **.Xdefaults**. Additionally, because of the design of X, users can name this file anything they want, so long as they specify it in the XENVIRONMENT variable. To embrace these users, you could use **sed** or a combination of **grep** and **cut** to extract the XENVIRONMENT value from the startup script.

There are many other ways to use **Xsession**, too. As noted, you can startup any client you want from **Xsession**. And if you don't allow users to have an **.xsession** file, you can guarantee a great amount of uniformity. For example, if you administer users who only use mail and desktop applications, or are setting up a turnkey system, you could effectively shut them out from ever using programs they could accidentally abuse, such as Xterm or any other client that permits access to the UNIX shell.

The .xsession Script

If you have read the previous sections, you have a good idea about the **.xsession** script. You should also have a good idea of the degree to which you want users to customize their X environment. Then, because you see yourself spending a lot of time on developing the **.xsession** script, you decide not to let users modify their **.xsession** script. So you make the script writable only by root:

```
chmod 550 .xsession
ls -ls .xsession

2 -r-xr-x-- 1 root system 1393 Apr 27 01:24 .xsession
```

Okay, whether you get this rigid depends on your approach to users. The one thing that is universal is that you have to provide a substantial **.xsession** file in one form or another. If you choose to let users write to their **.xsession** file—giving the users an opportunity to participate in a standard—you can block out the code with comments and warn users not to alter the code you have put in place. Or you can create an alternate file that **.xsession** executes:

```
# Exec user's startup file
  startup="$HOME/.xexec"
  exec $startup
```

The bottom line is that there *is* a bottom line. At some point, the user gets to add clients to the startup process. If you want to limit the user's access to clients, you must limit access to the clients themselves.

The actual **.xsession** script that is presented here continues the login menu example. You can use the script as a template for your own **.xsession** scripts, changing the names of the menu items in the **Xresources** file and the names of the applications in **.xsession**.

```
#!/sbin/sh
# .xsession, xdm startup file
# Syntax: exec .xsession arg
# Note: args available: fs, F5-F7

# System environment variables
```

```
  XAPPLRESDIR=/home/resources
  XBIN=/usr/bin/X11
  XMENU=/usr/xmenu
  PATH=$PATH:$XBIN:XMENU
  export PATH
  export $XAPPLRESDIR $XMENU $XBIN $PATH

# Load user's resources with xrdb
  if [ -f "$resources" ]; then
     xrdb -load $resources
  else
     xrdb -load $XBIN/Xdefaults
  fi

# Initial values
  arg=$1

# Test for user's personal failsafe session
  if [ "$arg" = "fs" ]; then
     xterm -bg black -fg green \
           -g 93x48 \
           -fn '*courier-bold-r*180*'
     exit
  fi

# Process Xsession function key args
  case $arg in

        F5) xloadimage -windowid 0x28 -colors 128 \
                       /usr/images/moon.gif ;;
        F6) xloadimage -windowid 0x28 -colors 128 \
                       /usr/images/july.gif ;;

        F7) xloadimage -windowid 0x28 -colors 128 \
                       /usr/images/night.gif ;;

         *) break ;; # All other go to default

  esac

# Load default set of clients
  xterm -name Xmenu &
  xclock -g +800+50 -bg 'light slate grey' &

# Run console in the foreground
  xterm -name console -C -iconic -n con
```

The example **.xsession** follows in the footsteps of the previous **Xsession** file because it assumes the window manager already has been loaded as a background process.

X FROM THE COMMAND LINE

When you use **xinit** to load the X Window System, configuration issues can often be dealt with much more easily, but you sacrifice the login box. If you administer your own system, or are responsible for a network of systems, you might use **xinit** for you own personal startup, but use **xdm** on other systems.

As with **xdm**, the **xinit** program is responsible for invoking the X server program. Despite this layering, you can be sure that working with **xinit** is as deep as you'll want to go, unless you plan on experimenting with different X servers—in which case, you can still use **xinit** because it lets you specify a unique X server from the command line. This is one of the three options that you have when you run **xinit**. The other two options let you specify the display—for example, **sparky:0**—and start a client program, either locally or remotely. The syntax for **xinit** looks like this:

```
xinit [[client]options] [—[server] [display]options]
```

Unless you are a system administrator, or at least fully responsible for your own system, you are likely to find few reasons for modifying the **xinit** server option. Among UNIX workstation users, there is little reason to stray from the standard X server. And specifying the display in **xinit** can be easily dealt with in the **.xinitrc** file. The client option, however, is more than a little interesting. By modifying it in a startup script, you get maximum control of a couple of items:

- Executing a remote client from a CPU-wealthy host and displaying it locally on selected systems across the network
- Establishing default values for the basic set of X resources, including window geometry, fonts, and background and foreground colors

Neither of these capabilities is unusual. In fact, you can do both from any level in X—whether you are a root user or a guest on someone's system. What is unusual about doing it at the **xinit** level is that you can exert control at the system and network level that cannot easily be undone by a regular user. For example, you might use an SCO platform as a mail server and want everyone in the organization to use **scomail** as their mail reader. The following command would go a long way to ensuring its continued availability, if not its use, on the local X system:

```
xinit /usr/bin/scomail ibmpc:0 -display $LOCAL:0
```

Doing this is a lot different from asking users to execute a remote session, fire up **scomail**, and read their important messages. There's nothing to stop a user from closing **scomail** and breaking the connection to the remote server, but the user won't have a good excuse when you ask why.

To complete the tale of the enforced mail reader you would also have to ensure that local systems allowed server access for mail programs. This is accomplished with the **xhost** command or by adding the server name to the **/etc/X.hosts** file; providing access to the server by listing the remote machine in **/etc/hosts.equiv** or **rhosts** in $HOME; or on systems employing user-based access, running the **xauth** command.

Using **xinit** to set some basic defaults for a client—usually Xterm—is also an interesting proposition. As you will see throughout the rest of this book, there are numerous ways to set resources, including defaults. But sometimes, everything kicks back to the most basic defaults set up by **xinit**. Using this capability of **xinit** can help build a distinctive appearance for your workstation or all the workstations at your site. Here is an example:

```
xinit -geometry =80x65+100+100 \
      -fn terminal-bold \
      -fg 'forest green' -bg 'black'
```

This sets the default Xterm's size, font and colors. You could also set numerous other resources. The default action of **xinit**, incidentally, is to start an Xterm, thus allowing the user to start other clients from the Xterm. The resources from the previous example apply to this Xterm and any other default Xterms, whether or not you specify additional startup information.

Where you provide additional startup information is up to you. You have two places from which you can start the window manager and other clients: the **startx** script or the **.xinitrc** configuration file.

The Startx Script

Before considering **.xinitrc**, you'll likely need to consider the file that starts X. As noted, this file goes by many different names, but **startx** is the standard file shipped by the MIT X Consortium. The following example of a **startx** file is rudimentary and closely resembles the **startx** shipped by DEC in a release of its OSF/1 operating system. (Individual lines are numbered for later reference.)

```
#!/bin/sh
# Sample implementation of a slightly less
# primitive interface than xinit. It looks
# for .xinitrc and .xserverrc files, then
# system copies of these files. Otherwise,
# xinit uses its default. The system , start a
# xinitrc read resources files and start clients.

userclientrc=$HOME/.xinitrc
userserverrc=$HOME/.xserverrc
sysclientrc=/usr/lib/X11/xinit/xinitrc
sysserverrc=/usr/lib/X11/xinit/xserverrc
clientargs=""
serverargs=""

if [ -f $userclientrc ]; then
    clientargs=$userclientrc
else if [ -f $sysclientrc ]; then
    clientargs=$sysclientrc
fi
fi

if [ -f $userserverrc ]; then
    serverargs=$userserverrc
else if [ -f $sysserverrc ]; then
    serverargs=$sysserverrc
fi
fi

whoseargs="client"
while [ "x$1" != "x" ]; do
    case "$1" in
 /''*|\.*) if [ "$whoseargs" = "client" ]; then
          clientargs="$1"
      else
          serverargs="$1"
      fi ;;
 -)  whoseargs="server" ;;
 *)   if [ "$whoseargs" = "client" ]; then
          clientargs="$clientargs $1"
      else
          serverargs="$serverargs $1"
      fi ;;
    esac
    shift
done
```

```
44  xinit $clientargs—$serverargs
```

The purpose of the **startx** script is to get X going based on what it finds—or doesn't find—in the way of startup files. In lines 9-14, **startx** sets variables for the various possible startup files, as well as variables for arguments to **xinit**. The first set of **if** statements, in lines 15-20, tests for the existence of **.xinitrc** in $HOME. If it exists, $userclientrc is set to it. If not, $userclientrc is set to the system **xinitrc** file, which is located in **/usr/lib/X11/xinit** in the example. In lines 22-26 similar testing is done for the existence of the **.xserverrc** in $HOME. This file assists X in establishing user-based authorization to the X server. The final block of code in **startx** gets the value in **$1** and passes it to **xinit**.

The .xinitrc File

For **xinit** users, the **.xinitrc** file is crucial for customizing how X starts. There are some basic things you must do in **.xinitrc**: set the DISPLAY environment variable, invoke the **xrdb** resource editor, and start the window manager (although this could be accomplished in the **startx** script, but it is not conventional to do so). Additionally, you might want to run an Xterm as a console in the **.xinitrc** for trusted users on workstations, but not for users on X terminals:

```
xterm -console
```

This is a minimal Xterm command, except that it specifies that Xterm should receive system messages and act as the console. Importantly, there is no **&** after the command, meaning that the Xterm is run in the foreground. Typically, you put this command on the last line in the **.xinitrc** file, meaning the **startx** script—which is reading **.xinitrc**—does not exit until you exit the Xterm. Of course, when you do this, you also exit X. If you start a second Xterm console from an X terminal, or anywhere else, the first Xterm console is disabled.

It is likely that you will encounter configurations in which the window manager is run as the foreground process. This is not advisable if you take some of the approaches used in the Xmenu software. For example, you cannot use the **kill** command to terminate Motif without also being kicked back to UNIX. But you can use the **f.restart** function, so you might ask what do you lose? The *Starting Motif* section in this chapter answers that question.

So you will likely decide to use an Xterm as the process that the **.xinitrc** runs in the background. This is a good choice for a number of reasons:

- Xterm's console option redirects UNIX, X, and Motif error messages to the Xterm display—an important consideration for debugging configuration files.
- An Xterm acting as a console usually guarantees access to the command line in case other windows are hung. In addition, in those rare instances when Motif won't restart for some reason, it is likely you can use the Xterm to kill a process or two.
- The diverse resources associated with Xterms let you create a custom console window, with special features such as a log file and large screen buffer.
- With Motif's custom menu capability, you can also create a special menu tailored to console activities.

In addition to starting Motif and a console Xterm in **.xinitrc**, you should also run **xrdb** to load the contents of **.Xdefaults**, or whatever resource file you are using, into the resource database. Additionally, you can run other X utilities and start as many X clients as you want in **.xinitrc**. Here is a minimal script:

```
# .xinitrc, minimal X startup file
# Designed to run OpenWindows or Motif

# Load the .Xdefaults file now
  if [ -f $HOME/.Xdefaults ]; then
     xrdb $HOME/.Xdefaults
  fi

# Uncomment this section for OpenWindows
# $OPENWINHOME/lib/openwin-sys &
# eval `svenv -env`
# olwm -3 &

# Execute the Motif window manager (mwm)
  mwm

# Set Xhost status
  xhost +`hostname` > /dev/null &
  xhost sparky5 > /dev/null &

  clock
  xterm -name Xmenu
  xterm -C -name Xmenu
  exec $HOME/.xexec
```

The example **.xinitrc** file is conventional. It assumes that users can modify it and are trusted enough not to interfere with its functionality. It also assumes that Motif is the window manager of choice and then proceeds to load several clients that users might need at startup. However, if you want to develop a startup method similar to the menu approach described for **xdm**, you need to do additional customizing. At this point, it is almost imperative to limit end user access to a special configuration file, such as the **.xexec** file used in the final line of the **.xinitrc** example. The **xexec** file would contain additional clients.

Starting Motif

In default configuration files, and other texts on X, you will find that Motif—or whatever window manager you are using—is loaded as a foreground process. So far, however, this book has advocated that you load it in the background. Why?

When you load the window manager in the foreground, you inexorably link the window manager to the X session. This makes sense for default configurations, in that vendors have wanted the window manager and X to appear like a seamless combination. SCO even takes it one step further and blends the X.desktop desktop manager into the seam.

But what happens when you want to change the window manager's resources? Normally, you have to restart the window manager to effect a change in resources, so if the window manager is the foreground process, you end up restarting X to restart the window manager. This takes time—and if you have extensive scripts to modify the window manager resources as the Xmenu program does—you don't want to add more time to the restart process.

In addition to loading resources, there are at least two other concerns when loading Motif or any other window manager:

- Creating special window manager startup routines that let you produce special menus and key and button bindings
- Knowing when the loading process is complete, so you can load other X clients cleanly

The next three sections briefly discuss the techniques involved in customizing window manager startup. The rest of the book revisits and implements these techniques. And from henceforth, Motif is used in examples and descriptions, but essentially, you can use the same techniques with other window managers.

Restarting Motif

There are two ways to restart Motif. The conventional way is to use Motif's **f.restart** function, which you make accessible to users by including it in one of Motif's root menus (programmable via the **.mwmrc** file). The unconventional way is to use the UNIX **kill** command, which is essential if you want a script or menu routine that implements a resource change and restarts Motif.

When you use **kill** in a script to terminate Motif, you can restart it in the same script. The following example provides a basic approach.

```
#!/bin/sh
# Suggested name: rmwm
# Script to restart Motif window manager
# Syntax: no options
# Copyright (c) Alan Southerton 1993
  pid=`ps -e | awk '/mwm/ && ! /awk/ {print $1}'`
  kill -9 $pid
# Now restart Motif
  mwm &
```

The script represents the most basic approach to do-it-yourself starting of Motif. The **-9** value to **kill** is a powerful kill value. It ensures that you override Motif's ability to trap a more standard **kill** signal, such as **-1** or **-15**, and as a result, display a feedback window that asks you whether you are sure you want to leave Motif (See Figure 2-3).

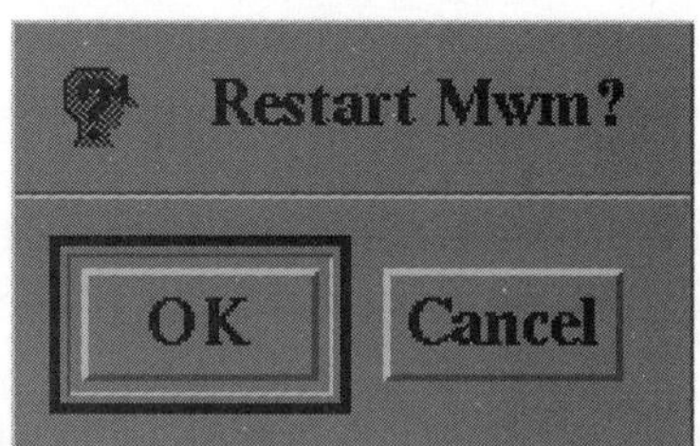

Figure 2-3 Motif restart window.

The problem with the previous script is there might be times when you want the feedback window to appear. Unfortunately there are no standard X tools that quickly tell you whether the feedback window has been displayed. If you are creating scripts for fast workstations, you might be tempted to use **xlswins** to poll the id numbers of windows, and then use the id with **xwininfo**. Here's how:

```
id=`xlswins -indent 0 -l | \
      grep "feedback.*301x119" | cut -d' ' -f3`
map=`xwininfo -id $id | \
      grep "Map State" | cut -d: -f2`
```

These lines of code yield the map state of the feedback window. If the feedback window is on-screen, **$map** equals **IsViewable**; otherwise, it equals **IsUnviewable**.

In order to obtain the restart feedback window, note that you must search for **feedback.*301x119**. The **301x119** values are the width and height of the feedback window. These dimensions are hard-coded into Motif. Before using them, check whether your version of Motif has the same dimensions. Whatever set it does have is consistent. There are no user-oriented ways to change them, although beginning with Motif 1.2, you can change the positioning of the feedback window with the **feedbackGeometry** resource.

Custom Motif Startup

What is the advantage of starting and restarting Motif with a script? Mainly, it lets you run custom scripts to modify X and Motif resource and configuration files (see Chapter 10). This is a major consideration, given that you can create scripts to retrieve system and network resources and build custom menus for these resources in Motif's main configuration file, **.mwmrc**.

The vehicle that you use to add this new layer of control to the Motif startup process is just a simple loader script. The purposes of the script is to allow you to perform some action between the time that you kill Motif and the time you start it again. In order to accomplish this, you must give the script the same name as the Motif executable—normally **mwm**—and then rename the Motif executable. Here is a skeleton version of the script:

```
#!/bin/sh
# mwm, script to load Motif

# Get system resources
   .
   .
   .
# Get network resources
   .
   .
   .
# Call renamed Motif executable
  /usr/bin/MWMEXEC
```

That's it. Just one line to load the Motif executable after calling whatever special routines you devise. In the example, the Motif executable has been renamed to **MWMEXEC**. The uppercase letters call attention to the renaming—both in the script and in output from the **ps** command.

The new **mwm** executable, the script, can be run in the foreground or the background. In either case, the script does not complete until Motif terminates. Note, however, that killing the **mwm** script will not kill the Motif executable. As a result, if you use both the **rmwm** script from the previous section, and the **mwm** script, you must replace **mwm** with **MWMEXEC** in the **rmwm** script.

After Motif Loads

If you have used X and Motif for awhile, you probably have noticed that clients run from either **.xinitrc** or **.xsession**—or just clients on the screen when you restart Motif—tend to appear before Motif loads. You can tell this has happened because the client part of the window—the main window area—appears without a frame and other window manager components.

Although this is harmless behavior, it is unsightly. It also might be disquieting to some users, and compared to an environment like Microsoft Windows, it also has the earmarks of a kludge. There is a way to avoid this. And speaking of kludges, the method used is a humdinger, but it works for Motif as well as OpenWindows.

The problem to be solved is how to make the startup process wait for Motif to finish loading itself in memory. If this can be accomplished, client programs load with the full accoutrement of window manager components. Well, the method involves generating an intentional error in Motif's **.mwmrc** file, redirecting Motif's standard error to a file, and then checking for the existence of the file from the startup script where you load clients. Here are the steps:

1. Insert an error in the **.mwmrc** file. Any error will do, such as a bad mnemonic key, or a faulty menu. For example, you could tack the following to the end of the **.mwmrc** file:

```
! Menu that creates intentional error
  Menu ErrorMaker
  {
     Error Error
  }
```

2. Redirect standard error to a file. If you are loading Motif by conventional means:

```
mwm 2> $HOME/.motifgo &
```

If you are loading Motif using the **mwm** script discussed in the last section:

```
/usr/bin/MWMEXEC 2> $HOME/.motifgo &
```

3. Use a **while** loop in the appropriate startup file to check for the existence of **.motifgo**. Here is a shell function that wraps the whole process into a single command:

```
# Function to load Motif and wait
  execwm() {
     $wm &
#    Make clients wait for window mgr
     while [ 1 ]
     do
        if [ -s $HOME/.motifgo ]; then
           rm $HOME/.motifgo
           break
        fi
     done
  return; }
```

The last step implements that actual wait loop. The **motifgo** file is not actually located until Motif finishes processing the **.mwmrc** file, which also happens to be one of the last things it does before it completes loading. When **.motifgo** does appear, the **execwm** shell function proceeds to remove it and break out of the while loop. At this point, you can begin loading any client programs.

A Startup Client

As noted several times, running the window manager in the background is important, because it lets you restart the window manager without restarting X. There are three consequences of this approach:

- The window manager restarts as quickly as possible, limited only by the size of its own configuration files.
- Native X configuration parameters, such as those put in place with the **xset** command, remain intact. Additionally, if you have displayed a bitmap or image on the root window, it remains.
- Another client program, such as an Xterm or the **xconsole** program, must be run in the foreground as the last command in your startup script (either **.xsession** or **.xinitrc**).

Selecting a startup client depends on your circumstances. If you are configuring X for yourself and other advanced users, the conventional client to choose is either Xterm or a special client provided by your system vendor. For example, Sun's **cmdtool** serves as a good startup client.

If you choose Xterm as the startup client, you'll likely want to use the **-C** option, which specifies that the Xterm receive all system-oriented messages. You might also want to add the **-iconic** option so the console opens as a Motif icon. The **-C** option, by the way, puts the string "console" in both the titlebar and icon label.

As another alternative—but one that requires user interaction with a menu—you might create a simple client to load before the window manager. You don't have to program in C to do so; rather, you just need to know how to create a menu using your window manager's menu configuration file. For example, you could add a menu to the **xlogo** program that gives the user the choice of opening a console window, loading the **.Xdefaults** file, restarting the window manager, or leaving X altogether. In Motif, you would orchestrate such an approach by creating a menu in the **.mwmrc** file that specifically served your startup window. The menu and window are linked with the **windowMenu** resource. Here are the steps for turning **xlogo** into a startup window:

1. Create a resource entry in **.Xdefaults** linking **xlogo** to its custom menu in **.mwmrc**:

   ```
   xlogo*windowMenu: XlogoMenu
   ```

2. Create the custom menu in **.mwmrc**:

   ```
   Menu XlogoMenu
   {
    "Session Manager"    f.title
    "Console window"     !"(xterm -C -iconic)&"
    ".Xdefaults"         !"(loadres)&"
    "Restart Motif"      f.restart
    "Restart X"          !"(xoff)&"
   "Minimize"            f.minimize
   }
   ```

3. Execute **xlogo** as part of your **.xinitrc** script (or **.xsession** script, if you use **xdm** and prefer to use **.xsession**).

For the time being, don't worry about the structure of the Motif menu; it is thoroughly explained in Chapter 6. The *Restart X* option does need some explanation, however. It is a script that kills X altogether and returns you to the system prompt, if you loaded X using **xinit**; or returns you to the **xdm** login box, if you used **xdm**. As a desktop customizer, you'll likely want to address both methods, especially as **xdm** becomes more popular. Some **xdm** systems also use special display managers, such as SCO's **scologin**, which you should take into account as a separate case.

In any event, arriving at a script that comes near to a universal approach helps customizers working on a heterogenous network. Here is a script that serves the purpose:

```
#!/bin/sh
# Suggested name: xoff
# Script to end X session
# Syntax: no options

# Dependencies
# $XSTARTUP defines startup mechanism
# $XDMHOME defines path to xdm directory
# $XSERVER defines path/name of server

case $XSTARTUP in
     xdm) kill -TERM 'cat $XDMHOME/xdm-pid' ;;

     xinit) pid='ps | grep $XSERVER \
               | grep -v grep | cut -c1-5'

     xinit) pid='ps -e | awk '/$XSERVER/ \
               && ! /awk/ {print $1}''
            kill -9 $pid ;;

     scologin) /usr/bin/X11/scosession -stop ;;
     *) echo 'Incorrect or no value for $XSTARTUP'
esac
```

Using environment variables for subsets of X is vital to writing scripts that work across different environments. Of the three environment variables in **xoff**, the $XSERVER variable is most crucial, because it defines the name of the server being used on a particular system. The $XSTARTUP variable is also crucial, in that it provides a simple way to supply the name of the startup method to the script. On the other hand, the $XDMHOME variable is somewhat superfluous, because on most systems that use **xdm**, it and its related files reside in **/usr/lib/Xll/xdm**.

The **xdm-pid** file is one related file. It contains the process id associated with the current **xdm** session, giving you a convenient way to obtain the pid for the **kill** command. Notice in the case of **xinit**, you have to obtain the id yourself. But also notice that in the SCO method, the kill process is streamlined into an option to the **scosession** client.

UNIX STARTUP FILES

Under X, the importance of the UNIX shell startup files depends on whether you use **xinit** or **xdm**. With **xinit**, shell startup files assume a more traditional role, but with **xdm** there is less need to perform all the traditional startup tasks and define all the environment variables that you would for a character-mode UNIX environment. In other words, because **xdm** doesn't source your shell startup files, you don't have to worry about setting system-specific information in the startup file—at least as far as **xdm** is concerned.

For **xinit**, you must define the initial operating environment in the shell startup files. There are two reasons: First, you will be logging into character-mode UNIX before you actually start X; and second, you need to pass the shell environment to X the first time you start it up. Thereafter, however, the **xinit** relationship to startup files is similar to that of **xdm**. For example, after you have started X, when next you call an Xterm you don't really need that Xterm to initialize by displaying the message of the day or running the **mailx** program. Instead, you want to remove as much of this traditional type of startup activity as possible from your startup files.

As for **xdm**, you need not concern yourself with defining the operating environment for X from the shell startup files. You do this in the **xdm-config** and **Xsession** files. For individual Xterm sessions, you must still define a path and environment variables for the session. For example, if you want your Xterm sessions to have a standard UNIX environment, plus access to X client programs, your path might look like this if you were using the Korn shell:

```
PATH=$PATH:$HOME/bin:
```

For C shell users, the situation is different. Because the C shell supports separate **.login** and **.cshrc** files, you can concentrate your efforts on building a **.cshrc** file that is totally suitable for Xterms. The reason is that unless you specify the **-ls** option to Xterm, it will not read the **.login** file. As a result, if you use **xinit**, you can tailor your **.login** file to starting up both character-mode and X environments, without worrying about later redundancies.

CHAPTER 3
Resource Infinity

RESOURCE FILES

Getting a solid grasp of resources is critical to controlling the look and feel of your X environment. Many of the things that you need to know about resources are straightforward, but sometimes you need a roadmap to understand the different resource files. This chapter summarizes general concerns about resources and provides examples to get you on your way.

There are two main categories of X resources: window manager resources and applications resources. Because the window manager has the status of an application, the division between system and application resources is somewhat blurred. You might even say it is an unnecessary distinction, but it is important to note because in some cases, window manager resources can overwrite application resources. The three basic resource-setting mechanisms break down into the following:

- Resource statements loaded via the **-xrm** command line option
- Command line options known by the client program
- Resource statements contained in resource files

The three mechanisms are listed in order of precedence. A healthy approach to the three mechanisms is to use command line options sparingly, and the **-xrm** option even more sparingly. Using resource files provides the basis for the most systematic way of dealing with X resources. Table 3-1 lists the various resource files and environment variables that you can use to control X resources.

Table 3-1 Setting Resources under X

Mechanism	Description
XENVIRONMENT	Environment variable to specify alternative name for the user's **.Xdefaults** file. If specified, the file takes precedence over $XAPPLRESDIR.
$HOME/.Xdefaults-*host*	File associated in the user's home directory that is used to for a given host on the network. The file is usually useful only when you use a single NFS-mounted home directory.
XAPPLRESDIR	Environment variable specifying special directory containing resource files named by the client application's class name.
$HOME/*app-file*	A file in your home directory named by the client application's class name.
$HOME/.Xdefaults	Individual user's resource file; most popular mechanism. Often loaded as part of a startup script by the **xrdb** utility. Otherwise, the server loads it automatically.
Xdefaults	Systemwide file that can be used if **.Xdefaults** does not exist in $HOME. Location varies, but usually found in **/usr/lib/X11/app-defaults**.
/usr/lib/X11/app-defaults	Directory of application resource files named by the client application's class name.

You might be wondering whether the X server reads all the files in Table 3-1 when an application loads. The answer is yes: The precedence of the files does not stop the server from reading files with lower precedence. It simply stops the server from accepting resource statements already defined in a file of higher precedence. For example, if **XTerm*Background** is defined in both $XAPPLRESDIR/**XTerm** and **/usr/lib/X11/app-defaults/XTerm**, the value from $XAPPLRESDIR/**XTerm** takes precedence.

One of the first places to consider setting resources is in a client application's resource file in the **app-defaults** directory. After all, this directory is set up for you when X is installed, and it is visible to applications without setting any special environment variables. Here are the caveats:

- Resources defined in **/usr/lib/X11/app-defaults** are visible to all users on a system.

- Remote clients don't read **/usr/lib/X11/app-defaults** on the local system. They read the copy of the system from which they are executed.

- Maintaining unadulterated copies of the shipped files in **/usr/lib/X11/app-defaults** gives users, customizers, and adminstrators a baseline reference.

The **/usr/lib/X11/app-defaults** directory typically contains resource files for the standard clients from the MIT X Consortium. The directory might also contain files for commercial software applications. It is a good idea to be aware of **/usr/lib/X11/app-defaults** and know how resources behave when loaded from a file in the directory. So, for the time being, we'll continue talking about **/usr/lib/X11/app-defaults**, but remember, you can override resources in the directory's files by using $XENVIRONMENT, $XAPPLRESDIR, $HOME/*app-file*, and $HOME/**.Xdefaults**.

When an X client consults **app-defaults**, it expects to find a file named after the class of an application. For example, **XTerm** with an uppercase **X** and **T** is the class name for Xterm windows. If it does not find a file, it doesn't consult any other file in **/usr/lib/X11/app-defaults**.

The class name of an application usually resembles the application's executable filename, except the first one or two letters are capitalized. If you ever are in doubt about a class name, you can use the **xprop** command to determine it. (The following example requires you to move the mouse to identify the window that you want **xprop** to evaluate. You can also use the **-name** option to **xprop** to obtain the name directly.)

```
xprop | grep WM_CLASS
```

Using this command on a standard Xterm window produces the following output:

```
WM_CLASS(STRING) = "xterm", "XTerm"
```

As you can see, the last field contains the class name. The middle field contains the instance name of the client resource name of the client application, which is the name of the executable file, unless you have specified a unique name for the application. See the *Named Resources* section in this chapter.

An application accesses resources in its **app-defaults** file whenever you load the application. Resources loaded from **app-defaults** files have two distinct characteristics:

- Changes made in **app-defaults** file take effect the next time you load the client application. No intermediate steps are required. No changes are made to any instances of the application that you may have running.
- Resources set in **app-defaults** files are not visible to the **xrdb** database maintained by the X server. Also, any resource loaded with **xrdb** overrides a resource set in an app-defaults file.
- The $XENVIRONMENT, $XAPPLRESDIR and $HOME/*app-file* files share the first characteristic of **app-defaults** files, but not the second characteristic. Because $XENVIRONMENT, $XAPPLRESDIR and $HOME/*app-file* have higher precedence, resources loaded into the **xrdb** database have no effect.

$XENVIRONMENT, $XAPPLRESDIR and $HOME/*app-file* expect to see a file named after the class of an application—just like the names of the files that you would put into **/usr/lib/X11/app-defaults**. For example, the presence of a file named **XTerm** in your home directory causes the X server to load any resource statements in it. Similarly, if you used $XAPPLRESDIR to specify **/home/resources**, you could then create a file called **XTerm** in it—or any other file named after a client application's class name.

It's not a good idea to have warring resource files, so you should plan your file schema carefully. Here are some considerations:

- On a host system that is accessed by X terminals or other X servers, you can use $HOME/*app-file* to localize resources to users.
- On workstations and UNIX PCs, which are likely to be used by a primary user, you can use the $XENVIRONMENT or $XAPPLRESDIR files.
- On all systems, you can use a combination of resources. The $XENVIRONMENT file especially lends itself to setting resources that you want to be in effect systemwide. You could then use the $XAPPLRESDIR or $HOME/*app-file* for user-specific resources.
- If you want to keep things as simple as possible, use **/usr/lib/X11/app-defaults** and rely on the **.Xdefaults** file in the user's home directory.

Why use any of the additional mechanisms to set resources? As detailed in the next section, the $HOME/**.Xdefaults** file is the most convenient place to set resources. But from a system administration point or view—or just from a neatness point of view—not every resource needs to be set in the **.Xdefaults** file. This is particularly true for named resources, which are explained in this chapter, as well as for any other resources you are not likely to change on a regular basis. And perhaps the best reason of all is the more resources you set in **.Xdefaults**, the more your X server performance is affected. The **xrdb** loading process also lengthens the X startup time.

If you want to be certain of which resources are being loaded for a given application, your system software may have a command that traces resources upon execution. On SunOS systems, this command is called **trace**. On SVR5 systems, the command is called **truss**. The **appres** command is also very useful for establishing which resources will be in effect when an application loads. To use **appres** to check the resources for the default Xterm window, enter:

```
appres XTerm xterm
```

To get the resources for an Xterm that has a special name of **bigterm** (again see the upcoming section *Named Resources*), enter:

```
appres XTerm bigterm
```

You can use **appres** for any X client. Commercial applications should have both a class and an instance name. For example, to get the resources that the WordPerfect word processor would load, enter:

```
appres Wp wp
```

If you don't have a copy of **appres** on your system, you should consider getting one. It is not only an interactive aid for customizers and administrators, it can be used in shell scripts for various purposes, including modifying resources before a client program loads, or just to provide critical information about a client. In Chapter 8, the **clone** script uses **appres** to get size values associated with internal components of Xterms. The values are then factored with other information to replicate an existing window.

For interactive use, you can get by without **appres**. In fact, the following **getres** shell script improves on **appres** in that it tells you the files associated with resources. Unlike appres, the **getres** script does not eliminate redundant resources. This might be good or bad, depending on your perspective, but **getres** is helpful if you have to debug multiple resource files.

```
#!/bin/sh
# getres, script to get resources
# Syntax: getres clientclass clientinstance
# Copyright (c) Alan Southerton 1993

# Operation: All resources are listed if they are
# contained in the standard resource files. The
```

```
# exception is key translation resources, which are
# just indicated by the opening statement.

# Dependencies
# /usr/lib/X11/app-defaults

# Check for valid number of arguments
  case $# in
    2) ;; # argument count okay
    *) echo "$0 clientclass clientinstance" 1>&2
       exit 1 ;;
  esac

# Initial values
  file=/tmp/getres.
  class=$1; instance=$2
  defhome="/usr/lib/X11/app-defaults/Xdefaults"

# Remove temporary file upon exit.
  trap "rm $file; exit 1 2 3 15"

# Define resource file locations
  places="$XENVIRONMENT \
          $XAPPLRESDIR/$class \
          $HOME/$class \
          /usr/lib/X11/app-defaults/$class \
          $HOME/.Xdefaults \
          /usr/lib/X11/app-defaults/Xdefaults"

# Loop through resource locations
  for arg in $places
  do
     if [ "$arg" = "$HOME/.Xdefaults" ]; then
          echo------------------------------------
          echo "$arg    [$class|$instance|*]"
          xrdb -query | egrep \
               "(^$class|^$instance|^\*)"
          echo
     elif [ "$arg" = "$defhome" ]; then
          echo------------------------------------
          echo "$arg    [$class|$instance]"
          xrdb -query | egrep \
               "(^$class|^$instance|^\*)"
          echo
     else
          if [ -r $arg ]; then
```

```
            echo------------------------------------
            echo "$arg     [$class|$instance|*]"
            echo
            egrep "(^$class|^$instance|^\*)" $arg
            echo
            fi
    fi
done
```

The **getres** file reads the various possible resource files if they exist. It also queries the **xrdb** database. All resources are displayed in order of precedence. Use **getres** as you would **appres**:

```
getres XTerm xterm
```

One shortcoming of the X resource scheme is the lack of a utility to tell you what resources are in effect for an existing application. If you need to track a resource, you might consider loading it via a command line option.

There are a few other things you should remember about the basic syntax of a resource statement. First, always make sure that you include a colon before the *value*. Omitting the colon is a common mistake, but the X resource manager doesn't inform you when you forget to include it. Second, if you need to comment a line in a resource script, begin the line with an exclamation point. Third, be wary of lines with trailing whitespace. Often, a trailing whitespace can cause a resource not to be loaded—and even more disconcerting, it can cause a resource not to be loaded in, say, a $XAPPLRESDIR file, even though it doesn't affect the resource when loaded from the **.Xdefaults** file.

THE .Xdefaults FILE

Often, the best place to set resources is in $HOME/**.Xdefaults**. You can design your customizing to take advantage of other resource files, but using **.Xdefaults** avoids conflicts with other users, as well as conflicts when you load client programs from other systems. Using **.Xdefaults** also eliminates a lot of concerns about where resources are being set.

The bad news is that it is impractical to set all resources in the **.Xdefaults** file. The more resources that you add to this file, the longer it takes the **xrdb** resource manager to load the file into the resource database. What's more, if you want to set systemwide resources for client programs, you should use the application's resource file in the **app-defaults** directory, the file pointed to by $XENVIRONMENT or $XAPPLRESDIR.

There are two ways that resources in the **.Xdefaults** file can be loaded:

- By loading **.Xdefaults** with the **xrdb** utility, which records the loaded resources into the server's database
- By simply creating a copy of **.Xdefaults** in your home directory and leaving the server to load it by default at startup

The second method is similar to the way that the X server treats other files such as those in **app-defaults** and those defined by XAPPLRESDIR. The server loads the resources, but you cannot later query them using **xrdb**. The reason is that only resources loaded with **xrdb** are recorded in the user-accessible server database. Thus, because **.Xdefaults** is a file that the end user is most likely to modify on a regular basis, it is usually loaded with **xrdb**. This is true whether a system starts X using **xinit** or **xdm**. Here is an example from a DEC OSF/1 system, which uses **xdm** and the **Xsession** startup script:

```
# Excerpt from DEC OSF/1 Xsession startup script
  resources="$HOME/.Xdefaults"
     if [ -f "$resources" ] &&\
         /usr/bin/X11/xrdb -load $resources
```

If you control your resources in **.Xdefaults**, you can generally be assured resource changes will take effect. The one exception is resources—such as window manager resources—that can be set with the **-xrm** command line option, which overrides previously set resources of the same name. The **-xrm** option is a good way to enforce window manager policy—either systemwide or with your own login.

In order for newly set resources in **.Xdefaults** to take effect, you must either restart X or load them with **xrdb**. By default, **xrdb** loads the specified file, although one of its many options is the **-load** option. In other words, the following two commands are identical:

```
xrdb $HOME/.Xdefaults
xrdb -load $HOME/.Xdefaults
```

It might be a good idea to use **-load** when building scripts. Normally, UNIX commands display some form of output when the command is entered without any options (default behavior). And the **man** page for **xrdb** acknowledges this, so it could lead one to wonder whether the MIT X Consortium might make **xrdb -query** the default behavior in a future release of the X Window System.

If you change window manager resources with **xrdb**, you must take the additional step of restarting the window manager. This is typically an option on the standard root window menu shipped with Motif. Desktop managers usually provide easy access to Motif's restart option, too. Additionally, as described in the previous chapter, you might implement a restart script such as **rmwm**. If you do, you might want to reload **.Xdefaults** before restarting Motif or another window manager.

The form of an **.Xdefaults** file is straightforward in nine out of ten cases. Individual entries in **.Xdefaults** consist of the *resource name*, followed by a colon, followed by a *resource value*. More often than not, you'll see one or more whitespaces or tabs after the colon. This is acceptable, but not required. However, if you prefer not to see whitespaces or tabs after the colon—the model that the **.xmenu** configuration file uses—you will have to do some filtering. The reason is that **xrdb** inserts tabs in its output. As a result, when you replace the contents of **.Xdefaults** with the output of **xrdb -query**—a technique used throughout the book—tabs will have returned to the file.

In some cases, such as when you specify fonts, you must ensure that no trailing whitespace occurs at the end of the resource value string. Resources files pointed to by $XAPPLRESDIR are also especially susceptible to this weakness.

If you have read this far, you have probably seen one or two **.Xdefaults** files in your day. Risking redundancy, here is a snapshot from the usually slightly larger **.Xdefaults** file that results from typical use of Xmenu. (The menu options, by and large, are responsible for adding most options to the **.Xdefaults** file used by the Xmenu software.)

```
Mwm*Background: #ab7665
Mwm*Foreground: #00627f
Mwm*IconPlacement: left top
Mwm*activeBackground: #004362
Mwm*activeForeground: #fbfafa
Mwm*client*foreground: #191970
Mwm*client*menu*background: blue
Mwm*client*topShadowPixmap: 75
Mwm*client.title.activeBackground: #3689de
Mwm*client.title.background: #9292b5
Mwm*colormapFocusPolicy: explicit

Mwm*errormsg*clientDecoration: \
          -minimize -maximize -menu -resizeh

Mwm*errormsg*matteBackground: #ff0000
```

```
Mwm*errormsg*matteForeground: #ff0000
Mwm*errormsg*matteWidth: 70
Mwm*fadeNormalIcon: True

Mwm*feedback*fontList: \
     "-adobe-times-bold-r-normal*18-180-75-75-p-99*"

Mwm*feedback*foreground: #000500
Mwm*fontList: "-adobe-times-bold-r-normal*180*"
Mwm*getinput*matteWidth: 15
Mwm*getinput.clientDecoration: none +title +border
Mwm*getstring*matteWidth: 25
Mwm*getstring.clientDecoration: none +title +border
Mwm*icon*background: #0094f1

Mwm*icon*fontList: \
      "-misc-fixed-bold-r-normal*15-140-75-75-c-90*"

Mwm*icon*foreground: #000900
Mwm*iconAutoPlace: True
Mwm*iconBoxSBDisplayPolicy: all
Mwm*iconBoxSize: 10x1
Mwm*iconBoxTitle: Icons
Mwm*iconDecoration: activelabel
Mwm*iconImageForeground: yellow
Mwm*iconImageMaximum: 50x50
Mwm*iconPlacementMargin: 0
Mwm*iconbox*clientDecoration: border +title
Mwm*iconbox*matteWidth: 0
Mwm*imgshow*matteBackground: #d7ee0a
Mwm*imgshow*matteForeground: #d7ee0a
Mwm*imgshow*matteWidth: 6
Mwm*interactivePlacement: False
Mwm*limitResize: false
Mwm*matteBackground: #bebfbd
Mwm*maximumMaximumSize: 1000x1000
Mwm*menu*DefaultWindowMenu*background: gray
Mwm*menu*GrabMenu*background: #228B22

Mwm*menu*GrabMenu*fontList: \
          "*times-bold-r-normal*180*"

Mwm*menu*background: #7288d5
Mwm*menu*foreground: #000000
Mwm*moveThreshold: 6
Mwm*passSelectButton: True
```

```
Mwm*purple*icon.background: #7288d5
Mwm*resizeCursors: True
Mwm*show*matteBackground: #ff0000
Mwm*show*matteForeground: #ff0000
Mwm*show*matteWidth: 24
Mwm*useIconBox: True
Mwm*wMenuButtonClick: True
Mwm*wMenuButtonClick2: True
Mwm*keyBindings: DefaultButtonBindings
Mwm*configFile: $HOME/.Mwmrc
Mwm*iconPlacement: left bottom
Mwm*iconBoxGeometry: 8x1+1-1

Mwm*client*fontList:\
     "-adobe-times-bold-r-normal*24-240-75-75-p-132*"

Mwm*resizeBorderWidth: 5

Mwm*menu*fontList:\
     "-misc-fixed-bold-r-normal*13-100-100-100-c-80*"

Mwm*showFeedback: all
Mwm*keyboardFocusPolicy: pointer
Mwm*focusAutoRaise: false
Mwm*client.background: #9b7e70
Mwm*buttonBindings: DefaultButtonBindings
Mwm*matteWidth: 15
```

You might have noticed that all the resources in the example are Motif resources. The explanation for this is the Xmenu scripts relegate other resources to files specified by the $XAPPLRESDIR environment variable. And the reason for not relegating Motif resources to an **Mwm** file in the $XAPPLRESDIR directory is that already loaded resources via the **xrdb** and **.Xdefaults** tandem make the Motif restart process go slightly faster. On slower workstations, this is meaningful, but if you have mostly fast workstations on your network, you might want to put many, if not all, of the Motif resources in the $XAPPLRESDIR directory, too. In fact, if you notice any performance degradation using the Xmenu approach, modify the Xmenu scripts so that $XAPPLRESDIR/**Mwm** becomes the home for Motif resources.

The one disadvantage to the Xmenu approach to the **.Xdefaults** file is that you cannot use C preprocessor directives in **.Xdefaults** (see the next section). The advantage, however, is that you can quickly and easily update both the current **xrdb** database and the **.Xdefaults** file. The **xrdb** program itself provides limited capabilities with its **-edit** option, but you can improve upon these capabilities with an approach similar to the following script.

```
#!/bin/sh
# Suggested name: xres
# Script to modify X resources known by xrdb
# Syntax: xres <client> <resource>

# Check for valid number of arguments
   case $# in
       3) ;; # argument count correct, do nothing
       *) echo "Usage: $0 client resource value"
1>&2; exit 1 ;;
     esac

# Query xrdb database, grep all lines but specified
# resource to temporary file; exit if xrdb fails.
# Otherwise, append resource to temporary file, move
# it to .Xdefaults, and lastly load new .Xdefaults.

  xrdb -query | grep -v "$1\*$2:" > /tmp/xrdb.$$
   if [ $? ] ; then
     echo $1\*$2:' '$3 >> /tmp/xrdb.$$
     cp $HOME./.Xdefaults $HOME/.Xdefaults.bak
     mv /tmp/xrdb.$$ $HOME/.Xdefaults
     xrdb -load $HOME/.Xdefaults
  else
     echo Could not create temporary file.
  fi
```

The **xres** script is a general-purpose implementation of the approach used by Xmenu scripts. The **xres** script itself is not called by any of the Xmenu scripts, but the sequence of querying the database, using **grep -v** to remove the specified resource, and then **mv** to update the **.Xdefaults** file is repeatedly used in the Xmenu scripts. Some of the Xmenu scripts also use the **egrep** command to process multiple resources at the same time. Additionally, the method of updating the **.Xdefaults** file is used on other resources files, including those in $XAPPLRESDIR.

To use **xres**, enter the resource name of the client, the resource itself, and the new resource value. For example, if you wanted to change the scroll buffer for standard Xterm windows, enter:

```
xres Xterm saveLines 1024
```

The **xres** script works fine to update the resources of a client program just before loading the program. It will seem to have no effect, however, when you use it to update the resources of the window manager—unless, of course, you restart the window manager.

The obvious next step is to use the restart option on the root window menu. This is a satisfactory approach, but in the interests of streamlining, you could rewrite the **rmwm** script from the previous chapter. Here is an example that assumes the **xrdb** database has been modified, without equal modifications occurring in **.Xdefaults**:

```
#!/bin/sh
#Suggested name: rmwm2
#Script to restart Motif window manager

# Get pid for renamed version of mwm executable
  pid=`ps -a | grep MWMEXEC | \
               grep -v grep | cut -c1-5`

# Make backup copy of .Xdefaults
  cp $HOME/.Xdfeaults $HOME/.Xdefaults.bak

# Query resource database and update .Xdefaults
  xrdb -query | sort -f > $HOME/.Xdefaults

# Kill Motif
  kill -9 $pid

# Restart Motif via special loader script
  mwm &
```

There are other ways that you can go about updating the resource database and restarting Motif. The Xmenu software, for example, does not use the approach in **rmwm2**. Instead, it relies on scripts that obtain changed resource values to update both the database and **.Xdefaults**. Then, whenever Motif is restarted, all changes are currently in server memory.

Finally, note that you can comment the **.Xdefaults** file even though you use the Xmenu method of updating it. The conventional way to comment **.Xdefaults** is to use the **!** character. You can also use **#**, but it generates an error—although a harmless one—when you load **.Xdefaults** with xrdb. Neither of these methods, however, is fruitful if you use the Xmenu updating method. The reason is that comments with either **!** or **#** are not loaded into the resource database. The workaround is to create comments like this:

`Mwm*client:` **Client Specific Resources**

When the **xrdb** program sees a line such as this, it loads it into the database along with valid resources. It has no way of knowing that it is not a valid resource. As a result, you can perform **xrdb -query**, obtain the comment, pass it through **sort**, update **.Xdefaults**, and have the comment reappear in its original place.

MORE ON XRDB

Because the **xrdb** program can use the C preprocessor, there are several features of **xrdb** that you may want to exploit. If you choose to do so, however, you must either use the **-edit** option to **xrdb** to update your **.Xdefaults** file, or design a system whereby you use the **#include** directive to assemble different files into a single file that you load with **xrdb**.

The **-edit** option allows you to preserve comments and preprocessor directives in **.Xdefaults**. The steps involved are slightly more tedious that the method used by the Xmenu software, and not as complete:

1. Load new resources into the database using either the **-load** or **-merge** option to **xrdb**.

2. Use the **-edit** option to copy the contents of the database to **.Xdefaults**. You can also use the **-backup** option at the same time to produce a backup file.

3. Edit the file to remove duplicate resource names.

If you use this approach in scripts, note that previously loaded resources with the same name as newly loaded resources are not replaced. Additionally, even though the **-edit** option adds new resources from the database to your resource file, it does so by appending them at the end of the file.

Compared with the Xmenu method of using **grep -v**, and then adding the new resource to a temporary file (which then replaces **.Xdefaults**), the **-edit** option is not as satisfying. Both methods, however, are portable across all X systems.

Among the different preprocessor features supported by **xrdb** are the **#include**, **#define** and **#ifdef** directives. These are the preprocessor's most powerful directives and C programmers would be at a loss without them. The Xmenu menus, in fact, use the **#include** directive to provide custom resource palettes (see Chapter 7) by assembling different files to load into the resource database. Here is an example:

```
# Form xrdb input with include statements.
echo \#include \"$HOME/.Xdefaults\" > $file
echo \#include \"$palette\" >> $file
xrdb -load $file
```

In this example, a temporary file called $file is created. The contents of $file is two **#include** statements. The first statement specifies the current **.Xdefaults** file. The second statement specifies a file with color resource statements. Finally, the temporary file is loaded into the resource database. One other note about include files: you can either specify an include file by its full path, as in the examples, or set a default include file directory. The **-I** option to **xrdb** allows you to set the default directory.

The **#define** directive can be as handy as **#include**. In essence, **#define** lets you create aliases for resource values that are otherwise too unruly to easily type and read. For example, some of the **Mwm*clientDecoration** resources can extend beyond a single line of text. Plus, wouldn't it be easier to enter an **Mwm*clientDecoration** value as a single word? Try this:

```
#define SIMPLE -minimize -maximize -menu -resizeh
.
.
.
Mwm*errormsg*clientDecoration: SIMPLE
```

Making font names more readable is another good use for the **#define** directive.* Here's a set of examples for the Times bold font:

```
#define TIMESB12 \
          "-adobe-times-bold-r-normal*120-75-75*"
#define TIMESB14 \
          "-adobe-times-bold-r-normal*140-75-75*"
#define TIMESB18 \
          "-adobe-times-bold-r-normal*180-75-75*"
#define TIMESB24 \
          "-adobe-times-bold-r-normal*240-75-75*"
```

You probably noticed that the defined names appear in uppercase letters. This is conventional, at least in C programming. There is no reason to extend the convention to resource files, however.

The third directive, **#ifdef**, yields another kind of power: it lets you develop conditional logic inside the **.Xdefaults** file. You could also use the hostname of a system as the condition for loading a given set of resources in **.Xdefaults**:

```
xrdb -D`hostname` -load $HOME/.Xdefaults
```

* You might prefer to use the X font database aliasing mechanism instead of the **#define** approach. It is equally valid, but you must be sure to maintain the font database across different systems when administering a networked environment.

In the example, the **-D** option is used to create the preprocessor symbol. A related option is **-U**, which removes symbols defined by **-D**.

You also use the **#ifdef** directive with predefined values, called symbols in preprocessor jargon. A common symbol to check for is COLOR, which was made internal to **xrdb** with X11R5 and allows you to create default resources for both monochrome and color systems. Table 3-2 lists the complete set of symbols recognized by the **xrdb** program.

Table 3-2 Preprocessor Symbols Known to Xrdb

Symbol	Description
BITS_PER_RGB	An RGB color specification's significant bits, which is the log base 2 of the number of distinct shades of each primary color supported by the system. This value is not typically related to the PLANES value.
CLASS	The visual class of the root window of the default screen. The value can be StaticGray, GrayScale, StaticColor, PseudoColor, TrueColor, or DirectColor.
COLOR	This.symbol is defined only if CLASS is one of the following values: **StaticColor**, **PseudoColor**, **TrueColor**, or **DirectColor**.
HEIGHT	The height of the root window of the default screen.
HOST	The hostname of the current display.
CLIENTHOST	The hostname for the system on which **xrdb** is running.
PLANES	The number of bit planes of the root window of the default screen.
RELEASE	The release number of the X server as set by the vendor, or developer, of the server.
REVISION	The X Protocol minor version number of the X server.
SERVERHOST	The hostname of the current display. Same as HOST.
VERSION	The X server version number. This is always **11**.
VENDOR	The name of the X server vendor or developer.
WIDTH	The width of the root window of the default screen.
X_RESOLUTION	The horizontal resolution of the root window of the default screen in pixels per meter.
Y_RESOLUTION	The vertical resolution of the root window of the default screen in pixels per meter.

Alternative Defaults

If you want to use preprocessor directives in your **.Xdefaults** file, yet also want to use many of the Xmenu scripts, you can have your cake and eat it, too. The simple answer is to add a line to the Xmenu scripts that includes a file containing your preprocessor directives. Here's a sample using the color palette example mentioned in the last section:

```
# mwmpalette, script to set canned resources
# Syntax: mwmpalette colorfile
# Copyright (c) Alan Southerton

# Defintions
    file=/tmp/xmenu.
    palette=$XSHELL/palettes/$1

# Remove temporary file on exit.
    trap "rm $file; exit 0 1 2 3 15"

# Form xrdb input with include statements, using
# xrdb's ability to override previously loaded
# resources.
    echo \#include \"$HOME/.Xdefaults.cpp" > $file
    echo \#include \"$HOME/.Xdefaults\" >> $file
    echo \#include \"$palette\" >> $file
    xrdb -load $file
```

This is the basic approach. The first **echo** statement adds an **#include** statement that calls a special file that contains your C preprocessor directives. (Note that the actual **mwmpalette** script, which appears again in Chapter 7, is more extensive than the one that appears here.)

NAMED RESOURCES

For lack of a better term, resources that are associated with a named instance of an X program can be called named resources. These resources are specifically designed for use with the named client. The only time they get used is when you execute a program and specify its predetermined name.

With the **-name** option supported by almost all X clients, command line users can quickly call up a custom window. For an Xterm defined in a resource file as **vi**—which is what you might name an Xterm window customized for the **vi** editor—users would enter the following at the command line:

```
xterm -name vi &
```

In writing scripts, named resources are a real time saver. First, they eliminate the need for many command line options. Second, they provide a method of organization that is easy to follow and duplicate, if users want to put their own custom tilt on things. Third, and very important, they let you override global resources on a selective basis, without having to reuse the class name of the resource. Among other things, this means that the default behavior and appearance remains intact—that the resource values specified in the **app-defaults** directory continue to be in effect when a user enters the generic command for a client. For example, **xman** brings up the default window, but **xman -name dtxman** brings up a special window.

Using a named resource solves the problem encountered in the **xlogo** startup client in Chapter 2—namely, when a second instance of **xlogo** is executed, it also has the singular characteristics that you created for the special startup client. The way to avoid this is to create an instance of **xlogo** that goes by a unique name, such as **smlogo**:

```
Mwm*smlogo*windowMenu: XlogoMenu
smlogo*iconic: true
smlogo*geometry: 100x125
smlogo*foreground: yellow
smlogo*background: black
smlogo*bitmap: /home/bitmaps/sm.xpm
```

To bring up this special **xlogo** window, enter:

```
xlogo -name smlogo
```

Other than creating a name for this special incarnation of **xlogo**, the resource statements effect only cosmetic changes. The geometry statement, for example, increases the height compared with the default version of **xlogo**, making it approximately the same size as the Motif menu. The iconic statement causes **xlogo** to open as an icon—and you just might want it to stay this way, given that you can access the Motif menu by clicking on the icon. The bitmap statement specifies a custom bitmap for **xlogo**, giving it even more of a custom feel. If you do open the **sm** version of **xlogo**, you will find that the **sm** version has a black background and yellow foreground. The **Mwm*smlogo*windowMenu** entry, as you'll see in later chapters, links the special Motif menu to **sm**.

The more options a client supports, the more you can customize it. For example, Xterm windows lend themselves well to customization and you will find that special instances of Xterms can serve in many situations, especially when you simply want to display data in a window, or want to get user input. For now, here is a complete example for the console window described in the previous section.

```
console*iconic: true
console*bitmap: /home/bitmaps/bm.xpm
console*geometry: 75x32+75+40
console*font: *adobe-courier-bold-r*180*
console*background: black
console*fogeground: green
console*internalBorder: 15
console*saveLines: 1024
console*scrollBar: true
console*thickness: 20
```

This example does many different things to the appearance and behavior of the Xterm window. First, it opens the window as an icon using a special bitmap. When the window opens, it is large, thanks to the geometry statement, but specifically because of the large font used. The colors of the Xterm are green on black, and a scrollbar, which uses the foreground color, has a width of 20 pixels. A border between the scrollbar and main window area has a width of 15 pixels. The scroll buffer is set to 1024 lines.

RESOURCE PRECEDENCE

The more specific you get about setting resources, the more concerned you have to be about precedence. The alternative, as presented in the previous section, is to name clients and have an array of differently named clients from which to choose.

X lets you specify values for any program as well as most user interface components in a program. Resources for these components range from the size of a dialog box to the color used in text in the titlebar of a window. You name it: It's likely controlled by a resource.

How deeply an application supports resources varies. Many commercial applications use resources in conjunction with a preferences dialog box. The user sets preferences in the dialog box and the application stores the user's choices as resources in **.Xdefaults** or a file in the directory specified by the $XAPPLRESDIR environment variable. The abstract syntax for precedence is:

```
program.object[object2...objectN].attribute: value
```

The *program* portion of the statement is obvious. Objects are nearly as obvious, but you need to know your program before you specify resources for them. Objects are typically any of several widgets (dialog boxes, menus, panels) that a program uses. The *attribute* is the characteristic of the object that you want to set, such as background and foreground colors. The *value* is the actual value you give the characteristic. Refer to the documentation supplied by the program to obtain actual names for attributes and values. Generally, you will be dealing with color names, font names, number values to specify windows sizing and screen positions, and Boolean values to specify whether a given attribute is turned on (true) or off (false).

So why are resource statements pesky? If you stay within the realm of setting basic resources, they aren't. But the minute you get fancy and want to set instances of an object within a class of objects, you need your fly-swatter. There are two basic rules to remember:

- Tight bindings have precedence over loose bindings.
- Instance definitions have precedence over class definitions.

A tight binding is simply a statement that specifically names an instance of an application. The most common way to explain this is via the Xterm window, which can be named according to the type of terminal emulation that you want the window to have. For example, you can specify a VT100 emulation with the following statement:

```
xterm.termName: vt100
```

After this, you can refer to the VT100 window by specifically mentioning it in your resource statement:

```
xterm.vt100.background: blue
```

Similarly, you can refer to all instances of **xterm** windows running VT100 emulation by capitalizing the class name

```
xterm.VT100.background: blue
```

In general, it is advisable to avoid tight bindings. For one thing, it makes it difficult to share resource files with other users. For another thing, when using them with applications, you can't be guaranteed that subsequent changes in an application won't invalidate the tight bindings. Note, too, that you have to use the dot character (**.**) before the instance name when specifying a tight binding.

As for classes versus instances, again it is not necessary to go into this much detail when setting resources, unless you have aesthetic or practical reasons for doing so. In order to determine to what class an instance belongs, you must study the resource definitions that accompany an application.

With the **xterm** window, for example, the resource **boldFont** is part of the class **font**. This means you can set **boldFont** in either of the two following ways:

```
xterm*Font:

xterm*boldFont:
```

Using instance names can be handy, but again, you should only bother to do so if you have a compelling reason. They provide an excellent way to customize applications for use by different groups of people, but for a standalone user, they serve little purpose and become a distraction.

CHAPTER 4

Shell Approach

REVERSAL OF TERMS

The server-client metaphor of the X Window System is confusing. Not only does it transpose the classical definitions of server (host) and client (terminal), it makes the word *client* synonymous with the word *application.*

The definitions of server and client are transposed because an X server usually runs on the local workstation, PC, or X terminal. The server is responsible for managing user input and display output. When you resize a window with the mouse, it is the X server's role to track the mouse and change the size of the window.

On the other side of the transposition, the X client sits waiting for input passed to it by the X server. The client can coexist with the server on the same machine (if you use a standalone UNIX workstation or UNIX-based PC). On a network, the client usually resides on a central machine. This machine is often referred to as a host, file server, or application server. This book uses *host* in most cases.

The client and server interact seamlessly. As a user, you rarely need to know that your application is designed to address the server-client metaphor. The main thing you need to know is the resource names that the client recognizes. For example, here are two resource statements used by the WordPerfect word processor:

```
Wp*editDialog*background: #D3D3D3D3D3D3
Wp*editDialog*foreground: #00000000CDCD
```

These examples represent the simplest form of a resource statement, because they have the fewest possible components: **Wp**, which is the name of the client; **editDialog**, which narrows the concern to the name of a subordinate window in WordPerfect; and **background** or **foreground**, which specify the resource you want. The hexadecimal numbers following the resource values are color definitions. Both numbers could be written in shorter form—**#D3D3D3** or **#0000CD**—but most, if not all, X servers recognize the longer form, even if their native format is a shorter one.

You can also use English-language names for colors, instead of hexadecimal numbers. And this choice gives rise to a debate between experienced X users. The hexadecimal method is cumbersome, but portable. Its major disadvantage is that each color set with a hexadecimal number uses one of 256 places in the system colormap. The alternatives—using the **rgb.txt** color database or the X11R5 X Color Management System, or Xcms—avoid this drawback. With these methods, you must maintain an external database, adding a layer of responsibility in a networked environment. But with the hexadecimal approach, all you have to do is write portable scripts.

All-in-all, almost every X application can have resources attached to it. This includes commercial applications, public domain software, clients from the MIT X Consortium, and importantly, whichever window manager you use. Using your window manager resources, you can standardize the look and feel of most applications. Some unruly applications can resist control by the window manager, but not many. The **xmag**, **xwd**, and **xwud** clients are prime examples of unruly applications (see Chapter 8).

COMMON RESOURCES

There is little standardization in what type of resources a given application supports. There is also little standardization in the names given to the resources that are supported. There are some major ones, however, and you should know the ones listed in Table 4-1.

Table 4-1 Resources Common to X Clients

Resource	Flag	Description
background	-bg	Window background color.
foreground	-fg	Window foreground color.
font	-fn	Text font in window.
iconic	-xrm*	Start window as icon.
geometry	-g	Window size and position.
translations	-xrm*	Keymap definitions in window.

* These options are usually available only through the **-xrm** flag, which lets you load resources at the command line. Xterm has an **-iconic** option, however.

The next section summarizes how to load resources using the **xrdb** client and by using command line options.

Loading Resources

If you have not done much work with resources, those listed in Table 4-1 are good ones to learn first. All of them produce some immediate effect. And in many programs, four out of the six have an equivalent command line option, allowing you to easily experiment with resources before setting them in a resource file:

```
xterm -bg blue -fg white -fn terminal-bold
```

You can also use the **xrdb** utility to experiment with resources. The **xrdb** utility is an important part of setting resources in the X Window System.

For desktop customizers, **xrdb** gives you an easy way to query the resource database maintained by the X server. As shown in Figure 4-1, the **xrdb** database is in a good position to control which resources are in effect. Using **xrdb**, you can override any resource not set at the system level. You can also set resources that weren't set at the system level.

The only resources you can't change are those set using the **-xrm** command line option. Almost all X programs support the **-xrm** option, which among other things, gives you a way to police resources. If you are working on your own system, you might want to set one or two resources with **-xrm** to prevent friends from changing critical parts of your window manager interface. Otherwise, the **-xrm** option really suits desktop customizers who are responsible for administering multiple systems in workgroups or in an entire site. To ensure that the Motif window manager always used point-and-click focus policy, for example, you would invoke Motif like this:

```
mwm -xrm 'mwm*keyboardFocusPolicy: explicit' \
    -xrm 'mwm*focusAutoRaise: true' &
```

For resources that are okay to change dynamically (this is not to say that changing focus policy is a serious offense; it is perhaps mostly an annoyance in a workgroup where people use each others' systems regularly), you should avoid the **-xrm** option and stick with **xrdb**, or load resources automatically via $XAPPLRESDIR files.

In its simplest form, **xrdb** can be invoked for interactive input. From an Xterm window, just type **xrdb** at the prompt, press Return, enter a valid resource statement, and press Ctrl-D. Here is an example:

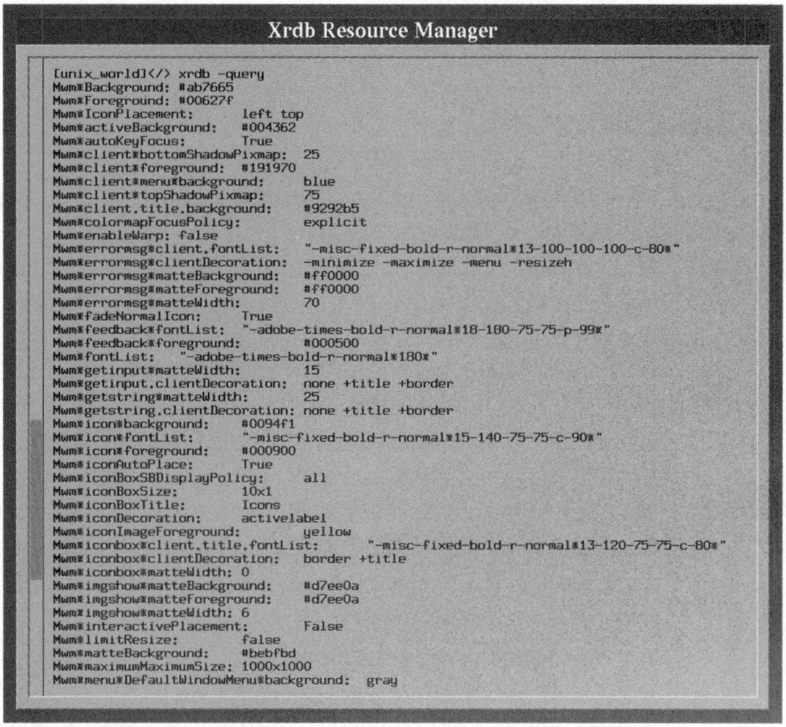

Xrdb Resource Manager

```
[unix_world]</> xrdb -query
Mwm*Background: #ab7665
Mwm*Foreground: #00627f
Mwm*IconPlacement:      left top
Mwm*activeBackground:   #004362
Mwm*autoKeyFocus:       True
Mwm*client*bottomShadowPixmap:  25
Mwm*client*foreground:  #191970
Mwm*client*menu*background:     blue
Mwm*client*topShadowPixmap:     75
Mwm*client.title.background:    #9292b5
Mwm*colormapFocusPolicy:        explicit
Mwm*enableWarp: false
Mwm*errormsg*client.fontList:   "-misc-fixed-bold-r-normal*13-100-100-100-c-80*"
Mwm*errormsg*clientDecoration:  -minimize -maximize -menu -resizeh
Mwm*errormsg*matteBackground:   #ff0000
Mwm*errormsg*matteForeground:   #ff0000
Mwm*errormsg*matteWidth:        70
Mwm*fadeNormalIcon:     True
Mwm*feedback*fontList:  "-adobe-times-bold-r-normal*18-180-75-75-p-99*"
Mwm*feedback*foreground:        #000500
Mwm*fontList:   "-adobe-times-bold-r-normal*180*"
Mwm*getinput*matteWidth:        15
Mwm*getinput.clientDecoration:  none +title +border
Mwm*getstring*matteWidth:       25
Mwm*getstring.clientDecoration: none +title +border
Mwm*icon*background:    #0094f1
Mwm*icon*fontList:      "-misc-fixed-bold-r-normal*15-140-75-75-c-90*"
Mwm*icon*foreground:    #000900
Mwm*iconAutoPlace:      True
Mwm*iconBoxSBDisplayPolicy:     all
Mwm*iconBoxSize:        10x1
Mwm*iconBoxTitle:       Icons
Mwm*iconDecoration:     activelabel
Mwm*iconImageForeground:        yellow
Mwm*iconbox*client.title.fontList:      "-misc-fixed-bold-r-normal*13-120-75-75-c-80*"
Mwm*iconbox*clientDecoration:   border +title
Mwm*iconbox*matteWidth: 0
Mwm*imgshow*matteBackground:    #d7ee0a
Mwm*imgshow*matteForeground:    #d7ee0a
Mwm*imgshow*matteWidth: 6
Mwm*interactivePlacement:       False
Mwm*limitResize:        false
Mwm*matteBackground:    #bebfbd
Mwm*maximumMaximumSize: 1000x1000
Mwm*menu*DefaultWindowMenu*background:  gray
```

Figure 4-1 This Xterm window shows representative output of the xrdb resource database program.

```
$ xrdb
 *background: blue
<Ctrl-D>
```

This interactive session with **xrdb** changes the background resource for all windows to blue. The ***background** specification is very general, however, and any windows without a more specific **background** statement would be overridden by ***background**. The section on *Resource Precedence* in Chapter 3 describes this situation.

The other frequently used options to **xrdb** are **-query**, **-merge**, and **-load**. All three options require a resource file as an argument. The **-load** option is actually the default for **xrdb** when you follow it with a filename:

```
xrdb mydefaults
```

Here **xrdb** simply loads a file called **mydefaults** into the X server database. Any previous contents in the database are deleted. The only resources in effect are those set in the **mydefaults** file, as well as any set at the system level and by the **-xrm** option.

Window Colors

Most PCs, workstations, and X terminals have color displays, with a minimum of 256 colors per color palette. If you attempt to exceed 256 colors—for example, by displaying a bitmap image on the root window while using one or more applications with fairly heavy color demands—the colors in one window or another may distort into an unrecognizable blur.

Aside from staying within the limits of your hardware, manipulating colors in X is straightforward enough. Colors available to you at the system level are listed in the **rgb.txt** color database file, which contains more than 700 English-language color names, ranging from the primary colors—**red**, **blue**, **green**—to exotic names like **deep sky blue**, **papaya whip**, and **navajo white**. The **rgb.txt** file resides in different directories on different systems, but it usually resides in the **/usr** hierarchy. In the MIT X Consortium release, it resides in **/usr/lib**.

When using the default **rgb.txt**, you have the choice of using either regular English-language words in all lowercase letters, or a German-style word, which combines more than one word and capitalizes the first letter of each word. Here are some examples:

```
navajo white          NavajoWhite
misty rose            MistyRose
white
darkslate gray        DarkSlateGray
darkslate grey        DarkSlateGrey
navy
navy blue             NavyBlue
aquamarine
dark green            DarkGreen
```

Probably because the **rgb.txt** file exists, all vendors don't feel compelled to include the **showrgb** client in their implementations of X. A handy way to overcome this is to create a script or alias that simply displays the file to the screen, such as in the following example for OSF/1 systems:

```
cat /usr/lib/X11/rgb.txt
```

A good name for the script or alias—if you don't want to use the **showrgb** name—is **xlscolors**. This provides consistency with the **xlsfonts** client explained in the next section. The one shortcoming of the **rgb.txt** file and the **showrgb** client is that neither tells you the hexadecimal number associated with a color.

The hexadecimal number is important if you are concerned with portability between different X systems. The reason for this is there is no standardization in the English-language names used for colors under X11R4. In X11R5, there is an approach to standardization, but at cost of clarity in naming conventions. X11R5 also supports the X11R4 method of naming colors, so any strategy you develop under X11R4 is useful in X11R5. On the other hand, the X11R5 Xcms system is an excellent tool for applications that require color consistency between displays and printers. For managing the desktop and its colors, it may be easier to stick with the X11R4 approach than convert.

Because X servers can handle up to 16 million colors, the hexadecimal number can get quite large. Depending on the number of colors supported by the system or whether, as in the WordPerfect example at the beginning of this chapter, you are dealing with resources set by an application seeking to achieve portability, you could encounter any of the following forms:

```
#rgb
#rrggbb
#rrrgggbbb
#rrrrggggbbbb
```

Working with hexadecimal numbers is not second nature to everyone. UNIX itself provides the **bc** and **dc** utilities, but both of these require some effort to use. The **bc** utility is interactive and you must work in its editor. The **dc** utility is more practical for desktop customizers and you can use it from the command line or in scripts:

```
echo "16o135p206p250p" | dc
```

This command is handy enough if you want to make a quick conversion on the command line. The only problem is each output number—**87 CE FA**—displays on a line of its own. In a script, you can overcome the problem:

```
#!/bin/sh
# dec2hex, converts three decimal numbers to hex
# Syntax: hex2dec num num num
  hexnums=`echo "16o$1p$2p$3p" | dc`
  echo hexnums
```

The one drawback to using **dc** is its sluggishness. To be sure, you can get by if you convert only a few numbers at a time. If you want build a script that converts many numbers from **rgb.txt**, you should probably use a simple C program like the following:

```
# dtoh, converts decimal numbers to hex
# Syntax: dtoh num1...numN

#include<stdio.h>
#include<stdlib.h>

void main(int argc, char *argv[])
{
     int i;
     for(i=1; i<argc; i++)
     { printf("%X ", atoi(argv[i])); }
}
```

The output from this program is a steady stream, with no embedded newline characters. To use it in reading the **rgb.txt** files, C programmers might want to just expand upon the program. Shell script writers can use it to create a simple filter for output from **rgb.txt**.

```
#!/bin/sh
# xchex, hexadecimal filter for rgb.txt

  while read
  do
     read R G B color || break
     dtoh $R $G $B; echo $color
  done
```

You can use **xchex** like any other filter. If you pipe the entire contents of **rgb.txt** with **cat**, the performance is lackluster at best. But using **grep** to pipe a set of colors through **xchex** produces quick results:

```
$ grep blue rgb.txt | xchex
     F0 F8 FF  alice blue
     19 19 70  midnight blue
     .
     .
     .
     8A 2B E2  blue violet
```

As already noted, the **background** and **foreground** resources are the main resources when it comes to color. Used in a resource statement with no other parameters, the **background** resource affects the work area and frame of a window. The **foreground** resource affects the text in the work area and any text in the frame. In addition, both resources can be used with smaller components than the window. For example, when you use the Motif window manager, you can write resource statements that effect color changes in most components, including titlebars and menus:

```
Mwm*client*title*background: powder blue
Mwm*menu*background: light slate blue
```

In these examples, as with most resource statements, the application name (in this case, Mwm) does not have to be part of the resource statement. It is simply included for clarity, but leaving it off would produce the same effect, plus immediately affect any clients that you happened to load before activating Motif.

In addition to resource statements, you can make some color changes in X by using the **xset** and **xsetroot** utilities. The **xset** utility **-p** option allows you to specify the name of the colormap entry. For general use, you will want to ignore this capability.

The **xsetroot** utility is more efficacious. With it, you can change the color of the root window; clear the root window by setting it to X's default, lightly rippled, gray pattern; reverse the foreground and background colors; or display a bitmap on the background with any foreground and background colors you specify. The following hints at what what you can do with **xsetroot**.

```
#!/bin/sh
# xwrite, script to write on root window
# Syntax: xwrite string
# Note: limitation of 7-chararcter string

# Set values
  string=$1; i=1; LINES=8; nl='echo \\\012'
  txfile=/tmp/txfile.$$
  lnfile=/tmp/lnfile.$$
  bmfile=/tmp/bmfile.$$

# Set trap
  trap "rm -f $txfile $bmfile $lnfile; exit" 0 1 2 3
15

# Format input
  banner "I ${string} I" | sed -e '
     s/ /-/g
     s/^...//g
```

```
      s/^##/#-/g
      s/###$/—/g
      s/#$/-/g
      p' > $txfile

# Create blank lines
  line=`sed -n '1,1s/#/-/gp' $txfile`
  line=`echo $line | sed 's/^-/#/'`
  while [ $i -le $LINES ]
  do
    echo $line >> lnfile
    i=`expr $i + 1`
  done

# Create bitmap file
  cat $lnfile $txfile $lnfile | atobm > $bmfile
  xsetroot -bg "#B0E0E6" -fg "#000000" -bitmap $bmfile
```

Font Resources

Font resources are the most difficult type of resources to handle in X because of the unwieldy text strings that define a given font (see Figure 4-2). In X11R5, system fonts have been enhanced, and include scalable fonts, but the methods you use under X11R4 continue to be effective in X11R5.

To obtain information about the fonts in use on a given system, you can use the **xset** client. The **-q** option to **xset** reports on systemwide X configuration information including the current font path. The font path simply consists of one or more directory hierarchies in which fonts are stored. On a DEC Alpha workstation running OSF/1, the default font path information is reported like this:

```
Font Path:
/usr/lib/X11/fonts/decwin/75dpi//usr/lib/X11/fonts/MIT/
```

Notice that different hierarchies are separated by a comma and that each path ends with a forward slash. If you want to reset the font path, you can use the **-fp** option. The **-fp** option can be used in several ways, as described in Table 4-2.

In general, you need only to use the **-fp** option to **xset** when you want to modify the directories that the X server searches for fonts. More often than not, the only time you will want to do this is if you are involved in adding a

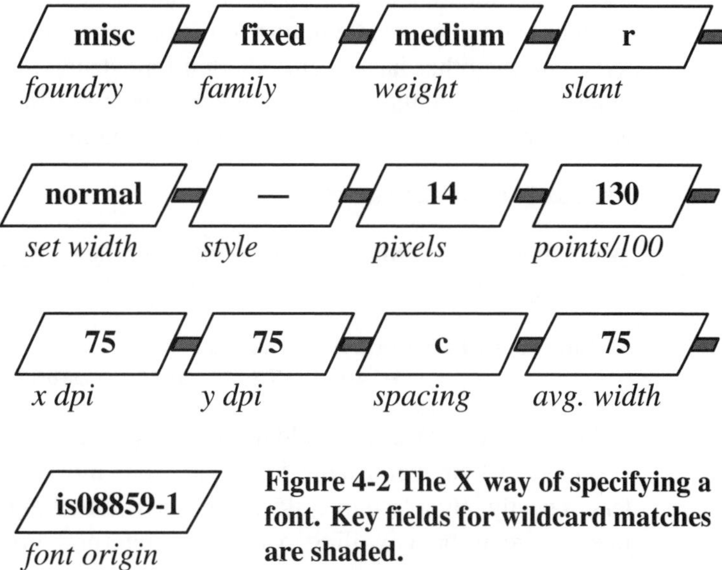

Figure 4-2 The X way of specifying a font. Key fields for wildcard matches are shaded.

new set of fonts to the system. The **mkfontdir** client and a new set of fonts are the prerequisites for this process.

Font resources can be loaded from the command line with most X clients. The **-fn** or **-font** switch is usually available. Xterm windows even have a second switch, **-fb**, which lets you specify a font to be used for displaying bold text. Typing in a font string, which can range from 50 to 70 or more characters in length, is not the thing to do. (Using this long a string in a resource file is undesirable; usually it is avoidable, but the practice occurs even in commercial software.)

Table 4-2 Font Path Options for Xset

Resource	Description
fp=*path*	Sets font path to the directory hierarchy specified by *path*.
fp default	Resets the font path to the system default.
fp rehash	Tells the server to reread the font databases in the current font path.
-fp or fp-	Deletes a directory hierarchy from the font path.
+fp or fp+	Adds a directory hierarchy to the font list.

The answer to long font strings is the * wildcard character. You can also use the **?** wildcard character to form a font string, but you would be likely use it only if you were attempting some form of conditional match. The asterisk, on the other hand, helps shorten font strings so that they are more practical to type at the command line. For example, the following 18-character string matches only 14-point courier medium fonts:

```
'*courier-m*-r*140*'
```

When used with the **xlsfonts** utility, the example string yields only a single matching font:*

```
-adobe-courier-medium-r-normal \
                    —14-140-75-75-m-90-iso8859-1
```

For brevity's sake, you could make your search strings even smaller. It is best to keep them identifiable, however, and in most cases, 18 or so characters fit neatly into a resource file. If you enter something from the command line, you're probably willing to accept misinterpretations of your string, so try **'*r-m*-r*140*'** and you will likely get the same results as in the previous example. Always try to be precise, however. The X server, unlike the **xlsfonts** utility, parses its font path and returns the first font string that it determines to be a match. For instance, typing **'*courier*140*'** is certain not to yield the results that you want.

There are several utilities that can be of help with fonts. As noted, there is **xlsfonts**, which can be likened to a **grep** specifically for the font database. Then there is **xfd**, which accepts the **-fn** option and displays the character set of the specified font in a window. The **xfontsel** utility also shows a single font, if one is specified, but importantly, **xfontsel** menu options allow you to examine all X fonts on the system. If you use the **-print** option with **xfontsel**, it prints the font you selected to standard output:

```
-adobe-courier-bold-r-normal—14-140-*-*-*-*-*-*
```

The sequences of **-*-** appear because this example results from selecting the first seven menu options in **xlsfonts**, which fills in the remaining fields with wildcards. What's neat about **xlsfonts**, given that its interface lacks the polish of a Motif application, is that it can be used inside a script to help you make entries into resource files. The following script, called **xsf**, is based on this idea.

* In some cases throughout the book, resource strings and other text is *escaped*. The \ symbol indicates that the line continues and ignores the invisible newline character. Some files on some systems do not accept this behavior. In these cases, allow the line to wrap to the next line.

```
#!/bin/sh
# xsf, script to set fonts
# xsf -c [client] -e [resource file]
# Note: if no option follows -c or -e, the script
# defaults to $HOME/.Xdefaults and xterm.

# Set values
  option=$1; object=$2; file=/tmp/xsf.$$
  if [ -z "$object" ] ; then object=xterm; fi
  usage="Usage: $0 [-x] [-cf [client||resource]]"

# Check for valid arguments
  case $# in
     0) xfontsel -print ; wait; echo; exit 1 ;;
     1|2) ;; # argument count okay
     *) echo $usage; exit 1 ;;
  esac

# Exec xfontsel with print option
  font='xfontsel -print'
  wait

# Process by option: -c loads client with new font;
# -r sets resource with new font; -x sends escape.

  case $option in
     -c) exec $object -fn $font & ;;
     -r) xrdb -query | \
               grep -v "${object}\*$font:" > $file
          if [ $? ] ; then
               echo "*${object}*font: $font" >> $file
               mv $file $HOME/.Xdefaults
               xrdb -load $HOME/.Xdefaults
          else
               echo Unable to create temporary file.
          fi ;;
     -x) echo "^[]50;$font^G"
  esac
```

The **xsf** script has three options. The **-c** option uses the font string returned from **xlsfonts** in an **exec** statement to execute the client specified in **$2** on the command line. If you don't specify a client, an Xterm is launched. The **-r** option, which also uses **xterm** by default, sets the font resource for any client you specify. The script removes any old resource matching the client name paired with the resource keyword **font**.

The last option in **xsf** brings up the special topic of using fonts in Xterms. What the **-x** option does is send an escape sequence to the Xterm window in which **xsf** is running. As a result of this particular escape sequence, the Xterm immediately changes its font. Additionally, in the Xterm's font menu, which you invoke by pressing Ctrl-Button 3, the "Escape Sequence" item is activated and retains the name of the font received from **xsf**. Each time you send an Xterm a subsequent escape with a different font, the "Escape Sequence" menu item retains the new font name.

In order to create a font escape sequence, you must use your text editor's mode for creating special characters. The reason is that you need a real escape character in the escape sequence. The escape character looks as though it is composed of two characters, ^[, but it is actually one character. The surest way to create an escape sequence is to **cat** into an open file. For example, type **cat > test**, and press return. This takes the standard input, the keyboard, and puts it in the file **escseq**. Now type **echo "ESC]50;'*courier-bold- r*140*'Ctrl-G"** and press Return. Then press **Ctrl-D** and execute **chmod +x**. The result is a simple script that changes an Xterm's font to 14-point courier bold.

Building a script based on escape sequences gives you dynamic control of fonts in a Xterm window. Additionally, if you use Xterms as a frontend to display messages to users, you can use font escape sequences to enhance the appearance of an Xterm. The script on page 85, called **xtf**, lets you access most fonts recognized by X. The exception is any font that is proportionally spaced. Proportionally spaced fonts, while acceptable for displaying messages in an Xterm, cannot be adapted for routine use at the command line. You can tell whether a font is a proportional (**p**), monospaced (**m**), or character cell (**c**) font by examining the eleventh field in the full font string.

Another way to dynamically control Xterm fonts is through the VT Fonts menu. As noted, the default way to pop up this menu is by pressing Ctrl-Button 3. Depending on your version of X, you could have four, six, or more menu selections to control fonts. The resource that controls the menu selections is called **fontMenu**—which, incidentally, is not documented in the manual pages, but is used in the default resource file located in the **app-defaults** directory.

One trick to specifying fonts through the **fontMenu** resource is that you must use the full font string. No quotation marks are necessary, but you must enter the string exactly as it appears in its **xlsfonts** listing, or minimally, as it appears as the result of using **xfontsel**. The point is you cannot use standard wildcard font matches; each field must be delimited in some form. Here is an example of a set of resource statements for the VT Fonts menu:

```
*fontMenu.Label: Xterm Fonts
*fontMenu*fontdefault*Label: Default
*fontMenu*font1*Label: Courier Medium 14
*VT100*font1: -*-courier-medium-r-*-*-*-140-*-*-*-*-*-*
*fontMenu*font2*Label: Courier Bold 14
*VT100*font2: -*-courier-bold-r-*-*-*-140-*-*-*-*-*-*
*fontMenu*font3*Label: Courier Medium 18
*VT100*font3: -*-courier-medium-r-*-*-*-180-*-*-*-*-*-*
*fontMenu*font4*Label: Courier Bold 18
*VT100*font4: -*-courier-bold -r-*-*-*-180-*-*-*-*-*-*
```

You can locate these resource statements anywhere, but you should probably leave the file in **app-defaults** alone, or at least make a backup. Most likely, the best place for it is in the directory pointed to by $XAPPLRESDIR, because there is also no reason to clutter up the **.Xdefaults** file with it. In addition, if you want to have different sets of VT Font menus available, you can use named Xterms. The following set of font resource statements would be fine. The arbitrary name of the Xterm is **xt**.

```
xt*fontMenu.Label: Xterm Fonts
xt*fontMenu*fontdefault*Label: Default
xt*fontMenu*font1*Label: Sony Medium 12
xt*VT100*font1: -*-sony-medium-r-*-*-*-120-*-*-*-*-*-*
xt*fontMenu*font2*Label: Sony Medium 15
xt*VT100*font2: -*-sony-medium-r-*-*-*-150-*-*-*-*-*-*
xt*fontMenu*font3*Label: Sony Medium 17
xt*VT100*font3: -*-sony-medium-r-*-*-*-170-*-*-*-*-*-*
xt*fontMenu*font4*Label: Sony Medium 23
xt*VT100*font4: -*-sony-medium-r-*-*-*-230-*-*-*-*-*-*
```

The other thing you should be aware of regarding the VT Fonts menu is the "Selection" choice. Before clicking on this item, which appears grayed out anyway, highlight a font string—most likely one that you have displayed using **xlsfonts**. The highlighted font becomes the Xterm's current font.

Font Aliases

Knowing how to manipulate font strings in the shell is the surest way to achieve font comparability between various X platforms. An easier way—but one that requires an extra step on each system that you configure—is to edit the **fonts.alias** file on each system you need to customize.

In Chapter 3, you saw how to create font aliases using the C preprocessor #define directive. The **#define** approach only creates aliases processed by

xrdb. If you use the **font.alias** file, you can create aliases recognized by the X server and therefore every other program run under X.

In the **fonts.alias** file, you assign an alias by entering the alias name in the first field and the full font string in the second field:

```
times14 -adobe-times-medium-r-normal \
              -14-140-75-75-p-74-iso8859-1
```

This example creates an alias for the standard 14-point Adobe Times font. When giving names, try to be consistent and concise:

```
times14b -adobe-times-bold-r-normal \
              -14-140-75-75-p-77-iso8859-1
```

By adding **b** to end of the alias, it is apparent to users who have worked with fonts that **times14b** is the boldface equivalent of **times14**. Next you can account for italic cases:

```
times14i -adobe-times-medium-i-normal\
              -14-140-75-75-p-73-iso8859-1
times14bi -adobe-times-bold-i-normal\
              -14-140-75-75-p-77-iso8859-1
```

When you add aliases to the **fonts.alias** file, be sure not to overwrite the file or delete existing aliases. You can also have more than one version of **fonts.alias** on a system, as long as each version is in a separate directory specified in the system's font path.

X11R5 Fonts

X11R5 did much to improve the font capability of the X Window System. The two major enhancements were:

- A font server, which runs on a host system and provides fonts to other systems on the network. The font server can read different types of font formats and is capable of passing off font requests to other font servers, if necessary.
- Scalable fonts, which give the desktop customizer a larger variety of fonts. Importantly, you can still use the same routines you developed in X11R4 with scalable fonts. The major difference is you can request any point size for a scalable font and the font server will fulfil the request.

If properly installed, scalable fonts do not require a change in approach such as that already described in this section. When you request a scalable font, the X server sends the single file matching your font request. After accessing the file, the X server sizes the font to your request. When you use **xlsfonts**, however, you get only one listing for any one scalable font. This suggests that you should avoid using **xlsfonts** as a frontend to obtaining a font string for any script file you might write, as shown in the previous examples in this section.

The font server effects more of a change for desktop customizers. It doesn't undo methods that you have developed for X11R5; it simply gives you access to a lot more fonts. The commands **fs**, **fsinfo**, and **fslsfonts** are new in X11R5 and act as the primary interface to font server.

Window Size and Positioning

The **iconic** and **geometry** resources fall into the category of size and positioning resources. You encounter other resources in this category, such as those used for the Motif icon box, or any unique ones you may find in a third-party application, but the **iconic** and **geometry** options are supported in most X applications.

The **iconic** resource is more like a "state" resource, rather than a size and positioning option. From the user's viewpoint, windows have a limited number of states: open, iconified, and perhaps, maximized, if you are using a Motif or Open Look window manager.

Bringing up a window in an iconified state is a useful technique. Don't overlook it because it is easy for all users to quickly iconify a window. An iconified window might serve as a tool in and of itself. For example, by attaching a custom menu to an icon, you can quickly build a tool for yourself and other users to easily access, yet take up a minimum of screen real estate.

The actual positioning of icons on-screen is the province of the window manager. As a result, if you encounter a resource such as **iconGeometry**, which is recognized by Xterm, it won't work in Motif and Open Look.

There's a much bigger story to tell for the **geometry** resource. First, the **geometry** resource is clever, but the flexibility of the way you set up its arguments is perhaps too clever for some users who might prefer a more readable command, even if it meant a longer command string. In any event, here is the syntax:

```
*geometry: [width][xheight][+/-x][+/-[y]
```

The breathless take on this is *width*, which can be specified by itself, times the height, optionally located *x* pixels from the side of the screen (left or right) specified by **+** or **-**, plus optionally located *y* pixels from the top or bottom of the screen, again as specified by **+** and **-**, yields the finished geometry statement.

Until you've experimented, the **geometry** resource may not handle like it is second nature. Besides, the width and height of Xterm windows are specified in row-by-column format, and this, too, is determined by the current font in use for the Xterm window. Not so bad, but there is yet another condition: You also have to consider the size of the monitor for the *x* and *y* coordinates. The good news is if you over- or underspecify a coordinate—such as specifying 1100 for a monitor with a 1024 width—the window won't appear off-screen.

The width and height values are straightforward when specified in pixels. You can specify just the width of a new window, if you like:

```
xedit*geometry: 1152
```

Or, by preceding a single value with the multiplication sign (x), you can specify just the height of the new window:

```
xedit*geometry: x900
```

Or you can specify both the width and height together:

```
xedit*geometry: 1152x900
```

All three statements ensure that the window spans the entire dimension of the screen, whichever dimension, or dimensions, are specified. The first example spans the vertical dimension on a 1152 by 900 monitor. The second example spans the horizontal dimension. The third example, which is a full-screen window, is the format you will most likely use. Specifying single numbers to geometry statements in resource files is a rare practice, but you might adopt the technique when you load client applications from the command line. See how fast you can type **ico -g 9999x9999**. Unless you write a shell script or alias, it's one of the fastest ways in X to cover up your monitor—any monitor, because the out-of-bounds numbers result in a full-screen window.

As for the *x* and *y* coordinates, if you relate to starting positions (see Table 4-3), latch onto **+0+0**. When you specify it in a geometry statement, the left and top borders of the window are flush against the screen's left and top borders. Your other choices, **+0-0**, **-0+0**, and **-0-0** position a window bottom-left, top-right, and bottom-right. The fact that you must precede each number with either a plus or minus sign can make you feel like a nonintuitive blob. You also might pull your hair out when you realize there are eight possible combinations for any two numbers when one of the two numbers is nonzero: **+20+0**, **+20-0**, **+0+20**, **+0-20**, **-20+0**, **-20-0**, **-0+20**, and **-0-20**.

Table 4-3 Window Starting Position Coordinates

Value	Example	Screen Reference
+x+y	600x500+100+200	Upper-left corner
+x-y	600x500+100-200	Lower-left corner
-x+y	600x500-300+200	Upper-right corner
-x-y	600x500-300-200	Lower-right corner

Note: The examples in this table create a window 600 pixels wide by 500 pixels high and place it in the same general screen area, half-way down the left side of the screen.

Overall, getting used to width and height dimensions mostly requires familiarity with the screen resolution of your monitor. If you want precision, you can use the **xwininfo** client. The **xwininfo** client provides the current width, height, and screen coordinates. To use **xwininfo** interactively, you enter **xwininfo** at the command line and click the mouse in the target window. The utility also lets you specify windows by id and name so you can use it without the mouse (in a script perhaps). Handily, the **xwininfo** utility lets you specify **-root**, so you can obtain a monitor's resolution, color depth, and installed colormap. The **xdpyinfo**, available on most X systems, also provides information on the monitor resolution, as well as numerous other display concerns.

As for Xterm windows, they require that you specify width and height in row-and-column format. This is an important difference, and it isn't easily reduced to a simple formula to convert between the two formats. The reason is the row and column sizes are based on the currently selected font. For on-screen positioning, however, Xterms do use pixel coordinates.

A reasonably sized Xterm window—for fonts ranging from the default **fixed** font to a 14-point Courier—can fall anywhere between 40x20 and 80x40. For instance, if your screen is smaller than 1024 by 864, say, the 80x40 size takes up a lot of real estate. If you have a larger screen, and want to use an 18-point font—definitely within the bounds of sensibility for an Xterm window—a size of 60x20 produces a reasonable window. Full screen on a 1024 by 864 monitor for an 18-point font requires a size of about 92x48.

If you haven't checked out the **xfontsel** client distributed with X, you should do so when making some initial choices about which fonts to use with Xterm windows. In the **spc** field in the **xfontsel** display menu, choose either **c** or **m** to examine appropriate fonts for Xterm windows. The **c** option specifies fonts designed in a character cell format for use in a Xterm. The **m** option specifies monospaced fonts, which often, but not always, work well in an Xterm. Lastly, you can examine the **ptSz** and **avgWdth** fields in the display menu. After you select a font, compare the values of these two fields with those in the same fields for the system's default fixed font (iso8859-1), which is a 13-point medium font, 130 pixels high (ptSz) by 80 pixels wide (**avgWdth**).

If you want to do more than estimate pixel-to-row/column conversions, the following formula yields a close approximation.

```
pixel_width/(avgWdth/10)*pixel_height/(ptSz/10)
```

You can test this approach by running a client such as **xedit** with pixel-based numbers, and then running an Xterm with the numbers produced by the formula. It is likely that the resulting windows will have identical widths, but you'll probably notice that the heights will be different. This occurs because Xterm allocates enough window height for *x* number of rows, with no remainder. It also occurs because you have to provide rounded numbers to Xterm. The following script, called **pxtell**, gives you a tool to convert numbers.

```
#!/bin/sh
# pxtell, converts pixel geometry for Xterms
# Syntax: pxtell font pwidth pheight
# Copyright (c) Alan Southerton

# Check for valid number of arguments
  case $# in
      2) ;; # argument count okay
      *) echo "Usage: $0 font pwidth pheight"; exit 1
;;
  esac

# Get valid font or exit
  fnstring=`xlsfonts "$1"`
  if [ "$fnstring" = ""] ; then exit 1 ; fi

# Extract values
  pixWdth=`echo $2 | cut -dx -f1`
  pixHigh=`echo $2 | cut -dx -f2`
  avgWdth=`echo $fnstring | cut -d- -f8`

# Convert numbers
  xtheight=`echo $fnstring | cut -d- -f8`
  xtwidth=`expr $avgWdth / 10`
  xtwidth=`expr $pixWdth / $xtwidth`
  xtheight=`expr $pixHigh / $xtheight`
```

```
# Display results
  /bin/echo -n Font string:
  /bin/echo $fnstring
  /bin/echo -n Rows/Columns:
  /bin/echo ${xtwidth}x$xtheight
```

To use **pxtell**, you must enter a valid font string, but you can also use wildcards as you would for the **xlsfonts** utility, which **pxtell** itself uses. For the second and third arguments, you simply enter the pixel width and height. If you enter an invalid font string, or the wrong number of arguments, the script exits. No other error checking is performed.

Key and Mouse Maps

There are two primary ways to set key and mouse click definitions in X. The first way is systemwide, in that it affects all windows maintained by the local X server. To take advantage of this capability, use the **xmodmap** client and specify a new key or mouse definition on the command line:

```
xmodmap -e 'keysym Backspace = Delete'
```

This sets the Delete key to the same functionality as the Backspace key. If you have many changes, you can also use **xmodmap** with a file containing your changes. You can name this file anything you want.

The alternative method to **xmodmap** involves the use of the **translation** resource and works with Xterms and selected other clients such as **xcalc**, **xedit**, and various third-party applications. As with other resources, you can tailor a set of key and mouse click translations to a named instance of any client. In Xterms, you can use the **translation** resource to map strings and functions to keys and mouse clicks.

Both **xmodmap** and the translation resource use a set of shorthand names for each keyboard press. These shorthand names are called *keysyms* to distinguish them from *keycodes*. A keysym can be an abbreviation, such as Caps_Lock and Shift_L, or it can be the letter, number, or English-language word associated with a given key. For special keys on some keyboards, you should note that the keysym name doesn't necessarily mirror the name on the physical key. For example, the "Do" key on some DEC keyboards has a keysym name of "Menu."

A keycode is the system-specific, nonportable, numeric value associated with a given key. Each keycode can accept either one or multiple keysym definitions. A second definition is required for keys that have different values when shifted; letter keys do not need a shifted definition.

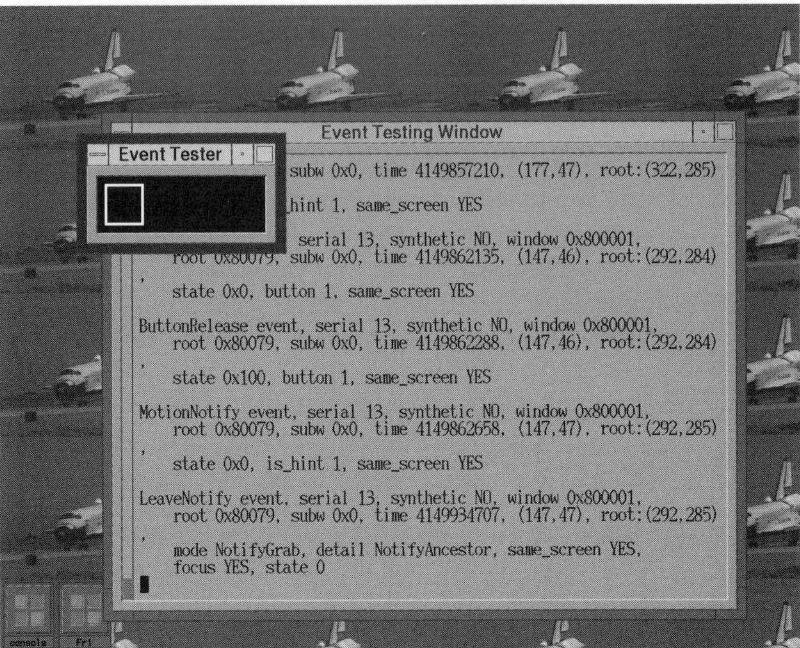

Figure 4-3 Example of the xev client. To use xev, move the mouse pointer into the xev window and then press a key or mouse sequence and watch the associated keysyms display in the window.

Other additional keysym definitions can be made to give multiple keys the same functionality. Also note that you cannot map keycodes to other keycodes. This is a vital restriction, in that the keycode always remains the base value.

Mouse clicks have obvious names. For example, **xmodmap** uses **pointer 1** to refer to the left button click on the mouse. The translation resource recognizes terms such as **Btn1Down** and **Btn3Motion** when dealing with the mouse. Mouse clicks and movements do not have an associated keycode.

Whether you use **xmodmap** or the translation resource, you should also know about the **xev** client. The **xev** client tracks server-related events, including key strokes and mouse clicks. For key clicks, **xev** displays both keycodes and keysyms. Figure 4-3 provides an example of **xev**.

For mouse activity, **xev** also lets you track when a mouse button was pressed (ButtonPress) and when it was released (ButtonRelease). It also lists the number of the button, but you should know that from left to right, the buttons are 1, 2, and 3.

Xmodmap

The **xmodmap** utility is useful for making many changes to the existing key mappings. It is commonly invoked at startup from a file such as **.xinitrc**, **.xsession** or **.X11Startup**, depending on your platform and its configuration. In general practice, **xmodmap** is used most often to redefine shift keys, or *modifiers*, and to reassign keysyms on nonstandard keyboards.

Setting mouse assignments with **xmodmap** is trivial. The **pointer** keyword is the only option supported. It lets you specify the order in which the mouse buttons are to be interpreted by the X server: 1,2,3; 3,2,1; or even 2,3,1 or 2,1,3. There is also a **pointer = default** command that you can give **xmodmap**, in which case 1,2,3 is mapped to the left, middle, and right buttons, respectively. If you want to customize button events further, you have to use the **translations** resource.

Before you begin to change any key settings, be sure that you retain a backup of your current settings. This is important when using **xmodmap** to associate keysyms with other, already defined, keysyms. (And as implied, it is not worthwhile at all if you are concerned only about mouse button settings.) If you do not have a file containing your default key settings, the following script produces one using the **-pk** option to **xmodmap.**

```
#!/bin/sh
# xmodef, script to store default key settings
# Syntax: xmodef [-display]
# Copyright (c) 1993 Alan Southerton
# Note: for keymaps with 1 to 3 keysyms per keycode,.
# repeat the 4th and 5th sed commands.
# Use screen 0 on local display by default
  if [ -z "$1" ] ; then
     DISPLAY=":0"
  else
     DISPLAY=$2
  fi
# Run xmodmap through sed commands
  xmodmap -display $DISPLAY -pk |
    sed 's/^.../keycode/p' |      # add command
    sed 's/(/##/1p' |             # set up 1st search
    sed 's/\ \ \ .*##/ = /p' |    # change ## to " = "
    sed 's/(/##/1p' |             # set up 2nd search
    sed 's/).*##/ /p' |           # change ## to space
    sed 's/).*(/ /p' |            # change more parens
    sed 's/)//p' |                # change last parens
    sed '/[0-9]\ \ .*$/d' |       # delete empty codes
    sed '1,4s/^/! /p' > .defkeysyms
```

Before using **xmodef**, run **xmodmap -pk | more** and examine the output. The **xmodef** script expects three spaces to begin each line and at least three more spaces after the keycode column. And as noted in the comment at the top of the script, you need to repeat the fourth and fifth **sed** commands if any one keycode has more than three keysyms.

With a default set of key mappings intact, you can go about adding custom settings. On a typical system, it is not necessary to make a lot of custom settings. Using **xmodmap** is handy for vexing problems, such as assigning a destructive backspace to the Delete key, disabling the CapsLock key, or reassigning the Escape key on DEC systems.

You can also use **xmodmap** to change the value of shifted comma and period keys, which usually represent the greater than and less than symbols (but some UNIX platforms vary). All in all, you might have enough keyboard and pointer changes that it would be worthwhile creating a custom settings file for **xmodmap**:

```
xmodmap -display sparky:0 .axpkeysyms
```

The file in which you place this type of command can have any name. In the example, it is **axpkeysyms**.

An **xmodmap** keysym file consists of two columns. The left-hand side is a value already known by the X server. For example, the numeric keycode, which can be expressed in decimal, hexadecimal, or octal format, is the base value associated with each key:

```
keycode 176 Caps_Lock
```

This is the default keycode for the CapsLock key on a DEC Alpha system. If you have already assigned a keysym to a keycode, you can use this keysym in the left-hand column. The keywords **clear**, **add**, and **remove** can also be used to adjust modifier keys.

Translations

The question of when to use the translation resource versus **xmodmap** should not be too hard to answer: Use **xmodmap** to set systemwide key and mouse settings; use the translation resource for everything else if you are using an Xterm; or use it for linking key and mouse actions to client-specific functions in other programs.

By far, Xterm offers unmatched flexibility when it comes to the translation resource. In fact, by using the translation resource extensively with Xterm, along with some other resources, and perhaps an escape sequence or two, you can create interfaces for old UNIX programs. The only thing that the translation resource has against it is that its format is delicate. To use the translation resource, create an entry in a resource file, specify either the keyword **#override**, **#replace**, or **#augment**, and escape the line return:

```
*VT100.Translations: #override \
```

You need to escape the line return because the translation resource statement, plus all the key mappings that follow it, must be one long continuous string. When the X server reads the string, however, it still needs to know where a line ends. Thus, mapping statements must end with a **\n** sequence, with no following whitespaces:

```
*VT100.Translations: #override \
  <Key>F17: string("ls -ls | more") string(0x0d) \n\
  <Key>F18: string("ps -ef | more") string(0x0d) \n\
  <Key>F19: string("df") string(0x0d) \n\
  <Key>F20: string("cd ..") string(0x0d)
```

This is a complete translations statement. The F17 through F19 entries have the **\n** sequence at the end of each line. The final entry has no **\n** sequence. The keyword **#override** is used, informing the X server to replace other defintions for the **VT100.Translation** resource, if they have been previously defined; otherwise, add them to the current set of mappings. A dot connects **VT100** and **Translations** for organizational purposes, indicating the intention that the key mappings are class-level fare. **Translations** is capitalized for the same reason.

The entries in the example show a little of the power of the translation resource. The keys have not been mapped to keysyms, as with **xmodmap**. Instead, they have been mapped to text strings representing UNIX commands. Each command inside the first instance of the **string** keyword is followed by a second instance of **string** that contains the hexadecimal code for a Return character.

Now here is another example containing one entry that does remap a keysym, plus several others that act as quick keys for the **vi** editor:

```
*vi*translations: #override \
     <Key>F1: string(0xff1b) \n\
     <Key>Insert: string("i") \n\
     <Key>Find: string("_") \n\
     <Key>Select: string("$") \n\
     Shift<KeyPress>Prior: string("1G") \n\
     Shift<KeyPress>Next: string("G") \n\
     <Key>Prior: string("^B") \n\
```

```
<Key>Next: string("^F") \n\
<Key>Up: string("k") \n\
<Key>Down: string("j") \n\
<Key>Right: string("l") \n\
<Key>Left: string("h") \n\
<Key>KP_F1: string(":set nu") string(0x0d)
```

This example is designed for a DEC LK201 keyboard, a 105-key keyboard that resembles the industry standard 101-key keyboard, but only in physical appearance. Keys such as Find and Select replace the standard Home and End keys. Thus, the example uses **vi** commands that would normally be associated with Home and End, instead of Find and Select. Besides screen movement keys, the example sets F1 to be the Escape key, which is geographically similar to the standard UNIX escape key. In order to do so, the hexadecimal number representing the Escape key is used; you cannot use the English-language keysym to remap one key to another key. (To get correct hexadecimal numbers for keys refer to your default **xmodmap** settings or use the **xev** client.)

Also in the example, note the two entries that use the **Shift<KeyPres>** sequence. These set Shift-Prior and Shift-Next to move to the top and bottom of the document, respectively. The following two lines then map Prior and Next themselves. Remember that shifted definitions must occur before unshifted ones. If they don't, the X server treats any event involving the primary key, such as Shift-Next, as equal to pressing Next alone. The example also uses one of the LK201's special PF keys, represented by KP_F1, to enable line numbering in **vi**.

Bitmaps

The X bitmap standard provides a way for you to introduce two-color bitmap images onto the desktop. With bitmaps, you can create images on the root window, create icons for use with a window manager, or convert bitmap font characters into images.

It is easy enough to learn **bitmap**, as well as other image editors available from third parties, so this section points you to the **man** pages and documentation for these products. The X11R4 version of **bitmap**, you will find, is adequate for many images, so long as they are black and white. The X11R5 version is still more improved.

One important tip when creating images for icons, be sure that you size the image appropriately. In most cases, an image for an icon should be sized between 48 by 48 pixels and 64 by 64 pixels. To specify the size of an image for the X11R4 version of **bitmap**, enter the filename followed by the pixel dimensions:

```
bitmap new.bmp 64x64
```

In the X11R5 version of **bitmap**, the syntax is more traditional:

```
bitmap -size 64x64
```

After you know how to make bitmaps, there are some questions and problems you have to address. One of the first questions you face is when is a bitmap not a bitmap, and instead a *pixmap*. The answer is when you introduce full color into a particular image file—and when you have produced the image file in an editor other than **bitmap**. Unfortunately, there is no inherent support in X11R4 or X11R5 for pixmap files, nor is there necessarily support for them in your window manager. Sun's OpenWindows and some versions of Motif for Sun do support pixmaps, so its worth investigating on your part.

In the interests of portability between different systems, the X bitmap format is the surest way to success. A lot can be done with bitmaps, too, because of the **atobm** and **bmtoa** conversion utilities included in the standard release of X. You can use bitmaps to create custom icons in Motif if, as noted, the system does not support pixmaps. The resource that you use to associate a bitmap with a client under Motif is **iconImage**. Under OpenWindows, you use the **Icon.Pixmap** resource for specifying a client's pixmap. And as illustrated in subsequent chapters, you can include bitmaps into Motif menus, a technique that can make your desktop distinctive.

The first order of business for many desktop customizers is to create unique icons for client programs. For regularly accessed programs, you can create these icons in **bitmap**—or again, on Sun systems, in a pixmap editor—and assign them using the appropriate window manager resources. On Motif systems, there are several resources that apply globally to icons, such as **iconIMage**, which assigns an icon to a client.

```
Mwm*iconImageAutoShade: True
Mwm*iconImageBackground: light blue
Mwm*iconImageBackgroundPixmap: unspecified_pixmap
Mwm*iconImageBottomShadowColor: yellow
Mwm*iconImageBottomShadowPixmap: unspecified_pixmap
Mwm*iconImageForeground: black
Mwm*iconImageMaximum: 64x64
Mwm*iconImageTopShadowColor: yellow
Mwm*iconImageTopShadowPixmap: unspecified_pixmap
Mwm*iconImage: mydefault.bmp
Mwm*vi*iconImage: vi.bmp
```

Besides using bitmaps for icons, you can use them in Motif menus (see Chapter 8), as well as third-party applications that make their menu structure accessible through resources. At the X server level, you will find the other major application for bitmaps: displaying them on the root window.

Depending on how you arrange your windows on screen, bitmaps and other images that are displayed on the root window can serve many different practical purposes. If you are inclined to have a lot of windows open, however, you might not see the immediate benefit of displaying information on the root window. Even so, as compared with other image formats such as GIF, which usually are sized 640 by 480 or greater, bitmaps can be used to provide information in small areas of the screen.

Loading a bitmap onto the root window is also a fast operation. The standard **xsetroot** client is the vehicle:

```
xsetroot -bitmap any.bmp -fg black -bg 'light blue'
```

In the example, the **.bmp** extension on **any.bmp** is totally arbitrary. The bitmaps contained in the standard release of X (see **/usr/lib/X11/bitmaps**) don't use any extension at all. But it is a good idea to use an extension when working with other types of image files as well. Otherwise, the example loads the bitmap and sets the foreground and background colors.

The format of a bitmap file is C language character array. The array defines the values of individual pixels in the pixel matrix defined at the top of the bitmap file. Here is an example for a file called **zen.bmp**:

```
#define zen_width 64
#define zen_height 64
static char zen_bits[] = {
     0xff, 0xff, 0xff, 0xff, 0xff, 0xff, 0xff, 0xff,
0xff, 0xff, 0xff, 0xff,
     0xff, 0xff, 0xff, 0xff, 0xff, 0xff, 0xff, 0xff,
0xff, 0xff, 0xff, 0xff,
     .
     .
     .
     0xff, 0xff, 0xff, 0xff, 0xff, 0xff, 0xff, 0xff,
0xff,0xff, 0xff, 0xff,
     0xff, 0xff, 0xff, 0xff, 0xff, 0xff, 0xff, 0xff};
```

Unless you want to manipulate the bitmap image from a C program, you rarely need to edit a bitmap file directory, although it is an ASCII file. If you change the name of a bitmap file, you might want to edit the **#define** statements in the file, or use the following script to change the names of standard X11 bitmap files:

```
#!/bin/sh
# mvbmp, rename bitmap files
# Usage: mvbmp src target

# Check argument count
  case $# in
      2) ;; # Correct number of args
      *) echo "Usage: $0 src target"; exit 1 ;;
  esac
# Set trap
  trap "rm -f /tmp/mvbmp.$$; exit" 0 1 2 3 15

# Define variables
  srcfile=$1; targetfile=$2
  srcdef=`basename ${srcfile} | sed 's/\..*$//p'`
  targetdef=`basename ${targetfile} | sed 's/\..*$//p'`

# Edit and rename file
  testvar=`grep ${srcdef}_ $srcfile`
  if [ "$testvar" = "" ] ; then
      echo "Error: Problem with src file"
  else
      cat $srcfile | sed -e "
      s/${srcdef}_/${targetdef}_/gp" > /tmp/mvbmp.$$
      mv /tmp/mvbmp.$$ $targetfile
      rm $srcfile
  fi
```

The **mvbmp** script edits the **#define** statements in the bitmap file, including those that define a hot spot if it has been declared. The script also uses **grep** to check whether the filename matches the **#define** name. Other error checking, such as the existence of the **src** file, is left to the shell.

In addition to the C language representation of a bitmap, you can have an ASCII text representation of a bitmap. In fact, you can create a bitmap in a text editor, if you feel especially creative with the # and **-** characters, the default marker characters in the ASCII representation. The **bmtoa** and **atobm** utilities convert between the two file types. Figure 2-4 provides a sample of of a bitmap that consists of three squares placed inside one another. The bitmap is 16 by 16 pixels in size.

Although you might not be inclined to use a text editor to create bitmaps, the ASCII component is useful because you can use **atobm** in shell scripts to create bitmaps from other data. For example, assuming you started your window manager at least once a day, you could run a **cron** process that updated the icon for a calendar-related program with the current date. Using

```
################
################
--##-------##---
##-##########-##
##-##########-##
##-##------##-##
##-##-####-##-##
##-##-####-##-##
##-##-####-##-##
##-##-####-##-##
##-##------##-##
##-##########-##
##-##########-##
--##-------##---
################
################
```

Figure 4-4 This is the ASCII rendition of an X11 bitmap. Note that the # character represents filled pixels and the minus character represents blank pixels.

similar techniques, you can also write to the root window. The following script provides a general purpose approach and is capable of accepting quoted UNIX commands as input.

```
#!/bin/sh
# xwrite, script to write on root window
# Syntax: xwrite [string1]...[stringN]
# Note: up to 9 characters per string

# Set values
  i=1; LINES=6
  txfile=/tmp/txfile.$$
  bmfile=/tmp/bmfile.$$
  lnfile=/tmp/lnfile.$$

# Set trap
# trap "rm -f $txfile $bmfile $lnfile; exit" 0 1 2 3 15

# Format input
  for arg in $*
  do
    banner "${1}I" | sed -e '
       s/ /-/g
       s/###$/—/
       s/#$/-/
       p' > ${txfile}.$i
            i=`expr $i + 1`
```

```
        shift
    done

# Join the various files
    paste -d\- ${txfile}* |
        sed -n 1,14p | sed p > ${txfile}.tmp

# Add some spacing
    sed 's/^/--------/' ${txfile}.tmp > $txfile

# Create blank lines
    line=`sed -n '1,1s/#/-/gp' $txfile`
    i=1
    while [ $i -le $LINES ]
    do
      echo $line >> $lnfile
      i=`expr $i + 1`
    done

# Add blanks and execute
    cat $lnfile $txfile $lnfile | atobm > $bmfile
    xsetroot -bg 'medium sea green' \
            -fg black -bitmap $bmfile
```

In the script, the **banner** command provides the initial capability to convert a string into ASCII format. For each command line argument entered, **banner** sees the argument, plus the letter **I**, ensuring there is some consistency to line endings. The subsequent **sed** commands key in on the # characters associated with the letter **I**, and make all line lengths uniform. The last **sed** command replaces blank spaces with hyphens, the default character representing a blank space in the ASCII version of a bitmap file. The entire **sed** operation is repeated as many times as there are command line arguments to **xwrite**. The output of each repetition is stored in a separate temporary file. The **paste** command then joins the temporary files in $txfile. Next some spacing and blank lines are added. And lastly, $lnfile, which contains blank lines, is piped with $txfile into **atobm**, which creates $bmfile for **xsetroot** to execute.

In addition to using strings with **xwrite**, you can also use UNIX commands when their output does not exceed nine characters per argument. For example, here's how you can put the date and time on your root window:

```
xwrite `date`
```

Many modifications to **xwrite** could be made to enhance the appearance of the output. If your needs are more specific than an all-purpose root writing utility, you could easily streamline some of the **xwrite** code. Alternatively, you might want to write a C program to replace **xwrite** to improve performance.

CHAPTER 5
Motif Resources

RESOURCE FLEXIBILITY

With the acceptance of Motif as the one standard window manager for the X Window System, the desktop customizer can feel comfortable in getting to know Motif resources well. Doing so gives you a passport into a world of great interface flexibility.

There are numerous categories of Motif resources, but some general distinctions can be made. The most obvious categories form along the lines of appearance, behavior, and functionality. Admittedly, these words have lost meaning because of their overuse, but they do apply in the case of Motif resources. The more straightforward definitions used in this book for these categories are:

- Appearance—affects the look of the window but has no functional purpose.
- Behavior—asserts limitations or characteristics on features.
- Functionality—turns features on and off.

In the appearance category, you can easily place several different kinds of resources—including color, fonts, and component sizing, such as adjusting the size of the window frame or increasing or decreasing the size of icons. Not coincidentally, resources that fall into the appearance category are the ones most frequently changed by users. With the exception of resizing components, appearance resources do not affect either the behavior or functionality of windows in Motif.

The behavior category—as contrasted with functionality—includes resources that affect the way Motif acts. Behavior resources are extensive in

Motif, not the least of which are focus policy resources. For focus policy, you can make the basic choice between explicit (click-to-type), and implicit (pointer). In these categories, you can vary many other behaviors, such as whether a window rises to the top of the stack when it gets the focus. Other resources in the behavior category include ones that affect window positioning; ones that affect button and key event handling; and others that affect the relationship of the primary window to its *transient*, or secondary, windows.

The functionality resources are the smallest—and probably the least used—group of resources in Motif. The functionality resources include those that affect whether a component such as a minimize button or window menu appears in a window; those that affect whether the window has minimize and menu functionality; and those that affect the presence and location of icons. Changing the functionality of a window is full of danger for the customizer who wants to stay within standards. At times, however, it represents a reasonable way to limit a user's options, especially when additional options are unnecessary. For example, there is no reason a user needs a maximize functionality for a window that contains a prompt for a string of text.

Dividing along the lines of appearance, behavior, and functionality departs somewhat from the way the Motif documentation from the Open Software Foundation categorizes Motif resources. It also has three categories:

- Component appearance resources
- Specific behavior and appearance resources
- Client-specific resources

The resources in these categories generally fit the categories used in this book. The difference is that client appearance resources are more apt to be grouped with component appearance resources.

APPEARANCE RESOURCES

In most cases, Motif is an excellent example of implementing resources under the X Window System. It is perhaps best when it comes to appearance resources, and offers so much flexibility, that application designers are advised in the Motif style guide not to do anything to restrict this flexibility—for users will come to expect it.

The most important thing to note about appearance resources is that you can use them on almost any distinct component in a Motif window, as well as on an entire window, or all windows. Well-written Motif applications emulate this approach, and you should be able to modify the appearance of dialog boxes, menus, and file boxes, among other things, that are specific to the application.

Table 5-1 Motif Appearance Resources

Name	Value	Default
Window Manager Context		
activeBackground	color	varies
activeBackgroundPixmap	string	varies
activeBottomShadowColor	color	varies
activeBottomShadowPixmap	string	varies
activeForeground	color	varies
activeTopShadowColor	color	varies
activeTopShadowPixmap	string	varies
background	color	varies
backgroundPixmap	string	varies
bottomShadowColor	color	varies
bottomShadowPixmap	string	varies
cleanText	true/false	true
fontList	string	fixed
foreground	color	varies
frameBorderWidth	pixels	5
resizeBorderWidth	pixels	10
topShadowColor	color	varies
topShadowPixmap	string	varies
Client Window Context		
iconImage	file	image (with pathname)
iconImageBackground	color	icon background
iconImageBottomShadowColor	color	icon bottom shadow
iconImageBottomShadowPixmap	color	icon bottom shadow pixmap
iconImageForeground	color	varies
iconImageTopShadowColor	color	icon top shadow color
iconImageTopShadowPixmap	color	icon top shadow pixmap
matteBackground	color	background
matteBottomShadowColor	color	bottom shadow color
matteBottomShadowPixmap	color	bottom shadow pixmap
matteForeground	color	foreground
matteTopShadowColor	color	top shadow color
matteTopShadowPixmap	color	top shadow pixmap

Again, the basic types of resources that affect appearance are color, fonts, and component sizing resources, but there are other types, such as resources that add bitmap patterns to windows. As you can see in Table 5-1, most of the resources address color and pixmaps used for shading components. The table also includes the **fontList** and **iconImage** resources, which address window fonts and the actual bitmap displayed by an icon.

Context Particulars

There are some behaviors you should know about when dealing with the different contexts in which resources exist. In the window manager context, when you are dealing with windows (clients), menus, icons, and feedback windows, you set resources on a class, or global, basis. The following syntax summarizes this:

```
Mwm*[client|menu|icon|feedback]*resource: value
```

For windows, you can also specify resources for the titlebar, including fonts and background and foreground colors. The syntax is:

```
Mwm*client.titlebar*resource: value
```

Still speaking globally, you can also set resources for menus on a menu-by-menu basis. The syntax here is:

```
Mwm*menumenuname*resource: value
```

In the context of an individual window, you can modify resources based on named windows, but in most cases you cannot override Motif resources set on a global basis. For example, you cannot override fonts and colors used in the window components. But you can override the window menu. In addition, there are numerous resources devoted to the window context.

Color Resources

Color resources exist in the window manager context and in the client window context when they involve matte colors. A secondary set of color resources controls icon appearance. In general, you can control colors separately for inactive windows—those without the keyboard focus—and the active window, the window with the keyboard focus. Matte, or pixmaps for Motif's optional inner window frame also have a set of color resources.

The default Motif colors are set to light gray for inactive windows and to cadet blue for the active window. There are three rules Motif uses in creating shadows for its 3-D effects:

- Top shadow colors are lighter than the background color.
- Bottom shadow colors are darker than the background color.
- A foreground shadow color is darker than the background shadow color.

In many cases, it is advisable to use this default scheme. In some cases, such as menus that have many separator lines and tend to blur, you might adjust the top and bottom shadow colors as a corrective measure (or just use a different color scheme). If you are using a matte, you might want to set the bottom shadow color to the same color as the matte for better contrast against the frame.

Window Colors

As noted, color resources exist in both window manager and client window contexts. In both contexts, color attributes of all components in a single class can be modified by placing an asterisk before the resource name:

```
Mwm*background: blue
```

or

```
Mwm*matteForeground: red
```

These examples change the color of all components that recognize the background resource, unless those resources are controlled by a more specific resource, such as ***title.background**. The second example, while possible, is unlikely because mattes are specialized and you will likely use them in the context of a named window. You can use them with a named window because they operate in the client context. Here is a more likely example:

```
Mwm*mywindow*matteForeground: red
```

You can also use color resources to modify components in the window. For example, to change the background color of all menus, enter the following into your **.Xdefaults** file or $XAPPLRESDIR/**Mwm** file:*

```
Mwm*menu*background: blue
```

You can also modify the color of any distinct menu without affecting the color of all other menus. This includes submenus:

```
Mwm*menu*ImageMenu*background: yellow
```

* As you should know by now, when you make changes in **.Xdefaults**, you must load it before restarting Motif. When you make changes in the $XAPPLRESDIR file, loading **.Xdefaults** is unnecessary and unrelated.

Finally, you can change the color of the window menu with:

```
Mwm*menu*DefaultWindowMenu*background
```

In all, Motif is very flexible with colors. Table 5-2 describes general resources that you can use to change window colors.

Table 5-2 Motif Color Resources

Resource	Description
activeBackground	Frame and titlebar colors for the window with the focus
activeBottomShadowColor	Lower and right bevel color for the window with the focus
activeForeground	Titlebar and other window manager text color in the window with the focus
activeTopShadowcolor	Upper and left bevel color for the window with the focus
background	Frame and titlebar color for windows without the focus
bottomShadowcolor	Lower and right bevel color for windows without the focus
foreground	Titlebar and other window manager text color for windows without the focus
topShadowColor	Upper and left bevel color for windows without the focus

Matte Colors

The matte is the optional inner window frame on primary windows (see Figure 5-1). It has no usefulness beyond extra decoration. You might want to use it for some windows to indicate that they are different from more standard windows.

As you will see in later chapters, the Xmenu software uses mattes for text input windows. Specifying colors for mattes is straightforward. There are no active colors associated with mattes. You turn on a matte with the **matteWidth** resource (see Table 5-3). A value greater than zero must be specified:

```
matteWidth: 5
```

This makes the width of the matte equal to the default size of the window border. You might also want to use matte in an asymmetrical manner, creating a very large matte, for instance, to highlight something in the center of a window.

Figure 5-1 Example of an image in a matted window. This image happened to originate as a photograph and was processed with Kodak Photo CD technology.

Table 5-3 Motif Matte Color Resources

Resource	Description
matteBackground	Background color of the optional inner border of a window
matteBottomShadowColor	Lower and right bevel color for optional inner border
matteForeground	Foreground color of the optional inner border
matteTopShadowColor	Upper and left bevel color for optional inner border

Icon Colors

The icon color resources (see Table 5-4) may seem redundant in that you can set the colors for icons in two other ways: by using the general **Mwm*background** statement you would use for windows; or more specifically, by using a component statement such as **Mwm*icon*background**. Other components, such as menus and feedback windows, do not have their own color resource statements as icons do.

The reason that the icon color resources are not redundant is you use them to set the colors of the inner area of the icon. The equivalent would be setting the color of the client area in a window, which is not possible in Motif (this is left up to the individual application). In any event, when you use the icon color resources it is possible to set colors for all parts of the icon, including the frame and label area if you use **Mwm*background** for these.

Table 5-4 Motif Icon Color Resources

Resource	Description
iconImageBackground	Background color of the inner area which is the actual icon image
iconImageBottomShadowColor	Lower and right bevel color for the icon image
iconImageForeground	Foreground color of the icon image
iconImageTopShadowColor	Upper and left bevel color for the icon image

Shading Resources

The shading resources produce 3-D effects by mixing the foreground and background colors. This mix is possible because Motif can use a bitmap as a reference for the color mix. You can use shading resources with menus, icons, and windows.

If you work on a color system, or administer color systems, it is advisable not to get carried away with the shading resources. A modification here or there, perhaps by changing the default value of the matte, is okay, but in general, shading does not enhance the appearance of windows on a color display, although on monochrome systems, shading can greatly enhance the appearance of windows. (The Xmenu software includes limited options for shading, because the harm of mindless setting of the shading resources obviously outweighs any benefits.)

By default, shading is not implemented on color systems. On monochrome systems, several resources are activated. Table 5-5 lists the various values that you can use to specify pixmap shading.

Table 5-5 Pixmap Shading Values

Value	Description
foreground	The current foreground color
background	The current background color
25_foreground	Crosshatch pattern using 25 percent of the foreground color and 75 percent of the background color
50_foreground	Crosshatch pattern using 50 percent of the foreground color and 50 percent of the background color
75_foreground	Crosshatch pattern using 75 percent of the foreground color and 25 percent of the background color
horizontal_tile	Horizontal lines that alternately use the foreground and background colors
vertical_tile	Vertical lines that alternately use the foreground and background colors
slant_right	Diagonal lines slanting right that alternately use the foreground and background colors
slant_left	Diagonal lines slanting left that alternately use the foreground and background colors

Window and Menu Shades

Six resources are supported for changing the shading of window components (see Table 5-6). Additionally, if you are working on a monochrome system, you can use the **cleanText** resource to improve the appearance of text against shaded backgrounds.

For both color and monochrome systems, you should experiment with the different bitmap patterns until you find a suitable 3-D effect. On color systems, most of the effects will be unnerving. You might like to adjust the top and bottom shadow pixmap resources for inactive windows, for instance, but might not like the effect it has on menus. The solution is to limit your resource statements to the client component:

```
Mwm*client*topShadowPixmap: 25_foreground
Mwm*client*bottomShadowPixmap: 75_foreground
```

You can also produce some reasonable effects by adjusting the top and bottom shadow pixmaps used by icon frames. Menus, however, generally deteriorate when you change any of the pixmap values.

Table 5-6 Window, Icon, and Menu Shading

Resource	Description
activeBackgroundPixmap	Background pixmap for the window with the focus. Value from Table 5-5.
activeBottomShadowPixmap	Lower and right bevel pixmap for the window with the focus. Value from Table 5-5.
activeTopShadowPixmap	Upper and left bevel pixmap for the window with the focus. Value from Table 5-5.
backgroundPixmap	Background pixmap for the windows without the focus. Value from Table 5-5.
bottomShadowPixmap	Lower and right bevel pixmap for windows without the focus. Value from Table 5-5.
cleanText	Set to true, text has a clear background. Otherwise, the text is drawn directly on the background.
topShadowPixmap	Upper and left bevel pixmap for windows without the focus. Value from Table 5-5.

Matte Shading

If you use a matte in a window, it is a good candidate for shading with a pixmap pattern (see Table 5-7). You can either specify a line pattern, such as **vertical_tile** or **slant_right** to produce a different effect, or **background** to better blend the frame and matte colors.

Table 5-7 Menu Shading Resources

Resource	Description
matteBottomShadowPixmap	Lower and right bevel pixmap for mattes. Value from Table 5-5.
matteTopShadowPixmap	Upper and left bevel pixmap for mattes. Value from Table 5-5.

Icon Image Shading

If you adjust the pixmap shading for the icon image, you should adjust it for the icon frame as well. This makes the shading effect consistent not only in the frame, but in the icon label area (see Table 5-8).

In the default case, the label area appears as the lower part of the icon. You can change this with the **iconDecoration** resource. You can eliminate the area altogether—a relatively aesthetic approach if you are using the **slant_right** pixmap. Alternatively, you could have **iconDecoration** set to **activelabel** (the default), in which case you might want to extend the pixmap to the active area. The following statements do the trick:

```
Mwm*icon*activeTopShadowPixmap: slant_right
Mwm*icon*activeBottomShadowPixmap: slant_right
```

You could also choose to use the above statements even if you did not modify the icon image pixmaps. The result would be to add a secondary highlighting feature to the active label. By default, the active label extends horizontally so that it can display all text assigned to the icon label.

Table 5-8 Icon Image Shading

Resource	Description
iconImageBottomShadowPixmap	Lower and right bevel pixmap for icon images. Value from Table 5-5.
iconImageTopShadowPixmap	Upper and left bevel pixmap for icon images. Value from Table 5-5.

Icon Bitmaps and Pixmaps

Some versions of Motif support color pixmap, or XPM2, images for use in icons. Most versions, however, just support monochrome bitmap, or XBM, files. Even with monochrome images, you can make a bitmap icon colorful by setting the different color and pixmap resources. But if you want to do something like put a graphic or photographic image in the icon, you're out of luck.

We have already discussed the special resources for setting colors and pixmaps for mattes and bevels (3-D shadowing). Table 5-9 repeats these for convenience sake, but see Chapter 4 and the discussions later in this chapter on icon behavior and functionality for additional information on bitmaps.

To specify a bitmap in a resource file, you use the **iconImage** statement, which was listed in the first table in this section, grouping appearance resources. The **iconImage** resource definitely belongs in this category, because if you don't modify it to some extent, your desktops lose visual functionality and look stale. Any experienced Motif user will tell you it is a relief not to see the OSF's default icon on a desktop.

Table 5-9 Icon Image Appearance Resources

Name	Value	Default
iconImage	file	image (with pathname)
iconImageBackground	color	icon background
iconImageBottomShadowColor	color	icon bottom shadow
iconImageBottomShadowPix	color	icon bottom shadow pixmap
iconImageForeground	color	varies
iconImageTopShadowColor	color	icon top shadow color
iconImageTopShadowPixmap	color	icon top shadow pixmap

The **bitmapDirectory** resource identifies a directory to be searched for bitmaps. The directory is searched if you simply set a resource statement to the name of a bitmap file. If you use a full pathname when setting the resource statement, the bitmap directory is not searched. Or, because the default value for **bitmapDirectory** is **/usr/include/X11/bitmaps**, you can store your bitmaps here—and then all you have to do is set the resource statement to the name of the bitmap file.

If you use this last method, you might want to move or back up the X Consortium bitmaps normally residing in that directory. Alternatively—in the interest of other users, who might have unique uses for the Consortium bitmaps—you might want to create a new bitmap directory and copy selected Consortium bitmaps into it. This is the approach of the Xmenu program.

The **iconImage** statement works in the context of windows, so it's a good tool to make Xterms and other applications distinct from one another. Simply use the named window approach:

```
Mwm*judy*iconImage: judy.xpm2
```

If you have access to a scanner, you can scan in photographs of other users on your network and turn the image files into pixmaps, given you are using a version of Motif that supports pixmaps in icons. This is a natural interface for a script that begins a **talk** session with another user, or a script that logs into another user's system. Figure 5-2 shows an example.

Figure 5-2 Various examples of icons that resulted from scanning photographs on a desktop scanner.

The steps necessary to convert a photograph into an image are numerous. First you need a photograph. Then you need a scanner. If you can't find a UNIX system with a scanner, look for someone who has one hooked up to a PC or a Macintosh. Most PC and Mac scanner software produces GIF files, which can be easily loaded in UNIX under **xloadimage** or **xv**. After you have displayed the GIF file, you can use the screen capture utilities in Chapter 8 to capture and convert an icon-sized version of part of the photograph.

Font Resources

The last distinct area of appearance resources is font resources. Controlled by the **fontList** statement, you can effect a font change on window components that contain text. This may also work with applications, provided that the application permits and you know the name of the associated resource.

For Motif components, you can use **fontList** whenever text is involved, including titlebars, icon labels, and menus. You can also specify on a global basis or by component. To set the window manager text consistently throughout all components, use a statement similar to the following:

```
Mwm*fontList: "courier-bold-r*140*"
```

You can use any font you like, but you will notice that character cell and monospaced fonts produce the best results (see Chapter 4).

After setting the global font, you might like to vary the font for components. A large font in the titlebar, for instance, yields very aesthetic results:

```
Mwm*client.titlebar*fontList: "times-bold-r*240*"
```

Next, to change the fonts in menus, do it on a global basis for all menus:

```
Mwm*menu*fontList: "courier-bold-r*140*"
```

You can also change on a menu-by-menu basis:

```
Mwm*menu*specialmenu*fontList: "times-bold-r*140*"
```

Finally, you can specify a font for feedback windows:

```
Mwm*feedback*fontList: "times-bold-r*140*"
```

Window Frame Size Resources

Although size is part of appearance, there are only two resources that control the size of window components: **frameBorderWidth** and **resizeBorderWidth** (see Table 5-10). You can also change the size of Motif components by changing the font as discussed in the previous section.

The default frame width is 10 pixels. This applies if windows use resize handles, which is the default condition. If the resize handles have been removed via the **clientDecoration** resource, the default frame width is 5 pixels. When resize handles are in effect, the **resizeBorderWidth** resource applies. When resize handles are absent, the **frameBorderWidth** applies.

The default values of 5 and 10 pixels are suitable for most users, but it is fairly acceptable to increase the width up to 25 pixels. A larger frame provides a boost in functionality if you have created special windows menus that pop up when you press a mouse button on the frame area. Implementing this technique with a smaller frame makes it difficult for the user to pop up the menu. To complement the larger frame, you should also increase the font size of the text in the window titlebar. The result is a larger-looking Motif.

Table 5-10 Window Frame Size Resources

Resource	Description
frameBorderWidth	Width of the window frame when resize handles are not used. Default is 5 pixels.
resizeBorderWidth	Width of the window frame when resize handles are used. Default is 10 pixels.

BEHAVIOR RESOURCES

It is an easy matter to draw the line between appearance and behavior. But drawing a line between behavior and functionality is harder. In this section, the criterion used to establish behavior resources (see Table 5-11) is to apply to them the test: Do they modify an existing behavior? If the answer is yes, they are in this section. If the answer is no, and they add or delete functionality, they appear in the next section, *Functionality Resources*.

Table 5-11 Motif Behavior Resources

Name	Value	Default
autoKeyFocus	true/false	true
autoRaiseDelay	milliseconds	500
bitmapDirectory	directory	/usr/include/X11/bitmaps
buttonBindings	string	DefaultButtonBindings
clientAutoPlace	true/false	true
colormapFocusPolicy	string	keyboard
configFile	file	.mwmrc
deiconifyKeyFocus	true/false	true
doubleClickTime	milliseconds	multi-click time
enableWarp	true/false	true
enforceKeyFocus	true/false	true
focusAutoRaise	true/false	varies
iconAutoPlace	true/false	true
iconClick	true/false	true
iconDecoration	string	varies
iconImageMaximum	width/height	50x50
iconImageMinimum	width/height	16x16
iconPlacement	string	left bottom
iconPlacementMargin	pixels	varies
interactivePlacement	true/false	false
keyBindings	string	DefaultKeyBindings
keyboardFocusPolicy	string	explicit
limitResize	true/false	true
lowerOnIconify	true/false	true
maximumClientSize	width/height	full screen
maximumMaximumSize	width/height	twice screen
moveThreshold	pixels	4
multiScreen	true/false	false
positionIsFrame	true/false	true
positionOnScreen	true/false	true
quitTimeout	milliseconds	1000
raiseKeyFocus	true/false	false
saveUnder	true/false	false
screens	string	varies
startupKeyFocus	true/false	true
useClientIcon	true/false	false
windowMenu	string	DefaultWindowMenu

The behavior resources fall into several categories:

- Keyboard focus
- Execution parameters
- Sizing and positioning
- Configuration resources

By and large, they operate in a global context. One exception is the **windowMenu** resource, which replaces the default window menu with one you specify in the **.mwmrc** file. The exception is partial because you can effect this change on a global basis, or by using named windows. Technically, it is a global resource, however. The same is true of the **maximumClientSize** and **maximumMaximumSize**.

Keyboard Focus Resources

Among experienced users, keyboard focus policy is one of the most religious issues for graphical user interfaces. There are basically two keyboard focus models:

- Explicit: also known as "click-to-type," this model requires the user to click in a window before the focus is transferred.*
- Implicit: also known as "focus-follows-mouse," this model transfers the focus according to the position of the mouse.

On the surface, there doesn't appear to be much to distinguish one model from another. But the minute you add the **focusAutoRaise** resource to the equation things change. With **focusAutoRaise** set to false in the implicit model, windows don't raise to the top of the stack when they get the focus. For experienced users, this is a boon, because you can type in a window, even though that window might be partially obscured by another window. The benefit is you can often see more window.

Click-to-type supporters might note that **focusAutoRaise** can be used in the explicit model. The difference means an extra mouse click, plus likely an additional mouse movement to get to the titlebar or window frame—all in all, a lot of moving and clicking if you're traversing several windows.

Whichever side you choose in the keyboard focus debate, there are other focus resources to be considered. These include the duration before a window rises to the top of the stack; whether a window gets the colormap focus; and whether windows automatically get the focus when they are opened, moved through the stack, or restored from an icon. Table 5-12 describes all the focus resources.

*Microsoft Windows and Apple Macintosh use only click-to-focus.

Table 5-12 Motif Focus Resources

Resource	Description
autoKeyFocus	Explicit mode only. When set to true, causes the previous window with the focus to get the focus again when the current window with the focus is closed or iconified. This is the default behavior.
autoRaiseDelay	Implicit mode only and **focusAutoRaise** must be set to true. The **autoRaiseDelay** resource specifies the time in milliseconds before a window rises to the top of the stack when it gets the focus. The default is 500 ms.
colormapFocusPolicy	Implicit and explicit modes. This resource sets the colormap focus policy. Set to **explicit** to automatically set the colormap, if possible. Set to **pointer** to wait to set the colormap until a window contains the mouse pointer. Set to keyboard to wait until the window gets the focus.
deiconifyKeyFocus	Explicit mode only. If set to **true**, a window receives the focus when it is restored from an icon.
enforceKeyFocus	Implicit and explicit modes. Setting this resource to **false** permits globally active windows to remain active without the focus. **True** requires direct transfer of the focus.
focusAutoRaise	Implicit and explicit modes. If set to **false** in implicit mode, the window rises to the top of the stack when it gets the focus. Conversely, you must set it to **true** for the same behavior in explicit mode.
keyboardFocusPolicy	Sets the focus policy: **explicit** sets click-to-type policy; **pointer** sets focus-follows-mouse policy.
raiseKeyFocus	Explicit mode only. If **true**, specifies that windows raised via the **f.normalize_and_raise** function receive the focus.
startupKeyFocus	Explicit mode only. Traditionally, this resource has slowed performance of Motif. Set to **true** it causes a window to get the focus when it is first opened.

Execution Parameter Resources

Resources that affect execution—ranging from the time Motif waits before closing a window to the management of multiple consoles—are sometimes desirable to adjust. For instance, if another user comes to you and asks if you know how to lengthen the time between mouse clicks for double-click actions, the **doubleClickTime** resource provides the answer (see Table 5-13).

Table 5-13 Motif Execution Parameter Resources

Resource	Description
doubleClickTime	Sets the maximum time in milliseconds between mouse clicks in a double-click operation. The default value is set automatically based on hardware parameters.
enableWarp	Designed for use with the window menu's resize and move options, this resource moves the pointer to the center of the window if set to true. Otherwise, it leaves the pointer in the area of the window menu.
moveThreshold	Sets the number of pixels that the mouse must move before a move operation begins. The default value is **4** pixels.
multiScreen	Tells Motif to manage more than one screen when set to true. Otherwise, Motif manages a single screen, which is the default.
quitTimeout	Sets the amount of time in milliseconds that Motif waits before it begins closing down well-behaved windows. The default is **1000** ms.
saveUnder	Tells the X server to save the contents of obscured windows. The obscured window must have its "save under" attribute bit set. The default is **false**, which disables this feature.
screens	Specifies the resource names for screens that Motif manages. The default names parallel screen names used by X (0,1,2...).
useClientIcon	Allows you to override an application's intent to use its own icon. Setting the resource to **true** permits the application to use its own icon.

You should exercise caution if you modify execution parameters. Although one user wants **doubleClickTime** lengthened, many other users might find the change uncomfortable. This is especially true of a resource such as **moveThreshold**, which controls the number of pixels the mouse needs to move before a move operation begins.

The **enableWarp** resource also presents an interesting dilemma when it comes to user preferences. If you accept its default behavior, a window pointer moves to the center of the window after selecting a move or resize operation from the window menu. Because **enableWarp** is primarily designed for keyboard users, this is what you expect. For mouse users, however, the automatic movement of the pointer to the center of the window is unexpected. Hence the rationale for this resource (although, in practice, most mouse users initiate move and resize operations elsewhere).

Sizing and Positioning Resources

The sizing and positioning resources help you define limits and behavior for windows and icons (see Table 5-14). Many of these resources assert limits on the size of windows and icons. Others establish the initial size and location of the window or icon.

The **interactivePlacement** resource is the one resource in the group that some users might expect. When set to true, **interactivePlacement** causes a tracking rectangle to appear when you first summon a window. The drawback to using this resource is that if you create any scripts that invoke Xterms—say, for information purposes, or to get user input—you must rely on the user to click the mouse before the window fully materializes.

If you're concerned about policy—perhaps you administer systems in which you have some cowboy users who like to modify their own resources—some of the sizing resources are a good deterrent. For example, you can use **iconImageMaximum** to limit the size of icons and **limitResize** to limit window resizing to a window's normal maximum size. Of course, if

Table 5-14 Sizing and Positioning Resources

Resource	Description
clientAutoPlace	Sets initial window position when **interactivePlacement** is **false**. The default initial position is top left. Setting **clientAutoPlace** to **false** lets application positioning, if any, take control.
iconAutoPlace	Sets icon positioning to a predetermined screen location (see **iconPlacement**). If set to **false**, sets icon positioning to last position of the full window.
iconImageMaximum	Sets icon size by setting the maximum size up to 128 by 128 pixels. The value you specify is the actual size, providing it is not less than the value of **iconImageMinimum**. The default is 50 by 50 pixels.
iconImageMinimum	Sets the minimum image size for the icon. Both the default and minimum sizes are 16 by 16 pixels.
iconPlacement	Specifies the screen area where icons are placed: **left top**, **right top**, **top right**, **bottom right**, **right bottom**, **left bottom**, **bottom left**, **top left**.
iconPlacement	Specifies the distance in pixels between any icon and the edge of the screen.

Table 5.14 continued

Resource	Description
interactivePlacement	Presents the user with a tracking rectangle to place newly opened windows. The default of **false** opens a window at the position specified by **clientAutoPlace**.
limitResize	Stops the user from sizing a window beyond its maximum size. See **maximumMaximumSize**.
maximumClientSize	Specifies the maximum size of the client portion of the window by using coordinates based on the type of data in the window. For example, set size according to columns and rows for Xterm windows.
maximumMaximumSize	Specifies the maximum window size. Can be used with named windows. Default is twice the screen size.
positionIsFrame	Specifies that Motif should handle positioning requests based on the window frame size. If set to **false**, it handles them based on the client area size.
positionOnScreen	Tells Motif to ensure that part of the window (upper left-hand corner) is visible when window positioning data would otherwise force it off-screen. If set to **false**, positioning data has precedence.

your cowboys are real gunslingers, you have to assert your authority by making the necessary changes using the **xrm** option to Motif—and you'll also have to sequester the Motif startup file in an execute-only script owned by root (see Chapter 2 for more on startup files).

Motif Configuration Resources

The various resources in this category address one configuration issue or another (see Table 5-15). In general, they are unrelated, although you can view the **buttonBindings**, **keyBindings**, and **windowMenu** as serving similar purposes.

The major difference between the bindings resources and the **windowMenu** resource is the bindings resources do not operate in a window context. You can change button and key bindings as you desire, but the change is always global. The button and key bindings do maintain default actions inherent in Motif, unless you specifically override these. For more information on menus and bindings, see Chapter 6.

The **configFile** resource is interesting. It gives you a way to switch between different versions of the **.mwmrc** file. Why do this? Even an individual user could take advantage of switching between different versions of **.mwmrc**, tailoring each version to a particular application environment. On a system level, the **configFile** resources gives you a built-in way to offer **.mwmrc** files of different complexity to users.

Table 5-15 Configuration Resources

Resource	Description
bitmapDirectory	Identifies a directory to be searched for bitmaps. The directory is searched if you simply use a filename for a bitmap file. Otherwise, you can set a full path in the resource statement. The default directory is **/usr/include/X11/bitmaps**.
buttonBindings	Specifies the name of the set of button bindings as contained in **.mwmrc**. The default is **DefaultButtonBindings**.
configFile	Specifies the pathname to a **.mwmrc** file. If this resource is not used, Motif searches several default paths. The usual location is $HOME.
iconClick	Tells Motif to post the system menu when an icon is clicked. If set to **false**, the system menu is not posted.
iconDecoration	Specifies whether icons appear as labels (**label**), images (**image**), images with labels (**label image**), images with labels that expand when the icon gets the focus (**activelabel**), or just labels that expand (**activelabel label**).
keyBindings	Specifies the name of the set of key bindings as contained in **.mwmrc**. The default is **DefaultKeyBindings**.
lowerOnIconify	Causes a window's icon to go to the bottom of the window stack when the window is minimized. If set to **false**, the window's icon retains the window's current place in the stack.

FUNCTIONALITY RESOURCES

The distinction between behavior and functionality resource is somewhat arbitrary, but two factors apply to functionality resources that don't necessarily apply to behavior resources:

- Functionality resources let you modify critical features of the basic Motif environment.
- Functionality resources give you the ability to undermine the Motif interface—something you want to avoid, of course.

Five resources you should avoid, except for special reasons, are:

- **clientDecorations**
- **clientFunctions**
- **transientDecorations**
- **transientFunctions**
- **showFeedback**

Each of these resources can remove functionality from a window. In the case of the transient resources, they can remove functionality from transient windows, which include dialog boxes and file boxes. If you are concerned about rigorous enforcement of interface policy, these resources are good candidates for an **-xrm** override in a sequestered startup file:

```
# Load Motif using -xrm option. Each resource
# requires -xrm. Lines must be escaped.
  mwm -xrm 'clientDecorations all' \
      -xrm 'clientFunctions all' \
      -xrm 'transientDecorations menu title resizeh' \
      -xrm 'transientFunctions -minimize -maximize' \
      -xrm 'showFeedback all' &
```

Some users might object to this approach, and you might want to grant leniency on a case-by-case basis, but even if you do grant leniency, you can maintain a record of users who are making exceptions to interface policy. In general, the functionality resources fall into the following categories:

- Decorations and functions
- Icon box resources
- Miscellaneous resources

Several, if not all, of the functionality resources (see Table 5-16) could be included in the sequestered startup file. For example, your site might object to the use of a matte as an unnecessary adornment. Or similarly, the icon box might be outlawed as a ludicrous invention, although many experienced users do prefer the icon box—so you should also take this into account. Whatever the case, regard the functionality resources with caution—or come up with a system that gives you an easy way to repair runaway interfaces, such as the Xmenu *Resources* menu described in Chapter 7.

Table 5-16 Motif Functionality Resources

Name	Value	Default
clientDecoration	string	all
clientFunctions	string	all
matteWidth	pixels	0
maximumClientSize	width/height	full screen
transientDecoration	string	system
transientFunctions	string	-minimize -maximize
useIconBox	true/false	false
iconBoxGeometry	string	6x1+0-0
iconBoxName	string	iconbox
iconBoxSBDisplayPolicy	string	all
iconBoxTitle	string	Icons
passButtons	true/false	false
passSelectButton	true/false	true
resizeCursors	true/false	true
wMenuButtonClick	true/false	true
wMenuButtonClick2	true/false	true
fadeNormalIcon	true/false	false
showFeedback	string	-kill

Decoration and Function Resources

As already noted, you should use care when modifying the Motif interface with the decoration and function resources. Proper use of these resources is well within the style parameters of the Motif interface, but removing window components and functions for the sake of a different look and feel is a preposterous idea. Table 5-17 lists the resources discussed in this section.

Table 5-17 Decoration and Function Resources

Resource	Description
clientDecorations	Removes and adds componentsto the window frame
clientFunctions	Removes and adds functions to the window
showFeedback	Gives you options to provide users with interface feedback
transientDecorations	Removes and adds components to transient window frames
transientFunctions	Removes and adds functions to transient windows

All five of the decoration and function resources work in the same manner by allowing you to specify which components and function are in effect. The resource statements recognize plus and minus signs in order to determine whether decorations and function should be included or excluded:

- When a resource value begins with a plus sign—or more simply, with a value—Motif determines that the following decorations or functions will be included.
- When a resource value begins with a minus sign, Motif determines that the following decorations or functions will be excluded.

The decoration and function resources have different keywords, although they parallel each other in the features they address. Tables 5-18 and 5-19 describe the various keywords.

Table 5-18 Decoration Keywords

Component	Description
all	All decorations. This is the default.
border	Window border.
maximize	Maximize button.
menu	Window menu (in title bar only).
minimize	Minimize button.
none	No decorations.
resizeh	Resize handles.
title	Titlebar including border.

Table 5-19 Function Keywords

Function	Description
all	All functions. This is the default.
close	Close the window.
minimize	Minimize the window.
maximize	Maximize the window.
move	Perform move operation.
none	No functions.
resizeh	Perform resize operation.

The one safe way to make liberal use of the decoration and function resources is by limiting them to named windows. In many cases, you will also find this appropriate because you should be able to easily pinpoint windows that require an aberration to the style guide. For example, you might find it silly that some software vendors have file boxes that you can maximize, even though the contents of the client window do not enlarge with the window.

Similarly, you might use Xterm windows to get user input for a shell script. If you do, you see no reason why the user should be able to maximize or resize this special Xterm. The following resource statement partially disarms the Xterm:

```
Mwm*getinput*clientDecoration: -maximize -resizeh
```

The reason this gets you only part of the way is that the window menu still contains options for minimizing and resizing. So you could add the following statement to your resource file to complete the job:

```
Mwm*getinput*clientFunctions: -maximize -resizeh
```

This does the trick, but aesthetically, you might still find something wrong with the text input window: Why have so many menu options? Why not just use the fewest necessary to satisfy both keyboard and mouse interfaces?

There's absolutely no reason not to take this tack. It is a popular tack in Microsoft Windows programs and in some Motif programs, although UNIX vendors tend to shy away from even appearing to break style guide rules. There is nothing in the *Motif Style Guide* that prohibits this behavior, by the way (see Figure 5-3).

```
Menu GetInput
{
     Restore    _R Alt<Key>F5   f.restore
     Move       _M Alt<Key>F7   f.move
     Minimize   _n Alt<Key>F9   f.minimize
     Close      _C Alt<Key>F4   f.kill
}
```

After this step, you need to specify the following resource so Motif knows about the Xterm's special menu:

```
Mwm*getinput*windowMenu: GetInput
```

Now you have a practical solution, but you could further reduce the menu options. If you wanted to rely on other users' ability to move, iconify, and

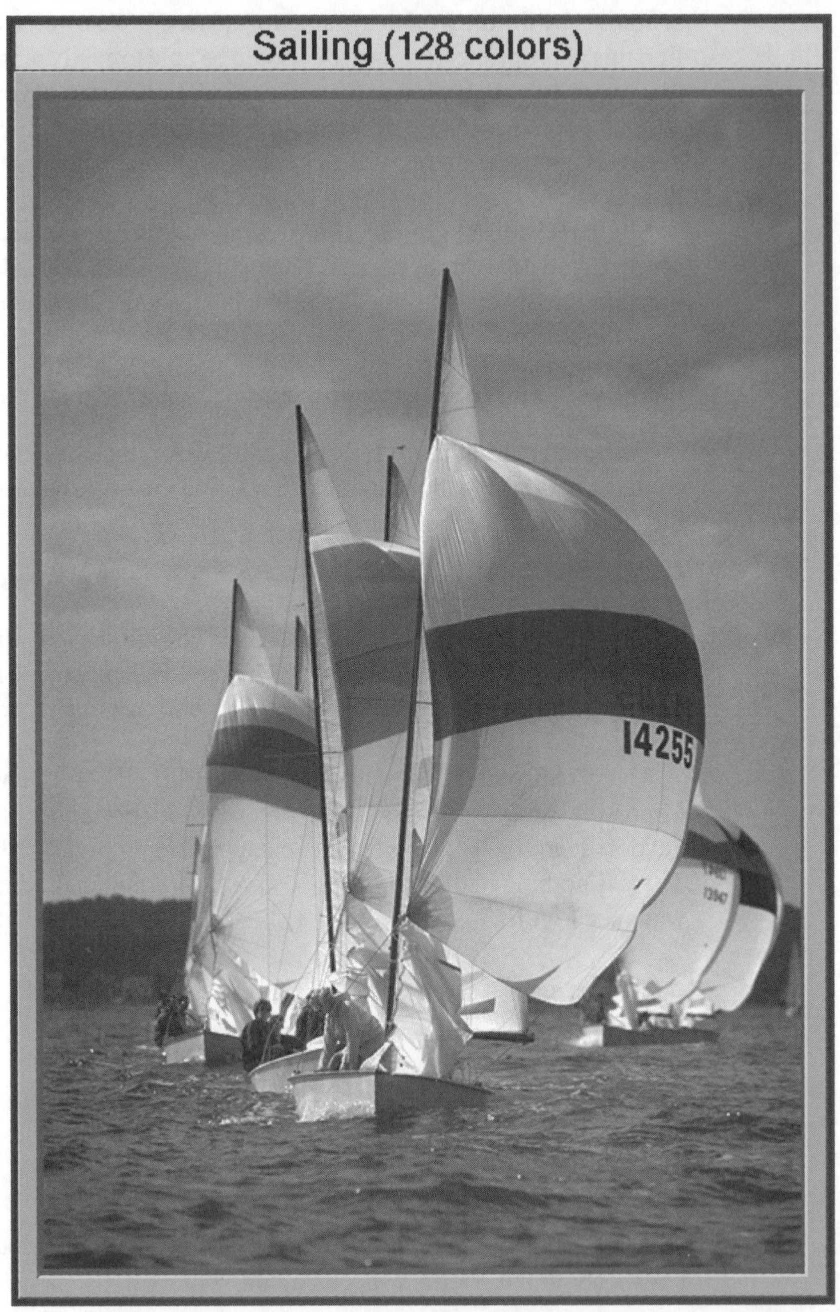

Figure 5-3 Nonstandard Motif window displaying a photograph using a public domain image utility run from the command line.

restore a window using the mouse and window decorations, or the keyboard and keybindings, you could feasibly reduce the menu to the Close option only. In any event, the question now becomes can you use a menu in **.mwmrc** and obviate the need to use the **clientFunctions** resource?

The answer is yes, but you should also use the **clientFunctions** resource. There is always the likelihood that the **maximize** and **resizeh** functions are bound to other key or button sequences. You, yourself, have probably created such bindings, and you and your users might habitually employ them. One way to cut down on redundancy, however, is not to use **clientDecorations** and **clientFunctions** for the same resource. You don't need to. The only time you should be using both is when you want to strip a window of an interface component, yet leave the functionality intact for the window menu or key or button binding.

As for feedback options, user preference should be the determining factor in most cases. Table 5-20 describes the various feedback options.

Table 5-20 Feedback Keywords

Option	Description
all	Show all feedback. This is the default.
behavior	Confirm behavior switch.
kill	Confirm if KILL signal received.
move	Show coordinates during move operation.
none	No feedback.
placement	Show coordinates and size for interactive placement.
quit	Confirm if user has chosen quit option.
resize	Show coordinates during resize operation.
restart	Display confirmation window for restart.

As you can see in Table 5-20, many of the feedback options are designed to help users, although other users might think they are a hindrance. On some systems, too, the coordinates display boxes for the resize, move, and placement options have been known to survive normal screen repainting.

From a site policy viewpoint, the two options you should insist on using are **kill** and **quit**:

```
Mwm*showfeedback: kill quit
```

To dress the message box up a bit, you might want to add a font change:

```
Mwm*feedback*fontList:"-adobe-times*bold-r-nor*180*"
```

The other feedback options are worth investigating. If you or your users are apt to accidentally restart Motif from the root menu, including the **re-**

start option to **showFeedback** prevents unnecessary restarting, although it adds a step—clicking Okay in the feedback window—which some users might protest. You also might want to include the **configure** option. It is less likely to be accidentally invoked, but when it is, it can confound users. The result of a behavior switch (see the description for **f.set_behavior** in Chapter 6) is that Motif switches to its default set of resources, including its default menu configuration.

Icon Box Resources

The icon box is not immensely popular, but it has a persistent following, especially among DEC sites, where it has existed on DEC's VMS implementation of Motif for a long time in computer industry terms. It's a worthwhile invention and you should give it a try if you never have. For systems with a minimum of screen real estate—especially PCs running an X server under Microsoft Windows—the icon box definitely makes organizing running applications a lot easier.

The icon box is an application that sits between Motif and other applications. Instead of icons appearing against the root window, they appear in the icon box (see Figure 5-4). The major difference in behavior caused by the addition of the icon box to the Motif interface is that opened icons—in other words, windows—still have an icon in the icon box. Icons normally disappear when you open them. This can lead to some user confusion, so the icon box supports a resource statement, **fadeNormal**, to gray-out any icons with a corresponding open window.

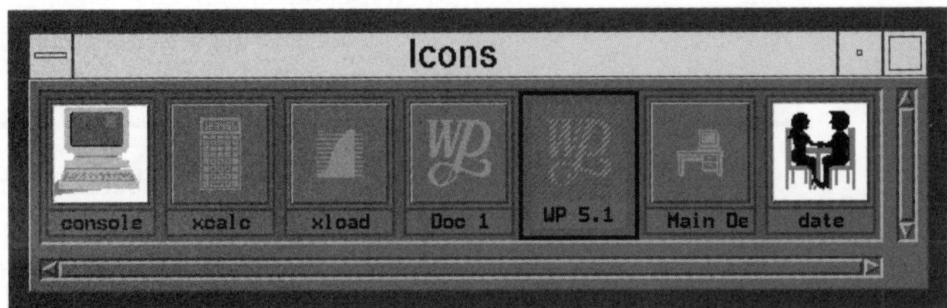

Figure 5-4 Standard version of the Motif icon box.

To use the icon box, set the **useIconBox** resource to true in your Motif resource file. Alternatively, because the icon box represents a major interface difference, you might want to use **xrm** and set the resource in your sequestered Motif startup file. (And if your site is against the use of the icon box, you might want to set **useIconBox** to false in the startup file.) Table 5-21 lists the icon box resources.

Table 5-21 Icon Box Resources

Resource	Description
fadeNormalIcon	Fades any icon in the icon box that corresponds to an open window. The default is **false**.
iconBoxGeometry	Sets the size of position of the icon box. Units of measure are the current size of icons. Pixels are used for positioning.
iconBoxName	Sets the resource name of the icon box. The default is **iconbox**.
iconBoxSBDisplayPolicy	Sets the horizontal and vertical orientation of scrollbars in the icon box.
iconBoxTitle	Sets the text that appears in the titlebar of the icon box. The default is **Icons**.
useIconBox	Tells Motif to use the icon box. The default is **false**, meaning not to use it.

One thing you have to be wary of with the icon box is that you can lose track of running applications. Not only will this affect system performance, it might drive you crazy opening multiple instances of documents and forgetting about them, or checking for running applications that you care about (versus the ones you might not care about—which are unfortunately the ones that are located in the visible area of the icon box).

Again, the major benefit to using the icon box is the savings in screen real estate. You define the size of the icon box with the **iconBoxGeometry** resource. You calculate the geometry string much the same way you calculate the geometry string for Xterm windows (see Chapter 4, "Window Size and Positioning"). The only difference with the icon box is you use the size of icons, versus the size of font characters. If you start from the mindset that you want an icon box that is eight icons wide and one icon deep, sizing the icon box is easy:

```
iconBoxGeometry: 8x1+1-1
```

This places the icon box in the lower left-hand corner of the screen. It extends from left to right and has both horizontal and vertical scrollbars. The horizontal scrollbars are unnecessary unless you resize the icon box to a smaller width. The vertical scrollbars become active when you add your ninth icon to the box—because you have specified **8x1**. Now, if you are pixel-minded, you can convert **8x1** by multiplying it against the value specified by **iconImageMaximum**, which specifies the size of icons. For a **50x50** icon, the conversion works out to be **400x50**. Next add the width of the scrollbars and window frame, and the true dimensions of an **8x1** icon box become something like **785x125**.

Figure 5-5 Modified Motif icon box. Notice that the minimize and maximize buttons have been removed from this version of the icon box.

The **+1-1** in the geometry string represents the *xoffset* and *yoffset* and follows standard X geometry logic (again, see Chapter 4, *Window Size and Positioning*). The default geometry for the icon box is **6x1+0-0**. This is almost identical to the example. But the example starts one pixel away from both edges of the screen. (This is a good habit to get into if you ever use the **xwd** utility to make screen captures. The added pixel in both directions gives a frame effect to the screen capture.)

The **iconBoxSBDisplayPolicy** is another resource that affects icon box geometry. It takes one of three possible arguments: all, horizontal, and vertical. The all argument adds both horizontal and vertical scrollbars to the icon box, and this has no effect on geometry. The horizontal argument tells Motif to size the icon box horizontally and sets the geometry, if a geometry statement doesn't exist. Similarly, the vertical argument sets the geometry for a horizontal orientation. The default icon box has both scrollbars.

In addition to setting the title of the icon box with the **iconBoxTitle** resource, you can configure it many ways using other resources. You might want to use a combination of **iconDecoration** and **clientDecoration** to produce a limited number of window manager controls for the icon box. Figure 5-5 shows the results of using the following resource statements:

```
Mwm*useIconBox: True
Mwm*clientDecoration: -minimize -maximize
Mwm*iconDecoration: label
Mwm*iconBoxTitle: Running Programs
Mwm*iconBoxSBDisplayPolicy: vertical
```

Miscellaneous Resources

The miscellaneous resources address four concerns: turning on mattes, passing button clicks to an application, resize cursors, and what happens when the user clicks on a window's menu button (see Table 5-22).

The **matteWidth** resource, as noted in the *Matte Colors* section in this chapter, turns on a window's matte. A matte is a 3-D rectangle abutting the window frame. A matte has no functionality. It gets its name from its appearance when you set it to a large number. A value of 100, for instance, makes a window appear as if it had been matted like a photograph.

The button resources—**passButtons** and **passSelectButton**—determine whether a window receives button input. In the case of **passButtons**, the default functionality is not to pass a button event to a client window when the button event is bound to a window manager operation. If you set **passButtons** to true, the button event is passed to the client window, but the window manager operation is still performed. The **passSelectButton** resource is similar. If you set it to true, the select button is passed to the client window after it performs a window manager function. Otherwise, a value of false limits the select button to the window manager.

The other resources in this category—**resizeCursors**, **wMenuButtonClick**, and **wMenuButtonClick2**—simply turn functionality on and off. The **resizeCursors** resource turns off the special window resizing cursor if you set it to false. The **wMenuButtonClick** resource determines whether the window menu is left posted after a single button click on the window menu button. The **wMenuButtonClick2** resource determines whether a double click on the window menu button closes the window.

Table 5-22 Miscellaneous Resources

Resource	Description
matteWidth	Activates window matte when set to value greater than zero.
passButtons	Passes window manager button events to the client window when set to **true**. The default is **false**.
passSelectButton	Passes a window manager select button event to the client window when set to **true**. The default is **false**.
resizeCursors	Deactivates the window resize cursors when set to **false**.
wMenuButtonClick	Disables the posting behavior of the window menu after a single click. The default of **true** leaves the menu posted.
wMenuButtonClick2	Prevents a window from being closed due to a double click on the menu button. The default of **true** allows this behavior.

CHAPTER 6
Making Menus

THE MENU APPROACH

An efficient way to coalesce utilities for the X Window System is through the root window menus available in OSF/Motif. Additionally, users of OpenWindows, **twm**, and Desqview/X have window manager menus.

Even if your site uses a desktop manager, which provides a drag and drop interface to utilities, you should not overlook the functionality of the window manager menus. They offer you a means to incorporate a consistent interface to X resources and any utilities you want on your systems. Moreover, if you work at a site with different window managers, the root window menu offers an essential sameness for users who must move between systems.

There are numerous issues associated with creating a menu interface to the X Window System. Many of these issues are described later in this chapter and other chapters, but they can be summarized as follows:

- Performance: The larger a root window manager interface becomes, the longer it takes for the window manager to restart.
- Structure: The design of root window menus requires the desktop customizer to use shell scripts to provide functionality, short of simple routines and built-in window manager features.
- Architecture: The menu interface sits between the X Window System and client applications, generally limiting its effect on clients, with the exception of loading and killing them.
- Availability: Window manager menus can be incorporated into clients and customized for a client, thereby providing a limited graphical interface for scripts and other character-mode utilities.

- Refinability: Window managers provide much of the interface for the end user, but leave many choices to the desktop customizer. Exact appearance of windows and many behavior features need to be refined on a site-by-site basis.

Surmounting the limitations of the menu interface, as well as exploiting the routine features, is the subject matter for much of the rest of this book. It should be noted that most of the development for this book was done using a Sun IPC workstation, Sun SPARCstation 2, and a 486 PC (50MHz) running SCO Open Desktop. These systems deliver adequate performance, but because of their older chip technologies, they also provided a baseline gauge as to how fast—or at times, how slow—the menu frontend could operate. If you are using a faster workstation, such as a Sun SPARCstation Classic or DEC Alpha system, performance is less of an issue. Remember, however, that if you are customizing for others, performance should remain a concern.

To create a professional menu interface, you must be aware of the way resources work in the X Window System. Refer to the previous chapters in this book for that information. It is especially important to know when it is necessary to use the **xrdb** resource manager or when you can rely on X to automatically load resources. Because of performance considerations, you should structure your menus as much as possible to rely on automatic loading of resources. For example, you will get better performance by modifying Xterm resources in the $XAPPLRESDIR/**XTerm** file rather than **.Xdefaults**, which requires the additional step of loading with **xrdb**.

MOTIF MENUS

At a fundamental level, Motif menus are easy to create. Even if you have not read about Motif menus, you can probably create a few menu options just by opening **.mwmrc** and copying a few lines and adding your own instructions.

The **.mwmrc** file is the one file in Motif that controls the contents of Motif menus as well as the keyboard bindings in effect at the root window level, and if desired, for specified client applications. The general syntax for a Motif menu item in the **.mwmrc** file looks like this:

```
menu item [mnemonic] [accelerator] function|command
```

Menu definitions always begin with the keyword **Menu**, followed by an opening French bracket, followed by menu statements, and are terminated with a second French bracket. Menu definitions can have keyboard accelerators such as Alt-F3 to lower a window, as well as keyboard mnemonics, or quick keys. These are indicated by an underscore next to the appropriate letter to press in the menu. Quick keys are excellent for anyone using the Motif menus as a frontend to a database: the quick key approach is universal among database products and appreciated by database users.

Inside the block of menu code are menu item definitions. Each definition can contain either a Motif-defined function, or a call to an executable file via the predefined **f.exec** function, which can also be represented by an exclamation mark. Here is an example from Xmenu's **.mwmrc** file:

```
Menu DefaultWindowMenu
{
     Restore    _R   Alt<Key>F5    f.normalize
     Move       _M   Alt<Key>F7    f.move
     Size       _S   Alt<Key>F8    f.resize
     Minimize   _n   Alt<Key>F9    f.minimize
     Maximize   _x   Alt<Key>F10   f.maximize
     Lower      _L   Alt<Key>F3    f.lower
     no-label                      f.separator
     "Shuffle Up"    Alt<Key>F1    f.raise_lower
     "Shuffle Down"  Alt<Key>F2    f.circle_down
     no-label                      f.separator
     Refresh         Ctrl<Key>Z    f.refresh_win
     Close           Alt<Key>F4    f.kill
}
```

This menu is similar to the standard window menu on many Motif installations. The name of the menu—in this case, and only this case—is special: upon startup Motif looks for a menu called DefaultWindowMenu, if no other menu has been specified through the **Mwm*windowMenu** resource. If you do not create a menu named DefaultWindowMenu—and you have not specified an alternative default menu via the **Mwm*windowMenu** resource—Motif uses an internally coded default menu, which would look like this if you were to duplicate it in the **.mwmrc** file:

```
Menu DefaultWindowMenu
{
     Restore    _R  Alt<Key>F5    f.normalize
     Move       _M  Alt<Key>F7    f.move
     Size       _S  Alt<Key>F8    f.resize
     Minimize   _n  Alt<Key>F9    f.minimize
     Maximize   _x  Alt<Key>F10   f.maximize
     Lower      _L  Alt<Key>F3    f.lower
     no-label                     f.separator
     Close          Alt<Key>F4    f.kill
}
```

It's good to remember the setup of the default menu. Users will be familiar with the options on the menu, so if you modify it, you should include the standard options. Usually, window manager style guides do not deter you from adding options to the menu. In fact, most system software vendors add one or two of their own options. DEC, for instance, adds a menu option for its workspace manager and help system.

In addition to the default window menu, you can have any number of menus defined in **.mwmrc**. The Xmenu program defines some 20 menus, which are associated with mouse and/or keyboard sequences, and named windows. In most Motif implementations, you will find at least one menu associated with one or all of the mouse buttons. This is traditionally called the root window menu. The Xmenu program has three root window menus, each associated with a different mouse button. In order to become familiar with them, and understand other references, here are the Xmenu root menus:

```
! Root Window Menu: Button 1 (left)
Menu ResourcesMenu
{
     " "                              f.nop
     no_label                         f.separator
     @/usr/xmenu/bitmaps/resmenu      f.title
     no_label                         f.separator
     no_label                         f.separator
     " "                              f.nop
     "     Goto Main"                 f.menu MainMenu
     no_label                         f.separator
     no_label                         f.separator
     " Motif Colors"        _C        f.menu MotifColors
     "        Fonts"        _F        f.menu MotifFonts
     "        Icons"        _I        f.menu MotifIcons
     "        Other"        _O        f.menu SystemRes
     no_label                         f.separator
     no_label                         f.separator
     "         Xrdb"        _X        f.menu XrdbMenu
     no_label                         f.separator
     no_label                         f.separator
     "      Refresh"        _f        f.refresh
     "      Restart"        _R        f.restart
     no_label                         f.separator
     no_label                         f.separator
     no_label                         f.separator
     no_label                         f.separator
     "         Exit"        _E        !"killx"
}
```

```
! Root Window Menu: Button 2 (middle)
Menu MainMenu
{
     " "                               f.nop
     no_label                          f.separator
     @/usr/xmenu/bitmaps/mainmenu   f.title
     no_label                          f.separator
     no_label                          f.separator
     " "                               f.nop
     "      Goto Xterm"                f.menu XtermsMenu
     no_label                          f.separator
     no_label                          f.separator
     "     Root Window"   _R           f.menu RWMenu1
     "       ImageShow"   _I           f.menu ImageShow
     "    File options"   _F           f.menu GrabMenu
     no_label                          f.separator
     no_label                          f.separator
     "       X clients"   _c           f.menu XClientsMenu
     "    Applications"   _A           f.menu Menu
     "   Unix commands"   _U           f.menu UnixCmdMenu
     no_label                          f.separator
     no_label                          f.separator
     " Desktop manager"   _D           f.nop
     no_label                          f.separator
     no_label                          f.separator
     no_label                          f.separator
     no_label                          f.separator
     "            Help"   _H           !"(xtermloader help)&"
}


! Root Window Menu: Button 3 (right)
Menu XtermsMenu
{
     " "                                  f.nop
     no_label                             f.separator
     @/usr/xmenu/bitmaps/xterms           f.title
     no_label                             f.separator
     no_label                             f.separator
     " "                                  f.nop
     "         Xterms"     _X             f.menu XSM
     no_label                             f.separator
     no_label                             f.separator
     "         Colors"     _C             f.menu XTcolors
     "          Fonts"     _F             f.menu XFM
     "       Pointers"     _P             f.menu XTP
```

```
        "          Scroll"      _S      f.menu XSB
        "            Misc"      _M      f.menu XtMisc
        no_label                        f.separator
        no_label                        f.separator
        "           Clone"      _C      !"($XMENU/clone)"
        no_label                        f.separator
        no_label                        f.separator
}
```

If you have read closely, you have likely noticed some peculiarities in the Xmenu root menus. Figure 6-1 shows what the menus look like to the user. The fact that menu items are aligned flush right, instead of flush left, requires the additional spacing before items in the code.

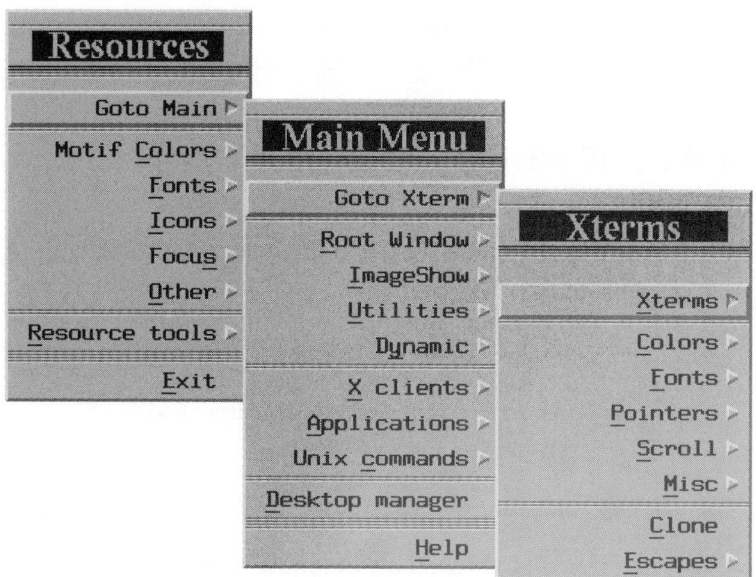

Figure 6-1 The Xmenu root menus.

The use of the **no_label** statement and the **f.separator** function creates lines between menu items. It is standard to use only one line between items, but multiple lines can create a more dramatic 3-D effect when the background color is a light shade.

Another trick—used again to heighten the 3-D effect—is to use spacing after separator lines. To create spacing, you can enclose one or more spaces in quotes and pair them with the **f.nop** function, which is the Motif function for performing no operation (like **:** in the Bourne shell). Beginning a menu with a space and **f.nop** function adds a comfortable amount of space to the top of the menu—compensating for Motif's otherwise flush-top approach.

Each of the three root menus in the Xmenu examples also loads a bitmap as a header to the menu. Bitmaps are loaded as menu items when you begin the menu line with a @ symbol. The @ symbol must be immediately followed by a valid file specification, such as **/usr/xmenu/resmenu**, **~/**, or the directory named by the **bitmapDirectory** resource.

You *cannot* use an environment variable instead of a pathname to specify the path to bitmap files (although you can use environment variables in other parts of the **.mwmrc** file).

One other design difference in the Xmenu root menus is the way the three menus can be called up in cascading fashion. The first two menus each have a function that calls up the menu to the right of it: ResourcesMenu calls MainMenu, and MainMenu calls XtermsMenu. This has appeal to users who continually—out of habit—press a single button. Beyond that, it shows how you can call one menu—already defined for use elsewhere—from any other menu. There is very little additional overhead.

MOTIF FUNCTIONS

Built-in functions for Motif are numerous, ranging from functions for manipulating windows to the **f.exec** function, which lets you execute commands from the **.mwmrc** file. You can associate a function with a menu item, or with a button or key press. The function syntax is straightforward:

```
menu item  function  [arguments]
```

or

```
key sequence  [context]  function  [arguments]
```

If you bind functions to mouse button and key sequences—a powerful method for providing interface shortcuts—you can make use of the optional *context* field. The context field simply tells Motif where the key binding has effect. The choices are **root**, **window**, and **icon**. For mouse buttons, you can also specify frame, title, border, and app. Here's the standard syntax:

```
context = object[|context]
object =  root|icon|window|title|frame|border|app
```

There are many helpful shortcuts you can implement using the key and button bindings. For example, because the standard behavior of Motif is to raise a window when you click the left mouse button on it, it makes sense that the right mouse button might lower the window. This is not standard behavior, but once you start using it, you'll likely never use Motif again without it. Here's the **.mwmrc** statement to establish this behavior:

```
<Btn3Down>   frame|icon  f.lower
```

As you can see, the context of this statement is constrained to the frame and icon areas of the window. This is the standard behavior for the raise option: When you click on the window frame or icon with the left mouse button, the window or icon comes to the top of the stack. Here's a look at some other standard behavior or Motif:

```
Buttons DefaultButtonBindings
{
  <Btn1Down>          icon|frame        f.raise
  <Btn3Down>          icon|frame        f.post_wmenu
  <Btn1Down>          root              f.menu RootMenu
  <Btn3Down>          root              f.menu RootMenu
  <Btn1Click2>        title             f.minimize
  Shift <Btn1Click2> icon              f.minimize
  Shift <Btn1Click>  icon|frame        f.lower
  Ctrl <Btn1Click>   root|icon|frame f.next_key
  Ctrl Shift <Btn1Click> root|icon|frame f.prev_key
  Meta <Btn1Click> root|icon|frame f.next_key transient

  !Following line escaped; does not work in all Motifs
  Meta Shift <Bt1Click> \
             root|icon|frame f.prev_key transient
}
```

These bindings are the same whether the window focus policy has been set to **explicit** or **pointer**. The default value of **f.lower** differs from the previous suggestion of binding **f.lower** to the Btn3Down. The standard behavior does not bind any other action to Btn3Down, however, and you can add it and still preserve Shift <Btn1Click> for users who might habitually use the binding.

As for whether a window rises to the top of the stack, the **f.raise** function is set to <Btn1Down>, but like the previous examples, is activated only when the user clicks on the icon or frame. Whether the window raises to the top of the stack when you click elsewhere in it depends on the value of the **focusAutoRaise** resource. The default value of **focusAutoRaise** is true when the focus policy is **explicit**; it is false when set to **pointer**.

Key bindings are also context specific, but as noted, they work only in the **root**, **icon**, and **window** contexts. As with button bindings, it is a good idea to be aware of the default Motif behavior. Here are the default bindings:

```
Keys DefaultKeyBindings
{
  Shift<Key>Escape    window|icon       f.post_wmenu
  Meta<Key>space      window|icon       f.post_wmenu
  <Key>F4             icon              f.post_wmenu
  Meta<Key>Tab        root|icon|window f.next_key
  Meta Shift<Key>Tab root|icon|window f.prev_key
  Meta<Key>Escape     root|icon|window f.next_key
  Meta<Key>F6         window    f.next_key transient
  Meta Shift<Key>F6   window    f.prev_key transient
  Shift<Key>F4   root|icon|window         f.menu RootMenu
  Meta Shift<Key>Escape   root|icon|window   f.prev_key
  Meta Ctrl<Key>exclam   root|icon|window   f.set_behavior

  !Following line escaped; does not work in all Motifs
  Meta Shift Ctrl<Key>exclaim \
                root|icon|window f.set_behavior
}
```

The default key bindings do three things: give you a way to return to the default Motif behavior, via the **f.set_behavior** function; post the window and root window menus; and provide a way to traverse the stacking order of windows. The latter is accomplished with the **f.prev_key** and **f.next_key** functions. When you specify the **transient** option to these functions, the traversal includes secondary windows within an application. Otherwise, the default behavior skips secondary windows. None of these functions operates, however, if the **keyboardFocus** policy is set to **pointer**.

Menu options exist in the context in which they are invoked. If you invoke an option from a root window menu, the option applies at the global level. If you invoke an option from a window menu, the option applies only to that window, unless it is a global level function that has been placed in the menu for convenience. Although this means you cannot use context keywords in menu items, it doesn't stop you from creating contexts for menus. The way to do so is to attach a menu to a button or key binding, using the **f.post_menu** or **f.menu** functions. This feature has many applications:

- Keyboard interfaces to the window manager
- Keyboard interfaces for specialized menus
- Custom keyboard interfaces for applications
- Command execution via key sequence
- Text macros for applications

- Context-sensitive mouse menus
- Context-sensitive mouse menus for named windows

Of these applications, providing a complete keyboard interface is often important. If you provide major functionality via mouse buttons, you should also think about providing it through function keys or key combinations. As with other functionality that can be controlled by application-specific resources, the window manager functionality can be overridden. Planning a consistent interface between the window manager, Xterms, and other applications is a task the desktop customizer should not ignore.

Sizing Functions

The sizing functions in Motif are basic (see Table 6-1). Four of the functions—**f.maximize**, **f.minimize**, **f.normalize**, and **f.resize**—appear in the default window menu. The fifth, **f.normalize_and_raise**, is used on a custom basis. It is a convenience function in the truest sense of the word and it is easy to appreciate, even at the cost of adding too much functionality. If you are worried about adding too much functionality, you might want to limit using **f.normalize_and_raise** to a shifted key sequence or to a single function key not commonly used.

Table 6-1 Sizing Functions

Function	Description
f.minimize	Window displays in icon form. Double-clicking on the icon, or selecting the *Restore* option from the icon's menu, redisplays the associated window.
f.maximize	Window displays at maximum size, which is full screen by default, but can be changed using the **maximumMaximumSize** resource.
f.normalize	Window displays in its normal state. Any secondary windows are also normalized. The associated window menu item is called *Restore.*
f.normalize_and_raise	Window displays in its normal state and rises to the top of the stack. Any secondary windows follow suit. The **raiseKeyFocus** resource must be **true** for this behavior.
f.resize	Window is interactively resized. When used, this function works with either cursor keys or the mouse.

Movement Functions

The movement functions provide an interesting excursion into overlapping functionality (see Table 6-2). If you use the **f.raise** and **f.lower** functions, the **f.circle_down** and **f.circle_up** functions become largely unnecessary when used in the window menu. If used in a root window menu, however, they provide a decent assist when you have to traverse numerous windows.

The idea behind **f.circle_down** and **f.circle_up** is to lower and raise windows in the window stack: The window at the top of the stack is lowered to the bottom of the stack when you use **f.circle_down**; and the window at the bottom of the stack is raised to the top when you use **f.circle_up**. With both functions, windows that are not obscured by other windows are not included in the window manager's shuffling through the stack. Secondary windows always move with their primary window.

The **f.raise_lower** function also has overlapping functionality. Unlike the shuffling functions, it only works in the window menu context. If you include it in a root window menu, it appears grayed out. The idea behind **f.raise_lower** is it moves an obscured window to the top of the stack, and unobscured windows to the bottom of the stack.

The last function in this category is **f.move**, which, like **f.resize** from the sizing functions, is designed for use with cursor keys.

Table 6-2 Movement Functions

Function	Description
f.circle_down	Window on top of the stack goes to the bottom. Unobscured windows are not affected.
f.circle_up	Window on the bottom of the stack goes to the top. Unobscured windows are not affected.
f.lower	Window with the context goes to the bottom of the stack.
f.move	Window is interactively moved. When used, this function works with either cursor keys or the mouse.
f.raise	Window with the context goes to the top of the stack.
f.raise_lower	Window with the context goes to the top of the stack if it is obscured; otherwise, it goes to the bottom of the stack.

Focus Functions

The focus functions—**f.focus_key**, **f.next_key,** and **f.prev_key**—work only when **keyboardFocus** is set to **explicit** (see Table 6-3). They are primarily designed for use in a keyboard interface to Motif. Using them in a menu and mouse interface is only useful from the root menu, although **f.focus_key** only works in window menus.

In general, the focus functions are provided so that you can have a keyboard interface to Motif. The **f.next_key** and **f.prev_key** functions shuffle

Table 6-3 Focus Functions

Function	Description
f.focus_key	Sets focus to the window or icon with current context.
f.next_key	Sets keyboard focus to the next primary window, icon, or secondary window in the window manager's window list.
f.prev_key	Sets keyboard focus to the previous primary window, icon, or secondary window in the window manager's window list.

through the stack of windows in the same way as some of the movement functions. Both **f.next_key** and **f.prev_key** also accept any of three arguments: icon, window, and transient. Of the three arguments, only **transient** adds functionality, in that it tells Motif to consider all icons and windows, including transient, or secondary, windows.

As for the icon argument, it limits the range of the **f.next_key** and **f.prev_key** to icons only. And the **window** argument limits the range to primary windows only. For examples of these functions, see the description of key bindings earlier in this chapter.

Colormap Functions

The colormap game in the X Window System can be confusing at times, and that's why you will find special colormap utilities from system software vendors, but the Motif colormap functions are there to lend assistance.

Of the three colormap functions—**f.focus_color**, **f.next_cmap**, and **f.prev_cmap**—the **f.focus_color** function is the most useful, especially if you display images on the root window (see Table 6-4).

To use **f.focus_color**, you must have **colomapFocusPolicy** set to **explicit**. Doing this enables Motif to automatically manage colormaps between windows. If for some reason Motif's automatic management does not work (for instance, you have installed a 192-color image on the root window), you can use **f.focus_color** to force a colormap change.

Forcing a colormap change lets you see the color image in the specified window, but if not enough colors are available, the screen blurs into a mesh of pixels (also known as *technicolor*). All in all, this is not a desirable situation, but until more advanced colors systems become the standard, you'll have to live with the 256-color shuffle.

Table 6-4 Colormap Functions

Function	Description
f.focus_color	Set colormap focus to window with the context.
f.next_cmap	Sets colormap to next available colormap for window with the context.
f.prev_cmap	Sets colormap to previously available colormap for window with the context.

Management Functions

Motif supports several functions that perform various operations, such as **f.quit_mwm**, which exits the window manager, and **f.refresh**, which refreshes the entire screen (see Table 6-5).

In general, the management functions are for convenience, and in some cases, they overlap with utilities available in UNIX and X. For example, you can use the **kill** command to exit the window manager and the **xrefresh** utility to refresh the screen. (This overlapping functionality is only pointed out, however, in case you find a Motif function inappropriate.)

Table 6-5 Management Functions

Function	Description
f.kill	Terminates a primary window.
f.pack_icons	Aligns icons in icon box.
f.quit_mwm	Exits the current Motif session, but not X.
f.refresh	Refreshes the entire screen.
f.refresh_win	Refreshes the window with the context.
f.restart	Restarts the window manager.
f.send_msg	Sends message to window with the context. The message is of type _MOTIF_WM_MESSAGES.
f.set_behavior	Resets Motif so it uses the default behavior, ignoring the contents of $HOME/**.mwmrc**. Invoked a second time, Motif restarts using the contents of $HOME/**.mwmrc**.

Menu and Bindings Functions

There are two menu functions: **f.menu**, which lets you specify any menu named in $HOME/**.mwmrc**; and **f.post_wmenu**, which lets you post the window menu as the result of an event such as a key sequence or button press. You can also use the **windowMenu** resource with **f.post_wmenu** to post a custom menu for a named window.

As for key bindings, the **f.pass_keys** lets you enable or disable the currently specified bindings. This is an effective function to include in an application window menu, especially if Motif key bindings conflict with the application's own key sequences (see Table 6-6).

Table 6-6 Menu and Binding Functions

Function	Description
f.menu	Binds a menu to a given event. Works in any context, but executes on a global basis.
f.pass_keys	Enables or disables the window manager's key bindings in a window context.
f.post_wmenu	Posts the window menu, which is the menu that appears when you click in the upper left-hand corner of a window.

The Execute Function

One of the most important functions supported by Motif is the **f.exec** function, which lets you run scripts and programs from menus. You can abbreviate **f.exec** to **!**, but in both cases, you must enclose the command to be executed in quotation marks and parentheses.

Multiple commands cannot be executed using **f.exec** or **!**, unless they are contained in a valid UNIX pipeline. To sidestep this limitation use scripts. You should always execute any command in the background using the **&** operator. If you don't, the window manager waits until the command completes. Here is an example:

```
!"(xtermloader default)&"
```

When a command executes, it uses the shell and environment information associated with the shell specified by the $MWMSHELL environment variable.If this variable is not set, Motif uses the $SHELL environment variable, if it is set. If no shell variables are set, Motif uses **/bin/sh**. Importantly, the environment information may differ from that associated with your log-in shell. One way to ensure consistency is to use environment variables or full pathnames for executable programs. Otherwise, be sure that $SHELL or $MWMSHELL are set correctly.

Internal Functions

Motif supports some internal functions for controlling menu appearances and behavior (see Table 6-7). The **f.title** and **f.separator** give you control over menu appearance and the **f.nop** and **f.beep** functions provide support.

Table 6-7 Internal Functions

Function	Description
f.beep	Causes a beep.
f.nop	Nothing is done. Text is grayed out. Use with a whitespace in quotes to add blank space to the menu.
f.title	Adds a title to the menu. Use with the @ symbol to load a bitmap as the title.
f.separator	Adds separator bars to the menu.

The **f.title** function is perhaps the most noteworthy of internal functions. With it, you can insert one or more titles in a menu, using either standard text or a bitmap. The bitmap approach can produce quality results and adds a certain presence to your menus. The downside to using bitmaps is it slows the reloading of the **.mwmrc** file. Here is the **f.title** statement used in the ResourcesMenu example earlier in this chapter:

```
@/usr/xmenu/bitmaps/resmenu f.title
```

On most Motif systems, you must use a hardcoded directory path when you want to load a bitmap. An environment variable would be preferable, but it does not work. Often, you can enhance the appearance of a title by adding space with the **f.separator** and **f.nop** functions:

```
" "                                f.nop
no_label                           f.separator
@/usr/xmenu/bitmaps/resmenu        f.title
no_label                           f.separator
no_label                           f.separator
" "                                f.nop
```

The first line in the example adds whitespace. The second line adds a separator bar above the bitmap. The next line adds the bitmap, which, as shown in Figure 6-2, is the word "Resources." The fourth and fifth lines add two more separators for effect. And the last line adds more whitespace.

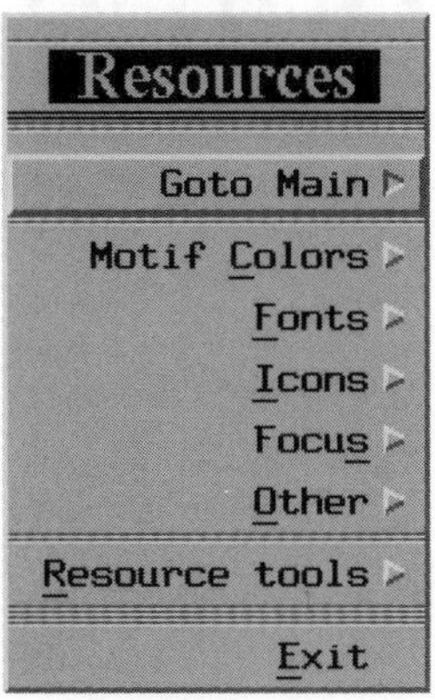

Figure 6-2 The Resources Menu.

In situations in which performance is not an issue, the **f.nop** function can be used to gray-out menu items, indicating they are not available to the user. To do this, your menu system should be lean and mean so that restarting Motif borders on the imperceptible. With some simple **sed** commands, it is an easy enough feature to code. To do it properly, you need a shadow **.mwmrc** file, so that you can always reinsert the correct values for a given menu item.

CHAPTER 7
Resourceful Menus

EASY RESOURCES

Although Motif has an extensive set of resources, it requires users to learn how to modify their environment the hard way. Some vendors, especially HP and DEC, have added utilities to their system software to help out with resource control. But even in these instances, the level of control is usually limited to the appearance of windows and the root window background.

A more complete interface to the Motif resources would cover behavior and functionality issues as well as appearance characteristics (see Chapter 5). For example, there should be an easy way for users to change the focus policy from implicit to explicit, and at the same time, stipulate that windows should not rise to the top of the stack when they get the focus

The Motif menu system lends itself well to creating your own end-user interface to Motif and X resources. The Motif root menus are a logical place to have such an interface, given that they exist at the system software level—and Motif supports numerous functions oriented toward window management. Indeed, in some cases, several Motif functions only work if a given resource is set appropriately.

One drawback to relying on the root window menus is the bigger you make the **.mwmrc** file, the longer it takes to restart Motif. This is especially critical for an interface to the Motif resources, because the only way to get a new Motif resource to take effect is by restarting Motif. A way to limit this exposure is to limit the role that **.Xdefaults** plays in your resource environment. To be sure, the **.Xdefaults** method is handy, because you can use the **xrdb** resource manager to query existing resources. But **xrdb** is not complete in its ability to know what resources are in effect. For example, it doesn't know anything about resources loaded from a file in the $XAPPL-

RESDIR directory. Additionally, you can build shell scripts to query resource files and simulate the work of **xrdb**, or you can use the **xprop** command on a window-by-window basis to obtain the current resources for a window. As a result, the benefits of using **xrdb** don't necessarily outweigh the performance benefits of not using it.

How do you limit the role of **.Xdefaults**? Simply by not putting any resource statements in it that you can put elsewhere, such as in a resource file in $HOME or $XAPPLRESDIR. Instead, you place only Motif resources in **.Xdefaults**. Then you can build scripts to work with your menus. Among other things, the role of the scripts is to append the modified resource to **.Xdefaults** and then execute **xrdb -load .Xdefaults**. By the time the user goes to restart Motif, even on slower workstations, the new Motif resources are loaded into the resource database.

The alternative is to have Motif read its resources from $HOME/**Mwm** or $XAPPLRESDIR/**Mwm**, which slows down the restart process. The reason for this is simple: Resources loaded by **xrdb**, which are formally said to be attached to the resource manager on the root window of screen 0, stay in memory throughout the Motif restart process.

The Xmenu software places all Motif resources that it manipulates in **.Xdefaults**. In your own development of Motif menus, you probably won't want to include as many resources. The motivation for doing so in Xmenu is to expose the reader to the various resources, as well as to make it easy to cut and paste the parts of Xmenu that you may want to implement.

Finally, a word about this chapter and the following two chapters. All three chapters contain descriptions of the three Xmenu root menus. In doing so, they present descriptions of the coding involved as well as rationales for structuring an overall interface to X and Motif resources. The descriptions cover both the portable and Sun versions of Xmenu.

RESOURCES MENU

Motif's **f.title** function lets you specify a title for any menu you create in the **.mwmrc** file. It is a straightforward function and is usually used with a one- or two-word text string. The Xmenu **.mwmrc** file does a little bit more as you can see in this listing for the *Resources Menu*:

```
! Root Window Menu: Button 1 (left)
Menu ResourcesMenu
{
  " "                             f.nop
  no_label                        f.separator
```

```
  @/xmenu/bitmaps/resmenu        f.title
  no_label                       f.separator
  no_label                       f.separator
  " "                            f.nop
  "      Goto Main"              f.menu MainMenu
  no_label                       f.separator
  no_label                       f.separator
  "   Motif Colors"       _C     f.menu MwmColors
  "           Fonts"      _F     f.menu MwmFonts
  "           Icons"      _I     f.menu MwmIcons
  "           Focus"      _s     f.menu MwmFocus
  "           Other"      _O     f.menu MwmResources
  no_label                       f.separator
  no_label                       f.separator
  " Resource tools"       _R     f.menu ResourceTools
  no_label                       f.separator
  no_label                       f.separator
  no_label                       f.separator
  no_label                       f.separator
  "            Exit"      _E     !"killx"
}
```

Besides the bitmap title and other appearance tricks (already described in Chapter 4), *Resources Menu* calls six submenus, and the **killx** script via the *Exit* menu option. The submenus will be dealt with in the sections following this one. As for the **killx** script, here is the listing:

```
#!/bin/sh
# killx: kills the X server

# Get process id for the X server
  pid_x='ps -e | awk '/Xws/ && ! /awk/ {print $1}'
# Kill the X server
  kill -KILL $pid_x
```

If your X server is simply called **X**, you can obtain the process id with a single **grep** statement. All you do is specify **X** followed by a whitespace:

```
#!/bin/sh
# killx: kills the X server

# Get process id for the X server
  pid_x='ps -e | grep "X "
# Kill the X server
  kill -KILL $pid_x
```

Unlike Motif, which can display a feedback window when it receives a kill signal, the X server blindly accepts its fate. To confirm whether the user really wants to kill the X server—and this is in keeping with the Motif feedback windows—the **killx** could prompt the user using an Xterm window. This technique is described later in this chapter.

Notice that all the menu options in the *Resources Menu* have mnemonic keys, but they do not have accelerators. The mnemonic keys are sufficient to provide a complete keyboard interface. However, because the Xmenu menus are extensive, the addition of keyboard accelerators would be an overwhelming proposition for the end user. By default, the Xmenu **.mwmrc** file binds the *Resources Menu* to Ctrl-F8, which enables the keyboard user to initially access the menus:

```
Ctrl<Key>F8   root|icon|window   f.menu ResourcesMenu
```

Mouse users might also be interested in this key sequence. For times when its hard to find a sufficient piece of the root window, the Ctrl-F8 sequence lets you pop up the Resources menu over any window. You then have the option of continuing through the menus with mnemonic keypresses or with the mouse.

Alternatively, you can usually find at least a sliver of the root window and invoke the root window menus with the mouse. You might or might not like what happens next: when the pointer rests along the right edge of the screen, the root window menus, instead of cascading off the screen, overlap one another as you go deeper into submenus. (Incidentally, Next Computer Inc., with the NextStep windowing system, disapproved so much of overlapping that it designed its menus to move toward screen-center when popped up along the right edge of the screen.)

Goto Main

The first item on the Resources menu is **Goto Main**. It illustrates the ability to call any menu from any other menu in the **.mwmrc** file. The option is designed for users who habitually use the same mouse button. The result of the option is to display the Main Menu, which is bound to button two in the Xmenu **.mwmrc** file.

One important note about the X bitmaps used in the Xmenu root menus: they are sized to be used with the 12-point fixed font. Using them with larger fonts causes the bitmap to be centered. This is not a bad effect, but if you want flush right and left as in the 12-point fixed font, you must edit the bitmap files. The easiest way to do this is in **bitmap** or another visual editor, although you could edit the ASCII version of the file (using the **bmtoa** and **atobm** utilities).

Motif Colors

There are any number of ways to give users the option to change colors from the **.mwmrc** menus. The simplest way is to use English-language text and offer a selection—perhaps, up to a dozen—of colors from which the user can choose.

A second method is to incorporate bitmaps into the **.mwmrc** file so that you can represent the colors visually. This only works on versions of Motif that support pixmap formats. It is an effective approach, but with cons as well as pros. It is a great technique to enhance the appearance of your Motif menus, but if you want to use it in many different places in your **.mwmrc** file, the overhead of loading bitmaps gets weighty.

The **.mwmrc** file has no way to define an object once and then make subsequent references to the internal definition. Instead, each time you want to display a bitmap for the color red, you have to load the corresponding bitmap. By making the bitmaps small—say, 16 by 16 pixels—you reduce the overhead somewhat.

Another method of setting colors in Motif is to call an independent application. There are any number of public domain utilities that suit the purpose here. The only requirement for such a program is that it return a color value, in text string format, to the shell.

The *Motif Colors* menu comes in two flavors: one that is portable across most Motif platforms; and one specifically written for Motif for Sun. In the portable version, color-setting routines are called directly from the menu; in the Sun version, submenus are called.

Portable Version

The portable version of the *Motif Colors* menu uses a public domain color editor called **xcoloredit**. Written by Richard Hesketh, at the University of Kent at Canterbury in England, **xcoloredit** is widely available from Internet archive sites. Moreover, it serves well for the Motif Colors menu because it returns a color value in string format to the shell. Figure 7-1 shows the *Motif Colors* menu.

Five types of colors are addressed in the *Motif Colors* menu. The window colors are the first menu item because it is most often the first menu item that users want to adjust. The number of options for each type—*Window*, *Active Window*, *Menu*, *Icon*, and *Other*—coincides with the number of resources that can be modified. For example, it is possible to modify four resources when dealing with window background color. But because you cannot specify a matte color for active windows, the *Active Window* choices are limited to three items. Here's the code for the portable version of the *Motif Colors* menu:

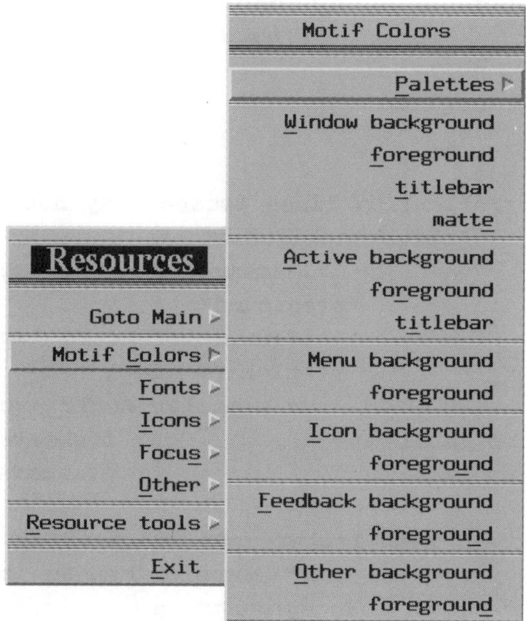

Figure 7-1 Motif Colors menu, portable version.

```
Menu MotifColors
{
  no_label                        f.separator
  no_label                        f.separator
  no_label                        f.separator
  no_label                        f.separator
  "Motif Colors"                  f.title
  no_label                        f.separator
  no_label                        f.separator
  " "                             f.nop
  "          Palettes"   _P       f.menu MwmPalettes
  no_label                        f.separator
  no_label                        f.separator

  !Followling lines escape; may not work in all Motifs
  "  Window background" _W \
               !"(mwmcolor WinBg 'xcoloredit')&"
    "        foreground" _f \
               !"(mwmcolor WinFg 'xcoloredit')&"
```

```
  "         titlebar" _t \
             !"(mwmcolor WinTb 'xcoloredit')&"
  "            matte" _e \
             !"(mwmcolor WinMt 'xcoloredit')&"
  no_label                    f.separator
  no_label                    f.separator


!Followling lines escape; may not work in all Motifs
"  Active background" _A  \
             !"(mwmcolor ActBg 'xcoloredit')&"
"         foreground" _r  \
             !"(mwmcolor ActFg 'xcoloredit')&"
"           titlebar" _i  \
             !"(mwmcolor ActTb 'xcoloredit')&"
no_label                    f.separator
no_label                    f.separator

"    Menu background" _M  \
             !"(mwmcolor MenuBg 'xcoloredit')&"
"         foreground" _g  \
             !"(mwmcolor MenuFg 'xcoloredit')&"
no_label                    f.separator
no_label                    f.separator

"   Icon background"  _I  \
             !"(mwmcolor IconBg 'xcoloredit')&"
"        foreground"  _u  \
             !"(mwmcolor IconFg 'xcoloredit')&"
no_label                    f.separator
no_label                    f.separator

"Feedback background"  _F \
             !"(mwmcolor FeedBg 'xcoloredit')&"
"         foreground"  _n \
             !"(mwmcolor FeedFg 'xcoloredit')&"
no_label                     f.separator
no_label                     f.separator

"  Other background"  _O  \
             !"(mwmcolor OtherBg 'xcoloredit')&"
"        foreground"  _d  \
             !"(mwmcolor OtherFg 'xcoloredit')&"
}
```

As in previous examples, you'll note the liberal use of the **f.separator** function. Beginning the menu with four calls to **f.separator** not only adds to the 3-D quality, but also is intended to denote that the *Motif Colors* menu is a submenu of some significance. Other important submenus in the Xmenu **.mwmrc** file resemble this menu, providing consistency for the end-user.

The first menu option, *Palettes*, offers the user a way to change all color resources at one time. The available palettes attempt to be unique, but it is easy to customize this option and add many more palettes yourself. The controlling script is **mwmpalette**, which takes one argument, the name of the palette to use.

The rest of the options on the *Motif Resources* menu call the **mwmcolor** script. There are two arguments to the script. The first denotes the given option, which, in the Sun version of the menu, also happens to be the submenu name. (The reason for this is you can change the color of some submenus in the Sun version.) The second argument to **mwmcolor** is the string returned by **xcoloredit**. Thanks to UNIX command substitution, the call to **xcoloredit** can be made directly from the **.mwmrc** file.

The one not-too-obvious selection on the *Motif Colors* menu is the *Other* item. You may or may not want to include this item in your own **.mwmrc** file. The reason is it defines the background and foreground window colors at the class level. This means that if you make no selections from the *Window* section of the menu—or from the menu and icon sections for that matter—the class definitions would be in effect for all window components. This includes feedback windows, if you chose not to set the feedback windows from the *Motif Colors* menu (and if no preexisting resource was in place for feedback windows).

The problem with setting the background and foreground colors at the class level is they are used in calculating the 3-D shadowing for windows and icons. The way to address this characteristic is to select colors that complement the 3-D effect. When you do this, however, you might not like the results on undefined components. So the answer is to get rid of the *Other* option altogether; create another option that deletes the **Mwm*Background** and **Mwm*Foreground** resources altogether; or include a menu that controls the 3-D shadowing. The Xmenu **.mwmrc** file uses the last approach.

Sun Version

Because some versions of Motif for Sun let you use color pixmaps (XPM2) in the **.mwmrc** file, you can take a different tack to provide a color selection mechanism. Namely, you can use bitmaps that represent colors. In addition, because you need to create another set of submenus to display the bitmaps, you can use the new submenus to display previously set colors. This is accomplished by changing the background color for the associated submenu.

This approach to the **.mwmrc** file is costly. On a SPARCstation 10 class and higher performing systems, you won't notice the additional time it takes to load the **.mwmrc** file. On older Sun systems, you'll notice the time delay. Depending on the systems you are customizing for, you'll want to be conservative in adding many pixmaps to menus. As for customizing the background color of menus—and the foreground color, too, for that matter—the overhead is minimal.

The Motif for Sun version of the *Motif Colors* menu is slightly different from the portable version. The main difference between the two versions is that submenus are called instead of **xcoloredit**:

```
Menu MotifColors
{
  no_label                                f.separator
  no_label                                f.separator
  no_label                                f.separator
  no_label                                f.separator
  "Motif Colors"                          f.title
  no_label                                f.separator
  no_label                                f.separator
  " "                                     f.nop
  "             Palettes"   _P   f.menu MwmPalettes
  no_label                                f.separator
  no_label                                f.separator
  " Window background"      _W   f.menu WindowBg
  "        foreground"      _f   f.menu WindowFg
  "          titlebar"      _t   f.menu WindowTb
  "             matte"      _e   f.menu WindowMt
  no_label                                f.separator
  no_label                                f.separator
  " Active background"      _A   f.menu ActiveBg
  "        foreground"      _r   f.menu ActiveFg
  "          titlebar"      _i   f.menu ActiveTb
  no_label                                f.separator
  no_label                                f.separator
  "   Menu background"      _M   f.menu MatteBg
  "        foreground"      _g   f.menu MatteFg
  no_label                                f.separator
  no_label                                f.separator
  "   Icon background"      _I   f.menu IconBg
  "        foreground"      _u   f.menu IconFg
  no_label                                f.separator
  no_label                                f.separator
```

```
  "  Feedback background"   _F  f.menu OtherBg
  "           foreground"   _u  f.menu OtherFg
  no_label                      f.separator
  no_label                      f.separator
  "  Other background"      _O  f.menu OtherBg
  "        foreground"      _d  f.menu OtherFg
  no_label                      f.separator
}
```

If you compare the Motif for Sun and portable versions, you'll notice that the submenus have familiar names: each submenu name is identical to the first argument to **mwmcolor** for the given menu item. The reason for this is to allow the same version of **mwmcolor** to work for both versions. The following submenu is typical of the submenus on the *Motif Colors* menu:

```
Menu WindowBg
{
  @/xmenu/skyblue    !"(mwmcolor WindowBg '#87CEFA')&"
  @/xmenu/cyan       !"(mwmcolor WindowBg '#00FFFF')&"
  @/xmenu/yellow1    !"(mwmcolor WindowBg '#FFFF00')&"
  @/xmenu/grnyellow !"(mwmcolor WindowBg '#ADFF2F')&"
  @/xmenu/violet     !"(mwmcolor WindowBg '#DB7093')&"
  @/xmenu/red        !"(mwmcolor WindowBg '#EE0000')&"
  @/xmenu/peachp     !"(mwmcolor WindowBg '#FFDAB9')&"
  @/xmenu/midblue    !"(mwmcolor WindowBg '#191970')&"
  @/xmenu/lgray      !"(mwmcolor WindowBg '#C0C0C0')&"
  @/xmenu/white      !"(mwmcolor WindowBg '#FFFFFF')&"
  @/xmenu/blue       !"(mwmcolor WindowBg '#4169FF')&"
}
```

The WindowBg menu uses the pathname because the **.mwmrc** file does not accept environment variables. Alternatively, you can locate the bitmaps in a directory pointed to by the **bitmapDirectory** resource.

TheWindowBg menu uses hexadecimal values to specify colors to be consistent with other examples in the book. You could use English-language names, however, because you don't have to worry about portability—the major advantage to using hexadecimal numbers.

The actual bitmaps are relatively small (16 by 16 pixels). Figure 7-2 shows the bitmap for skyblue.

There are several different ways that you could create this bitmap. If you do not have access to a bitmap or icon editor that creates XPM2 files, you could use utilities contained in the Extended Portable Bitmap Toolkit to convert from X bitmap format to XPM2 format. The **pbmplus** utilities, as the toolkit is also known, are mostly the work of Jef Poskanzer and are available from public domain archive sites.

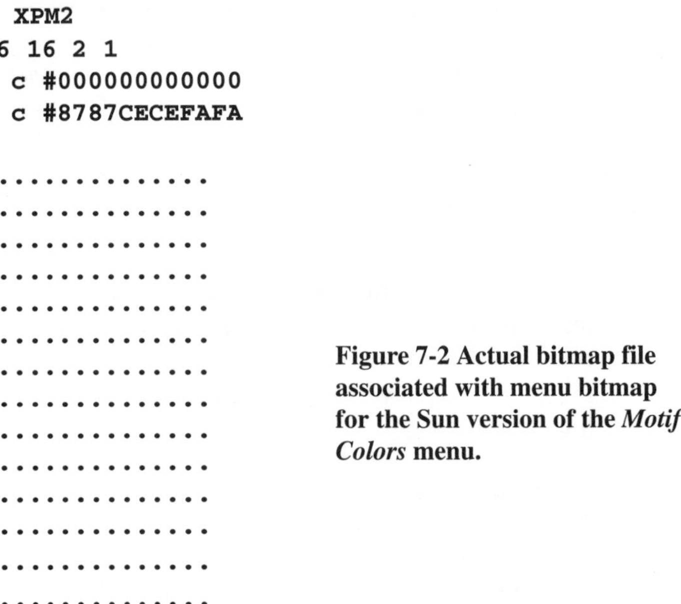

```
! XPM2
16 16 2 1
  c #000000000000
. c #8787CECEFAFA

 ..............
 ..............
 ..............
 ..............
 ..............
 ..............
 ..............
 ..............
 ..............
 ..............
 ..............
 ..............
 ..............
 ..............
```

Figure 7-2 Actual bitmap file associated with menu bitmap for the Sun version of the *Motif Colors* menu.

The only trick to converting from X bitmap format is that you must edit the converted file by hand in order to specify color information. This is not difficult. In the example bitmap file, note the third and fourth lines:

```
  c #000000000000
. c #8787CECEFAFA
```

Both lines specify color information. The first line says that all white-space characters in the file represent the color black. The second line says that all periods in the file represent the color skyblue. To change the colors, just edit the color values on these lines. With the **dec2hex** hexadecimal conversion program from Chapter 4, and a text editor, you can use this example file to make many more bitmaps, supplying your own colors. Also, note that the hexadecimal strings in XPM2 files are in the longer format.

When you establish the hexadecimal value you want, double it by repeating each two-digit sequence before proceeding to the next two digits:

```
#87CEFA = #8787CECEFAFA
```

Alternatively, because you are creating these for a Sun system, you probably have access to the **iconedit** program from Sun. You can use this to create XPM2 files, but the program has a limited color selection. You will likely to have to edit the resulting XPM2 files to specify the exact colors that you want.

The mwmpalette Script

For days when you're not in the mood to create your own color schemes, the **mwmpalette** script gives you a way to quickly change most Motif-managed colors. Xmenu comes with seven different color schemes, including one that wreaks color madness on various menus. For performance reasons, you'll likely avoid this option—but after using it once, you'll never forget that you can customize menu colors as much as you want. The rest of the palettes—*Gone Camping*, *Big blue*, *Radioactive*, *Alien mind*, *English lesson*, and *Civil War*—provide reasonable colors.

The **mwmpalette** script resembles other Xmenu scripts that modify resources, with one exception: It uses the C preprocessor's **#include** directive.

The C preprocessor, which **xrdb** calls automatically when loading resources, reads through an ASCII file and edits it according to the preprocessor directives. When used with **xrdb**, the number of directives is limited, but it does offer **#ifdef** as well as **#include**. Here is the **mwmpalette** script:

```
#!/bin/sh
# mwmpalette, sets canned appearance resources
# Syntax: mwmpalette colorfile
# Copyright (c) Alan Southerton

# Definitions
  file=/tmp/xmenu.$$
  palette=palettes/$1

# Remove temporary file on exit
  trap "rm $file; exit 0 1 2 3 15"

# Form xrdb input with include statements, using
# xrdb's ability to override previous resources.
  echo \#include \"$HOME/.Xdefaults\" > $file
  echo \#include \"$palette\" >> $file
  xrdb -load $file

# Load new resources; replace .Xdefaults if specified
  overwrite='grep SAVETOXDEFAULTS \
              $HOME/.xmenu | cut -d: -f2'
  if [ "$overwrite" = "yes" ] ; then
     cp $HOME/.Xdefaults $HOME/.Xdefaults.bak
     xrdb -query > $HOME/.Xdefaults
fi
```

By using the **#include** directive, the **mwmpalette** script can form the input to **xrdb -load** from multiple files. The **.Xdefaults** file, along with the specified color palette file, combine to feed **xrdb** the new set of resources. The script then takes advantage of the fact that **xrdb** overrides any previously set resource. In other words, if **Mwm*menu*DefaultWindowMenu-*background** is loaded from the **.Xdefaults** file, and then loaded from the color palette file, the value in the color palette file takes effect.

The **overwrite** variable—not to be confused with overriding resources—controls whether the script replaces the contents of **.Xdefaults** with the new values **xrdb** has just loaded.

The SAVETOXDEFAULTS variable in the **.xmenu** file controls the evaluation of *overwrite*. The user can change the value of SAVETOXDEFAULTS from the *Resource tools->save* menu. Basically, the $HOME/**.xmenu** file acts as a secondary resource file tailored to the Xmenu menus. The same approach is used with $HOME/**.xmenu** as with other resources files, namely using **grep -v** to obtain the contents of the file, minus the current resource; and then writing the contents to a temporary file, with the new resource.

All $HOME/**.xmenu** resources appear in uppercase letters and there is no space after the separating colon. Before the temporary file overwrites the current $HOME/**.xmenu** file, a backup file is made. There is no provision in the menu system to restore from the backup file, but the customizer, or advanced user, can edit it if necessary.

With command substitution, you can use the combination of **grep** and **cut** to get any value from **.xmenu**. The **-d** option to cut specifies a delimiter, which is always a colon in **.xmenu**. The **-f2** option says to cut the second field, which contains the value. If you prefer, you can use **sed** instead of **grep** and **cut**:

```
newvalue= \
      `sed -n s/SAVETOXDEFAULTS://p $HOME/.xmenu`
```

On most systems, the **grep** and **cut** method increases performance by a hair. You might prefer **sed**, however, if you are familiar with it.

A last word on palettes: They are a powerful tool for giving users color options. Importantly, by offering palettes you can avoid offering color-changing options on a component-by-component basis as the rest of the *Motif Colors* menu does. So, if you want a smaller and faster-loading version of Xmenu, you could eliminate many, or even all, of the other color options.

The mwmcolor Script

The **mwmcolor** script is short and to the point, but it serves both the portable and Sun versions of *Motif Colors* menu. The biggest obstacle the script overcomes is searching for the asterisk character in the output of **xrdb**

-query. This is accomplished by forming the full search string, using backslashes to quote asterisks and periods, and then passing it to **egrep** and **grep** as a variable.

```
#!/bin/sh
# mwmcolor, script to set Motif colors
# Syntax: mwmcolor restype resvalue
# Copyright (c) Alan Southerton

# Initial values
  file=/tmp/xrdb.$$
  menu=$1; value=$2

# Remove temporary file if untimely exit
  trap "rm $file; exit 1 2 3 15"

# Check if user closed out color editor
  if [ "$value" = "" ]; then
   exit 1
  fi

# Set correct resource name
  case "$menu" in
   WindowBg) resource="Mwm\*client\.background";;
   WindowFg) resource="Mwm\*client\.foreground";;
   WindowTb) resource="Mwm\*client\.title\.background";;
   WindowMt) resource="Mwm\*matteBackground";;
   ActiveBg) resource="Mwm\*activeBackground";;
   ActiveFg) resource="Mwm\*activeForeground";;
   ActiveTb) resource=\
              "Mwm\*client\.title\.activeBackground";;
   MenuBg) resource="Mwm\*menu\*background";;
   MenuFg) resource="Mwm\*menu\*foreground";;
   IconBg) resource="Mwm\*icon\*background";;
   IconFg) resource="Mwm\*icon\*foreground";;
   FeedFg) resource="Mwm\*feedback\*foreground";;
   FeedBg) resource="Mwm\*feedback\*background";;
   OtherFg) resource="Mwm\*Foreground";;
   OtherBg) resource="Mwm\*Background";;
  esac

# Check for version and create temporary
# file to update xrdb
  version=`grep XMENUVERSION \
                   $HOME/.xmenu | cut -d: -f2`
```

```
  if [ "$version" = "sun" ] ; then
     xrdb -query | \
     egrep -v "($resource|$menu)" > $file
     echo $resource: $value | sed 's/\\//g' >> $file
     echo Mwm\*menu\*$menu\*background: $value >> $file
else
     xrdb -query | grep -v "$resource" > $file
     echo $resource: $value | sed 's/\\//g' >> $file
fi

# Load new resources; replace .Xdefaults if specified
  xrdb -load $file
  overwrite=`grep SAVETOXDEFAULTS \
                     $HOME/.xmenu | cut -d: -f2`
  if [ "$overwrite" = "yes" ] ; then
     cp $HOME/.Xdefaults $HOME/.Xdefaults.bak
     mv $file $HOME/.Xdefaults
  else
     rm $file
  fi
```

After setting initial values, such as *menu* equal to **$1** and *value* equal to **$2**, the **mwmcolor** script evaluates the incoming string from **xcoloredit**. It is quite possible that the user could invoke **xcoloredit** and close it without setting a color. This results in a null value, so all you need to do is check for same. The preceding **trap** statement takes care of the untimely exit, but note that compared with **mwmpalette** the 0 has been dropped from the list of offending exit codes. The reason for the difference is that, later on in the script, the temporary file is eliminated by **mv** if $overwrite is **yes**. Otherwise, **rm** does the deed.

Next, a **case** routine sets the resource name for the given option. The string value for *resource* is especially prepared for use with **grep** and **egrep**. Because the asterisk and dot are special characters in **egrep** and **grep**, they must be escaped and the entire value for *resource* should be surrounded by double quotation marks. You might find that the statement seems to work without escaping the dot character, but **grep** uses this to match any character—perhaps a long-shot mismatch, but a match nonetheless.

The final block of code in **mwmcolor** starts by checking the version of Xmenu. The code on the distribution media associated with this book does not use this approach, but you might want to if you develop different versions of Xmenu. The code evaluates the version by using **sed** to check XMENUVERSION from $HOME/**.xmenu**. For the Sun version, **egrep** is used in order to extract all lines except those matching the two variables; compared with **grep** and **fgrep**, only **egrep** can check for two strings at once. In the portable version, **grep** is used. In both versions, new values are appended to results of **xrdb -query** and a new **.Xdefaults** is created. Finally, **xrdb -load** is executed on the new **.Xdefaults**.

Motif Fonts

Changing the fonts used by Motif is perhaps one of the most effective ways to enhance the window manager's appearance. It is ironic, in fact, that system software suppliers do not put a better foot forward by customizing the Motif fonts before shipping a system. Figure 7-3 provides an example of what can be done with fonts in the window titlebar; the figure also shows the font submenu on the Resources menu.

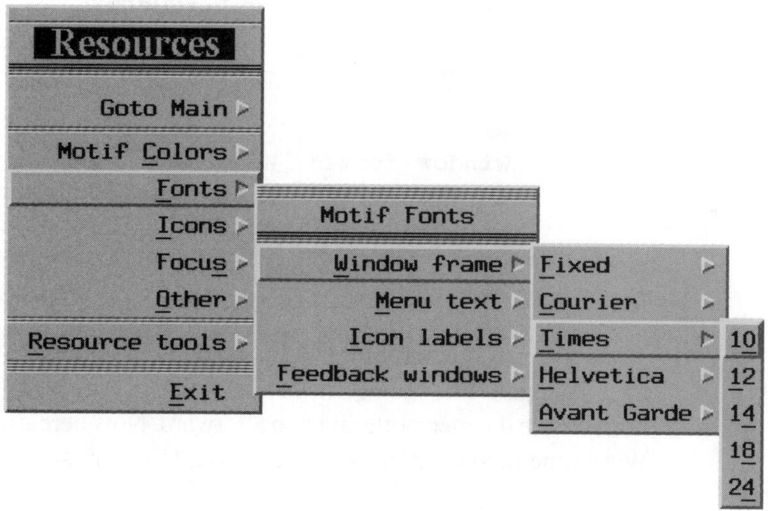

Figure 7-3 ***Fonts*** **submenu showing four levels of options.**

As you can see from Figure 7-3, the Xmenu **.mwmrc** file provides a limited selection of fonts. All have been tested for aesthetic appeal and are available on most X platforms. The menu is also designed to work with X11R4 systems, but if you are working on X11R5 systems exclusively, you can increase the variety of point sizes.

The same font menu (called MotifFonts in the **.mwnrc** file) is used in both Xmenu versions. In addition to changing the fonts for the components shown in Figure 7-3, you can change fonts in menus. The Xmenu menus do not demonstrate this, but you change a font in a menu by specifying the **.mwmrc** menu name in a **fontList** resource statement:

```
Mwm*style*fontList: "*times-bold-r-normal*180*"
```

The example sets a menu called style to use the 18-point Times bold font. This is a proportionally spaced font, as compared with a character cell or monospaced font. And even at 18 points, the results can be pleasing to the eye, especially on a large monitor. In the Xmenu menus, however, a proportionally spaced font would be inappropriate for right-justification of menu items. Nonetheless, you can use the same techniques shown in the following **.mwmrc** menu and scripts to build menus with proportionally spaced fonts. Here's the *Motif Fonts* menu:

```
Menu MotifFonts
{
   no_label                      f.separator
   no_label                      f.separator
   no_label                      f.separator
   no_label                      f.separator
   "Motif Fonts"                 f.title
   no_label                      f.separator
   no_label                      f.separator
   "      Window frame"  _W  f.menu FontsWinFrame
   "         Menu text"  _M  f.menu FontsMenuText
   "       Icon labels"  _I  f.menu FontsIconLabel
   " Feedback windows"   _F  f.menu FontsFeedback
}
```

As you can see, the Motif Fonts menu is simply a switchboard to other menus. Again, like the Motif Colors menu, it uses four **f.separator** functions before the menu title and two afterward. Now here's a look at the FontsWinFrame menu, which is typical of the four-font submenus:

```
Menu FontsWinFrame
{
  "Fixed"          _F   f.menu WinFixed
  "Courier"        _C   f.menu WinCourier
  "Times"          _T   f.menu WinTimes
  "Helvetica"      _H   f.menu WinHelvetica
  "Avant Garde"    _A   f.menu WinAvantG
}
```

That's right—another switchboard menu. The reason is it is more efficient in terms of menu code, not to mention user patience, to narrow down the font choices by cascading through submenus. In all, there are four menus that you traverse, including the top-level *Resources Menu*, before actually making a font selection. Here's the WinTimes menu, which again is typical:

```
Menu WinTimes
{
  "10" _0    !"(mwmfont client times 10-100-75-75-p-57)"
  "12" _1    !"(mwmfont client times 12-120-75-75-p-67)"
  "14" _4    !"(mwmfont client times 14-140-75-75-p-77)"
  "18" _8    !"(mwmfont client times 18-180-75-75-p-99)"
  "24" _4    !"(mwmfont client times 24-240-75-75-p-132)"
}
```

Each menu item in WinTimes calls **mwmfont** (as is the case with all the font menus at this level). Three arguments are specified: resource component, font family, and a font string containing point size and other data.

Why not use wildcards instead of a goodly portion of the font string? The best reason is that when you are working with so many different fonts, specifying fonts is much more readable with a meaningful segment of the font string. To test the hypothesis, create several font strings with wildcards and try to decipher them at a later date. Sure, you might recognize the point size, but in some cases the same font might have different pixel values for the same point size. And then there's always the question of dpi, which, in the WinFonts menu, is 75.*

The mwmfont Script

The **mwmfont** script resembles the **mwmcolor** script presented in the previous section. Instead of assembling the resource statement as in **mwmcolor**, the **mwmfont** script must assemble the font string. As an alternative to assembling the entire string and assigning it to a variable, the **mwmfont** script leaves the concatenation to the **echo** statement that writes the new font resource statement. Here is the script:

```
#!/bin/sh
# mwmfont, sets fonts for window manager
# Syntax: mwmfont resource fonttype spec
# Copyright (c) Alan Southerton

# Initial values
  file=/tmp/.xmenu.$$
  font=$1; resource=$2; spec=$3

# Remove temporary file if untimely exit
  trap "rm $file; exit 1 2 3 15"
```

* Throughout the book, and in the Xmenu code on the companion media, 75 dpi is used. If you intend on running the Xmenu menus on very high resolution monitors, you should use 100 dpi.

```
# Add proper font prefix; goes with $spec
  case "$font" in
        fixed) value=-misc-fixed-bold-r-normal;;
      courier) value=-adobe-courier-bold-r-normal;;
        times) value=-adobe-times-bold-r-normal;;
    helvetica) value=-adobe-helvetica-bold-r-normal;;
       avantg) value=\
        '-adobe-itc avant garde gothic-book-r-normal';;
  esac
# Create temporary file with new resource statements
  xrdb -query | grep -v \
              "Mwm\*$resource\*fontList:" > $file
  echo \
  Mwm\*$resource\*fontList: \"$value\*$spec\*\" >> $file
# Load new resources and replace .Xdefaults if specified
  xrdb -load $file
  overwrite=`grep SAVETOXDEFAULTS \
                      $HOME/.xmenu | cut -d: -f2`
  if [ "$overwrite" = "yes" ] ; then
     cp $HOME/.Xdefaults $HOME/.Xdefaults.bak
     mv $file $HOME/.Xdefaults
  else
     rm $file
  fi
```

There are other ways to handle the font string than that used in **mwmfont**. As noted, you could use wildcards. You could also pass the entire font string from the **.mwmrc** file. This method, however, makes the **.mwmrc** file hard to read, and before Motif 1.2, you could not use the escape character to continue lines. For readability's sake, this is the method Xmenu uses. It lets you easily add fonts to the script—just copy and edit three lines associated with an existing font. The rest of the script resembles the **mwmcolor** script.

As for fonts in general, it is a good idea to examine what fonts you can use on a given system. X has a core set of fonts that are available on most systems—and among them are the ones used in the Xmenu menus—but you'll probably encounter other fonts you want to use.

Motif Icons

The resources associated with icons are numerous. You have already seen that you can set fonts and colors for icons. You can also do things like change the size of the icon; specify where icons should be located on screen; and add the icon box, which is a special Motif window that manages the display of icons.

The *Icons* menu contains eight submenus. The need for so many submenus is an indication of the flexibility of the icon resources. All but one of the submenus terminate with the third-level menu. Figure 7-4 shows the *Parking lot* menu.

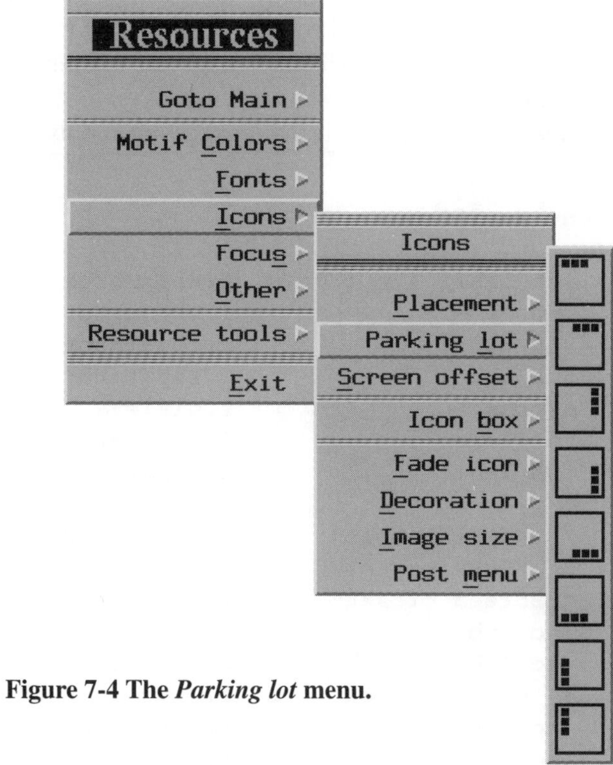

Figure 7-4 The *Parking lot* menu.

All icon resources work independently of one another, so you can use the icon menus without worrying about previous settings. In addition, the resources that apply to freestanding icons also apply to icons in the icon box. The one discrepancy you may encounter is that the icon box does not position itself on-screen as told to by the **iconPlacement** resource. This is supposed to be the default behavior, but a bug in some Motif implementations always places the icon box at the lower left side of the screen. The workaround is to set icon box coordinates via the **iconBoxGeometry** resource.

The main icons menu has a logical ordering of items. The first three items are the most general, because they apply to the organization of icons as well as to the icon box. The fourth item is the icon box, with double-bar separators to make it stand off. The last four items apply directly to the icons and their behavior, whether they are inside the icon box or freestanding.

The net result is that two of the most important icon resources appear at the top of the menu. Why is this important? Imagine that you have to use an associate's machine and **iconAutoPlace** is set to false. Well, if you're used to an icon box, this is a dramatic difference, and you'll appreciate the fact that you can use the *Icons* menu to alleviate the interface anxiety. Of course, when you finish working on the machine, you can use the menu again to restore the Motif resources to the way you found them.

The Motif for Sun and portable versions of Xmenu's **.mwmrc** file are the same for the *Icons* menu hierarchy. The only difference between the two implementations is that the Sun version uses pixmaps instead of bitmaps in the *Parking lot* menu. Here is the *Icons* menu and its submenus:

```
Menu MotifIcons
{
   no_label                 f.separator
   no_label                 f.separator
   no_label                 f.separator
   no_label                 f.separator
  "Icons "                  f.title
   no_label                 f.separator
   no_label                 f.separator
  " "                       f.nop
  "     Placement"     _P   f.menu IconAuto
  "   Parking lot"     _l   f.menu IconPark
  " Screen offset"     _S   f.menu IconSpace
   no_label                 f.separator
   no_label                 f.separator
  "      Icon box"     _b   f.menu IconBox
   no_label                 f.separator
   no_label                 f.separator
  "     Fade icon"     _F   f.menu IconFade
  "    Decoration"     _D   f.menu IconDecor
  "    Image size"     _I   f.menu IconImage
  "     Post menu"     _m   f.menu IconPost
}

Menu IconAuto
{
  " Automatic" _A  !"(mwmicon auto True)&"
  " User-only" _U  !"(mwmicon auto False)&"
}

Menu IconPark
{
  @/xmenu/p1  !"(mwmicon park 'left top')&"
  @/xmenu/p2  !"(mwmicon park 'right top')&"
  @/xmenu/p3  !"(mwmicon park 'top right')&"
```

```
  @/xmenu/p4  !"(mwmicon park 'bottom right')&"
  @/xmenu/p5  !"(mwmicon park 'right bottom')&"
  @/xmenu/p6  !"(mwmicon park 'left bottom')&"
  @/xmenu/p7  !"(mwmicon park 'bottom left')&"
  @/xmenu/p8  !"(mwmicon park 'top left')&"
}

Menu IconSpace
{
  "0"  _0  !"(mwmicon space 0)&"
  "1"  _1  !"(mwmicon space 1)&"
  "2"  _2  !"(mwmicon space 2)&"
  "3"  _3  !"(mwmicon space 3)&"
  "4"  _4  !"(mwmicon space 4)&"
  "5"  _5  !"(mwmicon space 5)&"
}

Menu IconBox
{
  " Open"         _O  !"(mwmicon box true)&"
  " Close"        _C  !"(mwmicon box false)&"
  " Title ..."    _T  !"(mwmicon boxtitle)&"
  " Size ..."     _S  !"(mwmicon setsize)&"
  " Matte ..."    _M  !"(mwmicon matte)&"
  " Scrollbars"   _b  f.menu IconBoxScroll
  " Decorations"  _D  f.menu IconBoxDecor
}

Menu IconBoxScroll
{
  " Both"         _B !"(mwmicon boxscroll all)&"
  " Vertical"     _V !"(mwmicon boxscroll vertical)&"
  " Horizontal"  _H !"(mwmicon boxscroll horizontal)&"
}

Menu IconBoxDecor
{
  " All"        _A !"(mwmicon boxdeco all)&"
  " None"       _N !"(mwmicon boxdeco none)&"
  " Maximize"   _M !"(mwmicon boxdeco maximize)&"
  " Menu"       _e !"(mwmicon boxdeco menu)&"  "
  " Minimize"   _z !"(mwmicon boxdeco minimize)&"
  " Resize"     _R !"(mwmicon boxdeco resizeh)&"
  " Titlebar"   _T !"(mwmicon boxdeco title)&"
}
```

```
Menu IconFade
{
  " Yes " _Y  !"(mwmicon fade True)&"
  " No "  _N  !"(mwmicon fade False)&"
}

Menu IconDecor
{
  " Image "   _I  !"(mwmicon deco image)&"
  " Label "   _L  !"(mwmicon deco label)&"
  " Both "    _B  !"(mwmicon deco 'label image')&"
  " Active "  _A  !"(mwmicon deco activelabel)&"
}

Menu IconImage
{
  " 35x50 "   _3  !"(mwmicon image 35x50)&"
  " 50x35 "   _0  !"(mwmicon image 50x35)&"
  " 50x50 "   _5  !"(mwmicon image 50x50)&"
  " 64x64 "   _6  !"(mwmicon image 64x64)&"
  " 96x96 "   _9  !"(mwmicon image 96x64)&"
  " 128x128 " _1  !"(mwmicon image 128x128)&"
}

Menu IconPost
{
  " Yes " _Y  !"(mwmicon post True)&"
  " No "  _N  !"(mwmicon post False)&"
}
```

As you can see, the icons section of the **.mwmrc** file is consistent with the colors and fonts sections. As a rule, menu items call a script tailored to handling icon resources. The script is **mwmicon**, which operates similarly to **mwmcolor** and **mwmfont** scripts. Here is the **mwmicon** script:

```
#!/bin/sh
# mwmicon, script to set Motif icon resources
# Syntax: mwmicon restype resvalue
# Copyright (c) Alan Southerton
# Initial values
  file=/tmp/xrdb.$$
  option=$1; value=$2

# Remove temporary file if untimely exit.
  trap "rm $file; exit 1 2 3 15"
```

```
# Set proper resource name
  case "$option" in
         auto) resource=iconAutoPlace ;;
          box) resource=useIconBox ;;
         post) resource=iconClick ;;
         fade) resource=fadeNormalIcon ;;
         deco) resource=iconDecoration ;;
        image) resource=iconImageMaximum ;;
        space) resource=iconPlacementMargin ;;
    boxscroll) resource=iconBoxSBDisplayPolicy ;;

     boxtitle) xterm -name getstring \
                    -title "Get Icon Box Title" \
                    -n GET \
                    -e xmenuget ICONBOXTITLE Title
               value='grep ICONBOXTITLE \
                         $HOME/.xmenu | cut -d: -f2'
               resource=iconBoxTitle ;;

      setsize) xterm -name getstring \
                    -title "Get Icon Box Size" \
                    -n GET \
                    -e xmenuget ICONBOXSIZE Size
               value='grep ICONBOXSIZE \
                         $HOME/.xmenu | cut -d: -f2'
               resource=iconBoxGeometry ;;

        matte) xterm -name getstring \
                    -title "Get Icon Box Matte Size" \
                    -n GET \
                    -e xmenuget ICONBOXMATTE Matte
               value='grep ICONBOXMATTE \
                         $HOME/.xmenu | cut -d: -f2'
               resource="Mwm\*iconbox\*matteWidth" ;;

      boxdeco) setibdeco $value
               exit ;;

         park) resource=iconPlacement
               size='grep ICONBOXSIZE \
                         $HOME/.xmenu | cut -d: -f2'
               case "$value" in
                'left top') value2="$size+1-2000"
                             resource2=iconBoxGeometry;;
               'right top') value2="$size+2000-2000"
                             resource2=iconBoxGeometry;;
```

```
                 'top right') value2="$size+2000-2000"
                              resource2=iconBoxGeometry;;
              'bottom right') value2="$size+2000-1"
                              resource2=iconBoxGeometry;;
              'right bottom') value2="$size+2000-1"
                              resource2=iconBoxGeometry;;
               'left bottom') value2="$size+1-1"
                              resource2=iconBoxGeometry;;
               'bottom left') value2="$size+0-0"
                              resource2=iconBoxGeometry;;
                  'top left') value2="$size+1-2000"
                              resource2=iconBoxGeometry;;
            esac ;;
  esac

# Create temporary file with new resource statements
  if [ "$option" = "park" ] ; then
     xrdb -query | \
     egrep -v \
        "(Mwm\*$resource:|Mwm\*$resource2:)" > $file
     echo Mwm\*$resource: $value >> $file
     echo Mwm\*$resource2: $value2 >> $file
  else if [ "$option" = "matte" ] ; then
     xrdb -query | grep -v "$resource" > $file
     echo $resource: $value | sed 's/\\//g' >> $file
  else
     xrdb -query | grep -v "Mwm\*$resource:" > $file
     echo Mwm\*$resource: $value >> $file
     fi
  fi

# Load new resources; replace .Xdefaults if specified
  xrdb -load $file
  overwrite=`grep SAVETOXDEFAULTS \
                  $HOME/.xmenu | cut -d: -f2`
  if [ "$overwrite" = "yes" ] ; then
     cp $HOME/.Xdefaults $HOME/.Xdefaults.bak
     mv $file $HOME/.Xdefaults
  else
     rm $file
  fi
```

The **mwmicon** script resembles the **mwmcolor** and **mwmfont** scripts in the previous sections. After establishing the resource and its new value, **mwmicon** queries the resource database, uses **egrep -v** or **grep -v** to remove the old value from the stream, and then loads the new resources (and optionally creates a new copy of **.Xdefaults**).

There are some different things going on in **mwmicon**. One of them is the workaround to correct the way the system places the icon box. Whenever the user selects the *Parking Lot option*, the request goes through a **case** statement that defines a geometric position for the icon box. For example, the request to set **iconPlacement** to **top left** generates an equal **iconBoxGeometry** statement. (A value of 2000 is used, in some cases, because it exceeds the size of the screen and thus harmlessly ensures that the icon box will be placed at the given edge of the screen.)

How does **mwmicon** know the previous size of the icon box? It queries the $HOME/**.xmenu** file, which serves several purposes throughout the Xmenu menus. In this case, it stores the current size of the icon box. If a user never sets the size, the ICONBOXSIZE value in Xmenu is **6x1**. It could be argued that the size of the icon box is not important, and that the default size could always be used, but some users might like to set the default size so they don't have to resize it each time they log in. A user might also decide to remove some, or most, of the window manager components from the icon box, making the default size—and the menu option to set it—crucial.

The **.xmenu** script is updated with the **xmenuget** script. This **mwmicon** script calls the **xmenuget** script three times. Each time it does, it does so in conjunction with opening an Xterm to get user input. The resources for the Xterm are tailored so that the Xterm best approximates a text input window (see Figure 7-5).

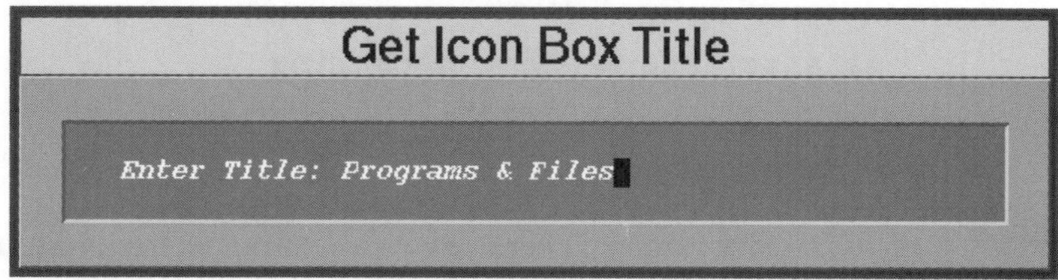

Figure 7-5 Xterm-based text input window.

The text input window is simple in design. As you will see in Chapter 9, it is possible to make better-looking and more efficient text input windows. For now, the resources for the text input Xterm—named **getstring**—are defined in two places: the $HOME/**.Xdefaults** file and the $XAPPLRESDIR/**XTerm** file:

```
! $HOME/.Xdefaults resources for getstring window
  Mwm*getstring.clientDecoration: none +title +border
```

```
  Mwm*getstring*matteWidth: 25

! $XAPPLRESDIR/XTerm resources for getstring window
  *getstring*background: #9c9386
  *getstring*font: *adobe-courier-bold*normal*140*
  *getstring*foreground: #ffffff
  *getstring*geometry: 55x3+365+435
```

The resources set up the appearance of the text input box. The two Motif resources must be defined either in $HOME/**.Xdefaults** or $XAPPLRESDIR/Mwm. The Xterm resources can be defined in any valid resource file. As noted before, the difference here is that Motif looks for certain resource files when it starts up and resources you want to set for Motif must be defined in these files. The same is true for Xterm, but restarting Xterms is not as consequential as restarting Motif.

If you have read previous chapters, the specific resources should be familiar. The **clientDecoration** resource is used to streamline the text input window; there is no point giving the user minimize and maximize capabilities, for example. The **matteWidth** is set to a relatively large size, giving the text input window a distinctive appearance. The Xterm-specific resources define the colors, font, and geometry for the window.

In the actual call to the named Xterm, **getstring** is specified as the parameter to the **-name** option. A title is then specified with the **-title** option, as is an icon label with the **-n** option. Finally, the **xmenuget** script is called using Xterm's **-e** option. The parameter to be passed to the script follows **xmenuget**. Here's another look at the **setsize** option:

```
setsize) xterm -name getstring \
               -title "Get Icon Box Size" \
               -n GET -e xmenuget Size
```

The **Size** parameter here serves two purposes. It tells the **xmenuget** script what to act upon; and it supplies the script with the string to use in its input prompt. Now let's take a look at **xmenuget**:

```
#!/bin/sh
# xmenuget, script to get iconbox name
# Syntax: xmenuget  <no options>
# Copyright (c) Alan Southerton

# Initial values
  file=/tmp/.xmenu.$$
  xshvar=$1; prompt=$2
```

```
# Display input text; get input
  echo
  /bin/echo -n "   Enter $prompt: "
  read value

# Update $HOME/.xmenu
  grep -v $xshvar $HOME/.xmenu > $file
  echo $xshvar:$value >> $file
  cp $HOME/.xmenu $HOME/.xmenu.bak
  mv $file $HOME/.xmenu
```

You will find that you can use the **xmenuget** script for many different tasks. All you need to do is supply the script a variable name and a string to complete the prompt in the Xterm window. The variable name, incidentally, need not exist before you write a new routine using **xmenuget**.

Why not just create a temporary file instead of using **.xmenu**? In the present case, a temporary file would not be as foolproof an approach, because **mwmicon** must know the name of the file, meaning you can include the process id (**$$**) in the temporary filename.

There are three values set in **.xmenu** used with **xmenuget**:

- ICONBOXSIZE
- ICONBOXTITLE
- ICONBOXMATTE

When control returns to the **mwmicon** script, the first order of business is to obtain the recently set value from **.xmenu**:

```
newvalue='grep ICONBOXSIZE \
               $HOME/.xmenu | cut -d: -f2'
```

Command substitution is then used, along with **grep** and **cut** to obtain the value from **.xmenu**.

One more thing about the **mwmicon** script is that it offers a way to add and subtract decorations to the icon box. The code for this is actually contained in the **setibdeco** script. The **setibdeco** script is self-contained and causes **mwmicon** to exit when control returns to it. Here's the script:

```
#!/bin/sh
# setibdeco, gets icon box decorations
# Syntax: setibdeco resource
# Copyright (c) Alan Southerton

# Intial values
```

```
  file=/tmp/boxdec.$$
  value=$1; found="no"

# Remove temporary file if untimely exit
  trap "rm $file; exit 1 2 3 15"

# Check for all and none options
  if [ "$value" = "all" -o "$value" = "none" ]; then
     found="yes"
     newstring=$value
  else
     oldvalue=`xrdb -query | \
     grep "Mwm\*iconbox\*clientDecoration" | cut -d: -f2`
     for arg in $oldvalue
     do
       #Remove plus sign from all positive cases
       testarg=`echo $arg | sed s/+//`
       if [ "$arg" = "+$testarg" ]; then
          arg=$testarg
       fi

       #Evaluate for matches with current value
       case $arg in
         "$value") found="yes"
                   newstring="$newstring -$value" ;;
        "-$value") found="yes"
                   newstring="$newstring +$value" ;;

        menu|minimize|maximize)
                   if [ "$value" = "title" ]; then
                      found="yes"; flag="title"
                      newstring="$newstring -$arg"
                   fi ;;

              none) flag=none
                   newstring="none "$newstring ;;
              all) flag=all
                   newstring="all "$newstring ;;
                *) newstring=$newstring" "$arg ;;
       esac
     done
  fi

# Take care of components previously not in effect
  case $flag in
     none) if [ "$found" = "no" ] ; then
```

```
                newstring="$newstring +$value"
                found="yes"
             fi ;;
        all) if [ "$found" = "no" ] ; then
                newstring="$newstring -$value"
                found="yes"
             fi ;;

      title) newstring="$newstring -$value" ;;
  esac

# Take care of oddball cases
  if [ "$found" = "no" ] ; then
   newstring="$newstring +$value"
  fi

# Create tempoary file with new resource statements
  xrdb -query | \
       grep -v "Mwm\*iconbox\*clientDecoration" > $file
  echo Mwm*iconbox*clientDecoration: $newstring >> $file

# Load new resources; replace .Xdefaults if specified
  xrdb -load $file
  overwrite='grep SAVETOXDEFAULTS \
                  $HOME/.xmenu | cut -d: -f2'
  if [ "$overwrite" = "yes" ] ; then
     cp $HOME/.Xdefaults $HOME/.Xdefaults.bak
     mv $file $HOME/.Xdefaults
  else
     rm $file
  fi
```

The idea behind the **setibdeco** script is to allow the user to reconfigure the icon box based on the current state of the icon box. For example, if the icon box has a maximize button, **setibdeco** examines the currently set icon box resources and sets the selected value to the opposite value. In other words, **+maximize** becomes **-maximize** and vice versa. If the currently set resource has neither a plus or a minus sign, it is assumed to be positive (the way Motif itself treats it).

The one drawback to this approach is if the user suddenly decides to change his or her mind and selects the maximize option two or more times in succession. The script takes care of this by indeed making the successive changes. There is no provision for the user who gets lost in a series of successive changes. In these instances, the best way to find out the current state of the icon box is to restart Motif.

One problem that **setibdeco** addresses is updating the decoration resources while making sense out of previously set resource values such as **all** and **none**. Recall from Chapter 5 that you can add and subtract values to the **clientDecoration** resource. You can also specify **all** and subtract resources:

```
Mwm*iconbox*clientDecoration: all -resizh -maximize
```

Or you can specify **none** and add resources:

```
Mwm*iconbox*clientDecoration: \
              none +menu +minimize +border
```

The two examples yield the same result: an icon box that has a border, menu, and minimize button, but no resize handles or maximize button.

After setting initial values and instituting the **trap** command, the **setibdeco** script begins its evaluation of the **all** and **none** cases. If the user has just specified **all** or **none**, the script proceeds to the fourth block where the $newstring value is set as preparation to modifying the **xrdb** database.

If the user requests a distinct decoration such as **resizeh** or **menu**, the script obtains the prior value of the **clientDecoration resource**:

```
else
   oldvalue=`xrdb -query | \
     grep "Mwm\*iconbox\*clientDecoration" | cut -d: -f2`
```

The **cut** command serves well here because it sees all values after the colon as a single string. If there are multiple decoration values in the string, the whitespace is maintained. This lets you address the string in a **for** loop:

```
for arg in $oldvalue
```

After this, each instance of $arg is compared with the currently requested decoration contained in $value. Both the add and subtract cases are evaluated:

```
case $arg in
        "+$value") found="yes"
                   newstring="$newstring -$value" ;;
        "-$value") found="yes"
                   newstring="$newstring +$value" ;;
```

If a match occurs, the $found variable is set accordingly and $newstring is appended with the new value. In the same **case** block, the **all**, **none**, and **title** decoration values are addressed. In the case of **title**, the script modifies **minimize**, **maximize**, and **menu** by testing for these values and setting positive values to negative ones. The reason behind this is if the user sees the titlebar in the current icon box, selecting title from the Xmenu menu assumes a desire to subtract the menu, minimize, and maximize buttons. As for the **all** and **none** cases, the script simply moves them to the beginning of $newstring and then appends the currently requested value.

Motif Focus

The issue of window focus is an important one. Many users might not realize this, because they have adopted Motif's default focus policy without giving the matter any thought. But even for these users, you would likely see a swift rebellion if their focus policy suddenly changed.

Because focus policy is a personal matter, it is a good tack to make the *Focus policy* menu easily accessible on systems that have multiple users. The Xmenu menus include it on the top-level *Resources* menu for this reason. Alternatively, for systems used primarily by a single person, the *Focus menu* could just as well be placed on a secondary menu. The only consideration here is that, as designed, the *Focus menu* extends three levels deep. Here is the top-level menu for setting the focus policy:

```
Menu MwmFocus
{
   no_label            f.separator
   no_label            f.separator
   no_label            f.separator
   " Motif Focus "     f.title
   no_label            f.separator
   no_label            f.separator
   no_label            f.separator
  " "                  f.nop
  "     Explicit"   _E f.menu MwmExplicitFocus
  "      Pointer"   _P f.menu MwmPointerFocus
   no_label            f.separator
   no_label            f.separator
  "     Colormap"   _C f.menu MwmCmapFocus
}
```

As you can see, the menu offers the two main choices for focus policy: *Explicit* and *Pointer*. If you prefer, you might want to use the word **implicit** instead of **pointer** to be consistent with the Motif documentation.

The third item on the menu is *Colormap*. A colormap's focus policy has no direct relation to the window focus policy, and all the menu items under *Colormap* operate independently from the other menu options. Placing the colormap focus policy on this menu, then, is merely a semantic consideration.

The second-tier menu in the *Focus policy* menus provides the user with additional branching to the final set of menus. Here are the rest of the menus:

```
Menu MwmExplicitFocus
{
  " Default"     _D  !"(mwmfocus explicit)&"
  " Raise"       _R  f.menu MwmRaise2Focus
  " Normalize"   _N  f.menu MwmNormFocus
  " Global"      _G  f.menu MwmGlobalFocus
  " Auto key"    _A  f.menu MwmAutoKeyFocus
  " Startup"     _S  f.menu MwmStartupFocus
}

Menu MwmRaise2Focus
{
  " Yes "   _Y  !"(mwmfocus raise2 true)&"
  " No "    _N  !"(mwmfocus raise2 false)&"
}

Menu MwmNormFocus
{
  " Yes "   _Y  !"(mwmfocus normal true)&"
  " No "    _N  !"(mwmfocus normal false)&"
}
Menu MwmGlobalFocus
{
  " Yes "   _Y  !"(mwmfocus global true)&"
  " No "    _N  !"(mwmfocus global false)&"
}

Menu MwmAutoKeyFocus
{
  " Yes "   _Y  !"(mwmfocus autokey true)&"
  " No "    _N  !"(mwmfocus autokey false)&"
}

Menu MwmPointerFocus
{
  " Default"  _D  !"(mwmfocus pointer)&"
  " Raise"    _R  f.menu MwmRaise1Focus
  " Global"   _G  f.menu MwmGlobalFocus
}

Menu MwmRaise1Focus
{
  " Yes "   _Y  !"(mwmfocus raise1 true)&"
```

```
  " No "    _N  !"(mwmfocus raise1 false)&"
}

Menu MwmCmapFocus
{
  " Explicit" _E  !"(mwmfocus cmap pointer)&"
  " Pointer"  _P  !"(mwmfocus cmap explicit)&"
  " Default"  _D  !"(mwmfocus cmap keyboard)&"
}
```

The only script called in the focus menus is **mwmfocus**. It handles both the explicit and implicit focus polices as well as the colormap focus policy.

None of the menu items require you to make more than one choice to effect a change in the focus policy. For example, if you select Focus->Explicit->Raise->Yes, the **Mwm*keyboardFocus** policy is set to **explicit** and the **Mwm*focusAutoRaise** resource is set to **true**. Also, the **autoRaiseDelay** resource is enabled, using the value of FOCUSRAISEDELAY in **.xmenu**.

On the other hand, if you select any of the other items on the *Explicit* selection menu, **Mwm*focusAutoRaise** and **Mwm*autoRaiseDelay** are unaffected. Again, however, **Mwm*keyboardFocus** is set to explicit, because in some cases, the user might be switching from a pointer, or implicit, focus policy. Looking at the **mwmfocus** script should reinforce this explanation:

```
#!/bin/sh
#mwmfocus, script to set Motif focus resources.
#Syntax: mwmfocus resource [value]
#Copyright (c) Alan Southerton
#Initial values
file=/tmp/xrdb.$$
option=$1; value=$2

#Remove temporary file if untimely exit.
trap "rm $file; exit 1 2 3 15"

#Irregular line lengths follow (limited indentation)

case "$option" in

#Explicit (click-to-type) focus policy resources
#
explicit)
xrdb -query | egrep -v \
"keyboardFocusPolicy|focusAutoRaise|autoRaiseDelay">$file
```

```
echo Mwm\*keyboardFocusPolicy: explicit >> $file
echo Mwm\*focusAutoRaise: true >> $file
raise=`grep FOCUSRAISEDELAY $HOME/.xmenu | cut -d: -f2`
echo Mwm\*autoRaiseDelay: $raise >> $file ;;


raise2)
xrdb -query | egrep -v \
"keyboardFocusPolicy|focusAutoRaise|autoRaiseDelay">$file

echo Mwm\*keyboardFocusPolicy: explicit >> $file
echo Mwm\*focusAutoRaise:  $value >> $file
raise=`grep FOCUSRAISEDELAY $HOME/.xmenu|cut -d: -f2`
if [ "$value" = "true" ]; then
   echo Mwm\*autoRaiseDelay: $raise >> $file
fi ;;


delay)
xterm -name getstring \
      -title "Get Window Auto-Raise Value" \
      -n GET \
      -e xmenuget FOCUSRAISEDELAY Milliseconds

xrdb -query | egrep -v \
"keyboardFocusPolicy|focusAutoRaise|autoRaiseDelay">$file
echo Mwm\*keyboardFocusPolicy: explicit >> $file
echo Mwm\*focusAutoRaise:  true >> $file
raise=`grep FOCUSRAISEDELAY $HOME/.xmenu | cut -d: -f2`
echo Mwm\*autoRaiseDelay: $raise >> $file ;;


autokey)
xrdb -query | \
egrep -v "keyboardFocusPolicy|autoKeyFocus" > $file

echo Mwm\*keyboardFocusPolicy: explicit >> $file
echo Mwm\*autoKeyFocus: true >> $file ;;


normal)
xrdb -query | egrep -v \
    "keyboardFocusPolicy|deiconifyKeyFocus" > $file

echo Mwm\*keyboardFocusPolicy: explicit >> $file
```

```
echo Mwm\*deiconifyKeyFocus: $value >> $file ;;


start)
xrdb -query | egrep -v \
"keyboardFocusPolicy|startupKeyFocus" > $file

echo Mwm\*keyboardFocusPolicy: explicit >> $file
echo Mwm\*startupKeyFocus: $value >> $file ;;


#Pointer (implicit) focus policy resources
#
pointer)
xrdb -query | egrep -v \
"keyboardFocusPolicy|focusAutoRaise|autoRaiseDelay">$file

echo Mwm\*keyboardFocusPolicy: pointer >> $file
echo Mwm\*focusAutoRaise: true >> $file ;;


raise1)
xrdb -query | egrep -v \
"keyboardFocusPolicy|focusAutoRaise|autoRaiseDelay">$file

echo Mwm\*keyboardFocusPolicy: pointer >> $file
echo Mwm\*focusAutoRaise: $value >> $file
raise=`grep FOCUSRAISEDELAY $HOME/.xmenu|cut -d: -f2`
if [ "$value" = "true" ]; then
   echo Mwm\*autoRaiseDelay: $raise >> $file
fi ;;


#This resource shared by explicit and pointer policies
global)
xrdb -query | \
grep -v "enforeKeyFocus" > $file
echo Mwm\*enforeKeyFocus: $value >> $file ;;

#Colormap focus policy
cmap1)
xrdb -query | \
grep -v "colormapFocusPolicy" > $file
echo Mwm\*colormapFocusPolicy: $value >> $file;;

esac
```

```
#Load new resources; replace .Xdefaults if specified
xrdb -load $file
overwrite='grep SAVETOXDEFAULTS \
                        $HOME/.xmenu | cut -d: -f2'
if [ "$overwrite" = "yes" ] ; then
   cp $HOME/.Xdefaults $HOME/.Xdefaults.bak
   mv $file $HOME/.Xdefaults
else
   rm $file
fi
```

Because focus policy resources are dependent on each, the code gets lengthy in the script. As it is presented, though, it serves as a learning tool for seeing the different relationships of the focus policy resources. In general, the script works similarly to other scripts in this chapter, but **egrep** is used more frequently because of the need to test for multiple resources.

One way to reduce the amount of code in **mwmfocus** would be to separate the treatment of different focus policies into different scripts, or different blocks in the same script. However, attempting to query the database after evaluating the previous and new resource statements—the method used in **mwmcolor**, **mwmfont**, and **mwmicon**—would make for much less readable code.

Other Resources

The *Other Resources* menu is the largest in the Xmenu menus. It contains items not easily grouped together, although the menu is arranged in four sections with each section containing loosely similar options. Again, liberal use of the **f.separator** function permits the grouping shown in Figure 7-6.

The first section of the *Misc Resources* menu contains items that generally relate to size and placement. The *Matte width* may not seem to affect window size, but if you specify a large matte, watch how your window grows.

The second section contains behavior-related items like *Show feedback*, which controls various ways Motif informs the user of an event. The third section has two options to change the appearance of Motif. The fourth section leads to a submenu from which you can specify custom key, button, and mouse bindings. Here is the *Misc Resources* menu:

```
Menu MwmResources
{
  no_label                    f.separator
  no_label                    f.separator
```

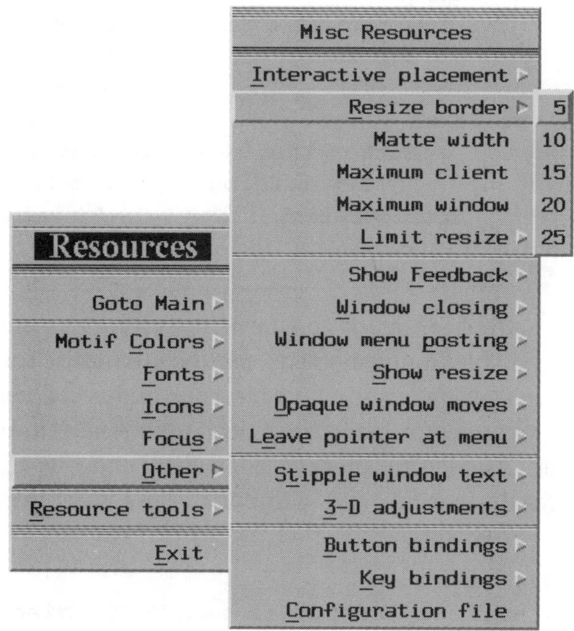

Figure 7-6 The *Other* menu and the *Resize border* option.

```
 no_label                      f.separator
 no_label                      f.separator
"Misc Resources"            _M f.title
 no_label                      f.separator
 no_label                      f.separator
" Interactive placement"    _I f.menu MwmWinPlacement
"          Resize border"   _R f.menu MwmResizeBorder
"            Matte width"   _a !"(mwmmisc matte)&"
"         Maximum client"   _x !"(mwmmisc cmax)&"
"         Maximum window"   _x !"(mwmmisc wmax)&"
"           Limit resize"   _L f.menu MwmLimitResize
 no_label                      f.separator
 no_label                      f.separator
"          Show Feedback"   _F f.menu MwmShowFeedback
"         Window closing"   _W f.menu MwmWinMenuClose
"    Window menu posting"   _p f.menu MwmWinMenuPost
"            Show resize"   _S f.menu MwmShowResizeCur
"    Opaque window moves"   _O f.menu MwmOpaqueMoves
" Leave pointer at menu"    _e f.menu MwmLeavePointer
 no_label                      f.separator
```

```
  no_label                        f.separator
 "   Stipple window text" _t f.menu MwmStipWinText
 "        3-D adjustments" _3 f.menu Mwm3DAdjust
  no_label                        f.separator
  no_label                        f.separator
 "        Button bindings" _B f.menu MwmBBindings
 "           Key bindings" _K f.menu MwmKBindings
 "    Configuration file" _C !"(mwmmisc config)&"
}
```

All of the options on the *Misc Resources* menu, whether or not they are available from a submenu, use the **mwmmisc** script. The **mwmmisc** script uses techniques from other scripts in this chapter and makes heavy use of **xmenuget** to obtain user input. Additionally, to adjust **showFeedback** values it adopts the model used in controlling the **clientDecoration** resources for the icon box (see **setibdeco**). Here is the **mwmmisc** script:

```
#!/bin/sh
# mwmmisc, script to set Motif misc resources
# Syntax: mwmmisc option value value2
# Copyright (c) Alan Southerton

# Initial values
file=/tmp/xrdb.$$
option=$1; value=$2; value2=$3

# Behavior resources
case "$option" in
    cmenu) resource=wMenuButtonClick2 ;;
    limit) resource=limitResize ;;
   opaque) resource=moveOpaque ;;
    place) resource=interactivePlacement ;;
    pmenu) resource=wMenuButtonClick ;;
  rcursor) resource=resizeCursors ;;
   resize) resource=resizeBorderWidth ;;
     stip) resource=cleanText ;;
   thresh) resource=moveThreshold ;;
     warp) resource=enableWarp ;;
   adjust) resource=topShadowPixmap
           resource2=bottomShadowPixmap ;;
   button) xterm -name getstring \
                 -title "Get Named Button Bindings" \
                 -n GET \
                 -e xmenuget BUTTONBINDINGS Name
           value='grep BUTTONBINDINGS \
```

```
                              $HOME/.xmenu | cut -d: -f2`
               resource=buttonBindings ;;
       config) xterm -name getstring \
                     -title "Get Named Configuration File" \
                     -n GET \
                     -e xmenuget CONFIGFILE Name
               value=`grep CONFIGFILE \
                              $HOME/.xmenu | cut -d: -f2`
               resource=configFile ;;

         cmax) xterm -name getstring \
                     -title "Get Maximum Client Area Size" \
                     -n GET \
                     -e xmenuget MAXCLIENTSIZE Size
               value=`grep MAXCLIENTSIZE \
                              $HOME/.xmenu | cut -d: -f2`
               resource=maximumMaximumSize ;;

          key) xterm -name getstring \
                     -title "Get Named Key Bindings" \
                     -n GET \
                     -e xmenuget KEYBINDINGS Name
               value=`grep KEYBINDINGS \
                              $HOME/.xmenu | cut -d: -f2`
               resource=keyBindings ;;

        matte) xterm -name getstring \
                     -title "Get Matte Width" \
                     -n GET \
                     -e xmenuget MATTEWIDTH Matte
               value=`grep MATTEWIDTH \
                              $HOME/.xmenu | cut -d: -f2`
               resource=matteWidth ;;

       showfb) setfeedback $value
               exit ;;

         wmax) xterm -name getstring \
                     -title "Get Maximum Window Size" \
                     -n GET \
                     -e xmenuget MAXWINSIZE Size
               value=`grep MAXWINSIZE \
                              $HOME/.xmenu | cut -d: -f2`
               resource=maximumClientSize ;;
esac
```

```
# Create temporary file; treat "adjust" differently
# Irregular line length follows (limited indentation)
if [ "$1" = "adjust" ]; then
   xrdb -query | egrep -v \
"Mwm\*client\*$resource:|Mwm\*client\*$resource2:">$file
   echo Mwm\*client\*$resource: $value >> $file
   echo Mwm\*client\*$resource2: $value2 >> $file
else
   xrdb -query | grep -v "Mwm\*$resource:" > $file
   echo Mwm\*$resource:' '$value >> $file
fi
# Load new resources; replace .Xdefaults if specified
xrdb -load $file
   overwrite=`grep \
           SAVETOXDEFAULTS $HOME/.xmenu | cut -d: -f2`
if [ "$overwrite" = "yes" ] ; then
   cp $HOME/.Xdefaults $HOME/.Xdefaults.bak
   mv $file $HOME/.Xdefaults
else
   rm $file
fi
```

The first set of resources, including **moveOpaque** and **resizeCursors**, are set up in a familiar arrangement. The main purpose of the code here is to set the appropriate resource name. Again, you could eliminate the step by specifying the full name in the **.mwmrc** file, but by specifying the name in the script, you enhance readability.

The second set of resources in **mwmmisc** uses the **xmenuget** script. Each call to **xmenuget** supplies the name of the **.xmenu** variable and a string to complete the prompt in the subsequently displayed Xterm. These blocks of code then use the **grep** and **cut** method to extract $value from **.xmenu**.

The last set, containing the **adjust** and **showfb** options, are anomalies. The **adjust** option, because it deals with 3-D shadowing, requires two values (and later, it requires its own routine to create a temporary file). The second option, **showfb**, manipulates the values of **showFeedback** and requires a separate script, called **setfeedback**:

```
#!/bin/sh
# setfeedback, set showFeedback resources
# Syntax: setfeedback resource
# Copyright (c) Alan Southerton
# Initial values
  file=/tmp/boxdec.$$
  value=$1; found="no"
```

```
# Remove temporary file if untimely exit
  trap "rm $file; exit 1 2 3 15"

# Check for all and none options
  if [ "$value" = "all" -o "$value" = "none" ]; then
     found="yes"
     newstring=$value
  #Else get current value and start parsing
  else
     oldvalue=`xrdb -query | \
               grep "Mwm\*showFeedback" | cut -d: -f2`
     for arg in $oldvalue
     do

     case $arg in
        "+$value") found="yes"
                   newstring="$newstring -$value" ;;
        "-$value") found="yes"
                   newstring="$newstring +$value" ;;
             none) flag="none"
                   newstring="none $newstring" ;;
              all) flag="all"
                   newstring="all $newstring" ;;
                *) newstring=$newstring" "$arg ;;
     esac
    done
 fi

# Take care of components previously not in effect
  if [ "$found" = "no" ] && [ "$flag" = "none" ]; then
     newstring="$newstring +$value"
  else
     if [ "$found" = "no" ] && [ "$flag" = "all" ];then
        newstring="$newstring -$value"
     fi
  fi

# Take care of oddball cases
  if [ "$found" = "no" ] ; then
     newstring="$newstring +$value"
  fi

# Create tempoary file with new resource statements
  xrdb -query | grep -v "Mwm\*showFeedback" > $file
  echo Mwm*showFeedback: $newstring >> $file
```

```
# Load new resources; replace .Xdefaults if specified
  xrdb -load $file
  overwrite='grep \
           SAVETOXDEFAULTS $HOME/.xmenu | cut -d: -f2'

  if [ "$overwrite" = "yes" ] ; then
     cp $HOME/.Xdefaults $HOME/.Xdefaults.bak
     mv $file $HOME/.Xdefaults
  else
     rm $file
  fi
```

The **setfeedback** script is similar to **setibdeco**, with the exception that it does not require as many unique handlers. When control returns to the **mwmmisc** script from **setfeedback**, **mwmmisc** exits.

Button and Key Bindings

On the surface, the menus controlling the **.mwmrc** bindings—buttons, keys, and the **config** filename—look like many other Xmenu menus. On second thought, though, you might wonder why the default set of bindings menus is skimpy. Here is a partial look at the menu hierarchy:

```
Menu MwmEventBindings
{
 " Button bindings"      _B f.menu MwmBBindings
 " Key bindings"         _K !"(mwmmisc key)&"
 " Configuration file"   _C !"(mwmmisc config)&"
}

Menu MwmBBindings
{
 " Default" _D !"(mwmmisc bbind DefaultButtonBindings)&"
 " Named"   _N !"(mwmmisc bname)&"

}
```

If you add different button bindings to your **.mwmrc** file, you will discover that this menu can grow. That's right. The Xmenu menus and scripts have a certain self-awareness, and button and key bindings are one of these areas. In the standard versions of Xmenu, the ability to update menus themselves is not built into the menu system. You can incorporate it, however, by creating menu items that call the **mwmbbind** and **mwmkbind** scripts. Here is the **mwmbind** script:

```
#!/bin/sh
# mwmbbind, script to configure button menus
# mwmbbind <no options>
# Copyright (c) Alan Southerton

# Initial values
  file=/tmp/.xmenu.$$
  opt="!\"(mwmmisc bbind"

# Remove temporary file if untimely exit
  trap "rm $file; exit 1 2 3 15"

# Check for Mwm*configFile or use HOME/.mwmrc
  cfgfile=`xrdb -query | \
               grep "Mwm\*configFile" | cut -d: -f2`
  cfgfile=`eval echo $cfgfile`
  if [ "$cfgfile" = "" ] || [ ! -f $cfgfile ]; then
     cfgfile=$HOME/.mwmrc
  fi

# Set string to contain all button bindings
  buttons=`grep "^ *Buttons " $cfgfile | \
               sed 's/Buttons //p'`

  set - `echo $buttons`

# Get and check total number of button bindings
  bnum=`sed -n "/Menu *MwmBBindings/,/}/p" $cfgfile | \
               grep mwmmisc | wc -l`

  if [ $# -gt $bnum ] ; then
   sed "/Menu *MwmBBindings/,/}/d" $cfgfile > $file
  fi

# Routine that inserts whatever button bindings were
# found in the previous config file. The routine also
# establishes acceptable mnemonics.

  echo "Menu MwmBBindings" >> $file
  echo "{" >> $file
  i=0;
  for item in $buttons
  do
    i=`expr $i + 1;`
    n=0; status=bad
    if [ $i -ne 1 ]; then
```

```
      while [ "$status" = "bad" ]
      do
         n=`expr $n + 1;`
         key=`echo $item | cut -c$n`
         if [ "$key" = "" ]; then
            echo Too many similar menu names
            exit 1
         fi
         #Parse through already set mnemonics
         for mnemonic in $letters
         do
           if [ "$key" = "$mnemonic" ]; then
              status=bad
              break
           fi
           status=good
         done
       done #endwhile

    #Else take care of first case
    else
         key=`echo $item | cut -c1`
    fi
    letters="$letters $key"

    #Make default name more sightly; then process
    if [ "$item" = "DefaultButtonBindings" ]; then
      item="Default"

      echo "\" $item\" _$key $opt \
             DefaultButtonBindings\)\"">>$file

    else

      echo "\" $item\" _$key $opt \
             $item\)\"" >> $file

    fi
  done

  echo "}" >> $file

# Make backup and then copy new config file
  cp $cfgfile $cfgfile.bak
  mv $file $cfgfile
```

The **mwmbbind** script initializes values, including setting $opt to part of a menu string, and then determines the correct name of the configuration file. In most cases, this will be $HOME/**.mwmrc**, but because Motif gives users the ability to change the name of the configuration file, you must check for any name changes:

```
cfgfile=`xrdb -query | grep \
                "Mwm\*configFile"|cut -d: -f2`
cfgfile=`eval echo $cfgfile`

if [ "$cfgfile" = "" ] || [ ! -f $cfgfile ]; then
   cfgfile=$HOME/.mwmrc
fi
```

First **mwmbbind** queries the resource database and obtains the name of the configuration file, using **grep** and **cut**. And then, because you can use environment variables to specify a path for the **xrdb** database, you need to evaluate the contents of $cfgfile; otherwise, the shell treats the environment variable in a literal fashion due to the previous command substitution. Next, **mwmbbind** checks the validity of $cfgfile. The first part of the **if** statement checks whether $cfgfile is null, which would be the case if **Mwm*configFile** did not exist in the database. The second part of the statement checks to see if the file indeed exists. If either condition is not met, the $cfgfile is set to $HOME/**.mwmrc**. For those of you who would like to carry the testing further, it wouldn't be a bad idea to also check for the existence of **.mwmrc**.

When **mwmbbind** gets down to the business at hand—checking for new button bindings—its does so using a combination of **grep** and **sed**. It stores the list of available buttons in the $buttons variable:

```
buttons=`grep "^ *Buttons " \
                $HOME/.mwmrc |sed 's/Buttons //p'`
set - `echo $buttons`
```

Because users might add their own bindings, either by typing them or copying them from someone else's **.mwmrc** file, you can't be sure of their indentation so the **grep** command uses the ^ * sequence to account for all whitespace before the keyword **Buttons**. The **sed** command, in the final part of the pipeline, then deletes the keyword, leaving you with the user-defined button bindings name, or in the case of the default bindings, **DefaultButtonBindings**.

Right after $buttons is defined, **mwmbbind** uses the **set** command as a quick way to obtain the number of values that $buttons contains. Because the **set -** notation allows you to fill the space normally occupied by command variables—**$1, $2...$9**—the special shell variable **$#** can be used to compare the number of new arguments against the number that currently exist in the MwmBBindings menu:

```
bnum=`sed -n "/Menu *MwmBBindings/,/}/p" \
              $HOME/.mwmrc | grep mwmmisc | wc -l`
if [ $# -gt $bnum ] ; then
   sed "/Menu *MwmBBindings/,/}/d" /.mwmrc > $file
fi
```

Before comparing the number of menu items, **mwmbbind** has to find the menu items. It does this by using a regular expression as an address for **sed**. In other words, **sed** reads through the **.mwmrc** file, and when it finds **Menu MwmBBindings**, it copies all text it encounters until it reaches **}**. Note the command between **/Menu *MwmBBindings/** and **/}/**. It is critical for portability, although some versions of **sed** do not require it.

In order to get the number of menu items, **mwmbbind** pipes the results of the **sed** command—which prints the pattern space, and only the pattern space, because **-n** is specified—into **grep** and **wc**. The **-l** option to **wc** causes only the number of total lines to be output, setting up the **if** statement that does the actual comparing of numbers. At this point, **sed** is given the same regular expression address. But this time, instead of printing the pattern space, it prints everything but. Notice that **-n** is now absent and the **d** edit option is used. The end result is that all of **.mwmrc**, with the exception of the MwmBBindings menu, is stored in a temporary file.

The following block of code begins constructing the new menu. The first thing **mwmbbind** does is write the menu header. It then starts a **for** loop to parse menu items on an item-by-item basis. During this stage, it enters a **while** loop, which in turn uses another **for** loop. Both of these loops are used to establish proper mnemonic characters for the menu item. With each iteration, the latest candidate for a mnemonic, represented in the variable $key, is compared with all previously accepted candidates. If a match does occur, the **while** loop resets with the help of the $status flag and the next character in $item is compared.

In the **while** loop, it is feasible that the characters in $item might match in all instances. Although this is highly unlikely, the script does include a test against the possibility:

```
if [ "$key" = "" ]; then
   echo Too many similar menu names
   exit 1
fi
```

This test assumes that you have run **mwmbbind** from the command line. If you do incorporate it or **mwmkbind** into a menu, you should add a routine to display the error message in an Xterm window. A method of doing this is described in the next section.

The last order of business, as usual, is to create a temporary file and replace the existing configuration file. Again, the script uses $cfgfile to represent the configuration file. By the way, if you intend on making different configuration files and incorporating Xmenu menus and scripts in them, you should avoid hard-coding the **.mwmrc** filename in your scripts.

Resource Tools

Unlike the other items on the *Resources* menu, the *Resource tools* menu does not set Motif resources. It does contain the *Restart* option to restart Motif, but otherwise, it is primarily concerned with manipulating the **.Xdefaults** file, **xrdb** database, and other system data.

In Chapter 10, you will find specific descriptions of the the utilities available on the *Resource tools* menu. In the meantime, don't hesitate to use the options. For example, *Database load->.Xdefaults* is a time-saver, and *format->Strip spaces* is a great way to ensure that you don't have any unwanted whitespaces at the ends of lines in **.Xdefaults**.

CHAPTER 8
Motif Army Knife

THE ROOT WINDOW

One thing that the Motif menus—or any other window manager menus—lend themselves to is a Swiss Army knife approach to desktop management. If an X client, shell script, or UNIX utility is on your system, or somewhere on the network, you can execute it from a menu. So this chapter takes a look at many different things that you can do from the Motif menus, including:

- Controlling the root window
- Displaying full color images
- Menu command recall
- Customizing UNIX utilities
- Loading X clients and programs

The Xmenu software wraps these various concerns into the *Main Menu*. It is bound to Button 2, the middle button, and incorporates a menu slide feature similar to that used by the *Resources Menu* (see Chapter 7). The only difference is that the slide feature pops up the *Xterms Menu*. Again, the feature is for users who compulsively click the same mouse button.

Internally, the *Main Menu* differs from the *Resources Menu* because it relies heavily on the **.xmenu** configuration file. Recall from Chapter 6 that only a few routines made use of the **.xmenu** file. With the *Main Menu*, however, most routines make use of **.xmenu**. The reason for the difference is that the *Main Menu* ventures into areas where client-defined resources are rare.

The principal behind the **.xmenu** file is similar to the **xrdb** database. Instead of having resources loaded into memory, where client applications can read them, the routines simply read the **.xmenu** file. Most of the routines use UNIX's **grep** and **cut** commands to obtain the value in an **.xmenu** statement. The **grep -v** command is typically used to remove a statement from a file. New and updated **.xmenu** statements are added to the file using **echo**. UNIX redirection is used extensively.

The **.xmenu** file looks something like an X resource file. There are two cosmetic differences: the resources appear in uppercase letters and are always one word in length; and the values, which are text strings, numbers, and true/false values, appear immediately after the colon. No whitespace follows the colon. You can use whitespace if you want if you choose to edit the **.xmenu** file by hand. Here are some sample resources:

- HOSTNAME:**digital2:0.0**
- IMAGELAST:**stars.gif**
- IMAGEPATH:**/usr/images**
- LASTCMD1:**/usr/xmenu/mwmres getall**
- MAXWINSIZE:**1152x900**

The samples show the range of the **.xmenu** resources. The HOSTNAME resource contains a typical value, the name of the host system, the display number, and the screen number. The IMAGELAST and IMAGEPATH resources contain the filename and path for the image last loaded onto the root window. The LASTCMD1 resource contains the last command executed via the menus. The MAXWINSIZE resource is a helper value for the **mwmmisc** script (see Chapter 7) that lets you use an Xterm to get user input.

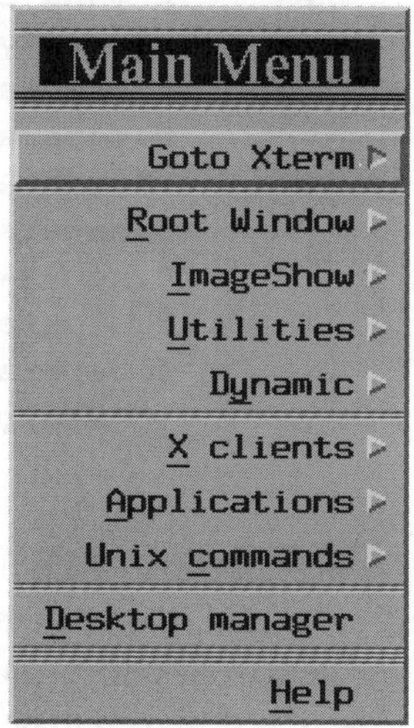

Figure 8-1 The *Main Menu* with options to change the root window, load utilities, and execute UNIX commands, among other things.

THE MAIN MENU

Similar in organization to the *Resources Menu*, the *Main Menu* offers eight options, including the menu slide to the *Xterms Menu* (right button). Figure 8-1 shows the *Main Menu*.

The goal of the *Main Menu* is to provide access to general utilities that enhance your work environment. You will likely modify the *Main Menu* for your own site, or even replace it entirely, but you will find many of its submenus interesting. Here is a look at the code for the *Main Menu*:

```
! Root Window Menu: Button 2 (middle)
  Menu MainMenu
 {
   " "                                  f.nop
   no_label                             f.separator
   @//usr/xmenu/bitmaps/mainmenu  f.title
   no_label                             f.separator
   no_label                             f.separator
   " "                                  f.nop
   "      Goto Xterm"                   f.menu XtermsMenu
   no_label                             f.separator
   no_label                             f.separator
   "     Root Window"       _R          f.menu RootWinMenu1
   "       ImageShow"       _I          f.menu ImageShow
   "       Utilities"       _U          f.menu SystemUtils
   no_label                             f.separator
   no_label                             f.separator
   "       X clients"       _X          f.menu SystemClients
   "    Applications"       _A          f.menu SystemApps
   " Unix commands"         _c          f.menu SystemCommands
   no_label                             f.separator
   no_label                             f.separator
   " Desktop manager"       _D          !"(xdt)&"
   no_label                             f.separator
   no_label                             f.separator
   no_label                             f.separator
   no_label                             f.separator
   "            Help"       _H          !"(xhelp 001)&"
}
```

Most of the menu items in the *Main Menu* lead to submenus. The *Desktop manager* and *Help* items are self-contained. If you do not have a desktop manager, you will want to delete the item from the *Main Menu*. It is included for completeness; the Xmenu software is designed to be complimentary to desktop managers. The *Help* item simply calls the **xtermloader** script (see Chapter 9), which then displays a text file. Using **xtermloader**, or a script like it, you could build an extensive help system for your site if you find one necessary.

ROOT WINDOW MENU

Most users like to decorate the root window background with one type of image or another. Included in the standard release of X is the **xsetroot** utility, which lets you display bitmap images on the background. Figure 8-2 shows the *Root Window* menu.

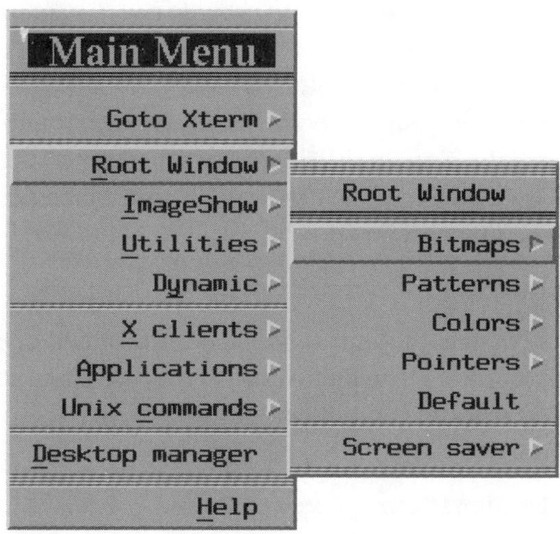

Figure 8-2 The *Root Window* submenu.

The first and second options on the Root Window menu use the **xsetroot** utility. Other options set the background and foreground colors. The code for the *Root Window* menu sets up a series of submenus:

```
Menu RootWinMenu1
{
  no_label            f.separator
  no_label            f.separator
  no_label            f.separator
  no_label            f.separator
  "Root Window"       f.title
  no_label            f.separator
```

```
    no_label                f.separator
    "          Bitmaps"     f.menu RootBitmaps
    "         Patterns"     f.menu RootPatterns
    "           Colors"     f.menu RootColors
    "         Pointers"     f.menu RootPointers
    "          Default"     !"(xsetroot -def)&"
    no_label                f.separator
    no_label                f.separator
    "     Screen saver"     f.menu RootScreenSave
    no_label                f.separator
    no_label                f.separator
}
```

With the exception of the *Default* option, the Root Window menu items call submenus to perform a particular task. The *Default* option itself uses the **-def** option to **xsetroot** to provide a way to return the root window to its default appearance.

The only other matter about the Root Window menu that deserves comment is its name: RootWinMenu1, which implies a second menu. If you have the Xmenu distribution media, notice that it contains a second Root Window menu. The difference between the two menus is RootWinMenu2 uses a bitmap for its title:

```
@/xmenu/bitmaps/rootmenu   f.title
```

The tale that this tells is an unfortunate one: In order to make a slight change to a menu that you want to reuse elsewhere on the desktop, you have to repeat the entire menu in the **.mwmrc** file. In the Xmenu **.mwmrc** file, RootWinMenu2 is bound to the Alt-Button1 combination:

```
Alt<Btn1Down>   root|frame   f.menu RootWinMenu2
```

Note here that you can invoke the Root Window menu by pressing Alt and Button 1 over the root window, or on top of a window frame.

Most of the routines used with the Root Window menu—or more accurately, its submenus—use the **rwin** script. In general, the **case** routines are similar, in that they set new values and maintain currently set values of related resources.

There is one break from the norm. It occurs in the two different ways of placing bitmaps on the root window. One method uses the approach found in all the other routines. The other method, which uses standard X patterns on the background, defines the filenames for the patterns in the script, not in the **.mwmrc** file. The reason for doing this is to illustrate an approach you can use if you want to speed up reloading of the **.mwmrc** file when Motif restarts. The idea behind it is you can use numbers instead of text strings to represent values. So here's a look at the **rwin** script:

```
#!/bin/sh
# rwin, script to set root window values in .xmenu
# Syntax: rwin resource value

# Dependencies
# $XMENU environment variables
# $XMENU/bitmaps directory

# Initial values
file=/tmp/.xmenu.$$
option=$1; flag=0

# This first loop reads the input and decides what
# variable in the .xmenu file is going to be set.

 case "$option" in
   bground) newvalue=$2
            bg=$2
            fg=`grep ROOTFGCOLOR $HOME/.xmenu | \
                           cut -d: -f2`
            pattern=`grep ROOTPATTERN $HOME/.xmenu | \
                           cut -d: -f2`
            resource=ROOTBGCOLOR ;;
   fground) newvalue=$2
            fg=$2
            pattern=`grep ROOTPATTERN $HOME/.xmenu | \
                           cut -d: -f2`
            bg=`grep ROOTBGCOLOR $HOME/.xmenu | \
                           cut -d: -f2`
            resource=ROOTFGCOLOR ;;
   pattern) case "$2" in
               1) pattern=blank ;;
               2) pattern=1x1 ;;
               3) pattern=2x2 ;;
               4) pattern=cweave ;;
               5) pattern=fuzz ;;
               6) pattern=dimple1 ;;
               7) pattern=dimple3 ;;
               8) pattern=dot ;;
               9) pattern=scales ;;
              10) pattern=star ;;
              11) pattern=starm ;;
              12) pattern=target ;;
              13) pattern=wweave ;;
              14) pattern=xlogo16 ;;
            esac
```

```
              newvalue=$pattern
              bg=`grep ROOTBGCOLOR $HOME/.xmenu | \
                             cut -d: -f2`
              fg=`grep ROOTFGCOLOR $HOME/.xmenu | \
                             cut -d: -f2`
              resource=ROOTPATTERN ;;
      bitmap) pattern=$2
              newvalue=$pattern
              bg=`grep ROOTBGCOLOR $HOME/.xmenu | \
                              cut -d: -f2`
              fg=`grep ROOTFGCOLOR $HOME/.xmenu | \
                              cut -d: -f2`
              resource=ROOTPATTERN ;;
     pointer) newvalue=$2
              pointer=$2
              flag=1
              resource=ROOTPOINTER ;;

        *) echo "Usage: $0 option value"
           exit 1 ;;
esac

# Execute the xsetroot command.
if [ "$flag" = 0 ] ; then
   xsetroot -bg "$bg" -fg "$fg" \
            -bitmap $XMENU/bitmaps/$pattern
else
   xsetroot -cursor_name $pointer
fi

# Having executed the command, supply .xmenu with the
# new bitmap pattern.

grep -v $resource $HOME/.xmenu > $file
echo $resource:$newvalue >> $file
cp $HOME/.xmenu $HOME/.xmenu.bak
mv $file $HOME/.xmenu
```

Compare the **bitmap)** and **pattern)** blocks in the script. The **bitmap)** block represents the method that relies on the **.mwmrc** file to pass the pertinent value. If you have a large **.mwmrc** file like the Xmenu **.mwmrc** file, this can add many seconds to the time it takes Motif to restart. The alternative is encapsulated in the **pattern)** block, which sets the values in the script. Of course, this method adds a slight processing penalty on the script-side of things, but a minimal one. Perhaps the major drawback is that it detracts from the overall readability of the various scripts needed to support the **.mwmrc** file. And it also detracts from the readability of the **.mwmrc** file itself.

Bitmaps

The *Bitmaps* menu resembles the color menus used in the Sun version of Xmenu, in that it associates a bitmap with each menu item. Instead of colors, though, the *Bitmaps* menu associates the actual bitmap that the user can select to have placed on the root window background. Figure 8-3 shows the *Bitmaps* menu.

You can use bitmaps of any practical size—square or rectangular—in a Motif menu. The *Bitmaps* menu uses 75-by-75 pixel bitmaps, which begins to approach the upper limit of practicality. Each menu item in Bitmaps calls the **rwin** script and specifies the actual bitmap filename. Here's a look at the menu:

```
Menu RootBitmaps
{
  @/xmenu/bitmaps/dsquares !"(rwin bitmap dsquares)&"
  @/xmenu/bitmaps/lsquares !"(rwin bitmap lsquares)&"
  @/xmenu/bitmaps/spiral   !"(rwin bitmap spiral)&"
  @/xmenu/bitmaps/woman    !"(rwin bitmap woman)&"
  @/xmenu/bitmaps/xlogo75  !"(rwin bitmap xlogo75)&"
  @/xmenu/bitmaps/geo4     !"(rwin bitmap geo4)&"
  @/xmenu/bitmaps/skyline  !"(rwin bitmap skyline)&"
  @/xmenu/bitmaps/loops2   !"(rwin bitmap loops2)&"
  @/xmenu/bitmaps/geo2     !"(rwin bitmap geo2)&"
  @/xmenu/bitmaps/geo3     !"(rwin bitmap geo3)&"
}
```

The **rwin** script processes the specified bitmap from the menu and actually loads the bitmap onto the root window. The **bitmap)** block, as already noted, is representative of other logic in **rwin**:

```
bitmap) pattern=$2
        newvalue=$pattern
        bg=`grep ROOTBGCOLOR \
                 $HOME/.xmenu | cut -d: -f2`
        fg=`grep ROOTFGCOLOR \
                 $HOME/.xmenu | cut -d: -f2`
        resource=ROOTPATTERN ;;
```

Figure 8-3 The *Bitmaps* submenu.

The different **case** blocks in **rwin** must handle associated resources. The **bitmap)** block handles the foreground and background colors, which ultimately is passed to **xsetroot**, along with the bitmap filename:

```
xsetroot -bg "$bg" -fg "$fg" \
        -bitmap $XMENU/bitmaps/$pattern
```

Finally, the **rwin** script updates the **.xmenu** file with the new bitmap name. The resource name is ROOTPATTERN, which is shared with the **pattern)** logic.

```
grep -v $resource $HOME/.xmenu > $file
echo $resource:$newvalue >> $file
cp $HOME/.xmenu $HOME/.xmenu.bak
mv $file $HOME/.xmenu
```

With the exception of the *Patterns* submenu, the remaining submenus on the *Root Window* menu closely follow the approach used in the *Bitmap* submenu. As a result, these sections treat these submenus in cursory fashion.

Patterns

As noted, the *Patterns* submenu relies on a different approach in the **rwin** script. Other than that—and other than the fact that it uses 16-by-16 pixel bitmaps—the *Patterns* submenu resembles the *Bitmaps* submenu. Here is the menu code:

```
Menu RootPatterns
{
  @/xmenu/bitmaps/blank      !"(rwin pattern 1)"
  @/xmenu/bitmaps/1x1        !"(rwin pattern 2)"
  @/xmenu/bitmaps/2x2        !"(rwin pattern 3)"
  @/xmenu/bitmaps/cweave     !"(rwin pattern 4)"
  @/xmenu/bitmaps/fuzz       !"(rwin pattern 5)"
  @/xmenu/bitmaps/dimple1    !"(rwin pattern 6)"
  @/xmenu/bitmaps/dimple3    !"(rwin pattern 7)"
  @/xmenu/bitmaps/dot        !"(rwin pattern 8)"
  @/xmenu/bitmaps/scales     !"(rwin pattern 9)"
  @/xmenu/bitmaps/star       !"(rwin pattern 10)"
  @/xmenu/bitmaps/starm      !"(rwin pattern 11)"
  @/xmenu/bitmaps/target     !"(rwin pattern 12)"
  @/xmenu/bitmaps/wweave     !"(rwin pattern 13)"
  @/xmenu/bitmaps/xlogo16    !"(rwin pattern 14)"
}
```

Instead of passing the filename associated with a pattern, each statement in the *RootPatterns* menu passes a number to the **rwin**. The number is then associated with the filename in the **rwin** script. For example:

```
5) pattern=fuzz ;;
```

This is from the **pattern)** block of code in the **case** statement in **rwin**. Again, the purpose for this approach is to help reduce the overall size of the **.mwmrc** file. (See the *Bitmaps* section for additional information on the **rwin** script.)

Colors

The *Colors* submenu lets you set the foreground and background colors of the root window. As with color selection submenus on the *Resources Menu*, the standard Xmenu version uses the **xcoloredit** program as the color-setting mechanism.

```
Menu RootColors
{
  " Background"    !"(rwin bground '$XMENU/xcol')&"
  " Foreground"    !"(rwin fground '$XMENU/xcol')&"
}
```

The Sun version does not use **xcoloredit**. Instead, like some of the *Resources Menu* options, it uses bitmaps in the **.mwmrc** to give the user color choices. Here's a representative menu:

```
Menu RBG
{
  @/xmenu/colors/skyblue   !"(rwin RBG #87CEFA)&"
  @/xmenu/colors/cyan      !"(rwin RBG #00FFFF)&"
  @/xmenu/colors/yellow1   !"(rwin RBG #FFFF00)&"
  @/xmenu/colors/grnyellow !"(rwin RBG #ADFF2F)&"
  @/xmenu/colors/violet    !"(rwin RBG #DB7093)&"
  @/xmenu/colors/red       !"(rwin RBG #EE0000)&"
  @/xmenu/colors/peachp    !"(rwin RBG #FFDAB9)&"
  @/xmenu/colors/midblue   !"(rwin RBG #191970)&"
  @/xmenu/colors/lgray     !"(rwin RBG #C0C0C0)&"
  @/xmenu/colors/white     !"(rwin RBG #FFFFFF)&"
  @/xmenu/colors/blue      !"(rwin RBG #4169FF)&"
}
```

This is certain not to satisfy some users. With the menus and other interface components, you can justify limiting colors to those that reflect best on the window manager. With the root window colors, you might want to make the menu larger, as a compromise. Or you might use some other technique, including a text input window (via Xterm) that lets the user enter the English-language name of the color.

Pointers

Pointers are a natural choice for using bitmaps in a menu. X supports numerous pointers and you can easily select from these to provide a menu of 6 to 12 pointers. Note that the pointers available on this menu affect only the current pointer for the root menu; application pointers are not affected.

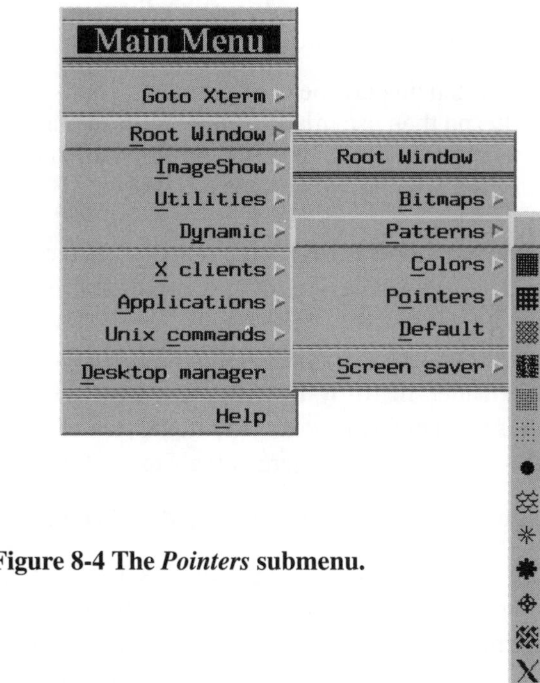

Figure 8-4 The *Pointers* submenu.

Alternatively, you can use the English names of the pointers for menu items. The problem here, however, is that many of the names are obscure, although **gumby**, for example, has endeared himself to at least two generations of computers users. Figure 8-4 shows a sample menu with pointer bitmaps, including **gumby**. The following code is the menu behind Figure 8-4.

```
Menu RootWinPointers
{
  @/xmenu/cur/arrows    !"(rwin RWC sb_h_double_arrow)"
  @/xmenu/cur/crossr    !"(rwin RWC cross_reverse)"
  @/xmenu/cur/bogo      !"(rwin RWC bogosity)"
  @/xmenu/cur/gumby     !"(rwin RWC gumby)"
  @/xmenu/cur/fleur     !"(rwin RWC fleur)"
  @/xmenu/cur/sailboat !"(rwin RWC sailboat)"
  @/xmenu/cur/arrow     !"(rwin RWC top_left_arrow)"
}
```

Specifying the bitmap files is the easy part. Finding the bitmaps is the hard part. The reason is that pointers don't already exist as bitmaps. You have to make them first. There are two ways you can do it:

- If your system uses the standard MIT font for pointers, called **cursor.snf**, you can use the **showsnf** utility to create ASCII files, which you can edit into a text editor and ultimately convert into bitmaps with the **atobm** utility.
- You can display the pointer font on your system with the **xfd** utility and then use image capture tools to magnify and save the font to a bitmap file. This way is preferred if you want to adjust the size of the pointer in its bitmap rendition.

Neither of these methods is automatic. When you use the **showsnf** utility, it produces an ASCII file from the **cursor.snf** file, but you must then edit it in a text editor to extract the pointer you want. Additionally, the pointers, which are called cursors when talking about them from the font perspective, are formatted in 16-by-16 character arrays. This many not be the size you want, so you have to take an additional step of doubling or tripling the lines (**sed** is the way to go). Here is the **showsnf** command:

```
showsnf cursor.snf > $XMENU/bitmaps/cursor.txt
```

On most systems that support the standard X Consortium pointers, the **cursor.snf** file is located in the **/usr/lib/X11/fonts/misc** directory. After performing the conversion, and editing the file so that you have a file with a single pointer in it—say, **gumby.txt**—you can convert it with the **atobm** utility:

```
atobm gumby.txt > gumby.xbm
```

Now you have one of the files referenced in the *Pointers* menu. Alternatively, you can use image editing tools to capture a display of the cursor and save it in X bitmap format. The **xfd** client program lets you display the entire cursor font. Simply enter **xfd cursor** at the command line. A display such as the one shown in Figure 8-5 appears.

To capture an image, you can use the **xmag** and **xwd** utilities, along with the **pbmplus** utilities, or you can use a commercial image editor. For the pointer bitmaps created for the Xmenu software, the SCO X.desktop bitmap editor was used.

Default

The *Default* item on the *Root Window* menu sets the background to the familiar stippled gray pattern. You can use this menu item or enter **xsetroot -def** at the command line to achieve this effect. Incidentally, entering **xsetroot** without parameters also produces the stippled gray background.

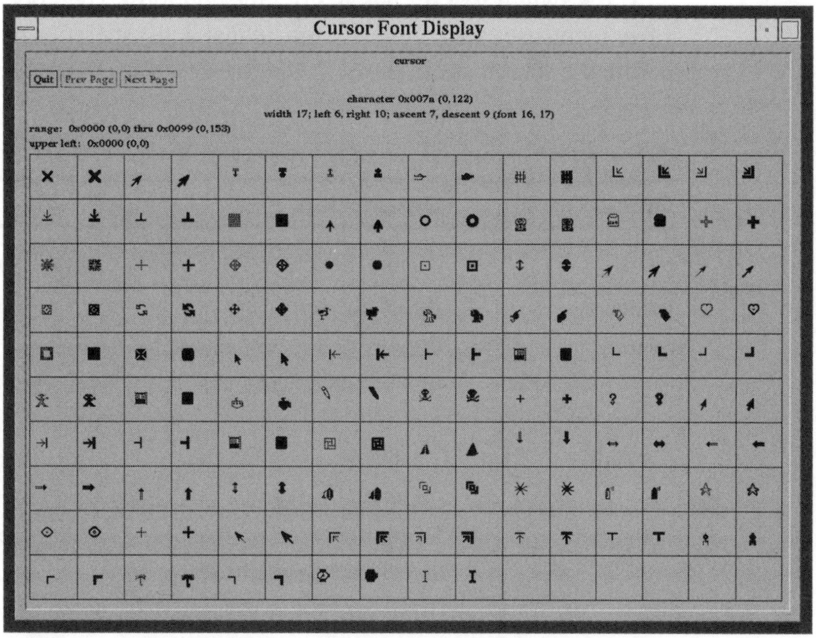

Figure 8-5 The Xfd client's display of the cursor font set.

Screen Saver

The *Screen saver* menu item is a simple utility. It uses the general purpose **xset** utility to blank the screen after a specified amount of time. As you probably know, it is important to either blank the screen or constantly update a screen saver image, so as to avoid "screen burn-in," which can severely diminish the display quality of monitors.

The **s** switch, without a **-** sign, tells **xset** to perform the screen saver operation. The **s** is followed by the time interval in seconds. Here's the *Screen Saver* menu as it appears in the **.mwmrc** file:

```
Menu RootScreenSave
{
 " 2 "    !"(xset s 120)&"
 " 4 "    !"(xset s 240)&"
 " 6 "    !"(xset s 480)&"
 " 8 "    !"(xset s 960)&"
 " 10 "   !"(xset s 1200)&"
 " 20 "   !"(xset s 2400)&"
}
```

The **s** switch to **xset** has many other options. The code for the *Screen saver* menu uses the simplest setup, in that it just specifies the length of time before the screen saver starts. Table 8-1 describes other **s** options.

Table 8-1 Screen Saver Options with Xset

Option	Description
blank	Blanks the screen. This option supersedes other options.
default	Resets the screen saver to its default settings.
expose	Permits servers without dedicated memory to store the current screen image and perform the screen saver option anyway.
noblank	Uses a background pattern as a screen saver, instead of blanking the screen.
noexpose	Permits only servers that have dedicated memory to perform screen saver operations.
off	Turns off the screen saver. This option supersedes other options.

ImageShow Menu

The *ImageShow* menu represents a departure from the standard tools in the MIT X Consortium release (see Figure 8-6). However, the main program used in the *ImageShow* menus is **xloadimage**.

The **xloadimage** program is in the MIT X Consortium's **contrib** collection, plus distributed as standard by several systems vendors. It is also included on the companion diskettes in source code. If you use any version of **xloadimage**, adhere to its copyright requirements, which require you to leave its existing copyright messages alone.

The only other departure is the Portable Bitmap Toolkit, known also as the **pbm** utilities, or **pbmplus**. You will definitely have to obtain this from a public domain archive site by either direct Internet access or via UUNET. There are also CD collections available from distributors and at trade shows and flea markets from which you can get the **pbmplus** utilities.

The *Image* menu has five options. Three of the options let you display images. One, the *Set defaults* submenu, lets you set image defaults. The fifth option, *File*, lets you capture, magnify, and save new images to a file. Here is the *ImageShow* menu as it appears in the **.mwmrc** file:

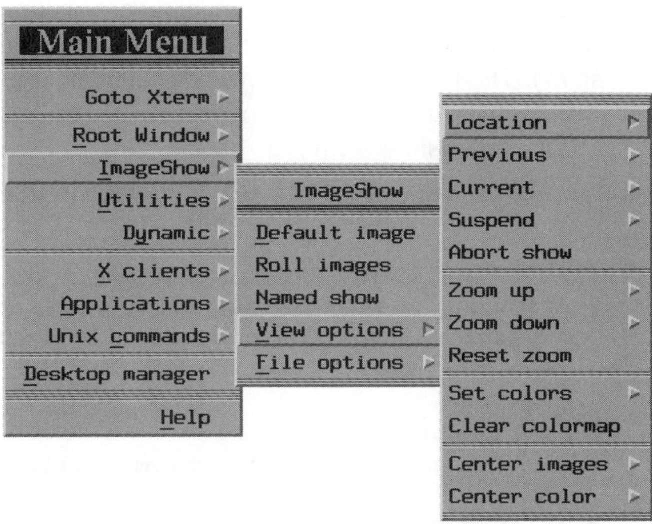

Figure 8-6 The *ImageShow* submenu.

```
Menu ImageShow
{
   no_label                 f.separator
   no_label                 f.separator
   no_label                 f.separator
   no_label                 f.separator
  " ImageShow "        _I   f.title
   no_label                 f.separator
   no_label                 f.separator
  " Roll images"       _R   !"(imageshow slides)&"
  " Named show"        _N   !"(imageshow named)&"
   no_label                 f.separator
   no_label                 f.separator
  " Default"           _D   !"(imageshow default)&"
  " Previous"          _P   f.menu ImagePrevImage
  " Current"           _C   f.menu ImageCurImage
  " Set defaults"      _S   f.menu ImageDefaults
   no_label                 f.separator
   no_label                 f.separator
  " File"              _F   f.menu ImageGrab
   no_label                 f.separator
   no_label                 f.separator
}
```

The image display options—*Roll images*, *Named show*, and *Default image*—let you display images on the root window. The *Roll images* and *Named show* options begin a slideshow of images (hence the name, image show). The Default image displays a single image, which you set in the **.xmenu** file. All three of these options, as you can see from the menu code, call the **imageshow** script:

```
#!/bin/sh
# Frontend to xloadimage. This script can be used
# standalone from the command line or incorporated
# into the .mwmrc file.

# Dependencies
# xloadimage (MIT X Consortium utility)

# Related Scripts
# getimage (gets imageshow name)
# runshow  (runs imageshow)
# Record this command
  lastcommand $0 $1 $2 $3 &
# Initial values
  file=/tmp/.xmenu.$$
  images=/tmp/images.$$
  imagespec=`grep ROOTIMAGESPEC $HOME/.xmenu | \
                      cut -d: -f2`

# Check and see if this is a request to kill the
# current instance of imageshow. If so, kill and exit.
  if [ "$1" = kill ] ; then
    showpid=`grep IMAGESHOWPID \
                  $HOME/.xmenu | cut -d: -f2`
  kill -1 $showpid
  grep -v ROOTSUSPEND $HOME/.xmenu > $file
  echo ROOTSUSPEND:0 >> $file
  mv $file $HOME/.xmenu
  exit
fi

# Begin the case block for different image shows.
  case $1 in
   #This block handles the default image
   default) defimage=`grep ROOTDEFIMAGE \
                  $HOME/.xmenu | cut -d: -f2`
            xloadimage -onroot -colors 64 $defimage & ;;
```

```
# This blocks handles the suspend option.
suspend) grep -v ROOTSUSPEND $HOME/.xmenu > $file
         echo ROOTSUSPEND:$2 >> $file
         mv $file $HOME/.xmenu ;;

#This option displays previous image in a window.
#The routine also suspends operation of the
#current slide show.
previous) grep -v ROOTSUSPEND $HOME/.xmenu > $file
          echo ROOTSUSPEND:1 >> $file
          cp $HOME/.xmenu $HOME/.xmenu.bak
          mv $file $HOME/.xmenu
          path='grep IMAGEPATH \
                     $HOME/.xmenu | cut -d: -f2'
          file=${path}/'grep IMAGELAST \
                     $HOME/.xmenu | cut -d: -f2'
          zlevel='grep ROOTZOOM \
                     $HOME/.xmenu | cut -d: -f2'
          xloadimage -onroot -onroot -colors 96 \
                    -zoom $zlevel $file & ;;

#This option puts the current image on the root
#window after Previous option has been used
current) path='grep IMAGEPATH \
                     $HOME/.xmenu | cut -d: -f2'
         file=${path}/'grep IMAGECURRENT \
                     $HOME/.xmenu | cut -d: -f2'
         zlevel='grep ROOTZOOM \
                     $HOME/.xmenu | cut -d: -f2'
         xloadimage -onroot -onroot -colors 96 \
                    -zoom $zlevel $file &
         sleep 10
         grep -v ROOTSUSPEND $HOME/.xmenu > $file
         echo ROOTSUSPEND:0 >> $file
         cp $HOME/.xmenu $HOME/.xmenu.bak
         mv $file $HOME/.xmenu ;;

slides) defslides='grep ROOTSLIDES \
                     $HOME/.xmenu | cut -d: -f2'
        echo $defslides > $images
        xterm -name imgshow -geometry 75x20 \
              -title "ImageShow" \
              -n Images -iconic \
              -e $XMENU/runshow $images &
        wait
```

```
                rm $images ;;

        named)  xterm -name imgshow -title "ImageShow"
                      -e getimage $images ;
                if [ ! -r $images ] ; then exit ; fi
                xterm -name imgshow -geometry 75x20 \
                      -title "ImageShow" \
                      -n Images -iconic \
                      -e runshow $images &
                wait
                rm $images ;;

 # This routine is for command line. Any file works.
           *) echo $* > $images
                xterm -name imgshow -geometry 75x20 \
                      -title "ImageShow" \
                      -n Images -iconic \
                      -e runshow $images &
                wait
                rm $images ;;
esac
```

The **imageshow** script can be run from a window manager menu or the command line. Many of the options in **imageshow** rely on the presence of the **.xmenu** file, but the default option, *), can be used to start a slideshow from the command line. Looking at the default *) routines exemplifies the way some of the other options in **imageshow** work.

As noted, the *) block is designed for the command line. If you supply an incorrect file specification to **imageshow**, the script lets **xloadimage** handle the error. Otherwise, the script accepts one or more filenames, or a wildcard specification, thanks to use of **$*** construct. The filenames are then redirected to a temporary file represented by $images. Next an Xterm is started in iconic fashion. Using the **-e** option, the Xterm calls the **runshow** script, supplying it the $images variable. Here's what **runshow** looks like:

```
#!/bin/sh
# runshow, runs the image show.
# Syntax: runshow filespec
# Copyright (c) Alan Southerton

# Note: An Xterm runs the show in order to display
# xloadimage messages in a window. The alternative is
# to let them display in the console window--or send
# them to /dev/nul or similar.
```

```
# Dependencies
# xloadimage (MIT X Consortium utility)
# imageshow  (main script)
# getimage (gets imageshow name)

# Initial values
  pid=XXX
  images=$1
  file=/tmp/.xmenu.$$

# Begin show by killing any previous shows.
  showpid=`grep IMAGESHOWPID \
             $HOME/.xmenu | cut -d: -f2`
  kill -1 $showpid
  grep -v IMAGESHOWPID \
               $HOME/.xmenu > $file  #update PID
  echo IMAGESHOWPID:$$ >> $file
  cp $HOME/.xmenu $HOME/.xmenu.bak
  mv $file $HOME/.xmenu

  for file in `cat $images`
  do
    suspend=`grep ROOTSUSPEND \
               $HOME/.xmenu | cut -d: -f2`
    while [ "$suspend" -ne 0 ]
    do
      suspend=`grep ROOTSUSPEND \
               $HOME/.xmenu | cut -d: -f2`
      sleep 30
    done

    zlevel=`grep ROOTZOOM $HOME/.xmenu | cut -d: -f2`
    colors=`grep ROOTCOLORS $HOME/.xmenu | cut -d: -f2`
    center=`grep ROOTCENTER $HOME/.xmenu | cut -d: -f2`
    border=`grep ROOTBORDER $HOME/.xmenu | cut -d: -f2`
    locate=`grep ROOTLOCATE $HOME/.xmenu | cut -d: -f2`
    grep -v IMAGECURRENT $HOME/.xmenu > $file

    echo IMAGECURRENT:$file >> $file
    mv $file $HOME/.xmenu

    if [ "$locate" -ne 0 ] ; then
       xloadimage -onroot -install \
                  -colors $colors \
                  -zoom $zlevel $file &
       sleep 3
```

```
      kill -1 $pid
      pid=`ps -aux | grep xloadimage | \
                     grep -v grep | cut -c10-14`

   elif [ "$center" -ne 0 ] ; then
      xloadimage -onroot -colors $colors \
                 -center -border $border \
                 -zoom $zlevel -onroot $file &
   else
      xloadimage -onroot -colors $colors \
                 -border $border -zoom $zlevel \
                 -onroot $file &
   fi

   sleep 48
   grep -v IMAGEPATH $HOME/.xmenu | \
                      grep -v IMAGELAST > $file
   echo IMAGEPATH:`dirname $file` >> $file
   echo IMAGELAST:`basename $file` >> $file
   mv $file $HOME/.xmenu
  done

# Finally, assign a dummy value to IMAGESHOWPID
  showpid=`grep IMAGESHOWPID \
                      $HOME/.xmenu | cut -d:  -f2`
  grep -v IMAGESHOWPID $HOME/.xmenu > $file
  echo IMAGESHOWPID:XXX >> $file
```

The **runshow** script must take care of assorted housekeeping. The first thing it must do is kill any previous image shows that are still running. This is not mandatory, but multiple image shows running in the background tend to consume system resources, as well as to be confusing to the user.

Inside the **for** loop that actually displays the images, the **runshow** script retrieves parameters from the **.xmenu** file. The parameters range from the zoom level of the image to whether the image has a border or not.

Finally, the script displays the images and either places them on the root window or in a regular window. Additionally, if the border parameter has been specified, the script places a border around the image as shown in Figure 8-7.

After the **runshow** script finishes its works, control returns to the **imageshow** script. In the *) block, the **wait** command ensures this. The last thing that occurs is that the file referenced by $images is deleted.

The Xterm that executes the image show uses a named set of resources called **imgshow**. These resources are defined in both **Xdefaults** and the

Figure 8-7 Image with a border around it.

XTerm file in the directory pointed to by the $XAPPLRESDIR variable. Here is what they look like:

```
!Define in $XAPPLRESDIR/XTerm
 *imgshow*background: black
 *imgshow*font: *adobe-courier-bold*normal*140*
 *imgshow*foreground: white
 *imgshow*geometry: 55x10+365+435
!Defined in $HOME/.Xdefaults
 Mwm*imgshow*iconImage: $XMENU/bitmaps/show.xbm
 Mwm*imgshow*matteBackground: #d7ee0a
 Mwm*imgshow*matteForeground: #d7ee0a
 Mwm*imgshow*matteWidth: 6
 Mmw*imgshow*clientDecoration: -maximize -resizeh
 Mmw*imgshow*clientFunctions: -maximize -resizeh
```

The **XTerm** resources set up the basic Xterm window, defining size, location, colors, and font. The **.Xdefaults** resources define Motif specific enhancements, including an icon image, window matte and matte colors. Additionally, the **clientDecoration** and **clientFunctions** resources remove the ability to maximize and resize the Xterm window. This is not necessary, but given that **imageshow** is not a vital client program, it is a good way to indicate to the user that it is practical to leave this Xterm alone.

Roll Images

The *Roll images* menu item closely follows the logic in the previous description. Instead of expecting command line input, however, it obtains the file specification for the image show from the **.xmenu** file:

```
defslides=`grep ROOTSLIDES \
               $HOME/.xmenu | cut -d: -f2`
echo $defslides > $images
```

The user can set the value of ROOTSLIDES by editing the **.xmenu** file directly. A wildcard specification such as **beach*gif** or ***.gif** suffices.

Named Show

The *Named show* menu item again resembles the previously described items. The only difference is it calls an Xterm in order to obtain user input:

```
xterm -name imgshow \
      -title "ImageShow" -e getimage $images ;
```

The input Xterm uses the same set of resources as the Xterm that actually runs the image show. Unlike the other routines that use the **imgshow** set of resources, however, the *Named show* routine doesn't change the preset geometry size (it was actually set with this routine in mind).

Next the routine calls the **getimage** script. Note that it passes the $images variable, which at this point doesn't reference a file, but will when the **getimage** script is through with it. (This is a handy technique for avoiding hard-coded temporary filenames). Here is the **getimage** script:

```
#!/bin/sh
# getimage, script to get user input
# Syntax: getimage filename
# Copyright (c) Alan Southerton
# Initial values
  images=$1

# Display message and get input
  echo
  echo " If you do not want to run the default image"
  echo " show, you can specify one here. Simply enter"
  echo " the path and filespec. For example, you might"
```

```
echo " enter /home/myimages/*.gif."
echo
echo
/bin/echo -n " Path and filespec: "
read ImageName
echo $ImageName > $images
```

When the **getimage** script returns control, **imageshow** immediately checks whether the user has entered a valid file specification:

```
if [ ! -r $images ] ; then exit ; fi
```

This is one of the rare instances in the Xmenu software where it is necessary to perform error checking. If the user does enter an invalid file specification, the **imageshow** script exits at this point. One side-effect of this is any previous instance of **imageshow** is killed.

Default

The *Default* option displays a single image on the root window. Parameters such as border and zoom level do not work with the *Default* option. It is meant to be a quick option so the user can put his or her favorite image on the root window.

As with other routines, *Default* retrieves the name of the image to load from the **.xmenu** file. Here is the relevant command from the **imageshow** script:

```
defimage='grep ROOTDEFIMAGE \
               $HOME/.xmenu | cut -d: -f2'
```

Next, **imageshow** calls the **xloadimage** program, specifying that the image should be displayed on the root in 64 colors. The color number is hardcoded in **imageshow** and you may want to change the value if 64 colors conflicts with other software that makes heavy use of the colormap.

```
xloadimage -onroot -colors 128 $defimage &
```

The *Set defaults* submenu offers a menu item to change the default image. You can use this routine or edit the **.xmenu** directly.

Previous

The *Previous* option redisplays the last image displayed on the root window or in a standard window, depending on the value of ROOTLOCATE in the **.xmenu** file. The *Previous* option also works with other display parameters in **.xmenu**. Let's look at the **previous)** block from **imageshow** again:

```
previous) grep -v ROOTSUSPEND $HOME/.xmenu > $file
            echo ROOTSUSPEND:1 >> $file
            cp $HOME/.xmenu $HOME/.xmenu.bak
            mv $file $HOME/.xmenu
            path=`grep IMAGEPATH \
                       $HOME/.xmenu | cut -d: -f2`
            file=${path}/`grep IMAGELAST \
                       $HOME/.xmenu | cut -d: -f2`
            zlevel=`grep ROOTZOOM \
                       $HOME/.xmenu | cut -d: -f2`
            xloadimage -onroot -onroot -colors 96 \
                      -zoom $zlevel $file & ;;
```

The **previous)** block contains a good summary of the various options to **imageshow**. The first thing that happens is the current image show is suspended. To restart **imageshow**, the user can select *ImageShow->Set defaults->Suspend->No* option.

To obtain the path and filename of the previous image, the **previous)** code uses grep to retrieve the values of IMAGEPATH and IMAGELAST from the **.xmenu** file. This is a two-step process, but the path and file end up in a single variable, $file. The script then goes on to retrieve the zoom level, contained in $zlevel, before executing **xloadimage**.

Current

The *Current* option should be selected after using the *Previous* option. Not only does it restart **imageshow**, it does so with the image that was displayed before the user selected the *Previous* option. Choosing *Current* without previously having chosen *Previous* is harmless. It simply lengthens the time that **imageshow** displays the image.

The code for the **current)** block is somewhat the inverse of the **previous)** block. Here's a look:

```
current) path=`grep IMAGEPATH \
                       $HOME/.xmenu | cut -d: -f2`
         file=${path}/`grep IMAGECURRENT \
                       $HOME/.xmenu | cut -d: -f2`
         zlevel=`grep ROOTZOOM \
                       $HOME/.xmenu | cut -d: -f2`
         xloadimage -onroot -onroot -colors 96 \
                   -zoom $zlevel $file &
         sleep 10
         grep -v ROOTSUSPEND $HOME/.xmenu > $file
```

```
echo ROOTSUSPEND:0 >> $file
cp $HOME/.xmenu $HOME/.xmenu.bak
mv $file $HOME/.xmenu ;;
```

The **current)*** code first retrieves the values it needs to display the current image, calls **xloadimage**, and then sleeps for 10 seconds. After this, it resets ROOTSUSPEND in the **.xmenu** file to 0, which tells the **runshow** script to resume operations. The **runshow** script itself sleeps for 30 seconds before displaying the next image. And, as always, the last item of business in the **current)** block is to make a backup copy of **.xmenu** before updating it with the temporary file.

Set Defaults

The *Set defaults* submenu gives you flexibility over displaying images. As noted already, this is the menu that lets you set the default image and the default slideshow, among many other things. Here is the *Set defaults* submenu:

```
Menu ImageDefaults
{
   no_label                   f.separator
   no_label                   f.separator
   no_label                   f.separator
   no_label                   f.separator
  "Suspend"            _S     f.menu ImageSuspend
  "Abort show"         _A     !"(imageshow kill)&"
   no_label                   f.separator
   no_label                   f.separator
  "Zoom up"            _u     f.menu ImageZoomUp
  "Zoom down"          _d     f.menu ImageZoomDown
  "Reset zoom"         _z     !"(setimage ROOTZOOM 100)&"
   no_label                   f.separator
   no_label                   f.separator
  "Set colors"         _c     f.menu ImageColors
   no_label                   f.separator
   no_label                   f.separator
  "Center images"      _i     f.menu ImageCenter
  "Center color"       _r     f.menu ImageCenterBg
  "Location"           _L     f.menu ImageLocation
   no_label                   f.separator
   no_label                   f.separator
  "Default image"      _e     !"(setimage defimage)&"
  "Default show"       _f     !"(setimage defshow)&"
}
```

The primary script used by the ImageDefaults menu is **setimage**, which contains the routines used to update the image resources in the **.xmenu** file:

```
#!/bin/sh
# setimage, set values in the .xmenu file
# Syntax: setimage

# Initial values
  file=/tmp/.xmenu.$$
  resource=$1; newvalue=$2

# Process default image requests
  case $resource in
     defimage) xterm -name getstring \
                     -title "Get Default Image" \
                     -n GET \
                     -e xmenuget ROOTDEFIMAGE Image ;;

     defshow) xterm -name getstring \
                    -title "Get Default Image" \
                    -n GET \
                    -e xmenuget ROOTDEFSHOW Image ;;
  esac

# Get all values from current $HOME/.xmenu and remove
# old instance of $newvalue if it exists. Then add the
# value of $newvavalue to the temporary file.
  grep -v $resource $HOME/.xmenu > $file
  echo $resource:$newvalue >> $file
  mv $file $HOME/.xmenu
```

The options and submenus that work with **setimage** generally set a numeric value or toggle a value between true and false. All the resources and values are contained in **.xmenu**. The **.xmenu** resource names used by **.mwmrc** are set in the **setimage** script. The values are set in $newvalue.

Suspend

The *Suspend* and *Abort* options let the user stop the slideshow. (This is a requirement for several reasons.) The *Suspend* option has a two-item menu:

```
Menu ImageSuspend
{
  " Yes"  !"($XMENU/imageshow suspend 1)&"
  " No"   !"($XMENU/imageshow suspend 0)&"
}
```

The way the suspend option works is that **runshow** polls the **.xmenu** file every 30 seconds:

```
while [ "$suspend" -ne 0 ]
do
  suspend=`grep ROOTSUSPEND \
                   $HOME/.xmenu | cut -d: -f2`
  sleep 30
done
```

You might consider adding another submenu to the *Set defaults* menu—that is, if it leaps out at you right now that there should be a menu option to adjust the delay between images. All told, the delay is equal to about 10 seconds, plus the value supplied by the **sleep** command. Some users might like to view images for a longer period. Some users, in fact, might like an option that allows more time to go by before the image changes.

Abort

The *Abort* option tells the **imageshow** script to kill the current image show. The UNIX **kill** command uses the process id for **imageshow** and sends a **-1** signal:

```
if [ "$1" = kill ] ; then
  showpid=`grep IMAGESHOWPID \
                  $HOME/.xmenu | cut -d: -f2`
  kill -1 $showpid
  grep -v ROOTSUSPEND $HOME/.xmenu > $file
  echo ROOTSUSPEND:0 >> $file
  cp $HOME/.xmenu $HOME/.xmenu.bak
  mv $file $HOME/.xmenu
  exit
fi
```

In addition to killing **imageshow**, the routine sets the ROOTSUSPEND value to 0 in case it had previously been set to 1. You might want to omit this, or document it for your users, but in practice, only users interested in a fragile lock against others would be interested in having ROOTSUSPEND equal 1 when an image show is not in progress.

Zoom Options

The two zoom options on the *Set defaults* menu are designed for the **zoom** option to **xloadimage**. This option uses 100 percent to represent the normal-sized image. Any nonzero value under 90 percent reduces, or zooms down, the image. Any value over 100 percent enlarges, or zooms up, the image. Here is the ImageZoomUp menu:

```
Menu ImageZoomUp
{
  "10"     !"(setimage ROOTZOOM 10)&"
  "20"     !"(setimage ROOTZOOM 20)&"
  "30"     !"(setimage ROOTZOOM 30)&"
  "40"     !"(setimage ROOTZOOM 40)&"
  "50"     !"(setimage ROOTZOOM 50)&"
  "60"     !"(setimage ROOTZOOM 60)&"
  "70"     !"(setimage ROOTZOOM 70)&"
  "80"     !"(setimage ROOTZOOM 80)&"
  "90"     !"(setimage ROOTZOOM 90)&"
}
```

In addition to the zoom menus included in the Xmenu **.mwmrc** file, you might want to make menus for the **xzoom** and **yzoom** options to **xloadimage**. You could either make menus that offer choices for each zoom direction, or you could make canned ratios as appear later in this chapter for one of the image capture menus.

Colormap Colors

The ImageColors menu offers a set of canned values for the **colors** option to **xloadimage**. This is an important option. Neither you nor your users want to have colormap conflicts. Therefore, the ImageColors menu might look a little conservative to someone who likes to view images at 240 colors and above, but the preset values are realistic for users running several applications at once. Here is the ImageColors menu:

```
Menu ImageColors
{
  "8"     !"(setimage ROOTCOLORS 8)&"
  "16"    !"(setimage ROOTCOLORS 16)&"
  "32"    !"(setimage ROOTCOLORS 32)&"
  "64"    !"(setimage ROOTCOLORS 64)&"
  "96"    !"(setimage ROOTCOLORS 96)&"
  "128"   !"(setimage ROOTCOLORS 128)&"
  "160"   !"(setimage ROOTCOLORS 160)&"
  "192"   !"(setimage ROOTCOLORS 192)&"
}
```

The best way to avoid colormap conflicts is to set the number of colors that **xloadimage** uses to a low value. In many cases, 64 colors yields acceptable image quality and doesn't conflict with applications that use a lot of colors. Most applications perform internal colormap adjustments and can exist comfortably as long as another application isn't hogging all the colors.

Centering Options

The *Set defaults* menu calls them centering options, but in photographic terms (or even in Motif lingo), the *Center images* and *Center color* options let your create a matte for images. For users who display images on the root window, this is somewhat of an impractical option, given that the center of the screen is often occupied with one application or another. For users who display images in a standard window, a matted photograph can have special appeal.

The **xloadimage** option to matte a photograph is also called **center**. Here is the simple menu that controls it:

```
Menu ImageCenter
{
    "Yes"  !"(setimage ROOTCENTER 1)&"
    "No"   !"(setimage ROOTCENTER 0)&"
}
```

The other centering option lets you specify a color for the matte. As with other color-setting needs, you can choose to use **xcoloredit**, bitmaps corresponding to colors, or English-language names for colors. (See the color-setting mechanisms in Chapter 7 for additional information.)

Location

The *Location* option is important because it lets users specify where the image should be displayed. The choice, as we've seen, is between the root window and a standard window. What hasn't been mentioned is you can change locations during an image show. The reason for this is that **imageshow** and **runshow** both retrieve the value of the display location (stored in ROOTLOCATE) for each image displayed.

Default Images

The *Default image* and *Default show* options give the user a quick and easy way to put images on the background. Once set, the user can leave these values intact for a long time, or change them as frequently as he or she wants. The point is that your favorite images are just a mouse click away.

Both default image routines go through **setimage** to invoke an Xterm and get user input. Here's a look at the routine that sets the default image show:

```
defshow) xterm -name getstring \
              -title "Get Default Image" \
              -n GET -e xmenuget ROOTDEFSHOW Image ;;
```

The routine uses the **xmenuget** script first described in Chapter 7. The routine doesn't do any error checking. The **xmenuget** script sets the new value of the specified resource and that's that. Error checking could be built in at this point, but a simple file existence test would prevent users from specifying images that they hadn't copied to a specified directory yet. Instead of checking for errors here, it is a better idea to check for the errors when the images are actually involved—at which point you can also rely on **xloadimage** to bypass nonexistent files.

File Option

The name *File* for this last item on the ImageShow menu is somewhat of a misnomer—except it is Motif style to use *File* as the menu name for file operations. But in addition to creating and saving files, the *File* submenu lets you capture and convert images. Figure 8-8 shows the *File* submenu.

The **xmag** client utility, which is part of the X Consortium's standard release (even though **xmag** itself is fairly nonstandard), is the workhorse of the *File* submenu. The reason is that the submenu relies on **xmag** to initially capture images, or parts of images, for the other options to use. Here's the code for the *File* submenu:

```
Menu ImageFileOptions
{
  no_label              f.separator
  no_label              f.separator
  no_label              f.separator
  no_label              f.separator
  " File Options "      f.title
  no_label              f.separator
  no_label              f.separator
  " Grab"          _G   !"(imgr grab)&"
  " Save"          _S   !"(imgr save)&"
  " Display"       _D   f.menu ImageDisplay
  " Print"         _P   !"(imgr prnt)&"
  no_label              f.separator
```

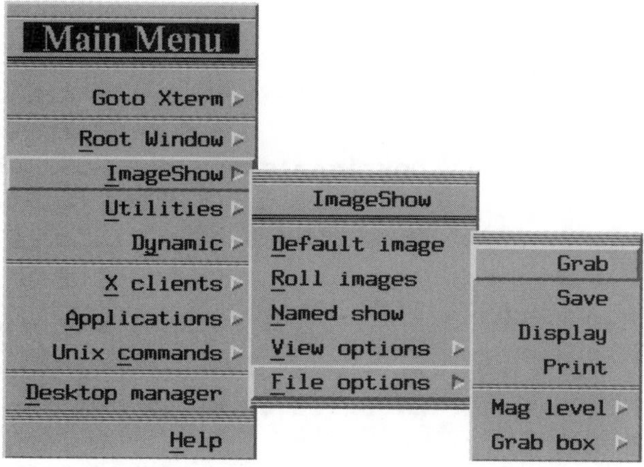

Figure 8-8 The *File* submenu for image shows.

```
    no_label                f.separator
    " Convert"      _C      f.menu ImageConvert
    no_label                f.separator
    no_label                f.separator
    " Mag level"    _M      f.menu ImageMagLevel
    " Grab box "    _b      f.menu ImageGrabBox
}
```

The last two items in the *File Options* submenu are critical to using most of the others. *Mag level* sets the all-important magnification factor; if you want to capture images and maintain their current size, be sure that you set the magnification factor to 1. The *Grab box* menu is just as important. It lets you set the size of the rectangle that outlines the part of the image you want to capture.

All of the options, including *Mag level* and *Grab box*, use the **imgr** script. Unlike most other scripts used by Xmenu, **imgr** does not set any values in resource files. It simply performs the specified file operation.

```
#!/bin/sh
# imgr, script for image file routines
# Syntax: $1 $2
# Copyright (c) Alan Southerton 1993

# Initial values
```

```
file=/tmp/.xmenu.$$
xwdfile=$$.xwd

case "$1" in
   grab) maglevel=`grep IMAGEMAGLEVEL \
                        $HOME/.xmenu | cut -d: -f2`
         boxsize=`grep IMAGEBOXSIZE \
                        $HOME/.xmenu | cut -d: -f2`
         xmag -mag $maglevel -source $boxsize ;;

    mag) grep -v IMAGEMAGLEVEL $HOME/.xmenu > $file
         echo IMAGEMAGLEVEL:$2 >> $file
         cp $HOME/.xmenu $HOME/.xmenu.bak
         mv $file $HOME/.xmenu ;;

    box) grep -v IMAGEBOXSIZE $HOME/.xmenu > $file
         echo IMAGEBOXSIZE:$2 >> $file
         cp $HOME/.xmenu $HOME/.xmenu.bak
         mv $file $HOME/.xmenu ;;

   save) xwd -nobdrs > $xwdfile
         grep -v IMAGEINBUFFER $HOME/.xmenu > $file
         echo IMAGEINBUFFER:$xwdfile >> $file
         cp $HOME/.xmenu $HOME/.xmenu.bak
         mv $file $HOME/.xmenu ;;

   disp) xwdfile=`grep IMAGEINBUFFER \
                        $HOME/.xmenu | cut -d: -f2`
         xwud < $xwdfile ;;

   name1) xterm -name getstring \
                -title "Get XWD Image" \
                -n GET \
                -e xmenuget XWDIMAGEFILE Image
         xwdfile=`grep XWDIMAGEFILE \
                        $HOME/.xmenu | cut -d: -f2`
         xwud < $xwdfile ;;

  print) xwdfile=`grep IMAGEINBUFFER \
                        $HOME/.xmenu | cut -d: -f2`
         xpr < $xwdfile ;;

  name2) xterm -name getstring \
                -title "Get XWD Image" \
                -n GET \
                -e xmenuget XWDIMAGEFILE Image
```

```
            xwdfile='grep XWDIMAGEFILE \
                          $HOME/.xmenu | cut -d: -f2'
            xpr < $xwdfile ;;

        *) exit ;;
esac
```

As you can see, the routines in **imgr** do not lend themselves to a general summary. The following sections explain each of the options.

Grab

The *Grab* option uses the **xmag** client to initially capture part or all of an image. It is designed for users who might run image shows and want to retain an image.

The **xmag** capture utility is especially useful if you are running **imageshow** and using a CD as the source of your image files. The CD might be in demand at your company—as new releases often are—or you might have to return it to a friend. Of course the alternative is to copy the entire image file and store it for later use. If you want to do this, and you are using the **imageshow** script, simply open the Xterm window associated with **imageshow** and obtain the image filename there.

When you select the *Grab* option, or run **xmag** from the command line, **xmag** takes control of the mouse and displays the image capture box, a rectangle that can you can move around the screen until you frame your target. When you are ready, press the left mouse button to capture the image. If you are running **imageshow**, it might be a good idea to use the *Suspend* option, because images that subsequently display could cause colormap problems for the image you just captured.

As noted, the *Grab* option depends on the values set using the *Mag level* and *Grab box* options. The default values for these in the **.xmenu** file are 1 and 150x150. Here is the **xmag** command again:

```
xmag -mag $maglevel -source $boxsize
```

By default, **xmag** assumes you want to magnify images that you capture. But because the Xmenu software uses it first and foremost as a straight capture utility, $maglevel is set to **1** in the **.xmenu** file as shipped. The **150x150** is adequate for capturing meaningful parts of images when $maglevel is set to **1**.

After you capture part of an image, **xmag** shows the captured image in a window. Inherent in **xmag** is the ability to examine the values of pixels in the image. When you press the left button over the window, a status line appears at the bottom of the window. In the status line, you will find the position of the associated pixel and its color value.

If, for some reason, you don't like the image that you have captured, you can make subsequent attempts without going back to the *Grab* menu option. To do so, just click the middle or right mouse buttons over the **xmag** window. This removes the **xmag** window and returns the capture rectangle. To leave **xmag** altogether, press **q**, **Q**, or Ctrl-C, or simply use the default Motif menu.

One thing that is irritating about **xmag** is that it does not let you put your own text string into the titlebar of its display window. You can make any number of attempts to surmount this, including referencing **xmag** as a named resource, but **xmag** is stubborn to a fault. The reason for the stubbornness is that **xmag** was not built using the standard X toolkit. In the end, the best you can do is remove the titlebar altogether by specifying the appropriate window manager resource. In Motif, enter the following into your **.Xdefaults** (or other resource) file:

```
clientDecoration: -title
```

Finally, if you have any display problems with other applications while using **xmag**, try the **-z** option. When you invoke **xmag** with **-z**, it ensures that **xmag** takes full control of the X server during capture operations.

Save

What good is capturing an image if you cannot save it? The **xmag** program has no capacity to save images, but other X clients come to the rescue. The *Save* option uses **xwd**, the standard X screen capture utility, to save images that you capture with **xmag**. Here's another look at the code in **imgr** for the *Save* option:

```
save) xwd -nobdrs > $HOME/$xwdfile
      grep -v IMAGEINBUFFER $HOME/.xmenu > $file
      echo IMAGEINBUFFER:$xwdfile >> $file
      cp $HOME/.xmenu $HOME/.xmenu.bak
      mv $file $HOME/.xmenu ;;
```

As you can see, a little more is being done here than just saving the file. First, the routine invokes **xwd**, which presents a crosshair cursor to the user, signaling that the user should click in the window that he or she wants to capture. The **nobdrs** option is used with **xwd** to ensure that the standard X border is omitted from the captured image.

Next, the **save)** block updates the **.xmenu** file with the filename of the **xwd** file. Because the process id is used in the filename, you can use this routine numerous times and be assured that each capture has a distinct filename. Ultimately, the **save)** code updates **.xmenu** so that you can further manipulate the last image that you saved into a file.

Display

After you have captured an image to disk, you might want to display it. The *Display* option allows you to display the previously captured image, or any named image, in a window. The *Display* option leads to the following submenu:

```
Menu ImageDisplay
{
    " Previous"     _P !"(imgr disp)&"
    " Named"        _N !"(imgr name1)&"
}
```

The first option displays the previous image by accessing the image filename in the **.xmenu** file. Here is the relevant code from the **imgr** script:

```
disp) file=`grep IMAGEINBUFFER \
                $HOME/.xmenu | cut -d: -f2`
      xwud < $file ;;
```

After the filename is obtained, you can use the **xwud** client to display the image. Note that **xwud** requires the use of redirection to get the filename. If you have any problem with this approach—and you might if you redisplay the image over a different image—try using the **-new** option to **xwud**, which forces a new colormap.

The second option in the *Display* submenu lets you specify any XWD file. This routine works like other routines that use Xterms to get user input.

```
name) xterm -name getstring \
          -title "Get XWD Image" \
          -n GET \
          -e xmenuget XWDIMAGEFILE Image
      xwdfile=`grep XWDIMAGEFILE \
                   $HOME/.xmenu | cut -d: -f2`
      xwud < $xwdfile ;;
```

This type of routine should be familiar by now. Once again, the **xmenuget** script is used to obtain the user input. Note that the routine does not affect the previously captured image in any manner whatsoever. In other words, the IMAGEINBUFFER resource in the **.xmenu** file remains unchanged. Also note that you can display XWD files with **xloadimage**, so the file loading routines on the *ImageShow* menu can be of assistance with the XWD files that you make.

Print

Another thing you might want to do with captured images is print them. The *Print* option handles this, using the standard **xpr** utility. Here is the submenu for the *Print* option:

```
Menu ImagePrint
{
    " Previous"     _P !"(imgr print)&"
    " Named"        _N !"(imgr name2)&"
}
```

The associated **imgr** routines follow the same pattern as those for displaying an XWD file:

```
print) xwdfile=`grep IMAGEINBUFFER \
                    $HOME/.xmenu | cut -d: -f2`
       xpr < $xwdfile ;;

name2) xterm -name getstring \
             -title "Get XWD Image" \
             -n GET \
             -e xmenuget XWDIMAGEFILE Image
       xwdfile=`grep XWDIMAGEFILE \
                    $HOME/.xmenu | cut -d: -f2`
       xpr < $xwdfile ;;
```

As written—and included on the distribution diskettes—the *Print* option uses **xpr** in its default state. There are a number of **xpr** options, however, including support for non-PostScript printers. If you want to make a more extensive menu—especially for a site that supports multiple printers—the **xpr** options could be adapted to additional **.mwmrc** menus. Table 8-2 summarizes the options.

In some cases when you use the **xpr** command, results will be unpredictable. This occurs with large and/or complex images. To try to remedy the problem, adjust the **scale** option or print the image over multiple pages.

Table 8-2 Options for the Xpr Utility

Option	Description
append	Lets you append one image to another image, as long as you have saved the first image to a file. You must specify the first image as an argument to **append**.
compact	Compresses white pixels if a PostScript printer has been specified as **device**.
cutoff	Modifies color to monochrome conversion for HP LaserJet printers. You must specify the level, which is a percentage of image brightness (e.g., **xpr -cutoff 75**).
device	Specifies the printer, including PostScript, HP Laserjet series, HP PaintJet, HP PaintJet XL, and monochrome PCL printers.
density	Specifies the dpi, or dots per inch, for HP printers. You must specify the dpi value as an argument to **density**.
gamma	Corrects color intensity for HP PaintJet XL printers. You must specify a floating point value between 0.00 and 3.00 as an argument to **gamma** (e.g., **xpr -gamma 1.23**).
grey	Converts a color image to grayscale. You must specify either **2**, **3**, or **4** as an argument to **grey**. The size of the image also increases by the factor specified.
header	Lets you add a header string to the printed output (e.g., **xpr -header "'date'"**).
height	Specifies the height of the printed page.
landscape	Specifies landscape mode.
left	Specifies the left margin using inches (e.g., **xpr -left 1.25**).
noff	Prints a subsequent image on the same page if the **append** option is also used.
output	Specifies the filename for redirected output. No printing occurs if this option is specified. See the **append** option.
scale	Sets the bit to grid translation, in that a bit in an image can be expanded into a grid of bits in the printed output. Values that you supply as an argument to scale could be 3x3, 4x4, etc.
noposition	Overrides header, trailer and positioning commands for HP printers.
plane	Sets the bit plane. For example, on an 8-bit plane system, you could enter 1 through 8 (e.g., **xpr -plane 4**).

Table 8-2 *(continued)*

Option	Description
portrait	Specifies portrait mode.
psfig	Turns off PostScript centering.
render	Special option for HP PaintJet XL printers. Refer to your HP documentation for algorithms that you must supply as an argument to **render**.
rv	Transposes background and foreground colors.
slide	Lets you create overhead transparencies with the HP PaintJet and HP PaintJet XL printers.
split	Splits images onto the number of pages that you specify as an argument (e.g., **xpr -split 3**).
top	Specifies the top margin (e.g., **xpr -top 2.25**).
width	Specifies the width of the page.

Mag Level

The *Mag level* option adjusts the magnification level for the **xmag** command. As available on the distribution diskette, the *Mag level* option presents a submenu of usable choices:

```
Menu ImageMagLevel
{
  "1"     !"($XMENU/imgr mag 1)&"
  "2"     !"($XMENU/imgr mag 2)&"
  "3"     !"($XMENU/imgr mag 3)&"
  "4"     !"($XMENU/imgr mag 4)&"
  "5"     !"($XMENU/imgr mag 5)&"
}
```

The **imgr** script processes the selection from the ImageMagLevel menu and updates the **.xmenu** file. All subsequent image captures will use the adjusted magnification level.

Grab Box

The *Grab box* option also references a submenu that presents a set of usable choices. You might want to modify these—more so than you would the magnification level choices—but the default choices cover a wide range.

```
Menu ImageGrabBox
{
   "100x100"    !"(imgr box 100x100)&"
   "100x150"    !"(imgr box 100x150)&"
   "100x200"    !"(imgr box 100x200)&"
   "100x250"    !"(imgr box 100x250)&"
   "100x300"    !"(imgr box 100x300)&"
   "150x150"    !"(imgr box 150x150)&"
   "150x250"    !"(imgr box 150x250)&"
   "150x300"    !"(imgr box 150x300)&"
   "150x350"    !"(imgr box 150x350)&"
   "150x400"    !"(imgr box 150x400)&"
   "200x200"    !"(imgr box 200x200)&"
   "200x300"    !"(imgr box 200x300)&"
   "200x400"    !"(imgr box 200x400)&"
   "300x300"    !"(imgr box 300x300)&"
   "300x400"    !"(imgr box 300x400)&"
   "300x500"    !"(imgr box 300x500)&"
   "400x400"    !"(imgr box 400x400)&"
   "400x500"    !"(imgr box 400x500)&"
   "500x500"    !"(imgr box 500x500)&"
}
```

As an alternative to this presentation, you could use an Xterm to get the user's preferred dimensions. Alternatively, you could modify the current method by breaking it into two submenus—one for horizontal coordinates and one for vertical coordinates. This would also require additional resource values in the **.xmenu** file.

UTILITIES

The next item on the *Main Menu* is *Utilities*. On this submenu, you find several general-purpose utilities that improve your efficiency in a windowing environment. The options on the *Utilities* menu range from command recall to dumping the contents of the X cut buffer to making image recordings of work sessions. Here is the *Utilities* menu:

```
!Note some lines are escaped for presentation
!purposes. Avoid this in your file.

Menu SystemUtils
{
 no_label                    f.separator
```

```
no_label                   f.separator
no_label                   f.separator
" Utilities "          _I  f.title
no_label                   f.separator
no_label                   f.separator
" !!"                  _!  !"(lastcommand exec 1)&"
" !-2"                 _2  !"(lastcommand exec 2)&"
" !-3"                 _3  !"(lastcommand exec 3)&"
no_label                   f.separator
no_label                   f.separator
" Refresh"             _e  f.refresh

" Save screen"         _r  !"(xwd -root > \
                                $HOME/xmenu.xwd)"

" Print screen"        _p  !"(xdpr -root)"
no_label                   f.separator
no_label                   f.separator

" Save buffer"         _S  !"(xprop -root -len 1000 \
                                CUT_BUFFER0>\$HOME/
cut.xsh)&"

" Append buffer"       _A  !"(xprop -root -len 1000 \
                       CUT_BUFFER0>>$HOME/cut.xsh)&"

no_label                   f.separator
no_label                   f.separator
" Show clipboard"      _C  !"(xclipboard -w)&"
" Update clipboard"    _U  !"(xcutsel)&"
no_label                   f.separator
no_label                   f.separator
" Record"              _R  f.menu SystemRecord
}
```

The various programs in the *Utilities* menu either call X clients directly or use different scripts. The following sections describe the X clients and scripts as appropriate. There is no section for the *Refresh* option, which simply uses Motif's **f.refresh** function to redraw the entire screen (see Chapter 6). Figure 8-9 shows the *Utilities* menu.

Command Recall

The command recall options borrow from C shell symbology and provide three easy-to-use options to recall menu commands. If you have paid close

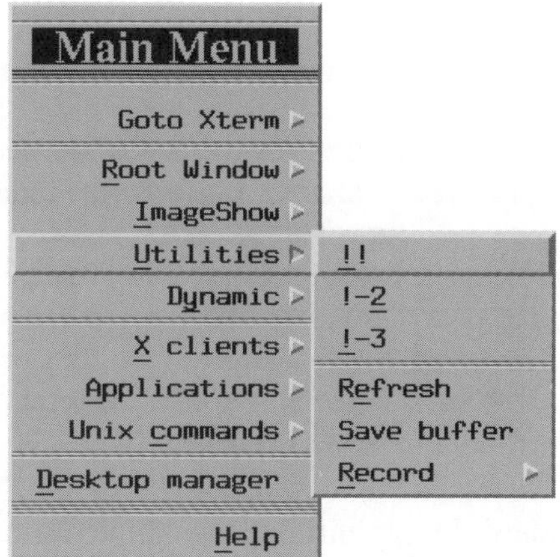

Figure 8-9 The *Utilities* submenu.

attention to the scripts in this book, you may have noticed that a certain comment and line of code has reappeared time and again:

```
# Record this command
  lastcommand $0 $1 $2 $3 &
```

What this command does is send the name of the current script file or X client, along with its parameters—up to three, because none of the clients or scripts in the Xmenu software exceed this number—to the **lastcommand** script. Here is the script:

```
#!/bin/sh -xv
# lastcommand, stores last command
# Syntax: lastcommand [options from previous cmd]
#         lastcommand -exec [1|2|3]
# Copyright (c) Alan Southerton 1993

# Initial values
  file=/tmp/.xmenu.$$
  exec=$1; n=$2

  if [ "$exec" = "exec" ]; then
     cmd='grep LASTCMD$n $HOME/.xmenu | cut -d: -f2'
     exec $cmd
```

```
        set - `echo $cmd`
    fi

# Now set the commands in .xmenu
    cmd1=$*
    cmd2=`grep LASTCMD1 $HOME/.xmenu | cut -d: -f2`
    cmd3=`grep LASTCMD2 $HOME/.xmenu | cut -d: -f2`
    grep -v LASTCMD $HOME/.xmenu > $file
    echo LASTCMD1:$cmd1   >> $file
    echo LASTCMD2:$cmd2   >> $file
    echo LASTCMD3:$cmd3   >> $file
    cp $HOME/.xmenu $HOME/.xmenu.bak
    mv $file $HOME/.xmenu
```

After defining initial values, **lastcommand** checks whether it has been invoked from the *Utilities* menu. If $exec equals "exec," this is the case and the script then executes the specified command. The $n variable contains the command number: either 1, 2, or 3. The command number is then combined with LASTCMD. For example, the next-to-last command is always LASTCMD2. As usual, the **.xmenu** file is used for storage purposes, and the **grep** and **cut** commands retrieve the value of LASTCMD*n*. Next, the **exec** command is used to execute the value of $cmd to ensure that the shell correctly parses the syntax of the command. Finally, the **set** command is used to fill the environment space with the filename and options from the just-executed command.

This brings us to the next block of code, which serves requests both from the *Utilities* menu and from scripts throughout Xmenu. The first thing that occurs here is to set $cmd1 (which represents the last command executed) equal to the contents of the environment space, represented by **$***. After this, the **lastcommand** script retrieves the values of other previous commands and sets them to $cmd2 and $cmd3. The script then updates **.xmenu** with all three values.

Screen Options

The *Save screen* and *Print screen* options are included on the SystemUtils menu to give the user a quick way of storing or printing the root window image. (Note that there is no display option; you can display an XWD file via options on the *ImageShow* menu).

The *Save screen* option uses the **-root** switch to **xwd** to inform it to immediately capture the contents of the entire root window, including any windows that overlap it. By specifying the **-root** switch, the interactive element of **xwd** is removed from the equation. Normally, if you just enter **xwd** at the command line, it presents you with a crosshair pointer and expects you to click in a window. You can also capture the root window this way.

The *Print screen* option uses the **xpdr** client, which is a hybrid of the **xwd** and **xpr** clients (see the *Print* section earlier in this chapter for information on **xpr**). Again, the **-root** switch is used. This time **xdpr** passes the switch to **xwd**, which captures the root window and passes the output to **xpr**. Because the *Print screen* option doesn't use the **-device** switch to specify a printer, **xdpr** passes the output to the default printer. If you decide to specify **-device** here, **xdpr** passes the switch onto **xpr**, which then formats the output for the given printer.

Buffer Options

The *Save buffer* and *Append buffer* options are everyday assets. The two options are almost identical. The *Save buffer* option saves the contents of the default system cut buffer to a file in the user's home directory. The *Append buffer* option appends the contents of the buffer to the same file.

The key to these options is the **xprop** utility which, in a single switch, **-len**, lets you specify the cut action and the amount of data you want to cut. Here's another look at the command for the *Append* option:

```
xprop -root -len 1000 CUT_BUFFER0 >> $HOME/cut.xsh
```

The **-root** switch tells **xprop** to query the resource database associated with the root window. As you will recall, this is the same place that **xrdb** stores resources. In addition to specifying the root window, you can specify other windows using either the **-id** or **-name** options to **xprop**. As for the **-len** switch, you can set this to any reasonable value. The unit for **-len** is bytes, not words or lines. Setting **-len** to 1000 yields about 150 to 250 words.

Clipboard Options

The clipboard options are useful if you want to give some type of organization to data that you cut and paste. Not all applications support the clipboard in X, but those that don't may support the system cut buffer, or CUT_BUFFER0. By default, Xterms support the cut buffer, but you can add a keyboard translation (see Chapter 9) that writes directly to the clipboard.

In any event, the **xcutsel** client can transfer data between the two buffers. The *Update clipboard* option invokes **xcutsel**. From this point, users are on their own. The interface to **xcutsel** is native X. It doesn't necessarily complement the Motif interface, but it makes up for it in functionality—especially if you like to use several Xterms, but need yet another window to store miscellaneous pieces of data.

Using **xcutsel** doesn't require any effort (see Figure 8-10), but the labels it uses for two of its three buttons are not user friendly—given that one of the definitions of *user friendly* is *user familiar.*

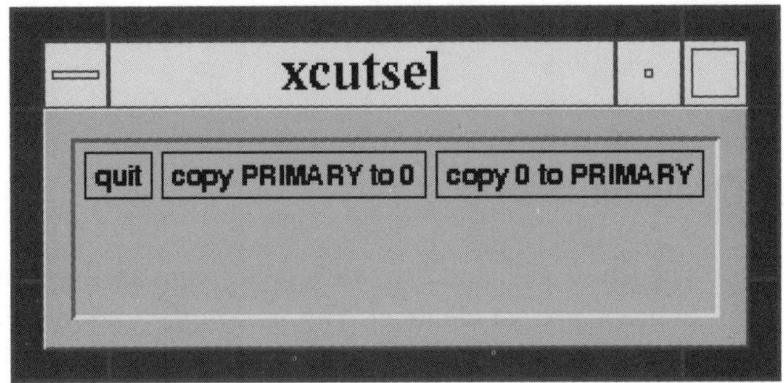

Figure 8-10 The Xcutsel window for pasting and copying text in conjunction with the X's built-in cut and paste mechanism.

The **xcutsel** button names are **copy PRIMARY to 0** and **copy 0 to PRIMARY**. Where these names come from is obvious: the first one copies from the primary buffer—the one that Xterm uses by default—and the second label copies from the clipboard buffer. Put this way—in terms of *from*, and with a little belief in user intuition—the labels could become **Primary** and **Clipboard**. Another alternative would be to use **To clipboard** and **From clipboard**. In any event, the good news is you can change the names of the labels:

```
XClipboard*set-cut: To clipboard
XClipboard*cut-sel: From clipboard
```

A third button, Quit, is also part of the **xcutsel** window. You can change this to Close if you prefer the Motif convention:

```
XClipboard: Close
```

Presenting the results of your activity with **xcutsel** is the job of **xclipboard**. The labels for these buttons are aptly named: Delete, New, Next,

Previous, and Quit. The resource suffixes for the buttons are delete, new, next, prev, text and quit. With the exception of **XClipboard*quit**, which you might want to give a value of **Close**, the buttons give a good indication of their function. Getting the text from the clipboard is the job of individual applications, but you can use the various buttons to display different text selections and then copy and paste them elsewhere. If you find yourself doing this a lot, check whether the application's keyboard translations can be modified to access the clipboard, as is the case with Xterm.

Record

The *Record* option lets users make a graphical log of their work by using the **xwd** command. Selecting *Record* brings up a submenu with options to begin and end recording. A third option lets you set the interval at which **xwd** takes a snapshot of the screen. Here is the *Record* submenu:

```
Menu SystemRecord
{
 " On"           _O   !"(xrecord on)&"
 " Off"          _f   !"(xrecord off)&"
 " Interval"     _I   f.menu SystemRecordTime
}
```

The menu to set the time interval contains five choices:

```
Menu SystemRecordTime
{
  "5"    _5   !"(xrecord 5)&"
  "10"   _0   !"(xrecord 10)&"
  "15"   _1   !"(xrecord 15)&"
  "20"   _2   !"(xrecord 20)&"
  "30"   _2   !"(xrecord 30)&"
}
```

Both menus use the **xrecord** script. The resulting XWD files are placed in the user's home directory and the filenames are constructed from the letters "xrec" and output from the **date** command. Here is the **xrecord** script:

```
#!/bin/sh
# xrecord, script to create visual log
# Syntax: xrecord [on|off|5|10|15|20|30]
# Copyright (c) Alan Southerton 1993
```

```
# Initial values
  arg=$1; i=0; seconds=`expr $arg \* 60`
  file=/tmp/.xmenu.$$
  id=`xdpyinfo | grep "root window id" | cut -d: -f2`
  pid=`grep XRECORDPID $HOME/.xmenu | cut -d: -f2`

# First attend to on/off status; in the last
# block attend to the actual recording mechanism
  case $arg in

    off) if [ "$pid" != "XXX" ]; then
            kill -9 $pid
            grep -v XRECORDPID $HOME/.xmenu > $file
            echo XRECORDPID:XXX >> $file
            cp $HOME/.xmenu $HOME/.xmenu.bak
            mv $file $HOME/.xmenu
            exit
         else
            exit
         fi ;;

     on) if [ "$pid" != "XXX" ]; then
            kill -9 $pid
         fi
         grep -v XRECORDPID $HOME/.xmenu > $file
         echo XRECORDPID:XXX >> $file
         cp $HOME/.xmenu $HOME/.xmenu.bak
         mv $file $HOME/.xmenu
         exit ;;

     5|10|15|20|30)
         seconds=`expr $arg \* 60`
         while [ 1 ]
         do
            xwd -id $id > $HOME/xrec`date + %m%d%H%M`
            sleep $seconds
         done ;;
  esac
```

Once started, **xrecord** continues working until the user terminates it with the *Off* option. This may not be desirable, given that some users may leave **xrecord** running indefinitely. Thus, it might be a good idea to add a routine to the **while** loop in the last **case** block. The routine would terminate **xrecord** after, say, a given number of XWD images had accumulated.

UNIX COMMANDS

As far as UNIX commands go, you could probably build a menu system devoted to them. The Xmenu software provides a few commands, more in the way of examples than anything else. Here is the *UNIX commands* menu:

```
Menu SystemCommands
{
  no_label          f.separator
  no_label          f.separator
  no_label          f.separator
  no_label          f.separator
  "Commands"        f.title
  no_label          f.separator
  no_label          f.separator
  " Calendar "      !"(unixcmd cal)&"
  " Processes "     !"(unixcmd ps)&"
  " Environment "   !"(unixcmd env)&"
  " Find file "     !"(unixcmd find)&"
  " List files "    !"(unixcmd ls)&"
  " Talk session "  !"(unixcmd talk)&"
}
```

Although you can call UNIX commands directly from the **.mwmrc** file—that is, if you use Xterm with its **-e** option to do so—the readability factor favors a different treatment. The way the Xmenu software does it is to use a script called **unixcmd**. Here is the **unixcmd** script:

```
#!/bin/sh
# unixcmd, script to run UNIX commands
# Syntax: unixcmd command
# Copyright (c) Alan Southerton 1993

# Initial values
  file=/tmp/.xmenu.$$
  arg=$1

# Process different commands
  case $arg in
      cal) xterm -name calendar -title "`date`" \
                 -n "`date +%m%d:%H%M`" \
                 -e cal_script ;;

       ps) xterm -name bigbox -title Processes \
```

```
                    -n ps \
                    -e ps_script ;;

         env) xterm -name bigbox -title Environment \
                    -n env \
                    -e env_script ;;

        find) xterm -name bigbox -title "Find Files" \
                    -n find \
                    -e find_script ;;

          ls) xterm -name bigbox -title "List Files" \
                    -n ls \
                    -e ls_script ;;

        talk) xterm -name getstring \
                    -e getany "User Name" $file
              user=`cat $file`
              xterm -name talk -n $user \
                    -title "Talking to $user" \
                    -e talk $user &
esac
```

Chapters 4 and 9 describe the Xterm command line options in detail, so there is no need to explain them again here. Suffice it to say that when it comes to Xterm options, the **unixcmd** script is skeletal. You will probably find yourself adding many more options—because in the case of running subordinate commands in a tailored fashion, it is advisable not to use too many resources. Otherwise, your resource files will be exploding with names such as **calendar**, **ls** and **talk**.

One important thing to notice about the **unixcmd** script is that all but one of the Xterms are run in the foreground. The initial call to **unixcmd** from **.mwmrc** is run in the background—relieving the system of a long wait—but you want **unixcmd** to wait for the Xterm and its UNIX command to complete. If you don't take this approach, **unixcmd** executes the command, the command output scrolls in the Xterm window, and the Xterm window disappears immediately. Let's look at the **ps_script** to continue the example:

```
#!/bin/sh
# ps_script, displays environment variables
# Syntax: ps_script

# Initial values
  file=/tmp/env_script.$$
```

```
# Begin procedure
# BSD: ps -aux > $file
  ps -ef > $file
  more < $file
  /bin/echo -n echo "Press RETURN to proceed"
  read key
  exit
```

The **ps_script** is straightforward. No new elements have been added to the X equation, but the one thing to notice is the read command: After the **ps** command finishes executing, the **/bin/echo -n** command displays a prompt, and the **read** command holds up further execution. And the further execution it holds up is the Xterm window closing. At this point, the user can either do as the prompt suggests—press the Return key—or use the window menu to close the window.

In **unixcmd**, the one exception to the foreground rule is the Xterm that runs the **talk** command. The reason for this is **talk** itself won't exit until the user explicitly requires it—thus obviating any need for an artificial wait with the **read** command. One other thing the **talk)** routine does is call the **getany** script, which is another general-purpose script similar to **xmenuget**. Here is the code:

```
#!/bin/sh
# getany, script to get user name
# Syntax: getany prompt file
# Copyright (c) Alan Southerton 1993

# Initial values
  prompt=$1; file=$2

# Begin routine
  echo
  echo -n "Enter $prompt: "
  read Anything
  echo $Anything > $file
```

The **getany** script uses a temporary file to place data that the calling script requires. You can modify the prompt as you see fit by specifying some string as the first argument to **getany**. And note that you must specify some word as the script is written. As an alternative to **getany**, you could use **xmenuget** by creating a new Xmenu resource specifically designed for holding temporary data. For example, you could name the resource XMENUTEMP.

HELP

Using window manager menus as a way to present a help system to users is a thoughtful practice. The Xmenu software does not come with a help system, but it could have. The *Help* option on the *Main Menu* is included for demonstration purposes. It simply brings up a copyright screen. The entry in the *Main Menu* for the help routine looks like this:

```
"              Help"      _H      !"(xhelp 001)&"
```

The script used by the *Help* option is similar to the **unixcmd** script described in the last section. If you plan on building a help system using Xterm windows, use the **xhelp** script as a starting point.

```
#!/bin/sh
# xhelp, script to display help files
# Syntax: xhelp filename
# Copyright (c) By Alan Southerton 1993

# Initial values
  helpfile=$1

# Begin routine

  xterm -name helpbox -title "Xmenu Menus" \
        -n xmenu -e help_script $helpfile
```

The script called **help_script** is necessary to avoid the waiting problems associated with Xterms loaded from the window manager menus. It simply uses **more** to display the specified file and then waits for the user to press Return.

```
#!/bin/sh
# help_script, more a help file
# Syntax: help_script filename
# Copyright (c) Alan Southerton 1993

# Initial values
  helpfile=$1

# Begin routine
  more $helpfile
  /bin/echo -n echo "Press RETURN to proceed"
  read key
  exit
```

Again, you could eliminate one step in this process by calling **help_script** directly from the **.mwmrc** file. For the sake of readability, the Xmenu software uses the intermediate step.

OTHER MENUS

Three menu options that appear in the *Main Menu* were not described in this chapter. These are the *X clients*, *Applications*, and *Desktop manager* options. Because these are site-specific concerns, little concrete explanation can be given. Additionally, because all of the programs that you would be likely to include in these menus are binary-executable programs, you can simply include the name of the program and run it in the background. For example, here's the *X clients* menu as included on the distribution diskettes:

```
Menu SystemClients
{
    no_label            f.separator
    no_label            f.separator
    no_label            f.separator
    no_label            f.separator
    " X Clients "       f.title
    no_label            f.separator
    no_label            f.separator
    " bitmap "          !"bitmap&"
    " ico "             !"ico&"
    " xbiff "           !"xbiff&"
    " xcalc "           !"xcalc&"
    " xclock "          !"xclock&"
    " xeyes "           !"xeyes&"
    " xload "           !"xload&"
}
```

Of course, the one thing wrong with this menu is that it is not designed for end users who are unfamiliar with X clients. This hasn't stopped many people who create **.mwmrc** menus, however. So the traditional role of X clients is included here for sentimental as well as example purposes.

CHAPTER 9
Epic Xterm

THE XTERM STANDARD

The Xterm is an underrated success story in the UNIX community. In other operating systems, with standard keyboard interfaces, this might go unnoticed. But for UNIX, the Xterm terminal emulator did something never accomplished before: It brought a standard keyboard interface to UNIX.

Of course, with the advent of the graphical user interface, the need for a standard keyboard interface diminishes. Application developers no longer write their applications to a hardware interface. Instead, they use callback functions to communicate key strokes and mouse button presses to the X server.

Some users find it hard to justify using Xterms. These users usually find a vendor-designed terminal emulator to be more comfortable. In the vendor implementations, however, you usually lose some amount of functionality. And, in fact, saying "some amount" is understating the case, because Xterms are so flexible that programmers who know the inner workings of Xterms can use them as translators for otherwise moribund character-mode applications.

With Xterms, you can do so many different things that it is sometimes hard just to remember what you can do. More than that, it is hard to remember *how* to do it. This is where vendor implementations succeed, because they usually offer menus and dialog boxes for customization and access to features. The built-in Xterm menus (see Figure 9-1) hardly compete with the user interface found on a terminal emulator such as Sun's **cmdtool** (see Figure 9-2) or the terminal emulators from other system vendors.

But Xterms are a standard in the X community. Every version of X ships with a copy of **xterm** in **/usr/bin/X11** or equivalent directory. Xterm is also

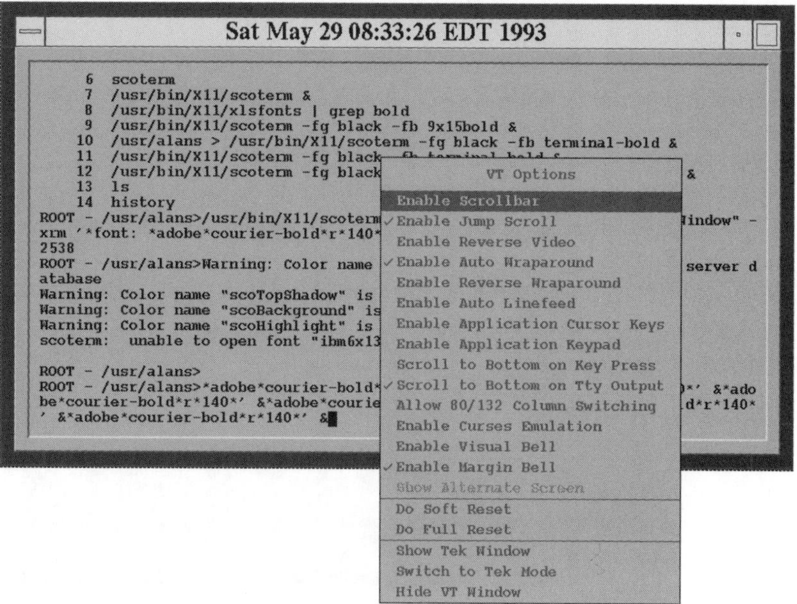

Figure 9-1 Built-in Xterm menu. Pressing and holding Ctrl-Button1 pops up this menu.

available on implementations for X on other operating systems, including DEC's OpenVMS and Quarterdeck's Desqview/X. And in its UNIXware, Novell Inc. sees fit to offer Xterm without providing an alternative terminal emulator. So you can't go wrong using Xterm. All you have to be wary of is that it is not easy for end users to learn all its features.

Given the right resources, Xterms can also appear more attractive than vendor implementations of terminal emulators. The *Default Xterm* section in this chapter makes an attempt at elevating the default existence of Xterm to this level. The rest of the chapter also describes how to make the Xterm experience better. In addition to a set of preconfigured Xterms, you will find numerous routines that let you set resources in order to get the kind of Xterm you want.

ANOTHER APPROACH

The scripts used for the *Xterms Menu* use a third approach to manipulating resources. Instead of relying on the resource database (like the *Resources Menu*), and instead of relying on a special configuration file (like the *Main Menu* relies on the **.xmenu** file), the *Xterms Menu* scripts use the **XTerm** file in the $XAPPLRESDIR directory.

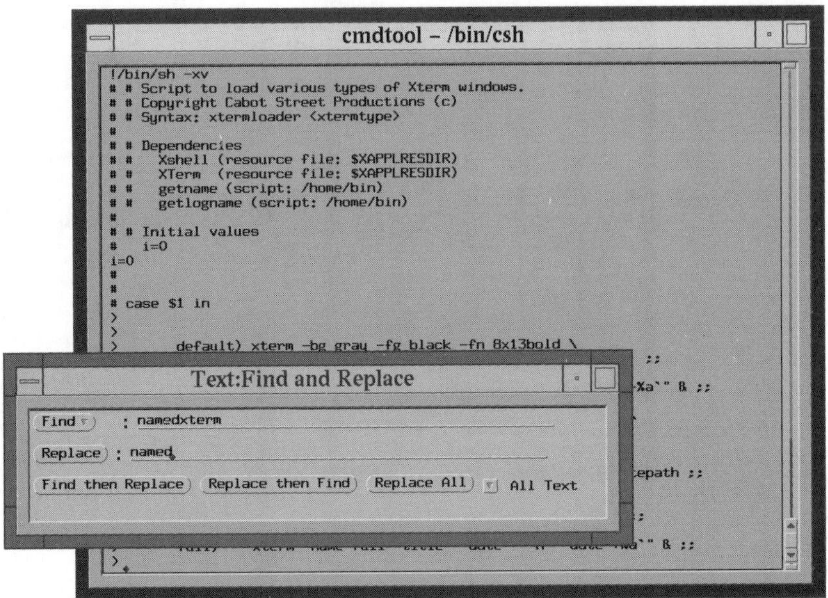

Figure 9-2 The cmdtool from Sun adds many features to the standard terminal emulator, including a search and replace function.

It's worthwhile to reflect on the three approaches to manipulating resources. The same scripting tools—**grep**, **cut** and redirection—are used to update the **XTerm** file. The **XTerm** approach—or more generally, the *application resources* approach is different from the **xrdb** approach, because its resources are not preloaded into server memory. It is similar to the homegrown approach of **.xmenu** for this reason. But it is unlike **.xmenu**, because Xterms automatically load the contents of **XTerm**. Here's a summary of the three approaches:

- *Database resources*, which the **xrdb** program loads into system memory so that they are there when you need them, should be associated with applications that you run frequently. The Xmenu software uses these exclusively for Motif resources, but you might rightly decide you want to use them for commonly used client programs, such as **XTerm**, a mail program, and other utilities. It is not advisable to use this approach for commercial applications, which tend to define many resources, and are not run as frequently as Xterms and utility programs.
- *Custom resources*, such as the **.xmenu** resources used with the *Main Menu*, let you simulate the X resource scheme. These are

appropriate for applications that don't support resources, as well as for applications that do support resources, but don't happen to support the functionality you want to achieve (see the treatment of the **xloadimage** client in Chapter 8). Additionally, custom resources can be used to store filenames, process ids, and other temporary data. The drawback to custom resources is you must write scripts to retrieve as well as set resources. Database and application resources are retrieved automatically.

- *Application resources*, which are usually stored in files the XAPPLRESDIR directory, but can be stored elsewhere such as in the user's home directory, are critical for many client programs. The **xclipboard** program, for example, hardly works without its associated resource file. What's more, you can make use of application resources if you are concerned about overloading the **xrdb** database. And application resource files are probably the best place to store keyboard translations, which do not lend themselves to script manipulation.

Splitting your attention among three methods of setting resources is time consuming. If you use the application resources method, you can't go wrong—that is, as long as you address another part of the equation: running remote applications on the local system. When you do this, the remote application will seek out an $XAPPLRESDIR file for the user loading the program. If it doesn't find one for the user, it will look elsewhere for resources files and won't find them. There are many known cures and probably a few you can dream up yourself. Here's a sampling:

- Use the UNIX standard Network Information Service (NIS) and Network File System (NFS). This propagates a single environment for users anywhere on the network.

- Use NFS, without necessarily using NIS, and have **xdm** be responsible for setting the X environment. The XAPPLRESDIR directory for all applications can then be set to an NFS directory seen by all systems.

- Create unique resource files for remote systems. Typically this file is called **.Xdefaults-***host*. You could can change the name of this file with the $XENVIRONMENT variable.

- Use yet another environment variable, $XFILESEARCHPATH, to a commonly mounted NFS system that acts primarily as a server. This is a convenient approach for mixed UNIX workstation, PC, and Apple Macintosh networks.

- Modify the **/usr/lib/X11/app-defaults** files on each system on the network, so that applications adhere to a standard set of resources on a site-specific basis. Then leave customization up to users, telling them to modify their $HOME/**.Xdefaults** file for further changes.

The Xmenu software uses the second approach to setting resources. The routines that work with the *Xterms Menu* are described in this chapter. The $XAPPLRESDIR solution is not necessarily better than others, but it gives you and end users flexibility. Presumably, $XAPPLRESDIR would point to a directory solely within each user's control such as $HOME/**resources**. If certain users don't like adding a new directory to $HOME, they can place resource files directly in $HOME. Client programs check here for resource files if $XAPPLRESDIR is not defined.

A brief word about the names of application-specific resource files: They are very specific. Most application resource files follow the convention of simply capitalizing the first letter in the filename of the associated executable file. But some don't. And Xterm is one of the ones that don't. Note that the "T" is also capitalized in **XTerm**. Other client programs that deviate from the standard are **xclipboard**, which looks for **XClipboard**, and **xcalc**, which looks for **XCalc**. So it goes.

THE DEFAULT XTERM

One thing wrong with the X Window System is it never puts its best foot forward. And nowhere is this more true than when it comes to Xterms.

The default Xterm—the Xterm that executes before anyone has any customized it—leaves much to be desired. The font is small, the background and foreground colors are uninspired, and the scrollbar needs to be activated. It is no wonder that new users make a quick decision to use an alternative terminal emulator, if one exists on the system.

But you can wash the Xterm blues away by making sure that the default Xterm on your system is well configured. And once you settle upon a configuration, don't change it. Use named Xterms to run Xterms for those times that the default won't do—and for other times, when you and your users prefer features not available in the default Xterm. Here, then, are some default **XTerm** resources worth keeping:

```
!Default Xterm Resources
!Note: some lines are escaped for presentation; this
!is not necessary in your file (and may not work).
```

```
  VT100.background: #010101
  VT100.foreground: #77e900
  VT100.pointerColor: #d74675
  VT100.pointerColorBackground: #fcfbfb
  VT100.scrollBar: true

  XTerm*alwaysHighlight: yes
  XTerm*background: gray
  XTerm*foreground: white

  XTerm*font: -adobe-courier-medium \
              -r-normal*14-140-75-75-m-90*

  XTerm*internalBorder: 10
  XTerm*marginBell: yes
  XTerm*pointerShape: bogosity
  XTerm*saveLines: 500
  XTerm*thickness: 10
  XTerm*visualBell: false
  XTerm*internalBorder: 15
  XTerm*VT100.cursorColor: #fbf9fb

!Arbitary comment
  XTerm*mycomment: "Say Anything"
```

Generally, the resources here do little in the way of turning on special functionality for the default Xterm. Instead, for the most part, they modify Xterm components usually available when you invoke the system's default Xterm. The one exception is the scrollbar, which does not come up with the system's default Xterm. The following line turns the scrollbar on:

```
VT100*scrollBar: true
```

You might be wondering why the **VT100** class name is used here. The reason is that Xterms can be designed from three different sets of resources: **VT100**, Tektronix (or **TEK4014**), and generic **XTerm** resources. In some instances, you cannot get the effects you want by simply using the generic **XTerm** resources. The scrollbar, which is a **VT100** component, is one of them. True, you could have used **XTerm*scrollBar** to activate the scrollbar, but you would run out of luck if you tried setting its color without using **VT100**. (See *The Colors Submenu* in this chapter for more information.)

The other resources in the example are typical settings. Things like the font, pointer shape, scrollbar thickness, and scroll buffer are set to provide a custom feel to the Xterm. You and your site may have different requirements. The idea, again, is to make the default Xterm more than the system's default version. The next two sections will help you attain this goal.

Xterm's Built-in Menus

Xterm comes with four built-in menus. By default, you invoke these menus by pressing the Ctrl key and pressing one of the mouse buttons. This accounts for the *Main Options*, *VT Options* and *VT Fonts* menus, respectively. The fourth menu, *Tek Options*, replaces the *VT Options* menu when you have invoked the Tektronix version of Xterm.

The *Main Options* menu provides little real assistance to users. It gives you numerous ways to terminate an Xterm, but this is useful only if the Xterm is hung for some reason. It does allow you to turn on a logging file, which is handy, but there is no way to modify the name or location of the logging file. There is a redraw option for the window, but if you have the same type of option on a root window menu, or your default window menu, it is a duplication of effort.

The *VT Options* menu is more useful. It allows you to do things such as toggle the scrollbar, enable reverse video, and open a Tektronix Xterm window. Alternatively, if you are working in a Tektronix window to start with, you use the *VT Options* menu to move to a VT100 window. The *VT Options* menu also offers some features that many users will simply ignore, including the ability to generate cursor escape sequences and a fix to **curses** emulation.

The *VT Fonts* menu is perhaps the most useful menu, at least for users who like to change fonts. It allows you to toggle between five default fonts, a font you have set with an escape sequence (see Chapter 4), and a font you have selected using the **xfontsel** client. You can change the alternate Xterm fonts using Xterm's **font1**, **font2**, **font3**, and **font4** resources. The default font is the system default font, which is the **fixed** font.

So now we have something additional that we can add to our default Xterm. And, along with the changes to the alternate fonts, let's change the menu item labels associated with them:

```
!Modified menu labels for Xterm
!Add to $XAPPLRESDIR/XTerm file
!Note: some lines are escaped for presentation; this
!is not necessary in your file (and may not work).

XTerm*fontMenu*font1*Label: Courier Bold 12
XTerm*VT100*font1: \
      -adobe-courier-medium-r-\
      normal—12-120-75-75-m-70-iso8859-1
XTerm*fontMenu*font2*Label: Courier Bold 14
XTerm*VT100*font2: \
-adobe-courier-medium-r-\
```

```
     normal—14-140-75-75-m-90-iso8859-1
XTerm*fontMenu*font3*Label: Courier Bold 18
XTerm*VT100*font3: \
     -adobe-courier-medium-r-\
     normal—18-180-75-75-m-110-iso8859-1
XTerm*fontMenu*font4*Label: Courier Bold 24
XTerm*VT100*font4: \
     -adobe-courier-medium-r-\
     normal—24-240-75-75-m-150-iso8859-1
```

When setting these resources, you have to do two things: Use the **XTerm** class designation, rather than beginning the resource statement with a * symbol; and specify the full font string, rather than using a wildcarded font string.

You can change other labels in the Xterm menus if you want. Unfortunately, you cannot remove a menu item through resources. The items are hardcoded into the Xterm application. If you want to edit the source code for Xterm, you can remove menu items. Check with your vendor before taking this step, however. Your vendor may have added some functionality to enhance performance.

The best resource for menu item label names, as well as for other defaults, is the **XTerm** file in **/usr/lib/X11/app-defaults**. This is an important file because it determines many of Xterm's defaults, even if you have Xterm resources specified in other resource files such as $XAPPLRESDIR/**XTerm** or $HOME/**XTerm**. If you institute you own Xterm defaults, you might want to make changes in this file. Make a backup copy first, so you have something to refer to later if necessary. For reference, here is the standard **XTerm** file as shipped by the MIT X Consortium:

```
! Xterm Resource Definitions
!Note: some lines are escaped for presentation; this
!is not necessary in your file (and may not work).

*SimpleMenu*BackingStore: NotUseful
*SimpleMenu*menuLabel.font: \
     -adobe-helvetica-bold-r-\
     normal—*-120-*-*-*-*-iso8859-*

*SimpleMenu*menuLabel.vertSpace: 100
*SimpleMenu*HorizontalMargins: 16
*SimpleMenu*Sme.height: 16
*SimpleMenu*Cursor: left_ptr
*mainMenu.Label:  Main Options
*mainMenu*securekbd*Label: Secure Keyboard
```

```
*mainMenu*allowsends*Label: Allow SendEvents
*mainMenu*logging*Label: Log to File
*mainMenu*redraw*Label: Redraw Window
*mainMenu*suspend*Label: Send STOP Signal
*mainMenu*continue*Label: Send CONT Signal
*mainMenu*interrupt*Label: Send INT Signal
*mainMenu*hangup*Label: Send HUP Signal
*mainMenu*terminate*Label: Send TERM Signal
*mainMenu*kill*Label: Send KILL Signal
*mainMenu*quit*Label: Quit

*vtMenu.Label: VT Options
*vtMenu*scrollbar*Label: Enable Scrollbar
*vtMenu*jumpscroll*Label: Enable Jump Scroll
*vtMenu*reversevideo*Label: Enable Reverse Video
*vtMenu*autowrap*Label: Enable Auto Wraparound
*vtMenu*reversewrap*Label: Enable Reverse Wraparound
*vtMenu*autolinefeed*Label: Enable Auto Linefeed
*vtMenu*appcursor*Label: Enable Application Cursor Keys
*vtMenu*appkeypad*Label: Enable Application Keypad
*vtMenu*scrollkey*Label: Scroll to Bottom on Key Press
*vtMenu*scrollttyoutput*Label: \
     Scroll to Bottom on Tty Output
*vtMenu*allow132*Label: Allow 80/132 Column Switching
*vtMenu*cursesemul*Label: Enable Curses Emulation
*vtMenu*visualbell*Label: Enable Visual Bell
*vtMenu*marginbell*Label: Enable Margin Bell
*vtMenu*altscreen*Label: Show Alternate Screen
*vtMenu*softreset*Label: Do Soft Reset
*vtMenu*hardreset*Label: Do Full Reset
*vtMenu*clearsavedlines*Label: \
     Reset and Clear Saved Lines
*vtMenu*tekshow*Label: Show Tek Window
*vtMenu*tekmode*Label: Switch to Tek Mode
*vtMenu*vthide*Label: Hide VT Window

*fontMenu.Label: VT Fonts
*fontMenu*fontdefault*Label: Default
*fontMenu*font1*Label: Unreadable
*VT100*font1: nil2
*fontMenu*font2*Label: Tiny
*VT100*font2: 5x7
*fontMenu*font3*Label: Small
*VT100*font3: 6x10
*fontMenu*font4*Label: Medium
*VT100*font4: 7x13
```

```
*fontMenu*font5*Label: Large
*VT100*font5: 9x15
*fontMenu*font6*Label: Huge
*VT100*font6: 10x20

!Application overrides fontescape and fontsel
*fontMenu*fontescape*Label: Escape Sequence
*fontMenu*fontsel*Label: Selection

!Resources for Tektronix emulation
*tekMenu.Label: Tek Options
*tekMenu*tektextlarge*Label: Large Characters
*tekMenu*tektext2*Label: #2 Size Characters
*tekMenu*tektext3*Label: #3 Size Characters
*tekMenu*tektextsmall*Label: Small Characters
*tekMenu*tekpage*Label: PAGE
*tekMenu*tekreset*Label: RESET
*tekMenu*tekcopy*Label: COPY
*tekMenu*vtshow*Label: Show VT Window
*tekMenu*vtmode*Label: Switch to VT Mode
*tekMenu*tekhide*Label: Hide Tek Window
*tek4014*fontLarge: 9x15
*tek4014*font2: 8x13
*tek4014*font3: 6x13
*tek4014*fontSmall: 6x10
```

Xterm Translations

Xterm gives you all the flexibility you need when it comes to mapping keyboard and mouse translations—making translations one of the most important resources that you can set at a default, systemwide level. To use the translation resource, you create an entry in a resource file, specify either the keyword **#override**, **#replace**, or **#augment**, and escape the line return:

```
*VT100.Translations: #override \
```

The reason you need to escape the line return is that the translation resource statement, plus all the key mappings that follow it, must be one long, continuous string. When the X server reads the string, it still needs to know where a line ends. As a result, for individual keyboard statements, you must terminate the line with **\n**. This means that most of your statements will look like this:

```
<Key>F19: hard-reset() \n\
```

You'll want to know what you can and cannot set with Xterm translation resources. You can refer to the Xterm man page for a full description of translations. Table 9-1 provides a summary of some of the more interesting translations. (One might argue that translations are different from resources and that's why they're called translations, not resources. But it's hard to deny that translations are not a resource for changing the interface.)

Table 9-1 Selected Xterm Keyboard Translations

Translation	Description
insert-selection	Inserts text from the specified buffer. Two arguments are required. The first is either PRIMARY, SECONDARY, or CLIPBOARD. The second is an optional buffer, ranging from CUT_BUFFER0 to CUT_BUFFER7.
keymap	Defines a new translation table. You can use this to create unique translations for named Xterms, but you don't have to use it to change the default translation table.
scroll-back	Scrolls backward through the buffer. One argument is required: page, halfpage, pixel, or line.
scroll-forw	Scrolls forward through the buffer. One argument is required: page, halfpage, pixel, or line.
select-start	Specifies the beginning of text selection.
select-end	Ends text selection. Two arguments are required. The first is either PRIMARY, SECONDARY, or CLIPBOARD. The second is an optional buffer, ranging from CUT_BUFFER0 to CUT_BUFFER7.
select-extend	Extends text selection. Must be a mouse event.
set-vt-font	Another way to set Xterm fonts. Two arguments are required. The first is the font coinciding with the items on the VT Fonts menu. Either the first letter or number in the item is used, so you have **d1234es** to choose from. The second argument is the font string. An optional third item lets you also specify the bold font, for times when an escape sequence displays text in boldface.
string	Inserts a text string. Ideal for often-repeated text strings. Also ideal for executing commands in the shell.
soft-reset	Resets the scrolling region.
hard-reset	Resets several default values, including scrolling region and window size. Also clears the screen.

If you need to know the names of key and mouse, you can use the **xev** client program to monitor them. As with most X clients, **xev** should reside in **/usr/bin/X11** (see Chapter 4).

For events that require modifiers, you use a ~ character before special key names such as Ctrl and Meta. You also put a whitespace between the modifier and the key or button event it is modifying:

```
~Meta <Btn1Down>: select-start()\n\
~Meta <Btn1Motion>: select-extend()\n\
Button1 <Btn2Down>: select-end(CLIPBOARD)\n\
~Meta <Btn2Up>: insert-selection(PRIMARY,CLIPBOARD)
```

This sequence of translations lets you paste data to the clipboard by pressing the left mouse button, extending the text selection, and then pressing the middle mouse button. It lets you retrieve the text by holding down the Meta key—usually, the Alt key—and pressing and releasing the middle mouse buttons. These and other translations could be added to the default Xterm. Here is a more extensive set:

```
*VT100.Translations: #override \
  <Key>F1: string(0xff1b) \n\
  Key>F2: string("!-2") string(0x0d) \n\
  <Key>F3: string("!!") string(0x0d) \n\
  <Key>F4: string("history") string(0x0d) \n\
  <Key>F5: string("ls -xf") string(0x0d) \n\
  <Key>F6: string("ls -ls | more") string(0x0d) \n\
  <Key>F8: string("ps -ef | more") string(0x0d) \n\
  <Key>F9: string("df") string(0x0d) \n\
  <Key>F10: string("who | more") string(0x0d) \n\
  <Key>F14: string("cd ..") string(0x0d) \n\
  <Key>F19: hard-reset() \n\
  <Key>F20: string("xterm") string(0x0d) \n\
  Button1 <Btn2Down>: select-end(CLIPBOARD)\n\
  ~Meta <Btn2Up>: insert-selection(PRIMARY,CLIPBOARD)\n\
  <Key>Menu: insert-selection(PRIMARY, CUT_BUFFER0) \n\
  <Key>DRemove: scroll-back(1,page) \n\
  <Key>Next: scroll-forw(1,page) \n\
  <Key>Insert: scroll-back(1,halfpage) \n\
  <Key>Prior: scroll-forw(1,halfpage)
```

These translations are in addition to those already defined in the default **XTerm** file. As a result, you do not need to define translations for selecting text. As in the previous example, this set of resources does allow you to cut and paste to the clipboard. And it also lets you paste from the primary cut buffer by pressing a key. In the example, a key called Menu (from a DECstation) is bound to this function. Other key names such as DRemove and Next are system specific, as is the number of function keys at your disposal. Most of the translations in the example bind UNIX commands to keys.

THE XTERMS MENU

Of the three root window menus, the *Xterms Menu* is the most compact. All of its menu options either load various Xterms or adjust resources associated with Xterms. Even the *Clone* option, which provides a technique for duplicating the resources of a running application, works with Xterms.

Unlike the other two root window menus, the *Xterms Menu* has no slide option. Recall that with the *Resources Menu* and *Main Menu*, you can slide to the next root window menu: *Resources Menu* slides to *Main Menu*, which slides to *Xterms Menu*. If you want a full loop between menus, add a slide function to Xterms so that it calls the *Resources Menu*.

The design of *Xterms Menu* is flexible enough so that it could become a submenu of another menu. The first option, again named *Xterms Menu*, provides a selection of different Xterms. Let's take a look at the menu.

```
! Root Window Menu: Button 3 (right)
Menu XtermsMenu
{
  " "                               f.nop
  no_label                          f.separator
  @//usr/xmenu/bitmaps/xterms       f.title
  no_label                          f.separator
  no_label                          f.separator
  " "                               f.nop
  "          Xterms"      _X        f.menu XtermChoices
  no_label                          f.separator
  no_label                          f.separator
  "          Colors"      _C        f.menu XtermColors
  "           Fonts"      _F        f.menu XtermFonts
  "        Pointers"      _P        f.menu XtermPointers
  "          Scroll"      _S        f.menu XtermScrolling
  "            Misc"      _M        f.menu XtermMisc
  no_label                          f.separator
  no_label                          f.separator
  "           Xmuse"      _C        !"(xmuse)"
  "           Clone"      _C        !"(clone)"
}
```

The purpose of the *Xterms Menu* is twofold: to provide a quick and consistent way to access a variety of Xterms. This is the intent of the *Xterms* submenu. The next five options also are submenus. And these fulfill the second purpose: to provide a quick and consistent way to change Xterm resources. The last two items, *Muse* and *Clone*, are different enough from each to stand alone, but you easily include them on the *Xterms* submenu.

XTERM CHOICES

The *Xterms* choices submenu (see Figure 9-3) provides a selection of different Xterms. The types range from small to large Xterms to ones that display the path in the titlebar to ones designed for creating log files.

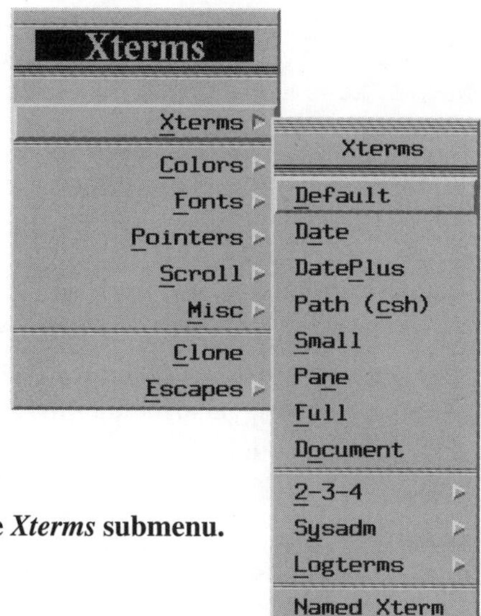

Figure 9-3 The *Xterms* submenu.

In the actual software, as you can see from Figure 9-3, the *Xterms* choices submenu is simply labeled *Xterms*. In this book, however, it is referred to as the *Xterms* choices submenu. Here is the **.mwmrc** code for the *Xterms* choices submenu.

```
Menu XtermChoices
{
  no_label                f.separator
  no_label                f.separator
  no_label                f.separator
  no_label                f.separator
```

```
  " Xterms"                       f.title
  no_label                        f.separator
  no_label                        f.separator
  " Default "           _D       !"(xtermloader default)&"
  " Date "              _a       !"(xtermloader date)"
  " DatePlus "          _P       !"(xtermloader date2)"
  " Path (csh) "        _c       !"(xtermloader path)"
  " Small "             _S       !"(xtermloader small)"
  " Pane "              _n       !"(xtermloader pane)"
  " Full "              _F       !"(xtermloader full)"
  " Document "          _o       !"(xtermloader doc)"
  no-label                        f.separator
  no-label                        f.separator
  " 2-3-4 "             _2       f.menu Xterm234
  " Sysadm"             _y       f.menu XtermSysAdm
  " Logterms"           _L       f.menu XtermLogging
  no-label                        f.separator
  no-label                        f.separator
  " Named Xterm "       _X       !"(xtermloader xname)"
}
```

There are eight predesigned Xterms immediately available on the *Xterms* choices submenu. There are more than ten others available on the submenus *2-3-4*, *Sysadm*, and *Logterms*. And with the *Named Xterm* option, you can summon any Xterm as named in a resource file.

As you can see from the menu, the **xtermloader** script executes the different Xterms. The script also handles the Xterm selections on the three submenus. Here is the code:

```
#!/bin/sh
# xtermloader, loads various Xterms
# Syntax: xtermloader <xtermtype>
# Copyright (c) By Alan Southerton 1993

# Dependencies
# Xmenu (resource file: $XAPPLRESDIR)
# XTerm  (resource file: $XAPPLRESDIR)
# getname (script: /home/bin)
# getlogname (script: /home/bin)

# Initial values
  file=/tmp/.xmenu.$$

# Remove temporary file on exit
  trap "rm $file; exit 0 1 2 3 15"
```

```
# Load the Xterm(s)
  case $1 in

    default) xterm -bg gray -fg black \
                   -fn terminal-bold \
                   -title Xmenu -n Xmenu &  ;;

    date)    xterm -name Xmenu -title "`date`" \
                   -n "`date +%a`" & ;;

    date+)   xterm -name Xmenu -title "" \
                   -n "`date +%a`" \
                   -e xtmulti1 ;; #no &

    path)    xterm -name Xmenu -n `pwd` \
                   -title "`hostname`:`pwd`" \
                   -e updatepath ;;

    doc)     xterm -name xtdoc & ;;

    full)    xterm -name full -title "`date`" \
                   -n "`date +%a`" & ;;

    console) xterm -name console -C -iconic \
                   -n console \
             -title "console:`hostname`:`date`" & ;;

    small)   xterm -name small -title "`date`" \
                   -n "`date +%a`" \
                   -geometry 78x12+15+40 & ;;

    pane)   xterm -name pane \
                -title "`hostname`:$USER:`date`" & ;;

    xname)  xterm -name getinput \
                  -title "Get Xterm Name" \
                  -e getany $file Xterm
            xterm -name `cat $file` & ;;

    terms)  terms=1
            while [ ${terms} -le $2 ]
            do
             xterm -name Xmenu \
                   -title "`date`" -n "`date +%a`"  &
              terms=`expr $terms + 1`
            done ;;
```

```
# Turn on logging with personal filename.
  log1) xterm -name getinput \
              -title "Get Log Filename" \
              -e xmenuget $file Log
        xterm -title "`date`" -n $USER \
              -l -lf `cat $file` ;;

 # Turn on logging and put date in file name.
   log2)  xterm -name Xmenu \
          -title "`date`" -n $USER \
          -l -lf "$HOME/log.`date +%m%d%y`" & ;;

 # Turn on logging and filter log file.
   log3)  xterm -name Xmenu \
               -title "`date`" -n $USER \
               -l -lf "| grep $USER \
               > $HOME/log.`date +%m%d%y`" & ;;

 # Turn on logging and keep filtered
 #  and regular logs.
   log4)  xterm -name Xmenu \
        -title "`date`" -n "`date +%m/%d`" \
        -l -lf "| tee -a \
        $HOME/log1.`date` +%m%d` \
        | grep $USER>$HOME/log.`date +%m%d`" & ;;

 # An Xterm with Ethernet address
 #  in titlebar for SunOS.
   ethernet) xterm -title "`dmesg | \
                          grep 'Ethernet'`" & ;;

 # An Xterm with logged-in users in titlebar.
   whoterm) users=`who | cut -c1-8 | sort -u`
            xterm -n $USER \
                 -title "`eval echo $users`" & ;;

 # The following Xterms are not associated
 # with the Xterms Menu in the .mwmrc file.
 # They are for utility purposes.

   help) xterm -name helpbox -title "Quick X" \
               -n "Quick X" -e help_script & ;;

      *) xterm -fn '*adobe-cou*bold*nor*140*' ;;
esac
```

You can use the **xtermloader** script from the command line as well as the **.mwmrc** file. You don't have to execute **xtermloader** in the background from the command line, because Xterms are loaded in the background by the script. Note, too, that the Xterms in **xtermloader** take advantage of resources defined in $XAPPLRESDIR/**XTerm**. The final Xterm, as occurs in the *) block, does not use any resources. The following sections describe some of the more interesting options. Those not described are self-explanatory.

The Default Xterm

The **xtermloader** script actually has two default Xterms. The first one is associated with the *Default* menu option. The second one, which needs no explanation, is the default for the **case** statement for users who run **xtermloader** from the command line. The *Default* option brings up an Xterm that is defined strictly by its command line.

```
xterm -bg gray -fg black -fn terminal-bold \
      -title Xmenu -n Xmenu &
```

The *Default* Xterm uses the system's **terminal-bold** font, which is an alias available on many systems (you may change this if necessary). It also specifies gray as the background color and black as the foreground color. Both the titlebar and icon label display the word "Xmenu."

The Date Xterm

The *Date* option produces an Xterm that displays the current date and time. Both the date and time remain static, however. This option is offered because it makes it easy to tell when you fired up a given Xterm. Here is the command line again:

```
xterm -name Xmenu \
      -title "`date`" -n "`date +%H:%M" &
```

The not-too-obvious thing here is that you must use double quotation marks around the command substitution for the **date** command. If you don't, Xterm attempts to load the first distinct string in the **date** command's output—and fails miserably.

The **-title** option loads the entire output from the **date** command into the titlebar. The **-n** option simply loads the time in *hours:minutes* notation. Also in the command line is the **-name** option, which makes this a named Xterm. Here are the resources associated with the Xterm called Xmenu:

```
Xmenu.VT100.background: #010101
Xmenu*alwaysHighlight: yes
Xmenu*marginBell: yes
Xmenu.VT100.cursorColor: #fbf9fb
Xmenu.VT100.pointerColor: #d74675
Xmenu.VT100.pointerColorBackground: #fcfbfb
Xmenu*font: -adobe-courier-medium-r-\
                    normal*14-140-75-75-m-90*
Xmenu*visualBell: false
Xmenu*internalBorder: 10
Xmenu*pointerShape: bogosity
Xmenu.VT100.foreground: #77e900
Xmenu.VT100.scrollBar: true
Xmenu*background: #bebfbd
Xmenu*foreground: #0066c0
Xmenu*thickness: 15
Xmenu*saveLines: 500
```

If you intend on using the *Date* Xterm—and other Xterms loaded by **xtermloader**—you should include the **Xmenu** resources in the $XAPPL-RESDIR/**XTerm** file. Note that some of these resources duplicate the default resources suggested earlier, so you could pair the list down somewhat.

The Date+ Xterm

For users who have no need for a static date and time, the *Date+* option is available. It uses a script called **timedaemon** to update the time each minute:

```
#!/bin/sh
# timedaemon, starts timedaemon script
# Syntax: timedaemon ptty ppid
# Copyright (c) Alan Southerton 1993
# Initial values
  tty=$1; ppid=$2

  while [ 1 ]
  do
```

```
    string="`date +'%A    %b %d    %I:%M %p        '`"
    /bin/echo -n ";`echo $string`/" > $tty
    seconds=`date +%S`
    nap=`expr 60 - $seconds`
    pid=`ps -e | grep -v timedaemon | \
                awk '/$ppid/ && ! /awk/ {print $1}'`
    if [ "$pid" != "" ]; then
       sleep $nap
    else
       break
    fi
  done
```

The **timedaemon** script immediately writes the current time to the titlebar of the Xterm specified by $tty. The next time through the **while** loop, however, it has adjusted the time to be correct to the current second. It does this by using command substitution to obtain the current value for $second. It then subtracts $seconds from **60** using the **expr** command.

How does the **timedaemon** script know when to end? The $ppid variable passed from **xkick** is vital here. The $ppid variable contains the process id associated with the Xterm window. This gives **timedaemon** something to evaluate. It does so by executing **ps** and piping the contents through **grep** and **awk**. The result from the operation, using command substitution, is stored in the $pid variable. The subsequent **if** statement checks to see whether $pid is null. If it is null, **timedaemon** exits.

Alone, **timedaemon** is hardly functional. It needs to be run as a forked process—and this is where **xkick** enters the scene. The Xmenu software executes **xkick** from the **xtermloader** script. Here is the relevant code from **xtermloader**:

```
xterm -name Xmenu -title "" -n "`date +%a`" \
      -e xkick  #no bg operation
```

Note two things about the command. First, the command is run in the foreground in order for **xkick** to stay active (although no **tty** is associated with the process). Second, no text is supplied to the title option, as indicated by the "" sequence. Now let's take a look at the **xkick** script:

```
#!/bin/sh
# xkick, starts timedaemon script
# Syntax: xkick
# Copyright (c) Alan Southerton 1993
# Initial values
  tty=`tty`; pid=$$
```

```
# Call timedaemon script
  $XMENU/timedaemon $tty $pid &

# Execute intermediate shell
  exec $SHELL
```

What is going on here? The need for executing a second shell in **xkick** arises because the shell that usually executes has been diverted using Xterm's **-e** option. During the diversion, **xkick** obtains the current device name using the **tty** command and starts up the **timedaemon** script. Critically, **xkick** passes $tty to **timedaemon**, which could not obtain the correct **tty** itself because, upon execution, it is disassociated with the Xterm. The **xkick** script ends the diversion by invoking a shell to associate with the Xterm.

The Path Xterm—C Shell Only

It is a time-honored practice to include the current path in the shell's command line prompt. Someday, it might be just as common to see the path in the titlebar of an Xterm window. The *Path* option puts the current path into the titlebar, thanks to Xterm escape sequences. Here's the command line:

```
xterm -name Xmenu -n 'pwd' \
      -title "'hostname':'pwd'" -e updatepath;
```

The *Path* Xterm works with the C shell, but not the Korn shell because its prompt setting mechanism is not flexible enough to accept an Xterm escape sequence. You could, however, use a Korn shell function—or Bourne shell function, for that matter—to update the path in the titlebar.

The key to updating the path is the following **if** statement contained in the C shell's startup file, **.cshrc**:

```
set pathtest = /tmp/'tty | sed -n
's/\/dev\///p''.'hostname'
if ( -e $pathtest )  then
  set prompt="[\! ^H][$cwd] "
  alias cd 'cd \!*; /bin/echo -n \
   "^[]0;'hostname':$cwd^G";set prompt="[\! ^H][$cwd] "'
  rm $pathtest
else
  set prompt="['hostname']<$cwd># "
  alias cd 'cd \!*; set prompt="['hostname']<$cwd> "'
endif
```

The **if** statement works by checking for the existence of a temporary file. The temporary file, which is stored in the **/tmp** directory and consists of output from **tty** and **whoami** commands, is created after the user invokes the *Path* option, but before the **.cshrc** file is read. The script that sets the temporary file is straightforward:

```
#!/bin/sh
# updatepath, create .cshrc test file
# Syntax: updatepath
# Copyright (c) Alan Southerton 1993

# Create test file
  file=/tmp/`tty | sed -n 's/\/dev\///p'`.`hostname`
  echo ON > $file
  csh
```

If the test file is created, the test routine in **.cshrc** goes on to alias the **cd** command to include an Xterm escape sequence that sends the hostname and current path to the titlebar. The escape sequence is **^[ ]0**. The actual string sent to the titlebar consists of the output of the hostname command and the value of the $cwd built-in C shell variable. As usual for a titlebar escape sequence, it is terminated by **^G** (which is to say Ctrl-G). In the last step in the script, the startup routine also sets the prompt for the command line.

The Console Xterm

Think carefully before including the *Console* option for other users. As a customizer or system administrator, you might find the *Console* option a real asset, because it redirects system messages to an Xterm, instead of splattering them on the screen.

But the console Xterm can cause problems. For one thing, when you execute a new console Xterm, any previously running console Xterm no longer operates as the console. And for another thing, the console Xterm can represent a security hole, especially if someone surreptitiously runs it from a remote location. In any event, here's the command line:

```
xterm -name console -C \
      -iconic -n console \
      -title "console:`hostname`:`date`" &
```

In addition to specifying the **-C** option, which starts the Xterm as a console Xterm, the command line loads special resources, thanks to the **-name** option:

```
console*background: black
console*font: *adobe-courier-bold-r-normal*180*
console*foreground: green
console*geometry: 75x32+75+40
console*internalBorder: 15
console*saveLines: 1024
console*scrollBar: True
console*thickness: 25
```

These resources are fairly standard. You'll notice that a larger-than-usual font is used. And after you run the console Xterm, you'll notice that the window is fairly large. Also, the scroll buffer is set to 1024 lines, which again is larger than normal. All of these features, however, are useful in a console window.

The Named Xterm

The *Named* option brings up a text input window so that you can specify an Xterm by its resource name. In the **xtermloader** script, an Xterm is run first to get the text input (using the **getany** script explained in Chapter 8):

```
xterm -name getinput \
      -title "Get Xterm Name" \
      -e getany $file Xterm

xterm -name `cat $file` &
```

When all is said and done, the command line for the Xterm that gets the text input is more complicated than the one for the named Xterm. One reason for this is that the command uses neither the **-title** nor the **-n** option. Instead, it lets Xterm automatically designate these by using the string from the **-name** option.

The 2-3-4 Submenu

The *2-3-4* submenu gives you a handy way of starting multiple Xterms. Sometimes, even at the beginning of a work session, you know you are going to need more than one Xterm. So why not start them all at the same time? Here's the **.mwmrc** entry:

```
Menu Xterm234
{
 " 2 "   !"(xtermloader terms 2)&"
 " 3 "   !"(xtermloader terms 3)&"
 " 4 "   !"(xtermloader terms 4)&"
}
```

Each entry calls the **terms)** routine in **xtermloader**. A small **while** loop takes care of loading the Xterms:

```
terms=1
while [ ${terms} -le $2 ]
do
  xterm -name Xmenu \
        -title "'date'" -n "'date +%a'"  &
  terms='expr $terms + 1'
done
```

The familiar **Xmenu** set of resources sets up the Xterms for the *2-3-4* option. The equally familiar time and date string appears in the titlebar window.

The Sysadm Submenu

Two of the three Xterms on the *Sysadm* submenu provide ways to mix UNIX commands with Xterms. The other option brings up a console window (see *The Console Xterm* earlier in this chapter). You might note, however, that placing the console Xterm on the *Sysadm* submenu is okay, but don't give access to inexperienced users. Here's the submenu code:

```
Menu XtermSysAdm
{
 " Who "            !"(xtermloader whoterm)"
 " Console "        !"(xtermloader console)"
 " Ethernet "       !"(xtermloader ethernet)"
}
```

The two new items call separate routines. Here is the command line for the *Who* option:

```
users='who | cut -c1-8 | sort -u'
       xterm -n $USER -title "'eval echo $users'" &
```

Using command substitution, the variable $users is set equal to the set of users. The variable is then echoed, again with command substitution, so the titlebar receives the necessary text string.

The other option, *Ethernet*, requires a system-specific command that delivers up a system's Ethernet address. On Sun systems, you can get the address from the output of the **dmesg** command:

```
xterm -title "`dmesg | grep 'Ethernet'`" &
```

Again, command substitution is used to obtain the string for the **-title** option. The resulting display in the titlebar is handy if you're one of the many people who have trouble remembering Ethernet addresses.

The Logterms Option

Of the three *Xterms* submenus, the *Logterms* submenu has the most to offer. It gives you four different types of logfiles to choose from, plus a mechanism for customizing your own type of logfile. Here is the submenu:

```
Menu XtermLogging
{
 "Personal"     !"(xtermloader log1)&"
 "Date"         !"(xtermloader log2)&"
 "Filter"       !"(xtermloader log3)&"
 "Maximum"      !"(xtermloader log4)&"
}
```

Because Xterm doesn't give you an interactive way to name a logfile, GUI users must resort to the command line to specify a unique name for a logfile, or accept the default name, which is $HOME/**XtermLog.$$**. The first option, *Personal*, solves this problem.

The *Personal* option uses another Xterm to get text input before executing the logterm. Here is the code from **xtermloader**:

```
log1)    xterm -name getinput \
               -title "Get Log Filename" \
               -e xmenuget $file Log

         xterm -title "`date`" -n $USER \
               -l -lf `cat $file` ;;
```

As usual, the temporary $file is passed to **xmenuget**, which places the user's input into it. The second Xterm command—the one that actually loads the logterm—uses the **-l** switch to specify the logterm function and the **-lf** switch to specify the name for the logfile. The **-title** switch takes the familiar **date** output and **-n** takes the user name.

The second logterm, invoked by the *Date* menu item, assumes the user doesn't need a unique name for the file—that the date appended to a filename can suffice. Here's the command line:

```
xterm -name Xmenu \
      -title "`date`" -n $USER \
      -l -lf "$HOME/log.`date +%m%d%y`" &
```

The only difference between *Date* logterm and the previous one is the information fed to the **-lf** switch. Here, what you get is a filename comprised of the word **log** plus the month, day, and year. This type of filename gives you a convenient way to later go back and examine the contents of a logfile for a given date. Yes, you could argue that the shell itself maintains the date associated with a file, but if you rely on the shell's date, be sure you don't edit the logfile—which updates the shell's date.

The *Filter* logterm is for users who want to trim the size of their logfiles, yet retain important information. What the *Filter* logterm does is to only retain text with a specified string in it. Here's the command line:

```
xterm -name Xmenu
      -title "`date`" -n $USER \
      -l -lf "| grep $USER > \
          $HOME/log.`date +%m%d%y`" &
```

Again, the only change to the command is in the **-lf** switch. Instead of merely specifying a filename for **-lf**, a piped command is specified. Whenever you begin the argument space to **-lf** with the pipe symbol, it recognizes that what follows is a command. This creates many possibilities, but in this command, **grep** simply filters the logterm's output. Ultimately, all strings containing $USER are redirected to the logfile, which is named using the word **log**, plus the month, day, and year.

The *Maximum* option combines features from the previous three examples and allows you to create two logfiles. Here's the command line:

```
xterm -name Xmenu \
      -title "`date`" -n "`date +%m/%d`" \
      -l -lf "| tee -a $HOME/log1.`date` +%m%d` \
          | grep $USER > $HOME/log.`date +%m%d`" &
```

The important new element here is the UNIX **tee** command. Using the **tee** command's **-a** switch, you can redirect the current piped stream to a file, yet continue the pipe. This is exactly what happens as **tee** redirects the logterm output to a file called **log1** plus the month and day. After this, the stream is piped into **grep**, which filters the $USER string and sends the output to a file called **log** plus the month and day.

MORE XTERM OPTIONS

The *Xterms Menu* has five submenus. On these menus, you will find items to set most regularly used Xterm options, including colors, fonts, pointers, and scrolling features.

Most of the customization for Xterms is handled by the **setxterm** script. This script is like other resource scripts used by the Xmenu software, but makes use of the $XAPPLRESDIR/**XTerm** file. For most of its options, you can also invoke it from the command line:

```
#!/bin/sh
# setxterm, script to set Xterm resources
# Syntax: setxterm <resource> <value>
# Copyright Alan Southerton

# Initial values
  newfile=/tmp/.xmenu.$$
  oldfile=$XAPPLRESDIR/XTerm
  arg=$1

# Loop reads input and decides what variable in the
# .xmenu file is going to be set. Resource variables
# include syntax because both "*" and "." are used.

case "$arg" in

     bg) new='$XMENU/xcoloredit \
                -title "XTerm Background"'
         resource='.VT100.background' ;;

     fg) new='$XMENU/xcoloredit \
                -title "XTerm Foreground"'
         resource='.VT100.foreground' ;;

    sbg) new='$XMENU/xcoloredit \
                -title "Xterm Scrollbar Background"'
         resource='\*background' ;;
```

```
sfg) new='$XMENU/xcoloredit \
            -title "XTerm Scrollbar Foreground"'
     resource='\*foreground' ;;

cc1) new='sed -n \
            's/^\*Xmenu\.VT100\.foreground://p' \
            $oldfile | sed 's/ //gp''
     resource='.VT100.cursorColor';;

cc2) new='$XMENU/xcoloredit \
            -title "XTerm Cursor Color"'
     resource='.VT100.cursorColor' ;;

pc1) new='sed -n \
            's/^\*Xmenu\.VT100\.foreground://p' \
            $oldfile | sed 's/ //gp''
     resource='.VT100.pointerColor' ;;

pc2) new='$XMENU/xcoloredit \
            -title "XTerm Pointer Color"'
     resource='.VT100.pointerColor' ;;

pc3) new='$XMENU/xcoloredit \
            -title "XTerm Pointer Color"'
     resource='.VT100.pointerColorBackground' ;;

 fx) new=-misc-fixed-medium-r-normal\*$2\*
     resource='\*font' ;;

 fb) new=-misc-fixed-bold-r-normal\*$2\*
     resource='\*font' ;;

 cm) new=-adobe-courier-medium-r-normal\*$2\*
     resource='\*font' ;;
 cb) new=-adobe-courier-bold-r-normal\*$2\*
     resource='\*font' ;;

 so) new=-sony-fixed-medium-r-normal\*$2\*
     resource='\*font' ;;

 sh) new=-schumacher-clean-medium-r-normal\*$2\*
     resource='\*font' ;;
 sb) new=-schumacher-clean-bold-r-normal\*$2\*
     resource='\*font' ;;
 po) new=$2
     resource='\*pointerShape' ;;
```

```
        sbb) new=$2
             resource='\.VT100.scrollBar' ;;

        sbl) new=$2
             resource='\*saveLines' ;;

        sbs) new=$2
             resource='\*thickness' ;;

        # Options for Misc menu in .mwmrc
        inb) new=$2
             resource='\*internalBorder' ;;

        hlc) new=$2
             resource='\*alwaysHighlight' ;;

        mar) new=$2
             resource='\*marginBell' ;;

        viz) new=$2
             resource='\*visualBell' ;;

esac

# Get all values from current $XAPPLRESDIR file and
# remove old instance of $newvariable, if it exists.
# Then add the  value of $newvariable to the temporary
# file and do an mv. The eval command is used to
# accommodate "*" and "." in string.

  grep -v "Xmenu${resource}" \
              $XAPPLRESDIR/XTerm > $newfile
  eval echo "\*Xmenu${resource}\:\ ${new}" >> $newfile
  cp $XAPPLRESDIR/XTerm $XAPPLRESDIR/XTerm.bak
  mv $newfile $XAPPLRESDIR/XTerm
```

There is one general note about **setxterm**. In most cases, the asterisk wildcard character serves fine for delimiting resources, but sometimes it is necessary to be more specific and use the dot character. In turn, because **grep** needs to read these values, all asterisk and dot characters are escaped. Ultimately, the **eval** command is used with **echo** to write new resource statements to the $XAPPLRESDIR/**XTerm** file. Note that this is a slightly different method from the one used in Chapter 7 for Motif resources.

The following sections describe each of the *Xterms* submenus. To illustrate descriptions, relevant parts of **setxterm** are excerpted.

The Colors Submenu

Similar to other color-setting menus in Xmenu, the Xterm *Colors* submenu lets you set colors for various Xterm components. You must set the colors before you execute an Xterm for the change to take effect. Here is the submenu for the standard version of Xmenu:

```
Menu XtermColors
{
  no-label                   f.separator
  no-label                   f.separator
  no-label                   f.separator
  no-label                   f.separator
  "Xterm Colors"             f.title
  no-label                   f.separator
  no-label                   f.separator
  " Window background"       !"(setxterm bg)&"
  " Window foreground"       !"(setxterm fg)&"
  " Scrollbar background"    !"(setxterm sbg)&"
  " Scrollbar foreground"    !"(setxterm sfg)&"
  " Cursor color "           f.menu XtermCurColor
  " Pointer color "          f.menu XtermPntColor
}
```

Setting colors in Xterm can be a bit tricky. You can set them as you would set resources for Motif windows, or any client program, but you might not always get the result you want. For example, you can't set the color of the scrollbar with a resource specification such as **Xterm*scrollbar*background**. But you can set the scrollbar colors. You do it by setting the most general specification for Xterm color resources, such as **XTerm*background**. From there on, you use the most specific naming scheme available to define the color for other components, such as **XTerm.VT100.background**. Compare the routines from **setxterm** that set colors for the two different Xterm components:

```
 bg) new='$XMENU/xcoloredit
            -title "XTerm Background"'
  resource='.VT100.background' ;;
  .
  .
  .
sbg) new='$XMENU/xcoloredit
             -title "Xterm Scrollbar Background"'
   resource='\*background' ;;
```

The routines call the **xcoloredit** program and specify a related string for the titlebar of **xcoloredit**. The only other step is to intercept the output from **xcoloredit** and put it into a variable—making sure to add the correct delimiter, either an asterisk or dot character.

The first four items on the *Colors* menu work the same way. The next two items call submenus, but still use the **setxterm** script. Let's take a look at *Pointer color* submenu:

```
Menu XtermPntColor
{
  " Same as foreground "   !"(setxterm pc1)&"
  " Set foreground "       !"(setxterm pc2)&"
  " Set background "       !"(setxterm pc3)&"
}
```

The difference between this and the other color setting options on the *Colors* submenu is the **pc1** routine, which sets the pointer color to the same color as the foreground:

```
pc1) new=`sed -n \
          's/^\*Xmenu\.VT100\.foreground://p'\
          $oldfile | sed 's/ //gp'`
     resource='.VT100.pointerColor' ;;
```

Two **sed** statements are used in the **pc1)** block. The first extracts the line containing ***Xmenu.VT100.foreground** and the second one extracts the color value. The whole thing occurs within command substitution so $new ends up continuing the color value. The *Cursor color* submenu has a similar option and uses the same mechanism in the **cc1)** routine.

The Fonts Submenu

The *Fonts* submenu (see Figure 9-4) supports several monospaced and character cell fonts for use with Xterms. For routine work in an Xterm, it is necessary to use a font in which one character equals a single-character row and column coordinate. Both monospaced and character cell fonts fill the bill.

It would be ideal to have the Motif menus display fonts as they appear in an actual Xterm. And although the *Fonts* submenu doesn't take this approach, you can change fonts on a menu-by-menu basis.

In order to simplify the menu hierarchy—and it would take many menus so that none of them shared different fonts, sizes, and styles—the Xmenu

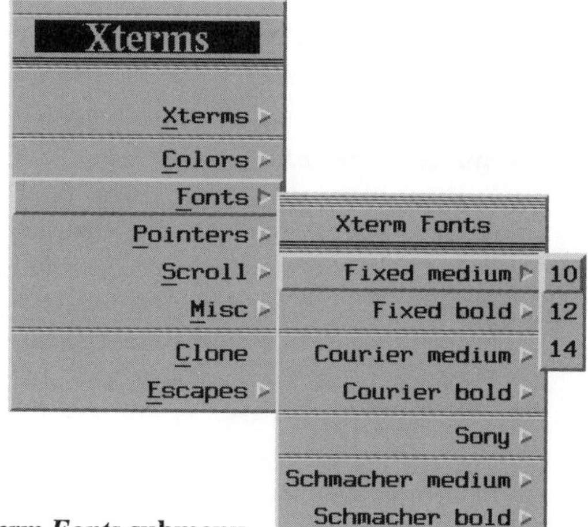

Figure 9-4 The *Xterm Fonts* submenu.

menus forgo this type of enhancement. If you want to provide a pleasing font interface, and are not using the various Xmenu scripts and menus, you might consider this approach.

The *Fonts* submenu supports six additional submenus, which in turn support another submenu so you can select the font and point size with a single menu action. Here is the the *Fonts* submenu:

```
Menu XtermFonts
{
  no-label              f.separator
  no-label              f.separator
  no-label              f.separator
  "Xterm Fonts"         f.title
  no-label              f.separator
  no-label              f.separator
  "     Fixed medium"   f.menu XtermFont1
  "       Fixed bold"   f.menu XtermFont2
  no-label              f.separator
  no-label              f.separator
  "  Courier medium"    f.menu XtermFont3
  "     Courier bold"   f.menu XtermFont4
  no-label              f.separator
  no-label              f.separator
  "             Sony"   f.menu XtermFont5
  no-label              f.separator
  no-label              f.separator
  "Schmacher medium"    f.menu XtermFont6
  "  Schmacher bold"    f.menu XtermFont7
}
```

By ordering the font selections by family and slant together, instead of family and then another submenu, the next submenu in the hierarchy is the last one in the chain:

```
Menu XtermFont3
{
  "10"      !"(setxterm cm 10-100-75-75-m-60)"
  "12"      !"(setxterm cm 12-120-75-75-m-70)"
  "14"      !"(setxterm cm 14-140-75-75-m-90)"
  "18"      !"(setxterm cm 18-180-75-75-m-110)"
  "24"      !"(setxterm cm 24-240-75-75-m-150)"
}
```

The other font menus look similar. Because some of the menus have both medium and bold options, an abbreviation, or variable, is used as the first argument to **setxterm**. The actual font-setting code from **setxterm** looks like this:

```
cm) new=-adobe-courier-medium-r-normal\*$2\*
    resource='\*font' ;;
```

If you prefer, you could shorten the font string more than in the example. In this particular case, you could minimally delete the word "normal" from the string.

The Pointers Submenu

The *Pointers* submenu is almost identical to the pointers menu for the root window (see Chapter 8). Pointers lend themselves to bitmap representation so you can opt to create a graphical menu.

The pointers used in Xterms remain in effect only for a given Xterm. This means you can have different Xterms with different pointers. And, if you have read about pointers in Chapter 8, you also know that an Xterm pointer has no effect on the pointer that is active for the root window and vice versa. Here is the *Pointers* submenu.

```
Menu XtermPointers
{
 @/xmenu/cur/arrows     !"(setxterm po sb_h_double_arrow)"
 @/xmenu/cur/crossr     !"(setxterm po cross_reverse)"
 @/xmenu/cur/bogo       !"(setxterm po bogosity)"
 @/xmenu/cur/gumby      !"(setxterm po gumby)"
```

```
 @/xmenu/cur/fleur     !"(setxterm po fleur)"
 @/xmenu/cur/sailboat !"(setxterm po sailboat)"
 @/xmenu/cur/arrow     !"(setxterm po top_left_arrow)"
}
```

Creating bitmap representations of pointers requires some special attention. Refer to Chapter 8 for two methods of doing this.

The Scroll Submenu

The Xterm *Scroll* menu has some handy options. Especially useful is its submenu that lets you set the buffer size. As you know, the larger the buffer size, the more memory your Xterm uses. Thus, it is convenient to have a quick way to set the size to a large value, start an Xterm, and then return the size to a small value. Here are the *Scroll* submenus from **.mwmrc**:

```
Menu XtermScrolling
{
  no-label             f.separator
  no-label             f.separator
  no-label             f.separator
  no-label             f.separator
  "Xterm Scrolling"    f.title
  no-label             f.separator
  no-label             f.separator
  " Scrollbar "        f.menu XtermScrollbar
  " Scrollbar size "   f.menu XtermSbSize
  " Buffer size "      f.menu XtermBuffer
}

Menu XtermScrollbar
{
  "On"    !"(setxterm sbb true)&"
  "Off"   !"(setxterm sbb false)&"
}

Menu XtermSbSize
{
  "10"   !"(setxterm sbs 10)&"
  "15"   !"(setxterm sbs 15)&"
  "20"   !"(setxterm sbs 20)&"
  "25"   !"(setxterm sbs 25)&"
  "30"   !"(setxterm sbs 30)&"
}
```

```
Menu XtermBuffer
{
  "100"   !"(setxterm sbl 100)&"
  "250"   !"(setxterm sbl 250)&"
  "500"   !"(setxterm sbl 500)&"
  "750"   !"(setxterm sbl 750)&"
  "1000" !"(setxterm sbl 1000)&"
  "1500" !"(setxterm sbl 1500)&"
  "2000" !"(setxterm sbl 2000)&"
}
```

The various menus are straightforward. The first submenu is admittedly yet another way turn the scrollbar on and off. This brings the total to five, if you include escape sequences and keyboard translations. The *Scroll* submenu is handy and gives the user a convenient way to experiment with different-size scrollbars. And the last submenu, as noted, is great for creating one or two Xterms with large buffers, and then resetting the value in $XAPPLRESDIR/**XTerm**.

Miscellaneous Xterm Resources

The *Misc* option on the *Xterms Menu* provides access to some otherwise hard-to-categorize features, including cursor highlighting, the size of the internal border, and warning bells. The following menus conclude the selection of Xmenu's Xterm options.

```
Menu XtermMisc
{
  "Highlight cursor" f.menu XtermHlightCur
  "Internal border"  f.menu XtermInBorder
  "Margin bell"      f.menu XtermMargBell
  "Visual bell"      f.menu XtermVizBell
}

Menu XtermHlightCur
{
  " No "   !"(setxterm hlc no)&"
  " Yes "  !"(setxterm hlc yes)&"
}

Menu XtermInBorder
{
  " 0"  !"(setxterm inb 0)&"
```

```
  " 5"   !"(setxterm inb 5)&"
  "10"   !"(setxterm inb 10)&"
  "15"   !"(setxterm inb 15)&"
  "20"   !"(setxterm inb 20)&"
}

Menu XtermMargBell
{
  " No "    !"(setxterm mar no)&"
  " Yes "   !"(setxterm mar yes)&"
}
```

The *Misc* menus use the **setxterm** script like other Xterm menus. All of the options are interesting, if you happen to use them, but these are not the most popular resources in the first place. The internal border resource is perhaps the most noteworthy. By setting the internal border value to 10 or 15, you can add another component to the Xterm, giving it a distinctive appearance. The border separates the scrollbar and main client area of the window.

THE XMUSE OPTION

The *Muse* option opens up a channel of communication with another Xterm using the **-l** and **-lf** options used to create logterms. This is an excellent built-in feature of the X Window System, but one that has not deserved proper attention. In fact, with the necessary devotion, you could build a robust computer-based teaching (CBT) environment.

When you use the *Xmuse* option, two Xterms appear. If you don't specify a hostname in the Xterm input window that immediately follows your selection, both Xterms appear on the local monitor. If you do specify a hostname, the second Xterm appears on that host. The **xmuse** script, along with the **xgetptty** script, services the *Xmuse* option. Here is the **xmuse** script:

```
#!/bin/sh
# xmuse, display output on second Xterm
# Syntax: xmuse [display]
# Copyright (c) Alan Southerton 1993

# Initial values
  file=/tmp/.xmenu.$$

# Remove temporary file
  trap "rm $file; exit 0 1 2 3 15"
```

```
# Get hostname for 2nd Xterm
  xterm -name getstring -e $XMENU/getany Title $file
  title='cat $file'
  rm $file
  if [ "$display" = "" ]; then display='hostname'; fi

  # Execute 2nd Xterm and get ptty number
  xterm -name Xmenu -display $display:0 \
        -title Muse2 -n muse2 -e $XMENU/xgetptty
  $file &
  while [ 1 ]
  do
    if [ -s $file ]; then
       ptty='cat $file'
       break
    fi
  done

# Execute 1st Xterm to begin log connection
  xterm -name Xmenu \
        -title Muse1 -n muse1 -l -lf $ptty &
```

After getting the hostname for the second Xterm via a text input window, **xmuse** has to take care of some important housekeeping. In other words, it has to establish the **tty** device number for the second Xterm, so that the first Xterm has somewhere to write its logfile output. Notice that the script uses $ptty instead of $tty. Both names are conventional (a **ptty** is a pseudo-terminal and has a **/dev/ptty*n*** file associated with it).

The key thing that **xgettyptty** does is to write the **tty** device number to a temporary file that is visible to both **xmuse** and **xgetptty**. Here is the **xgetptty** script:

```
#!/bin/sh
# xtrack, gets window info
# Syntax: xtrack <window name>
# Copyright (c) Alan Southerton 1993

# Initial values
  file=$1;

# Create the temporary file
  tty > $file

# Now start a subsehll
  exec $SHELL
```

As you can see, **xgetptty** is responsible for more than writing the output from **tty** to $file. In addition to this critical step, it performs another critical step: It starts up a subshell, without which the second Xterm would just complete executing and close itself. With the subshell, however, the Xterm acts like all other Xterms.

Back to the **xmuse** script. The **while** loop serves as the mechanism that makes the first Xterm wait for the completion of the **xgetptty** script. Once the temporary file is created, the script sets the $ptty variable and exits the loop. Now all that is left to do is execute the first Xterm and specify $ptty as the name of the logfile.

All in all, the *Xmuse* option gives you the basis on which to make many modifications and expand the functionality using the Motif menus. For example, you could use it in conjunction with a submenu of host connections (see Chapter 10 for a script to get hostnames dynamically). You could also include other submenus to display **xmuse** Xterms on more than one remote system. And although it is not necessarily a menu consideration, sites with maximum security interests could use the **xmuse** script for a way to monitor systemwide Xterm usage. (Security is a real concern at many businesses. And just the knowledge that real-time, visual Xterm monitoring is possible might be enough to deter an employee from a villainous act.)

From the counter perspective, the logfile mechanism represents a large security hole. Using the Trojan horse method, a villain can supersede your normal **xterm** executable with a script that redirects output to a remote location. The best defense against this is tight overall security, plus extra attention to the permission on the directories where you store your X client programs.

It should also be pointed out that Xterm's built-in *Secure Keyboard* option (the *Main Options* menu, via Ctrl-Button 1 menu) does not have any effect on an **xmuse** session. If the user of the first Xterm selects *Secure Keyboard*, the normal thing happens: the Xterm reverses its colors and the user thinks he or she cannot be monitored. The **xmuse** connection between the two Xterms is also fully functional. The user on the second Xterm gets an exact copy of what's happening on the first Xterm. Note that the second Xterm, like the first Xterm, does not echo passwords.

THE CLONE OPTION

The *Clone* option allows you to duplicate any Xterm, or almost any other X client for that matter. It is intended for those times when you have resized a program window and would like to have another version of the program running, without going through the fuss of resizing it again.

The one problem facing anyone who wants to design a clone utility is the problem of the different units of measure that X uses to size windows. Recall from Chapter 4 that Xterm measures windows in terms of rows, columns, and font size. And in Chapter 7, you saw how the Motif icon box uses bitmaps for its units of measure. Fortunately, most X clients use pixels, but minimally, you need to address the Xterm measurement scheme—because it is likely one of the best candidates for cloning.

The following script, called **clone**, can be executed from the command line or included as a menu option in **.mwmrc**. Because it uses **xwinifo** as its frontend, the user can interactively select a target window. The familiar crosshair pointer of **xwininfo** is the primary user interface mechanism. Just move the cursor to the window that you want to clone and click the left mouse button.

```
#!/bin/sh
# clone, script to clone an existing window.
# Syntax: clone
# Copyright (c) Alan Southerton 1993

# Operation: Clone duplicates any window as it
# appears on the screen, unless resources for
# the window are changed between times. Thus,
# changing fonts, scrollbar size, or internal border
# size will result in a different size window.

# Set values
  xtcheck=false; echeck=false
  file=/tmp/clone.$$

# Remove temporary file upon exit.
  trap "rm $file; exit 0 1 2 3 15"

# Initial values
  sbar=""; thickness=""; internal=""
  value=""; i=0;

# Generic function to get resource values
  getresvalue() {
  client=$1
  resource=$2
  resclass=$3

  #The following function returns the value for
  #a given resource based on the resource
```

```
#with the highest precedence. The use of
#the -i option to grep presupposes sane,
#as opposed to insane, resources.

str=`appres XTerm $client | grep -i "$resource:"`
if [ "$str" = "" ]; then return; fi
   set - `echo $str`

   for arg in $*
   do
     if [ "$arg" = "$client.VT100.$resource:" ]; then
        shift; value=$1; return
     fi
     if [ "$arg" = "$client.VT100*$resource:" ]; then
        shift; value=$1; return
     fi
     if [ "$arg" = "$client*$resource:" ]; then
        shift; value=$1; return
     fi
     if [ "$arg" = "$client*$resource:" ]; then
        shift; value=$1; return
     fi
  shift
done

set - `echo $str`
for arg in $*
do
  if [ "$arg" = "XTerm.VT100.$resource:" ]; then
     shift; value=$1; return
  fi
  if [ "$arg" = "XTerm.VT100*$resource:" ]; then
     shift; value=$1; return
  fi
  if [ "$arg" = "XTerm.VT100*$resclass:" ]; then
     shift; value=$1; return
  fi
  if [ "$arg" = "XTerm*VT100*$resclass:" ]; then
     shift; value=$1; return
  fi
  if [ "$arg" = "XTerm*$resclass:" ]; then
     shift; value=$1; return
  fi
  shift
done
```

```
  value=`appres XTerm $client | \
               grep "^\*$resource" | cut -d: -f2`

  return
}

# Get window information
  xwininfo -stats -size > $file


  id=`sed -n "s/xwininfo.*0x/0x/p" \
                        $file | cut -d' ' -f1`
  width=`sed -n "s/^.*Width: //p" $file`
  height=`sed -n "s/^.*Height: //p" $file`
  xinc=`sed -n "s/^.*x resize increment: //p" $file`
  yinc=`sed -n "s/^.*y resize increment: //p" $file`

# Get command string
  xprop -id $id > $file
  newwindow=`sed -n \
        /WM_COMMAND/,/WM_ICON/'s/^.*{//p' $file | \
        sed s/}$//p | \
        sed s/,//gp`
  program=`echo $newwindow | cut -d' ' -f1`

# Take care of different Xterm geometry. Geometry
# does not reflect internal Xterm components so
# must factor scrollbar and internal border sizes.
# The first block of code begins by parsing for
# a default Xterm.

  xtcheck=`sed -n \
      's/WM_CLASS(STRING).*\"XTerm\"/true/p' $file`

  if [ "$xtcheck" = "true" ]; then
     name=`echo $newwindow | \
           sed -n 's/^.*\"\-name\" //p' | \
           sed -n s/\"//gp | cut -d' ' -f1`
     if [ "$name" = "" ]; then
         name=xterm
     fi

     getresvalue $name scrollBar ScrollBar
     sbar=$value; value=""
     #Clean tabs and spaces from sbar variable
     sbar=`echo $sbar | sed 's/    //gp'`
```

```
#Check for default (no scrollbar) and for
#turn-off option on the command line
case $sbar in
    [Tt]rue) echo $newwindow | grep -q "\"+sb\""
             if [ "$?" = "0" ]; then
                 sbar=false
             else
                 sbar=true
             fi ;;
          "") sbar=false ;;
esac

#Check for turn-on on the command line
if [ "$sbar" = "" ]; then
    echo $newwindow | grep -q "\"-sb\""
    case $? in
       0) sbar=true ;;
       1) sbar=false ;;
    esac
fi

if [ "$sbar" = "true" ]; then
  getresvalue $name thickness Thickness
  thickness=$value; value=""
  : ${thickness:=10}
else
  thickness=0
fi

#Now have to check for internal border
getresvalue $name internalBorder InternalBorder
internal=$value; value=""

#Now have to check for border on command line
 echo $newwindow | grep -q "\"-b\""
 case $? in
       0) internal=`echo $newwindow | \
            sed -n \'s/^.*\"\-b\" \"//p' | \
            sed -n \s/\"//gp | cut -d' ' -f1` ;;
       1) : ${internal:=0} ;;
  esac

# Do calculations for internal components
  internal=`expr $internal + $internal`
  width=\`expr \( $width - $thickness \
                     - $internal \) / $xinc`
```

```
            height=`expr \( $height \
                             - $internal \) / $yinc`

     fi
     echo internalBorder=`expr $internal - $internal`
     echo scrollBar=$sbar
     echo thickness=$thickness
     echo width=$width
     echo height=$height

  # Set new geometry for command string
     echo $newwindow | \
          egrep "(\"\-g\"|\"\-geom\"|\"\-geometry\")"
     case $? in

       0) newwindow=`echo $newwindow | \
            sed "s/\"\-geometry\".\"...../\"\-geometry\" \
                    \"${width}x${height}/p" | \
            sed "s/\"\-geom\".\"...../\"\-geom\" \
                    \"${width}x${height}/p" | \
            sed "s/\"\-g\".\"...../\"\-g\" \
                    \"${width}x${height}/p"` ;;

       1) geometry="\"-geometry\" \"${width}x${height}\""
            newwindow=`echo $newwindow | \
                    sed -n "s/^$program/& $geometry/p"`

     esac

  # Execute cloned window
     eval $newwindow &
```

The **clone** script begins by saving the output from **xwininfo** to a temporary file. It then runs **sed** operations on the file to obtain the following information:

- Window id (any option)
- Width
- Height
- Horizontal resize increment
- Vertical resize increment

Both the **-stats** and **-size** options provide the window id, width, and height of a window, but only the **-size** option provides the horizontal and vertical resize increments. You don't need to use both options, in fact, but the **-stats** option has a cleaner output to filter through **sed**.

The next step for **clone** is to obtain the current command line string associated with the window. You can do this by using the **xprop** command and extracting information following WM_COMMAND. The script takes this information and stores it in a variable called $newwindow.

Now the work begins because **clone** needs to know whether it is dealing with an Xterm or a window using pixel coordinates. It is easy to perform the evaluation because the WM_CLASS message displayed by **xprop** contains the word "**XTerm**" if, indeed, the window is an Xterm.

In cases when the window is an Xterm, the **clone** script calls the **getresvalue** function. The primary role of **getresvalue** is to determine what type of resources have been used with the Xterm. For example, have the resources been set by naming VT100 widget in the resource statement?

The **set** command is used in **getresvalue** to conveniently place the individual values in $str in the shell's parameter space. The arguments are then evaluated against $resource and $resclass variables passed to the **getresvalue** function. When a match occurs, **clone** uses the **shift** command and sets $value equal to the next new value in the **$1** slot. The entire goal of this process—and of the **getresvalue** function—is to obtain the current value associated with $resource. The reason so many **if** statements are required is Xterm has so many different ways to set resources. The **if** statements are in sequence according to resource precedence (see *Resource Precedence* in Chapter 3).

It is important to get the size of the Xterm scrollbar because Xterm constructs its overall size based on scrollbar width, internal border width, and its standard geometry settings. Much of the remaining code in the script simply takes care of the math necessary to determine the true size of the Xterm. Note that if the window isn't an Xterm, very little code is required to duplicate it. The final task of the script is to execute the duplicated window with the **eval** command, which evaluates the possible clutter of whitespace and quotation marks in the $newwindow variable.

CHAPTER 10
Configuration Wrap

TOWARD DYNAMIC

The Motif menus give you a way to provide a consistent interface to most elements of modern computing. Time and again, the Motif menus will prove to be an efficient way to execute lengthy commands that are otherwise hard to remember.

For users who have little knowledge of shell commands, the Motif menus are hard to rival. In fact, only desktop managers offer equal capability. True, desktop managers offer drag and drop functionality, which is a good reason to implement a desktop manager with Motif menus, but when it comes to executing UNIX commands, or a series of UNIX commands in a script, the desktop manager relies on a scripting approach, too.

Combining the resources of the UNIX shell with the **.mwmrc** files opens up various possibilities for reconfiguring the user environment. Much of this book concerns itself with reconfiguring the user environment at the workstation level—and this chapter describes the *Resource Tools* menu to review this level of configuration. Additionally, this chapter explores ways to reconfigure Motif menus based on information that you can glean from the system as well as from the network.

This where dynamic configuration enters the scene. True, it is not dynamic in the sense that it occurs on-the-fly, but given the features that you can access, it is dynamic enough considering that all you have to do is restart Motif. And when more dynamic built-in routines for Motif become available, as they are available in Sun's OpenWindows, you can easily adapt most of the reconfiguration routines in this chapter.

RESOURCE TOOLS

The *Resource Tools* menu is a submenu on the main *Resources* menu that you pop up with the left button over the root window. You can also access the

Resource Tools by pressing Ctrl-F8. Because it is such a handy menu, you might also consider providing access to it from the default window menu—at least, in your personal version of the Motif menus, or any system administration version that you create.

The primary responsibility of the *Resource Tools* menu is to provide the user with a way to use the standard X tools to update resources. It was not discussed with the other options on the main root window *Resources* menu (see Chapter 7) because many of the issues its addresses require an overview of the Motif menu approach. Additionally, you might not want to make all the options on the *Resource Tools* menu available to end users. Figure 10-1 shows the *Resource Tools* menu.

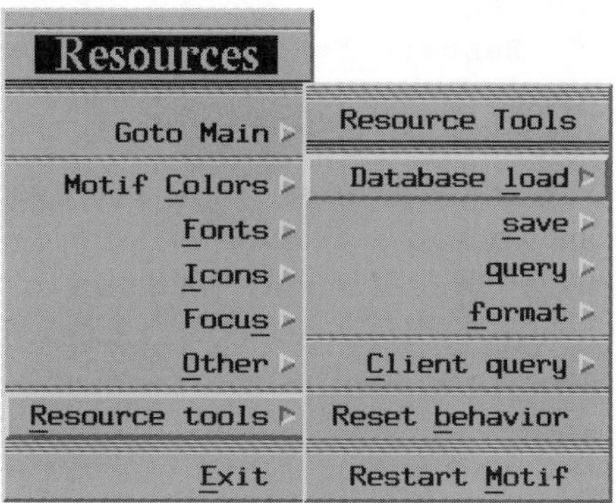

Figure 10-1 The *Resource Tools* submenu.

The **xrdb** utility is the main X client used in *Resource Tools* menu. But besides just using the **xrdb** options, some UNIX scripting tricks are employed to make resource files more presentable. Also, the *Resource Tools* menu uses the **xprop** client for displaying general information and resources about programs; the Motif **f.set_behavior** function for changing to the default Motif look and feel; and the Motif **f.restart** function for restarting Motif. Here is the code for the *Resource Tools* menu:

```
Menu ResourceTools
{
     no_label                 f.separator
     no_label                 f.separator
     no_label                 f.separator
     no_label                 f.separator
     "Resource Tools"         f.title
     no_label                 f.separator
     no_label                 f.separator
```

```
    "  Database load"  _l  f.menu XrdbLoad
    "           save"  _s  f.menu XrdbSave
    "          query"  _q  f.menu XrdbQuery
    "         format"  _f  f.menu XrdbFormat
    no_label               f.separator
    no_label               f.separator
    "   Client query"  _C  f.menu XrdbClient
    no_label               f.separator
    no_label               f.separator
    " Default Motif"   _D  f.set_behavior
    no_label               f.separator
    no_label               f.separator
    no_label               f.separator
    no_label               f.separator
    "  Restart Motif"  _M  f.restart
}
```

There are two items on the *Resource Tools* menu that you will summon time and again: the *Database load* items, which give you access to options to load $HOME/**.Xdefaults** file in server memory; and the *Restart Motif* item, which restarts the window manager. See Chapter 6 for information on the Motif functions. The other menu items are described in the following sections.

Xrdb Utilities

The Xrdb utilities allow you to update, modify, and aesthetically format the $HOME/**.Xdefaults** file. The utilities comprise the four menus, called *XrdbLoad*, *XrdbSave*, *XrdbQuery*, and *XrdbFormat*. Figure 10-2 shows the *XrdbSave* menu, which is somewhat typical.

Descriptions for the four menus are presented in the following sections. The script that the menus use is presented here:

```
#!/bin/sh
# mwmres
# Syntax: mwmres restype resvalue
# Copyright (c) Alan Southerton

# Record this command
  lastcommand $0 $1 $2 $3 &

# Remove temporary file on exit
  trap "rm $file; exit 0 1 2 3 15"
```

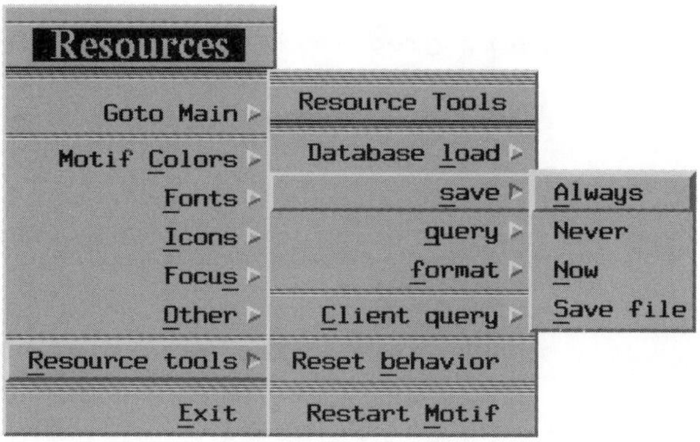

Figure 10-2 The *Xrdb save* submenu.

```
# Initial values
  file=/tmp/.xmenu1.$$
  file2=/tmp/.xmenu2.$$
  option=$1;

case $option in

    standq) cmd="xrdb -query | sort -f | more"
            xterm -name xbox \
                  -T "Xrdb Query" -n xrdb \
                  -e xshowbox "$cmd"
            exit ;;

    namedq) xterm -name getstring \
                  -T "Name Resource to Query" \
                  -n GET \
                  -e getany Resource $file
            resource=`cat $file`
            cmd="xrdb -query | grep $resource | \
                        sort -f | more"
            xterm -name xbox \
                  -T "Named Xrdb Query" -n xrdb \
                  -e xshowbox "$cmd"
            exit ;;

    always) grep -v SAVETOXDEFAULTS \
                    $HOME/.Xdefaults > $file
```

```
            echo "SAVETOXDEFAULTS:yes" >> $file
            exit ;;

    never) grep -v SAVETOXDEFAULTS \
                     $HOME/.Xdefaults > $file
            echo "SAVETOXDEFAULTS:no" >> $file
            exit ;;

      now) xrdb -query > $HOME/.Xdefaults
            exit ;;

     save) xterm -name getstring \
                  -T "Name for Resources File" \
                  -n GET \
                  -e getany Filename $file
            filename='cat $file'
            xrdb -query > $filename
            exit ;;

     file) xterm -name getstring \
                  -title "Name Save File" \
                  -n GET \
                  -e xmenuget SAVERESDB Filename
            xrdbfile='grep SAVERESDB \
                         $HOME/.xmenu | cut -d: -f2'
            xrdb -query > $xrdbfile
            exit ;;

esac

if [ ! -f $HOME/.Xdefaults ]; then
   cmd="echo Error: No .Xdefaults file found"
   xterm -name errormsg \
         -T "Warning...Warning...Warning" \
         -e xshowbox "$cmd"
   exit
fi

case $option in

   xdef) xrdb -load $HOME/.Xdefaults ;;

   load) xterm -name getstring \
               -title "Alternate Resource File" \
               -n GET \
               -e xmenuget SAVERESDB Filename
```

```
          xrdbfile=`grep SAVERESDB \
                       $HOME/.xmenu | cut -d: -f2`
          xrdb -load $xrdbfile ;;

   diffq) cmd="diff -tb $file $file2 | more ; \
                if [ $? ]; then \
                echo No differences found! ; fi"
          xrdb -query | sort -f > $file
          sort -f $HOME/.Xdefaults > $file2
          xterm -name xbox \
                -T "Xrdb Diff" -n xrdb \
                -e xshowbox "$cmd" ;;

    sort) sort -f $HOME/.Xdefaults > $file
          cp $HOME/.Xdefaults $HOME/.Xdefaults.bak
          mv $file $HOME/.Xdefaults ;;

    tab)  cp $HOME/.Xdefaults $HOME/.Xdefaults.bak
          sed 's/:/: /g' $HOME/.Xdefaults > $file
          cp $HOME/.Xdefaults $HOME/.Xdefaults.bak
          mv $file $HOME/.Xdefaults ;;

  space)  cp $HOME/.Xdefaults $HOME/.Xdefaults.bak
          sed 's/: /:/g' $HOME/.Xdefaults > $file
          cp $HOME/.Xdefaults $HOME/.Xdefaults.bak
          mv $file $HOME/.Xdefaults ;;

 tspace)  cp $HOME/.Xdefaults $HOME/.Xdefaults.bak
          sed 's/:/:/g' $HOME/.Xdefaults | \
              sed 's/: /:/g' > $file
          cp $HOME/.Xdefaults $HOME/.Xdefaults.bak
          mv $file $HOME/.Xdefaults ;;

trailer) cp $HOME/.Xdefaults $HOME/.Xdefaults.bak
          sed 's/ $//g' $HOME/.Xdefaults > $file
          cp $HOME/.Xdefaults $HOME/.Xdefaults.bak
          mv $file $HOME/.Xdefaults ;;


#XrdbClient Menu Options

 getall) set - `xprop | \
                grep WM_CLASS | \
                sed 's/^.*= //' | \
                sed -n 's/[\"\,]//gp'`
```

```
            for arg in $*
            do
                appres $1 >> $file
                shift
            done
            xterm -name xbox \
                  -T "Client Resources" \
                  -n client \
                  -e xshowtxt $file
            exit ;;

    getcur)  set - `xprop | \
                    grep WM_CLASS | \
                    sed 's/^.*= //' | \
                    sed -n 's/[\"\,]//gp'`
                         appres $1 > $file
             xterm -name xbox \
                   -T "Client Resources" -n client \
                   -e xshowtxt $file
             exit ;;

   getprop)  cmd="xprop"
             xterm -name xbox \
                   -T "Window Properties" -n xprop \
                   -e xshowbox "$cmd"
             exit ;;

   esac
```

Database Load

The *Database load* submenu provides some basic operations for manipulating the $HOME/**.Xdefaults** file, including a way to restore a backup copy of **.Xdefaults**. Here is the menu:

```
Menu XrdbLoad
{
   " .Xdefaults"    _X  !"(mwmres xdef)&"
   " Named file"    _N  !"(mwmres load)"
   " Backup file"   _B  !"(xrdbrestore)&"
}
```

The first two options on the *Database load* submenu load the contents of an associated file into the resource manager's root window memory area.

Both options use the **mwmres** script. The first option performs a straightforward loading of $HOME/**.Xdefaults**. The second option allows you to specify an alternate file:

```
load) xterm -name getstring \
            -title "Alternate Resource File" \
            -n GET \
            -e xmenuget SAVERESDB Filename

      xrdbfile=`grep SAVERESDB \
                     $HOME/.xmenu | cut -d: -f2`

      xrdb -load $xrdbfile ;;
```

Although this option might be too much for end users, it is useful for experienced users, and anyone who wants to test different sets of resources. The **load)** routine displays an Xterm to get the alternate resource filename, which it stores in the **.xmenu** variable SAVERESDB. The **xmenuget** script, as you have seen elsewhere, allows the communication between **mwmres** and the text input Xterm.

The third option on the *Database load* menu lets you restore the previous version of $HOME/**.Xdefaults**. The *Always* option on the *Xrdb save* menu lets you specify that the Xmenu scripts always make a backup copy of $HOME/**.Xdefaults**. You do not need to use this option in order to use the *Backup file* option on the *Xrdb load* submenu, but it helps.

Because of the importance of restoring $HOME/**.Xdefaults**, the *Backup file* option uses a separate script. You and your users can use this script either from the menus or from the command line:

```
#!/bin/sh
# xrdbrestore, restores previous .Xdefaults file,
# by loading it into the resource database and
# restarting the window manager
# Syntax: xrdbrestore
# Copyright (c) Alan Southerton 1993

# Check for existence of backup file
  if [ -f $HOME/.Xdefaults.bak ] ; then
     cp $HOME/.Xdefaults.bak /tmp
     cp $HOME/.Xdefaults $HOME/.Xdefaults.bak
     mv /tmp/.Xdefaults.bak $HOME/.Xdefaults
     xrdb -load $HOME/.Xdefaults

  else
```

```
    xterm -name errormsg \
          -T "Warning...Warning...Warning" \
          -e errormsg1
fi
```

The script assumes that the backup copy of $HOME/**.Xdefaults** is also located in the home directory and that it has a **.bak** extension. This is the convention that Xmenu uses.

Xrdb Save

The *Xrdb save* submenu gives you a way to choose when you want the current set of resources saved to $HOME/**.Xdefaults**. Some users might want any changes they make to their resource environment automatically saved. Other users might want to save their current resources when they have decided they like them better than a previous set of resources.

With the *Xrdb save* submenu, you have flexible control over the way you save resources. You can decide to always save them; save them at a given moment; or save them into an alternate file. Here is the *Xrdb save* submenu:

```
Menu XrdbSave
{
   " Always"      _A  !"(mwmres always)&"
   " Never"       _N  !"(mwmres never)&"
   " Now"         _w  !"(mwmres now)&"
   " Save file"   _S  !"(mwmres save)&"
}
```

The Xmenu interface is designed with the first option in mind. The various Xmenu scripts take a conditional approach to updating $HOME/**.Xdefaults**. Here is a typical example:

```
# Load new resources/replace .Xdefaults if specified
  xrdb -load $file
  overwrite='grep SAVETOXDEFAULTS \
                $HOME/.xmenu | cut -d: -f2'
  if [ "$overwrite" = "yes" ] ; then
     cp $HOME/.Xdefaults $HOME/.Xdefaults.bak
     mv $file $HOME/.Xdefaults
  else
     rm $file
  fi
```

As usual, the routine loads $file, which is a temporary file containing modified resources plus the previous resources obtained using **grep -v**. The second line of code comes into play when the user selects *Always* from the *Xrdb save* submenu. The **mwmres** script sets the value of SAVETODEFAULTS to **yes**, using the following routine:

```
always) grep -v SAVETOXDEFAULTS \
                    $HOME/.Xdefaults > $file
        echo "SAVETOXDEFAULTS:yes" >> $file
        exit ;;
```

The *Never* option does the reverse. When scripts are ready to overwrite the previous version of $HOME/**.Xdefaults**, they check the $overwrite variable. If it equals **yes**, the script is overwritten. If it equals **no**, the script removes the temporary file (which is unnecessary in most of the scripts, because the **trap** command is used to remove most temporary files; but it is included for readability's sake).

The *Now* option on the *Xrdb save* submenu is for users who have chosen the *Never* option. From time to time, users want to save changes they have made to their resources. For these times, the **mwmres** script uses an **xrdb -query** operation and saves the results directly into $HOME/**.Xdefaults**.

The last option on *Xrdb save* is the *Save file* option. Users who choose the *Named file* option on the *Xrdb load* submenu will probably want to use the *Save file* option. The **mwmres** routine, like other text input routines, displays an Xterm and uses the **xmenuget** script to store the filename. As in the *Now* option, a standard **xrdb -query** operation is used.

Xrdb Query

The *Xrdb query* submenu lets you display the contents of the resource database in a window. Xterm is integral in displaying the results of the query operations, but you can do some things with resources to tailor the appearance of Xterm for the job as shown in Figure 10-3.

The resources used with the *Xrdb query* routines are any current defaults, plus those associated with the named Xterm called **xbox**. Here are the **xbox** resources:

```
!From $XAPPLERESDIR/XTerm
 *xbox*background: white
 *xbox*font: *adobe-courier-bold-r-normal*140*
 *xbox*foreground: black
 *xbox*geometry: 60x17+15+40
 *xbox*internalBorder: 20
```

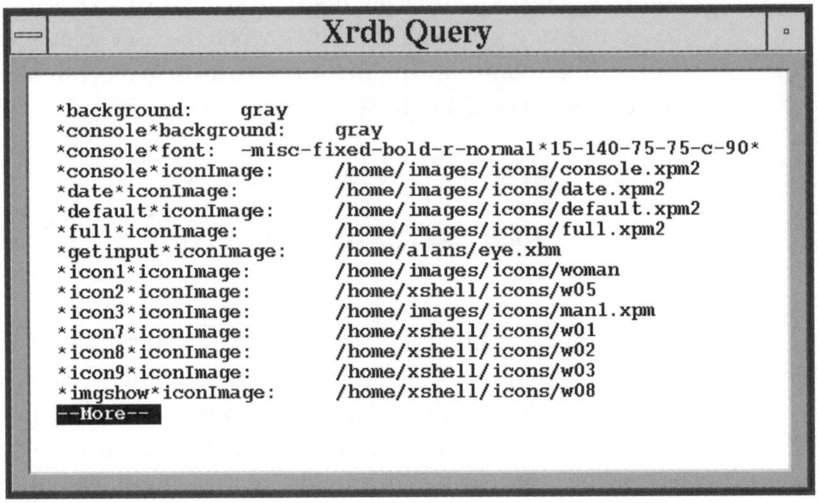

```
Xrdb Query

*background:    gray
*console*background:    gray
*console*font:  -misc-fixed-bold-r-normal*15-140-75-75-c-90*
*console*iconImage:     /home/images/icons/console.xpm2
*date*iconImage:        /home/images/icons/date.xpm2
*default*iconImage:     /home/images/icons/default.xpm2
*full*iconImage:        /home/images/icons/full.xpm2
*getinput*iconImage:    /home/alans/eye.xbm
*icon1*iconImage:       /home/images/icons/woman
*icon2*iconImage:       /home/xshell/icons/w05
*icon3*iconImage:       /home/images/icons/man1.xpm
*icon7*iconImage:       /home/xshell/icons/w01
*icon8*iconImage:       /home/xshell/icons/w02
*icon9*iconImage:       /home/xshell/icons/w03
*imgshow*iconImage:     /home/xshell/icons/w08
--More--
```

Figure 10-3 An Xterm configured to display the results of a resource query operation using Xrdb.

```
!From $XAPPLERESDIR/Mwm
 Mwm*xbox*matteBackground: #ff0000
 Mwm*xbox*matteForeground: #ff0000
 Mwm*xbox*matteWidth: 24
```

The first set of resources are Xterm specific and are therefore stored in the $XAPPLRESDIR/**XTerm** file. The second set of resources, which are Motif specific, are stored in $XAPPLRESDIR/Mwm. You could also store these in $HOME/**.Xdefaults**, if you use the Xmenu scheme of storing only Motif resources in $HOME/**.Xdefaults**. In any event, all three options on the *Xrdb query* menu use **xbox**. Here is the *Xrdb query* menu:

```
Menu XrdbQuery
{
  " All"     _A   !"(mwmres standq)&"
  " Diff"    _D   !"(mwmres diffq)&"
  " Named"   _N   !"(mwmres namedq)&"
}
```

The first option does a standard **xrdb -query**. The **standq)** routine in **mwmres** is a little out of the ordinary, however, because it formulates the query command and stores it in the variable $cmd. The *Diff* and *Named* options also use this approach, which is often absolutely necessary for displaying the output of complex commands in an Xterm window:

```
standq) cmd="xrdb -query | sort -f | more"
        xterm -name xbox \
              -T "Xrdb Query" \
              -n xrdb \
              -e xshowbox "$cmd"
        exit ;;
```

In addition to formulating the command, the routine passes the command to the **xshowbox** script, using Xterm's **-e** option. The **xshowbox** script's purpose is to prevent the Xterm from exiting after the command in $cmd finishes. It resembles other Xmenu scripts that make an Xterm wait:

```
#!/bin/sh
# xshowbox, reusable routine to display output
# Syntax: xshowbox cmdstring
# Copyright (c) Alan Southerton 1993

  eval $1
  echo
  /bin/echo -n Press Return to Exit
  read keypress
```

This represents a complete approach to displaying command output using standard X and Motif tools. If you can program in X, or use a programming interface such as Metacard (Metacard Inc.) or XVT (XVT Corp.), you can create a more efficient text output window. From a portability perspective, however, you can't beat the Xterm approach.

The next item on *Xrdb query* is the *Diff* option. After all, what would any query operation be like without the **diff** command entering the scene: Whether you understand the archaic **diff** output, or not, it is a great indicator of whether changes have been made in one file as compared with another. Here is the routine from **mwmres**:

```
diffq) cmd="diff -tb $file $file2 | more ; \
          if [ $? ]; then \
          echo No differences found! ; fi"
       xrdb -query | sort -f > $file
       sort -f $HOME/.Xdefaults > $file2
       xterm -name xbox \
             -T "Xrdb Diff" -n xrdb \
             -e xshowbox "$cmd" ;;
```

Here, the **diffq)** routine takes real advantage of storing a command in a command variable. The efficiency of the technique especially shines considering you can store multiple filenames in $cmd. If the **diff** command finds no differences, it issues a message to that effect. In both cases, **xshowbox** is used and the text display Xterm waits for the user to press Return or use the Close option on the default window menu.

The last item on *Xrdb query* allows you to perform a named query. The *Name* item has one of the few routines in Xmenu that uses an Xterm for both text input and output. The combination of the two uses of Xterm, however, opens up a lot of possibilities for frontends to UNIX commands. Here is the **namedq)** routine:

```
namedq) xterm -name getstring \
              -T "Name Resource to Query" \
              -n GET \
              -e getany $file Resource
        resource=`cat $file`
        cmd="xrdb -query | \
               grep $resource | sort -f | more"
        xterm -name xbox \
              -T "Named Xrdb Query" -n xrdb \
              -e xshowbox "$cmd"
        exit ;;
```

Performance is a consideration when you use two Xterms to accomplish a single menu item selection. On older UNIX workstations, the operation could take longer than 10 seconds if there is a significant load on the system. So it might be time to reexamine the resources that you use for the input and display Xterms. One way to improve performance, at least marginally, is to set the **saveLines** resource to 0. This effectively eliminates the scroll buffer, obviating the need for Xterm to set it up during its loading process.

Xrdb Format

At first blush, the *Xrdb format* submenu might seem like it was designed for perfectionists. After all, its primary function is to reformat the $HOME/**.Xdefaults** file. But if you have ever been confounded when a resource didn't go into effect, only to discover that the culprit was an invisible whitespace at the end of the offending resource statement, you'll like this menu. Here's the code from the **.mwmrc** file:

```
Menu XrdbFormat
{
  " Sort"                _S  !"(mwmres sort)&"
  no_label                   f.separator
  no_label                   f.separator
  " Strip tabs"          _t  !"(mwmres tab)&"
  " Strip spaces"        _r  !"(mwmres space)&"
  " Tabs & spaces"       _b  !"(mwmres tspace)&"
  " Trailing spaces"     _p  !"(mwmres trailer)&"
}
```

The first item, *Sort*, does exactly what it says: it performs an alphabetical sort, treating both uppercase and lowercase letters identically. Here is the routine from **mwmres**:

```
sort) sort -f $HOME/.Xdefaults > $file
      cp $HOME/.Xdefaults $HOME/.Xdefaults.bak
      mv $file $HOME/.Xdefaults ;;
```

The **-f** option to sort tells it to ignore the difference between uppercase and lowercase letters. Also, you should note that any resources that begin with an asterisk will appear at the beginning of the resource file after it has been sorted.

The next item on *Xrdb format* has appeal if the irregular tab spacing that results from an **xrdb -query** operation bothers you. Here is the routine for stripping tabs:

```
tab)  cp $HOME/.Xdefaults $HOME/.Xdefaults.bak
      sed 's/:{TAB}/: /g' $HOME/.Xdefaults > $file
      cp $HOME/.Xdefaults $HOME/.Xdefaults.bak
      mv $file $HOME/.Xdefaults ;;
```

Note that in the example (but not in the previous listing of the **mwmres** file), the tab is represented by *{TAB}*. If you enter this script, you must use the actual tab character. This done, **sed** searches for any tab that appears after colon and replaces it with a space. If you want, you could modify this so that **sed** replaces each **:*{TAB}*** sequence with just **:** instead—because resource files don't require the space after the colon; it is only a convention. Finally, if you think that some lines in your resource file contain more than one tab, you can run the *Strip tabs* option a second time.

And speaking of convention—or not following convention—the next item on *Xrdb format* gives you a way to remove spaces after the colon. Here's the routine for the *Strip spaces* item:

```
space)   cp $HOME/.Xdefaults $HOME/.Xdefaults.bak
         sed 's/: /:/g' $HOME/.Xdefaults > $file
         cp $HOME/.Xdefaults $HOME/.Xdefaults.bak
         mv $file $HOME/.Xdefaults ;;
```

The **sed** command works similarly to the one in the routine for *Strip tabs*. Using the two routines together is a quick way to remove all tabs and spaces, but an even quicker way is to use the *Tabs and spaces* routine:

```
tspace)   cp $HOME/.Xdefaults $HOME/.Xdefaults.bak
          sed 's/:{TAB}/:/' $HOME/.Xdefaults | \
                 sed 's/: /:/' > $file
          cp $HOME/.Xdefaults $HOME/.Xdefaults.bak
          mv $file $HOME/.Xdefaults ;;
```

The only change in this routine is that output from the tab stripping command is fed into a second **sed** command that strips the spaces.

Finally, the command that might save you the most grief is the *Trailing spaces* command. Here is the routine:

```
trailer)  cp $HOME/.Xdefaults $HOME/.Xdefaults.bak
          sed 's/ $//' $HOME/.Xdefaults > $file
          cp $HOME/.Xdefaults $HOME/.Xdefaults.bak
          mv $file $HOME/.Xdefaults ;;
```

The **sed** command keys on spaces at the ends of lines, thanks to the **$** symbol, which represents the ends of lines in this context. If you think you have more than one space at the ends of lines in your resource file, use the *Trailing spaces* option successive times.

Client Query

The *Client query* submenu is similar to the Xrdb menus, except that it works on a specified client and it lets you query resources that aren't necessarily in effect. Again, the associated script is **mwmres**. Here is the *Client query* menu:

```
Menu XrdbClient
{
  " All"          _A   !"(mwmres getall)&"
  " Current"      _C   !"(mwmres getcur)&"
  " Properties"   _P   !"(mwmres getprop)&"
}
```

As its name indicates, the *All* option gives you a way to query all the resources linked to a currently running client. The client name, and its associated class name, is obtained using the **xprop** utility. The **xprop** utility presents the user with a crosshair cursor to interactively select a window. Here is the routine for the *All* option:

```
getetall) set - `xprop | \
                grep WM_CLASS | \
                sed 's/^.*= //' | \
                sed -n 's/[\"\,]//gp'`
          for arg in $*
          do
            appres $1 >> $file
            shift
          done
          xterm -name xbox \
                -T "Client Resources" \
                -n client \
                -e xshowbox $file
          exit ;;
```

The script uses a **sed** command to extract the client name and its associated class name—that is, the value paired with WM_CLASS—from the output of the **xprop** utility. It then uses the UNIX **set** command to place the two names, which are clearly delimited by a whitespace, into the shell's argument space. After this, a **for** loop can easily process the list.

The important command in the **for** loop is **appres**, which is a client program included in the standard release of X. In order to get the full set of resources that pertain to an application, you must supply **appres** with both the *class* and *instance* name of the application. For example, the following command would yield all the resources for an Xterm named **Xmenu**:

```
appres XTerm Xmenu
```

Note that **XTerm** is used as the class name. If you are unfamiliar with a program's class name, you can usually guess it because it is frequently the same name that you use in the $XAPPLRESDIR directory. To be more precise, just use **xprop**, which shows both the instance and class names in its WM_CLASS line.

The **appres** client can also be used to query client resources known to **xrdb**. This is equivalent to using **xrdb** to query the resource database and then **grep** to extract the resource statements relevant to a given client:

```
appres Xmenu
```

On some systems at least, this command lists the **xrdb** resources associated with **Xmenu**. However, the manual page for **appres** indicates that the command should display all the resources associated with the given client. In any event, using **xrdb** to query the database and **grep** to filter is a tad quicker than **appres**, so you won't be guilty of the sin of *using two commands when one would do.*

The next routine, **getcur)**, is similar to **getall)**. The difference is that **getcur)** is concerned only about getting resources currently in effect for the window. Therefore all you need to supply to **appres** is the instance name. The **set** command is used again, because it conveniently places the instance name into the first position in the shell's argument space.

The last routine, **getprop)**, simply executes the **xprop** command. The user, accordingly, must select a window using the pointer. By specifying the command in the **-e** option to Xterm, **xprop** doesn't present its crosshair pointer until the Xterm window opens. You might want to reverse this behavior, but the Xterm, plus its titlebar (in this case, "Window Properties"), gives the user another cue as to what is happening.

DYNAMIC MENUS

There are plenty of things, many of them site dependent, that can be handled by menus to give users an up-to-the-minute interface to system and menu resources. This section presents a technique to accomplish this through the **.mwmrc** file and describes procedures for implementing some more common examples. Creating dynamic menus involves one of two approaches:

- Rename the **mwm** executable, so you can use a frontend script to load Motif. The frontend script must be called **mwm** and be located in the same directory as the original **mwm** executable.
- Use the UNIX **cron** facility to have menus updated during work-sessions or some other regularly scheduled time. This method is less obtrusive, but does not let the user initiate an update at will.

The Xmenu software uses the **mwm** frontend method. The original **mwm** is renamed **MWMEXEC**. Uppercase letters are used to indicate that, indeed, something very different is going on. Note that when you use the frontend method, you must restart Motif by using the **kill** command on the current instance of the Motif executable. Refer to the **rmwm** script in Chapter 2.

In the renamed **mwm**, you can do just about anything you want as a precursor to loading Motif. The Xmenu example (shown later in this section) simply inserts calls to various routines that gather network and system resources and then create appropriate menus. The only thing remaining is to decide where to locate these menus. In Xmenu, a submenu called *Configure* appears on the *Main Menu* (middle button). Initially, you can add a placeholder to the **.mwmrc** file. In Xmenu, until a user actually adds a dynamic menu, the placeholder looks like this:

```
Menu SystemConfig
{

}
```

You also have to add a menu item to the *Main Menu*. One way to do it is to use the **f.nop** function, so the menu item appears grayed out. The renamed **mwm** script, or its associated scripts, would be responsible for removing the **f.nop** when a menu was actually added. At this point, you would replace **f.nop** with **f.menu SystemConfig**. However, if you start at this point—the approach taken by Xmenu—the effect is harmless. Try it and see. The result is a small empty menu pane that appears if you select the *Configure* item.

Another reason to make the *Configure* item functional is so you can add calls to submenus. At this point, you definitely do use **f.nop**:

```
Menu SystemConfig
{
  "    Network hosts"  _N  f.nop
  " Logged-in users"   _L  f.nop
  "           Images"  _I  f.nop
  "        Configure"  _C  !"(xmenucfg)&"
}
```

By having a menu like this preconfigured, you reduce the amount of work necessary to update the **.mwmrc**. You also provide a cue for the user: If the menu isn't currently activated, **f.nop** causes the menu item to be grayed-out, which is even better, because it also alerts the user to the fact that a menu such as *Networks hosts* can exist. This leads us to another option: *Configure*, which is the last item on the *SystemConfig* menu. The **xmenucfg** script, which *Configure* calls, replaces the executable **mwm** with the frontend **mwm** shell script:

```
#!/bin/sh
# xmenucfg, script to add mwm frontend
# Syntax: xmenucfg
# Copyright (c) Alan Southerton 1993
```

```
# Script assumes mwm is in /usr/bin; please edit.
  mv /usr/bin/mwm /usr/bin/MWMEXEC

# Copy and rename mwm.exec from $XMENU directory.
  cp mwm.exec /usr/bin/mwm

# Remove the .motif error file if it happens to exist
  rm $HOME/.motifgo
```

The script simply renames **mwm** to **MWMEXEC**, copies **mwm.exec** to **mwm**, and removes **.motif** if it exists. The script assumes **mwm** is originally located in **/usr/bin**, but you should check this and make corrections as appropriate. The **.motifgo** file, which was introduced in Chapter 2, is generated automatically when Motif loads. The way to have Motif do this is to include an intentional error in the **.mwmrc.** The error used in Chapter 2 was the following:

```
Menu ErrorMaker
{
 Error Error
}
```

At the other end of the configuration spectrum, you must check for the existence of **.motifgo** before executing Motif. The way to do this is to use the **execwm** function in either a systemwide startup file, or in **.xsession** (**xdm** systems) or **.xinitrc** (**xinit** systems). The **execwm** function, which returns only after the **mwm** frontend finishes its chores, is repeated here:

```
execwm() {
  $wm &
  # Make clients wait for window mgr
    while [ 1 ]
    do
      if [ -s $HOME/.motifgo ]; then
         rm $HOME/.motifgo
         break
      fi
    done
return; }
```

After including the function in your startup script, you can start the window manager like this:

```
execwm ; mwm &
```

Depending on your startup scripts, the method could be more elaborate. Using the systemwide **Xsession** to load Motif would require a window manager startup routine something like this:

```
# Test for .xsession; start Motif and exec .xsession
  if [ -x "$HOME/.xsession" ]; then
     execwm
     exec $startup $*
  fi
```

So what does the actual **mwm** frontend script—or **mwm.exec** as it is stored in the $XMENU directory—look like? Anything you want it to, of course, but the one included with Xmenu simply calls subordinate scripts. In the case of the example, it calls **gethosts**, **getusers**, and **getimages**. (The following three sections describe these scripts; you will probably want to create your own based on the techniques they use.)

Using **mwm** frontend and related scripts is pretty straightforward. There is no intention to automate the entire process, but simply to automate some routines so the end user need not get involved in script configuration. There is a burden on the desktop customizer or administrator. You are required to manually update the **mwm.exec** and **.mwmrc** files to some extent. With **mwm.exec**, you must add the calls to subordinate scripts; with **.mwmrc**, you must edit the *Configure* submenu to add and remove items. If you choose, you could automate some of these procedures—but when it comes to software configuring itself, it is good to draw a line in the sand. If other users who use your software want to configure additional menus, they can call upon your services—or learn how to edit **mwm.exec** and **.mwmrc**.

Cron Alternative

If you are sensitive to the time its takes Motif to go through the restart process, you can use cron to edit the **.mwmrc** file behind the scenes. Depending on the importance of a feature, you can schedule **cron** to run reconfiguration scripts at different intervals.

In your **crontab** file, set up the **cron** timing so **gethosts**, **getusers**, and **getimages** get called on a regular basis, but not so regularly that a noticeable load is placed on the system. Call them at different increments every hour or so, or longer if updating the menu is not so important. When you establish settings in your own **crontab** file, you can make changes to other users' **crontab** files, or give them the option to make the changes on an **.mwmrc** menu. Here are some **crontab** examples:

```
# .mwmrc configuration scripts
  15 * * * * * /home/bin/Crons/gethosts
  30 * * * * * /home/bin/Crons/getusers
  45 * * * * * /home/bin/Crons/getimages
```

Another advantage to using **cron** is you can continue to use the **f.restart** option instead of killing and reexecuting Motif.

Network Hosts Option

The *Network hosts* option requires a little bit of persistence on the part of system administrators—in that the **/etc/hosts** file needs to be maintained in a uniform manner—but it adds a powerful mechanism to any set of Motif menus. Figure 10-4 shows a typical submenu consisting of hosts found on the network.

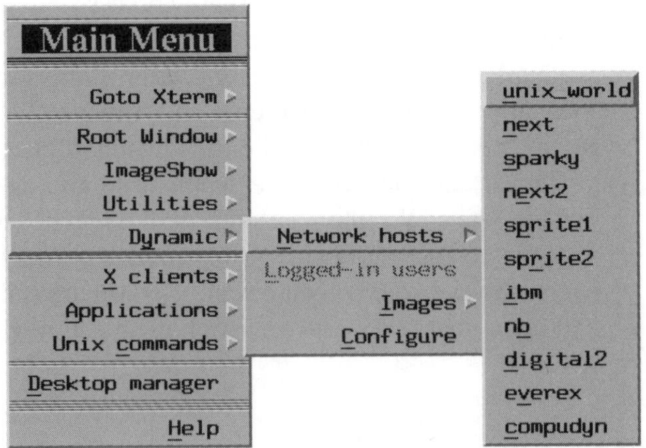

Figure 10-4 The *Network hosts* submenu.

The **gethosts** script associated with the *Network hosts* option expects to find a recognizable **/etc/hosts** file. This is important because it reduces the number of **sed** commands necessary to guarantee that different ways of ordering data in **/etc/hosts** are evaluated by **gethosts**. The alternative—writing enough **sed** routines to take into consideration any number of random whitespaces, tabs, and comments—could be mind-boggling. So guaranteeing a format such as the following one makes things a lot easier:

```
# Host Database
#
# If NIS running, this file is only consulted when
# booting. Also, use tabs for separators
#
127.0.0.1 localhost
#
192.9.200.1     sparks  IPC          # This SPARC
192.9.200.2     pelica alpha3000     # DEC Alpha
192.9.200.3     sparky               # Sparcstation2
192.9.200.5     next next68040       # Next
192.9.200.10    sprite1 dvx1         # DesqView/X
192.9.200.14    sprite2 dvx2         # DesqView/X
192.9.200.31    ibm                  # IBM 386
192.9.200.32    nb notebook zeos     # Notebook
192.9.200.107   compaq               # Pentium
```

From this **/etc/hosts** file, the *Network hosts* menu gets its menu options. The **localhost** designation is ignored. Here is the **gethosts** script:

```
#!/bin/sh
# gethosts, obtain currently networked hosts
# Syntax: gethosts <no options>
# Note: script requires well formed hosts file

# Initial values
  file=/tmp/.xmenu.$$
  opt="!\"(xterm -name remote -e telnet "

# Remove temporary file if untimely exit
  trap "rm $file; exit 1 2 3 15"

# Routine to get hostnames
  sed -n /192/,/192/p /etc/hosts > $file
  hosts=`cat $file | cut -d'  ' -f2 | cut -d' ' -f1`
  #Remove  set - `echo $hosts`

# Get and check total number of button bindings
  sed "/^Menu *NetworkHosts/,/}/d" $HOME/.mwmrc > $file

# Construct new hosts menu
  echo >> $file
  echo "Menu NetworkHosts" >> $file
  echo "{" >> $file
```

```
i=0;
for host in $hosts
do
  i=`expr $i + 1;`
  n=0; status=bad

  if [ $i -ne 1 ]; then
     while [ "$status" = "bad" ]
     do
        n=`expr $n + 1;`
        key=`echo $host | cut -c$n`
        if [ "$key" = "" ]; then
           echo Too many similar menu names
           exit 1
        fi
        #Parse through already set mnemonics
        for mnemonic in $letters
        do
          if [ "$key" = "$mnemonic" ]; then
             status=bad
             break
          fi
          status=good
        done
     done #endwhile

   #Else take care of first case
   else
        key=`echo $host | cut -c1`
   fi
   letters="$letters $key"

   echo "\" $host\" _$key $opt $host)\"" >> $file
 done
 echo "}" >> $file

 cp $HOME/.mwmrc $HOME/.mwmrc.bak
 mv $file $HOME/.mwmrc
```

After setting initial values and a **trap** command for temporary files, the script retrieves the hostnames in the third block of code. The first **sed** command keys on **192** in the host address. The script then deletes any existing *NetworkHosts* menu. The **sed** command used to do this requires that you specify the beginning and ending of the address, using precise string matching.

The script then goes on to build the new menu in $file. Much of the script is spent evaluating letters to use as mnemonics for the menu items. The **else** case inside the main **for** loop sets the first mnemonic to the first letter. If this is unacceptable, in that a previous item has already been set to that letter, the entire **while** loop is repeated. Using **cut** with the **-c** option lets you do this, as well as a loop counter, thanks to **expr**. The resulting menu looks like this:

```
Menu NetworkHosts
{
" sparks" _u !"(xterm -name remote -e telnet sparks)"
" pelica" _n !"(xterm -name remote -e telnet pelica)"
" sparky" _s !"(xterm -name remote -e telnet  sparky)"
" next" _e !"(xterm -name remote -e telnet next)"
" sprite1" _p !"(xterm -name remote -e telnet  sprite1)"
" sprite2" _r !"(xterm -name remote -e telnet  sprite2)"
" ibm" _i !"(xterm -name remote -e telnet ibm)"
" nb" _b !"(xterm -name remote -e telnet  nb)"
" compaq" _c !"(xterm -name remote -e telnet  compaq)"
}
```

Except for the format—columns don't line up and all entries are flush left—the automatically created menu is no different from one that you would create yourself. Note that after running **gethosts**, or any other script that edits **.mwmrc**, you should visually check the results. The **gethosts** script makes a backup file, but **$HOME/.mwmrc.bak** is overwritten the next time you use **gethosts**.

More Dynamic Options

You can probably think of many different things that you would like to automate. Some possibilities include **telnet**, **ftp**, the so-called **r** commands, **talk**, email, Netnews, **cu** and **uutry**.

The requirements for a general script to implement many menu options are not that different from those in **gethosts**. Additionally, because you will want to add site-specific options, a general script to handle many options is a good idea.

On the execution end of things you can have another general script, making maintenance of the configuration scripts relatively easy. Having an execution script also makes the **.mwmrc** file more readable if the *Network Hosts* menu happens to end up unwieldy.

Remember, even before you use a configuration script, you should have placed a corresponding **f.menu** statement elsewhere in the **.mwmrc** file.

With that proviso, here is **cfgmenus**, which presents a more general approach than the **gethosts** script:

```
#!/bin/sh
# cfgmenus, script to add submenus
# Syntax: cfgmenus <routine>
# Copyright (c) Alan Southerton 1993

# Initial values
  file=/tmp/.xmenu.$$
  item=$1; i=0

# Remove temporary file if untimely exit
  trap "rm $file; exit 1 2 3 15"

  case $item in

   #Routine to get user names
   users) items=`who | sed 's/ /:/' | cut -d: -f1`
          menu=LoggedInUsers
          opt="!\"(cfgexec talk " ;;

   email) items=`cut -d' ' -f1 $HOME/.mailrc`
          menu=EmailUsers
          opt="!\"(cfgexec email " ;;

   hosts) sed -n /192/,/192/p /etc/hosts > $file
          hosts=`cat $file | \
                    cut -d'    ' -f2 | cut -d' ' -f1`
          opt="!\"(cfgexec hosts " ;;

     ftp) sed -n /192/,/192/p /etc/hosts > $file
          hosts=`cat $file | \
                    cut -d'    ' -f2 | cut -d' ' -f1`
          opt="!\"(cfgexec ftp " ;;

  images) seed=`date +%S | cut -c2`
          max=`expr $seed + 10`
          path=`grep IMAGEPATH \
                    $HOME/.xmenu | cut -d: -f2`
          for image in $path/*.gif
          do
            if [ $i -gt $seed ]; then
               items=$items" "`basename $image`
               echo $image
               echo $items
```

```
            fi
            if [ $i -gt $max ]; then
               break
            fi
          i=`expr $i + 1`
          done
          menu=ConfigImages
          opt="!\"(imageshow $path/" ;;

  esac

# Delete previous instance of menu, if any
  sed "/^Menu *${menu}/,/}/d" $HOME/.mwmrc > $file


# Construct new menu
  echo >> $file
  echo "Menu ${menu}" >> $file
  echo "{" >> $file
  i=0;
  for item in $items
  do
    i=`expr $i + 1;`
    n=0; status=bad

    if [ $i -ne 1 ]; then
       while [ "$status" = "bad" ]
       do
          n=`expr $n + 1;`
          key=`echo $item | cut -c$n`
          if [ "$key" = "" ]; then
             echo Too many similar menu names
             exit 1
          fi
          #Parse through already set mnemonics
          for mnemonic in $letters
          do
            if [ "$key" = "$mnemonic" ]; then
               status=bad
               break
            fi
          status=good
          done
       done #endwhile

      #Else take care of first case
```

```
    else
         key=`echo $item | cut -c1`
    fi
    letters="$letters $key"

    echo "\" $item\" _$key $opt$item)\"" >> $file
done
echo "}" >> $file

cp $HOME/.mwmrc $HOME/.mwmrc.bak
mv $file $HOME/.mwmrc
```

The **cfgmenus** script implements four new options and you can probably think of many more. To call **cfgmenus**, you simply specify the name of the option you want. For example:

```
cfgmenus ftp
```

The parameter is then used throughout the script as well as passed to the **cfgexec** script. The **cfgexec** script, included on the distribution diskettes, executes the appropriate command using the **-e** option to Xterm.

The one routine presented in **cfgmenus** that needs further explanation is the **images)** routine. Using a very simple random number seed, the **images** routine uses a **for** loop to parse through a set of images. The example hard-codes the directory **/usr/images**. You will likely have to change this. One idea is to use the image directory specified in **.xmenu**. To do this, you would insert the following into the routine:

```
path=`grep IMAGEPATH $HOME/.xmenu | cut -d: -f2`
```

Note, too, that instead of **cfgexec**, the **image)** routine specifies that the associated menu items should call **imageshow**. See Chapter 8 for more information on **imageshow**.

Multiple Configurations

Having different versions of **.mwmrc** file available is another approach to providing custom environments. You may or may not want to use these files in conjunction with dynamic reconfiguration. The point is you can have different environments for different sets of users. You can create a special menu to allow users to change between the environments, or you can refrain, depending on whether you want a given user to have access to a given environment.

The Xmenu software does not provide alternative **.mwmrc** files to create different environments. The procedure behind it is straightforward, although you might want to create unique resources files—**.Xdefaults**, **XTerm**, and **.xmenu**, to name a few—for different **.mwmrc** files. The hardest part is the labor required to create sets of special resources and ensure that scripts that move and copy the resource and **.mwmrc** files create backup files and otherwise work accurately.

APPENDIX A
Performance Notes

MEMORY USAGE IN XMENU

Depending on the memory available to your system, you might want to strongly consider the effects of scripts and subshells on performance. In most modern workstations, it is advisable to have at least 16 megabytes of memory, and definitely preferable to have 32 megabytes of memory. Considering the cost of other workstation components, the relatively small amount for workstation memory is not that significant.

There are some things that you can do when configuring resources to prevent additional memory usage. One thing is keep your **.Xdefaults** files to a reasonable size. Another thing is to keep Xterm scroll buffers small except when necessary. Keep your **.mwmrc** file small (if that is possible after reading this book). Most of all, be sure you have adequate swap space to support your environment, including commercial applications, which place the highest demands on swap space.

To find out information about memory usage, use the **ps** command. The BSD **ps -aux** and the System V **ps -** reports on memory usage.

XMENU DIRECTORIES

It is recommended that the Xmenu software be installed in a common directory with access to all users on a given system. The Xmenu scripts should be executable for all users and it is a good idea to include the directory in the system path. This step is not necessary for the files on the distribution diskette if you set the $XMENU variable to point to the directory.

When you include directories that contain resource files, there are seven directories that can come into play:

- $HOME—contains normal shell startup files, **.mwmrc**, **.Xdefaults**, **.xmenu**, and possibly client resource files. The Xmenu scripts also make backup copies of **.mwmrc**, **.Xdefaults**, and **.xmenu** in the home directory.
- $XAPPLRESDIR—contains client resources files and is a location suggested by and known to X.
- $XMENU—contains the scripts that service the Xmenu software, plus subdirectories.
- $XMENU/**bitmaps**—contains bitmaps for the Xmenu software and for Xterms used with the menus.
- $XMENU/**palettes**—contains alternative color resources that you can use through the Xmenu software.
- $XMENU/**misc**—contains miscellaneous scripts not used in the Xmenu software, but useful for command line users.
- $XMENU/**menus**—contains the Xmenu menus broken down into smaller units, so you can configure a smaller version of **.mwmrc** if you want.

You can easily streamline the menus if you want and place all scripts and files in the $XMENU directory. If you choose to do something like this, remember that bitmap files used in the **.mwmrc** file are hardcoded. You will have to edit them by removing the old path and adding the new one. The total disk space used by the Xmenu software, as available on the distribution diskette, is 000K.

PUBLIC DOMAIN SOFTWARE

As you get deeper into customizing the X and Motif environment, you are more than likely going to want to use public domain software. Already, because of *The Shell Hacker's Guide to X and Motif*, you are confronted with compiling at least two public domain programs, **xcoloredit** by Richard Hesketh, at the University of Kent at Canterbury in England; and **xloadimage** by Jim Frost of Saber Software. The book also mentions other public domain utilities, and you are strongly advised again to get a copy of the Extended Portable Bitmap Toolkit, or **pbmplus** for short.

There are no guarantees in compiling public domain software. The author of the software usually has created the program for a specific environment, but has done so with portability in mind. The author may have tested the software on other environments—and may even provide documentation on how to compile the software—but again, there are no guarantees. But if it were a perfect world, the following steps would produce a compiled version of a public domain program:

1. **md /tmp/xcoloredit**
2. **cp xcolordtr.z /tmp/xcoloredit**
3. **cd /tmp/xcoloredit**
4. **mv xcolrdtr.z xcolrdtr.Z**
5. **uncompress xcolrdtr.Z**
6. **tar xovf xcolrdtr**
7. **cd xcoloredit**
8. **xmkmf**
9. **make**

Steps 1 through 3 might not be necessary, depending on how the file you are dealing with "untars" in Step 6. When you untar many public domain programs, the process creates a subdirectory, usually with the same name as the executable file for the program. This is true with the version of **xcoloredit** on the distribution diskette. Thus, after you uncompress and untar the file in Steps 5 and 6, you end up with:

/tmp/xcoloredit/xcoloredit

After you finish compiling the software, you can worry about moving compiled files and directories to a better location. In fact, after you have compiled many public domain programs, you don't need to keep any files on hard disk other than the program's executable file. In the meantime, don't worry that **/tmp/xcoloredit/xcoloredit** looks strange. Hold on for the hard part, Steps 8-9.

In Step 8, the suspense begins. The **xmkmf** script, contained in /usr/bin/X11, runs the **imake** program, which is supposed to generate a valid **Makefile** from another file, called **IMakefile**. A **Makefile** is necessary to adapt the compiling process to your system by specifying the location of various object libraries and other dependencies. Even if everything seems to work fine, and a **Makefile** is produced, you could still have problems in the **Makefile** and the program won't compile. At this point, if you haven't done so already, you should consult any **readme** files for information pertinent to your system. After this, you will probably have to edit the **IMakefile**.

USING GREP AND CUT

The scripts that support the Xmenu software make frequent use of the **grep** and **cut** commands. The **grep -v** command proves invaluable because it extracts all lines from a file except those that contain the specified string:

```
grep -v SAVETOXDEFAULTS $HOME/.Xdefaults > $file
```

This command outputs all lines in $HOME/**.Xdefaults** and they are placed in $file thanks to redirection. As a result, a new value for SAVETOXDEFAULTS can now be added to $file, and from there, as different Xmenu scripts illustrate, a new copy of **.Xdefaults** is made.

Another important use of **grep** in the Xmenu scripts is in a pipeline with **cut**. Together, the two commands give you a quick way to extract a value from a line of text. It is given, of course, that there will be only one line of text that matches the **grep** search pattern. Here is a typical example:

```
overwrite=`grep SAVETOXDEFAULTS \
                $HOME/.xmenu | cut -d: -f2`
```

Here the command reads the $HOME/**.xmenu** file and extracts the entire line containing SAVETOXDEFAULTS. The output is then piped into the **cut** command, which further extracts just the value to the right side of SAVETOXDEFAULTS. The **-d** switch to **cut** specifies a field delimiter. In this case, the delimiter is a colon. The **-f** switch tells **cut** which field to extract.

You can also extract values with **sed**. From a script programming viewpoint, you might prefer this approach, in that the Xmenu scripts also make extensive use of **sed**. Here is an equivalent **sed** command:

```
sed -n 's/SAVETOXDEFAULTS://p' $HOME/.xmenu
```

One slight annoyance with the **sed** approach is that it is a bit slower than **grep** and **cut**. But the speed difference should not be significant enough to deter you.

There is no reason not to consider **awk** either. Again the performance compared to **grep** and **cut** might be slightly slower. Here is the equivalent **awk** statement:

```
grep SAVETOXDEFAULTS $HOME/.xmenu |\
                          awk -F: '{print $2}'
```

If you are not accustomed to using **awk**, don't let that stop you from using **awk** in situations where you need to cut data from a file. For one thing, you can do floating point arithmetic with **awk** when you use it as a data cutting tool.

NAMED PIPES

If performance is an issue, you can always make UNIX scripts run a bit faster by using named pipes (that is, if the scripts use temporary files). To create a named pipe, you must use the **mknod** command:

```
mknod xmenutmp p &
```

One consideration is that the named pipe (which you name anything you like within normal file-naming conventions) should exist before you use the Xmenu scripts. If you create the named pipe in scripts, and then remove it before the script exits, the additional steps defeat the purpose of using the named pipe in the first place—namely, performance.

The user's home directory is one place to create the named pipe, but it is important that you sequester named pipes as much as possible. One reason is that some UNIX commands, such as **grep**, will get hung if they access the named pipe. And, as you know, many users are likely to use **grep** with a wildcard, putting the named pipe in the path of **grep**.

Restricting access to a file—or, in this case, a named pipe—is a subject with many conclusions. UNIX's numerous ways of protecting files—and the various methodologies that sites can implement—can lead to different ways to restrict and provide access. The most efficient method is to set the user id (SUID) or group id (SGID) on programs that require special access to files. Using this approach, you can store the named pipes for Xmenu scripts in an otherwise restricted directory. For example, you might want to create a directory in $XMENU called **pipes**. Be careful when you use SUID and SGID. Generally, avoid allowing nonprivileged users from running a subshell within an SUID or SGID script. If this safeguard is not taken, scurrilous users can acquire the privileges of the executing script.

There are different ways you can optimize with named pipes. The idea is to put as much data as possible into the named pipe before copying it to a real file. For example, because most of the Xmenu scripts query either the **xrdb** database (in server memory) or an existing resource file, you might want to combine your and read and write operations:

```
pipe=$XMENU/pipes/$USER
{ xrdb -query | grep -v $1; echo $1: $2; } > $pipe &
cp $pipe $HOME/.Xdefaults
```

The {} operators in the example let you group commands together. The result is that the output from the commands is streamed together before being redirected to the pipe. Pay particular attention to the whitespace used with the {} operators and the semicolons. Each command requires whitespace before and after it. Each command must also be terminated with a semicolon.

If you don't want to use the {} operators—and this would be the case on systems in which the Bourne shell starts a subshell to run the commands inside the {} operators—try the following:

```
pipe=$XMENU/pipes/$USER
xrdb -query | grep -v $1 > $pipe &
cp $pipe $HOME/.Xdefaults
echo $1: $2 >> $HOME/.Xdefaults
```

Here, the named pipe is used to receive the filtered output from the Xrdb database. This represents most of the data involved, so the actual writing of the new value to $HOME/**.Xdefaults** adds little overhead to the process.

MISCELLANEOUS TIPS

The performance that you get from X and Motif depends a lot on the type of hardware you are using. Although X has been around for a long time, it is only with the arrival of fast RISC workstations in the UNIX market that it is capable of exceptional performance. But not everyone or every business can afford fast RISC workstations, so it is important that your systems configuration do as much as it can to add, instead of detract, from performance. The following tips could be helpful:

- Limit the number of X clients running on a workstation at any given time. This is a common sense suggestion, but it is amazing the number of times that one sees computers filled with Xterms and other windows—and the owner of the workstation doesn't even know why they are all running.
- Whenever possible, run a fair number of X clients on remote machines. In some cases, running a client on a remote machine can actually be faster than on the local machine—because X doesn't have to switch between managing the server and client.
- Limit the number of fonts used by your X clients. The Xmenu software provides several basic fonts for use in Xterms. Your commercial applications will likely add other fonts. The net result is more memory usage. If you choose to limit your fonts, leave a fully workable set, because you must remove the remaining fonts from X server's font database.
- Define the X environment variable $DISPLAY as :0.0 so that X clients that run on the local system can take advantage of high per-

formance routines in the X server. Remote clients, which must have $DISPLAY defined to the hostname (0, or 0.0 are optional), cannot take advantage of these routines. (DEC workstations come with $DISPLAY defined to :0.0).

- So the system doesn't start falling all over itself when you start X and Motif, place brief **sleep** commands after each X client you start in your **.xinitrc** or **.xsession** file. Set to one or two seconds, the **sleep** statements actually let the system catch its breath between initializations of the X server, Motif, and your various X clients. The net result could be a faster overall loading time.

- For Heaven's sake, go easy on displaying images on the root window if you have memory-intensive tasks to perform. If you are running an image show, terminate it before starting up a memory-intensive application. You might also want to remove any current image from the root window.

- Make sure that Motif does not move its windows using opaque moves. An opaque move is when you can move the window, yet still see the window and its contents. Set **Mwm*moveOpaque** to **false** to drop this feature, which causes a severe performance penalty. The default behavior of Motif is to move windows in tracking-outline form.

APPENDIX B
Tracking Xterm

INTERCLIENT BLUES

Although a great deal of interclient communication goes on between windows and the window manager, the desktop tools that come standard with the system don't provide an easy way for end users to participate in managing windows outside of normal conventions. This appendix addresses the lack of a method to send an Xterm escape sequence from a window manager menu or, for that matter, from one Xterm to another Xterm.

In specific terms, the problem results from the fact that you cannot easily obtain data on the three identities of an Xterm window. To review, here's a summary of the three identities:

- ptty number—Each Xterm is assigned a pseudo-terminal device number corresponding to a device file. You can obtain the filename by using the UNIX **tty** command.
- window id—All windows, including Xterms, are assigned a window id by the X server. The id is in hexadecimal format. It can be obtained by using **xwininfo**.
- window name—All windows have a name corresponding to the the text in the titlebar. Don't confuse this with the name used with the **-name** option, which specifies an instance or class name for the window.

As you can see, it is possible to get plenty of information on a window. In addition to the three identities, the **xwininfo** and **xprop** commands tell you almost everything you need to know from an X viewpoint. And from a UNIX viewpoint, you don't have to stop with **tty**; you can use **ps** to get lots more information on the window's associated UNIX processes.

The problem remains, however: How do you get both the window id and the ptty number to be visible to the same shell script? The answer lies in using the window name as it appears in the titlebar. The difference between using the window name and using the window id is that you can record the window name when you first invoke an Xterm. This is an important distinction, because obviously just as there is no way to query the window id and ptty number at the same time, there is no way to query the window name and ptty number together. The following script, called **xtrack**, implements the approach:

```
#!/bin/sh
# xtrack, gets window info
# Syntax: xtrack <window name>
# Copyright (c) Alan Southerton 1993

# Initial values
  file=/tmp/.xmenu.$$
  name="$*"; tty=`tty`

# Get the window id
  id=`xwininfo -name "$name" | \
    sed -n "s/xwininfo.*0x/0x/p" | \
    cut -d' ' -f1`

# Now update the .xmenu file
  grep -v $tty $HOME/.xmenu > $file
  echo "$id:$tty" >> $file
  cp $HOME/.xmenu $HOME/.xmenu.bak
  mv $file $HOME/.xmenu

# Finally execute a subshell
  exec $SHELL
```

Most of the activity in **xtrack** occurs before the Xterm window is ready to use. The Xterm comes up, but does not display the UNIX prompt for a few seconds (unless you are using a fast workstation).

As you can see, the **xwininfo** utility uses its **-name** option to tell it which window to evaluate. (The default behavior of **xwininfo**, remember, is to require the user to select the window with the pointer.) Next a **sed** command extracts a string of text containing the window id. The **cut** command finishes up by cutting unnecessary text from the string.

Next the **xtrack** script uses $HOME/**.xmenu** to store the information it has obtained. By now, the script has obtained the window id, as described, as well as the ptty number. The latter is accomplished right off the bat in the

"Initial Values" block. Nothing is unusual about updating $HOME/**.xmenu**, but as you will notice, unlike the majority of **.xmenu** statements, this addition to Xmenu does not use a predetermined resource name (in uppercase letters). Instead, the entry in $HOME/**.xmenu** looks like this:

```
0x280000d:/dev/ttyp5
```

One thing you should note about the code that updates $HOME/**.xmenu**: It is responsible for deleting the previous statement, if any, associated with the current ptty number. This is necessary because the **xtrack** script exits after it executes the subshell:

```
exec $SHELL
```

If **xtrack** didn't exit here, you would have an instance of the shell unnecessarily hanging around. Because it exits here, however, you can use a **trap** command to ensure that the outgoing Xterm removes its window id entry in $HOME/**.xmenu**. In any event, as written, **xtrack** exits long before the subshell exits.

You also have to pay attention to how you call the Xterm when you use **xtrack**. If you do not specify an initial title and pass it on to **xtrack**, nothing is going to work. Here is an example:

```
xterm -name Xmenu -title Scripts -e xtrack Scripts &
```

The example uses a single word title, but you don't have to worry about multiple words. The reason is $name is set to **$*** in **xtrack**. Thus, you can use a command like this:

```
xterm -name Xmenu -title "`date`" -e xtrack `date`&
```

If you want to improve the performance of **xtrack**, you can run its two major routines in the background. Here's a second look:

```
#!/bin/sh
# xtrack, gets window info
# Syntax: xtrack <window name>
# Copyright (c) Alan Southerton 1993

# Initial values
  name="$*"

  xshgetid "$name"
  exec $SHELL
```

To complete the circuit, you need **xshgetid**, which in concept presents itself as a candidate for a reusable script. But because of the flip-flop of resource and value (window id and ptty number), you should probably make it a specific routine. Here's **xshgetid**:

```
#!/bin/sh
# xshgetid, gets window id
# Syntax: xshgetid <window name>
# Copyright (c) Alan Southerton 1993


# Initial values
  file=/tmp/.xmenu.$$
  name=$*; tty=`tty`

# Get the window id
  id=`xwininfo -name "$name" | \
    sed -n "s/xwininfo.*0x/0x/p" | \
    cut -d' ' -f1`

# Now update the .xmenu file
  grep -v $tty $HOME/.xmenu > $file
  echo "$id:$tty" >> $file
  cp $HOME/.xmenu $HOME/.xmenu.bak
  mv $file $HOME/.xmenu
```

The performance improvement in the second version of **xtrack** will be slight, if noticeable at all. But the second version has this to offer and nothing going against it: Even if you exit an Xterm immediately after using **xtrack**, the background **xshgetid** can run its course without harm. The next Xterm with the salient ptty number, as you have seen, will delete the previous reference from $HOME/**.xmenu**.

NOW FOR THE GAIN

Besides opening an unimpeded avenue to communicating with Xterms, **xtrack** is a delight for Xterm users. Because the window id and ptty number are now contained in $HOME/**.xmenu**, you can build any number of scripts to take advantage of it. The most compelling ones are scripts that send Xterm escape sequences.

In Chapter 4, the **xsf** script provides a thorough example of dealing with font escape sequences. The script includes error checking and plenty of options. You can use this as the basis on which to build other scripts that access $HOME/**.xmenu** for the window id and ptty number information. Presented here is the basic routine to send an escape sequence to an Xterm by using the new $HOME/**.xmenu** statement. For variety, the script modifies the titlebar to show process information associated with the ptty.

```
#!/bin/sh
# sendps, updates titlebar
# Syntax: sendpath <no options>
# Copyright (c) Alan Southerton 1993

# Initial values
  file=/tmp/.xmenu.$$

# Get the window id
  id=`xwininfo | \
    sed -n "s/xwininfo.*0x/0x/p" | \
    cut -d' ' -f1`

# Get the ptty number
  tty=`grep $id $HOME/.xmenu | cut -d: -f2`

# Define variable for escape sequence
  cmd=`ps aux -t $tty | grep -v TIME | grep -v grep`

# Send escape sequence
  /bin/echo -n "^[]0;`echo $cmd`^G" > $tty
```

After the script gets the window id (from **xwininfo**) and the ptty number (from $HOME/**.xmenu**), it puts together a string of text to send to the target Xterm. In the example, the **ps** command is used to generate the string. Note that although the **ps** command strips the **ps** header and **grep** entry, it does not strip additional subprocesses. You might view this as a feature, or you might like to limit the titlebar output to the initial process associated with the Xterm. The following replacement to define $cmd does the trick:

```
# Define variable for escape sequence
  set - `ps aux -t $tty | \
              grep -v TIME | grep -v grep`
  i=0
  for arg in $*
  do
     if [ $i -gt 12 ]; then break; fi
     i=`expr $i + 1`
     cmd=$cmd" "$arg
  done
```

Here the output from the **ps** command is placed in the shell's argument space with the **set** command. The **for** loop then cycles through the argument space. When the loop reaches 12, the number of fields in the **ps aux** command, a break is executed. This is a highly specific implementation of **ps**, in that it uses BSD compatibility (a feature of OSF/1 on DEC Alpha systems). If you use other flags, be sure you adjust the number of fields in the **if** statement.

There are plenty of other text values that you can send to the titlebar in Xterm windows. In fact, you can probably think of enough to know that it might be worth a more comprehensive script to manage sending Xterm escape sequences. Here is a starter script:

```
#!/bin/sh
# sendesc, send escape sequences
# Syntax: sendesc <option>
# Copyright (c) Alan Southerton 1993

# Initial values
  file=/tmp/.xmenu.$$
  option=$1

# Get the window id
  id=`xwininfo | \
     sed -n "s/xwininfo.*0x/0x/p" | \
     cut -d' ' -f1`

# Get the ptty number
  tty=`grep $id $HOME/.xmenu | cut -d: -f2`

  case "$option" in

    ps) cmd=`ps aux -t $tty | \
                  grep -v TIME | grep -v grep` ;;

  date) cmd=`date` ;;
  time) cmd=`date "+%I:%H %p"` ;;
  host) cmd=`hostname` ;;
  user) cmd=`echo $USER` ;;
  text) xterm -name getstring \
              -e getany Title $file
        if [ -s $file ]; then
           cmd=`cat $file`
        else
           exit
        fi ;;

  esac
```

```
# Send escape sequence
  /bin/echo -n "^[]0;`echo $cmd`^G" > $tty
```

The **sendesc** script gives you six choices, including one that puts up an Xterm window so you can enter text. In each **case** statement, all output from commands, as well as text from the input Xterm, is stored in the $cmd variable. Now you can add to these at will. The one drawback is that you cannot add commands that display environment-specific information about an Xterm. For example, you cannot show the current path. If you want to be able to set this type of information, one way to do it is through your shell prompt. For example, in your prompt alias, you could execute the **set** or **env** commands and maintain that file in a commonly known location. Next, in the **sendesc** script, you would add a routine that reads that file for the current path, among other things. See the *Path Xterm—C Shell Only* section in Chapter 9 for additional information.

The next step, if you haven't already guessed, is to make the **sendesc** script available to the Motif menus. The Xmenu software on the distribution media includes a menu called *Escape* on the *Xterms Menu*:

```
Menu XtermEscapes
{
  "Process"      _P  !"(sendesc ps)&"
  "Date"         _D  !"(sendesc date)&"
  "Time"         _T  !"(sendesc time)&"
  "Hostname"     _H  !"(sendesc host)&"
  "User name"    _U  !"(sendesc user)&"
  "Input text"   _T  !"(sendesc text)&"
}
```

APPENDIX C
Quick Scripts

COMMAND LINE HELP

This appendix contains suggested scripts not found in Xmenu. Many of them resemble functions, or tools, to help you build larger scripts. For example, the **xshwrite** script makes it easier to write to the **.xmenu** file. Similarly, **xshread** makes it easier to read from the **.xmenu** file. You should adapt these and other scripts in this appendix to your own needs.

senddate. The **senddate** script sends the date to the titlebar of an Xterm window. You execute **senddate** from the command line in the Xterm window that you want to affect. See the **sendesc** script in Appendix B for sending escape sequences to different Xterms.

```
#!/bin/sh
# senddate, updates titlebar
# Syntax: sendpath <no options>
# Copyright (c) Alan Southerton 1993

# Send path to ptty from command line
  /bin/echo -n "^[]0;`date`^G" > `tty`
```

sendpath. This script sends the current path to the titlebar of an Xterm window. You must execute **sendpath** in the same Xterm that you want to affect. It is a command line tool only.

```
#!/bin/sh
# sendpath, updates titlebar
```

```
# Syntax: sendpath <no options>
# Copyright (c) Alan Southerton 1993

# Send path to ptty from command line
  /bin/echo -n "^[]0;'pwd'^G" > 'tty'
```

sendtitle. The **sendtitle** script posts a text input Xterm and lets you enter a string of text to have inserted in the current Xterm's titlebar. Use this from the command line only. Similar to a routine in **sendesc** (see Appendix B), but it does not require the user to select an Xterm.

```
#!/bin/sh
# sendtitle, updates titlebar
# Syntax: sendpath <no options>
# Copyright (c) Alan Southerton 1993

# Initial values
  file=/tmp/.xmenu.$$

  xterm -name getstring -e getany Title $file
  title='cat $file'

  /bin/echo -n "^[]0;$title^G" > 'tty'
```

spymwm. This script evaluates currently running windows using the **xlswins** command. It lets you specify an English-language widget resource name and come up with the associated window id. If **spymwm** returns a window id, you can use **spymwm** a second time to extract related windows with similar ids. The script takes a single argument, which can be any text string acceptable to **grep**. The first time you use **spymwm**, start with a string of a widget-level resource name, such as **iconbox** or **feedback**.

```
#!/bin/sh
# spymwm, check for X widget level resource
# Syntax: spymwm <widget name>
# Example: spymwm iconbox

# Initial values
  widget=$1
  file=/tmp/.xmenu.$$
```

```
# Evaluate windows
  while [ 1 ]
  do
    xlswins > $file
    output='grep $widget $file'
    break
  done
  echo $output
```

tileterm. This is a script for Sun 1152x900 monitors. Many factors affect the size of an Xterm window, including the value given to the resize border, and the value of the current font. This script checks the resize border size and accommodates borders of 5 and 10 pixels. As for fonts, the script simply uses terminal-bold. For other display sizes, adjust the **-geometry** option in the various Xterm command lines. (See the **clone** script in Chapter 9 if you want to develop a script that automates Xterm sizing for any monitor.)

```
!#/bin/sh
# tileterm, start four Xterms
# Syntax: tileterm <no options>
# Copyright (c) By Alan Southerton

# Upper left-hand corner
  xterm -name tileterm \
          -geometry 68x27+0+0 -fn terminal-bold &

# Lower left-hand corner
  xterm -name tileterm \
          -geometry 68x27+0-0 -fn terminal-bold &

# Upper right-hand corner
  xterm -name tileterm \
          -geometry 68x27-0+0 -fn terminal-bold &

# Lower right-hand corner
  xterm -name tileterm \
          -geometry 68x27-0-0 -fn terminal-bold &
```

xshwrite. The **xshwrite** script lets you write a new value to the $HOME/**.xmenu** file. The script also removes the old value associated with the resource you specify. You must pass two arguments to **xshwrite**. The first argument is the Xmenu resource name. The second argument is the new value.

```
#!/bin/sh
# xshwrite, add item to .xmenu file
# Syntax: xshwrite <item> <value>
# Copyright (c) Alan Southerton 1993

# Remove temporary file if untimely exit
  trap "rm $file; exit 1 2 3 15"

# Initial values
  file=/tmp/.xmenu.$$
  item=$1; value=$2

# Add item to .xmenu file
  grep -v $item $HOME/.xmenu > $file
  echo "$item:$value" >> $file
  cp $HOME/.xmenu $HOME/.xmenu.bak
  mv $file $HOME/.xmenu
```

xflicker. The **xflicker** script displays alternates between two specified bitmaps every two seconds. The two arguments to **xflicker** are the bitmap filenames. Each must also have a full path specified unless you run **xflicker** from the directory containing the bitmaps. A suggested use is with a bitmap that has two versions, one the reverse of the other. (See Chapter 4 for information on using the the X11 bitmap editor.)

```
#!/bin/sh
# xflicker, alternates root bitmaps
# Syntax: xflicker <bitmap1> <bitmap2>
# Copyright (c) Alan Southerton 1993

  while [ 1 ]
  do
    xsetroot -bitmap $bitmap1
    sleep 2
    xsetroot -bitmap $bitmap2
    sleep 2
  done
```

xdim. This script uses the **-root** option to **xwininfo** and extracts the size of the root window. The script also formulates the results into easy-to-read sentences.

```
#!/bin/sh
# xdim, get monitor dimensions
# Syntax: xdim <no options>
# Copyright (c) Alan Southerton

# Initial values
  file=/tmp/xdim.$$

# Remove temporary file
  trap "rm $file; exit 0 1 2 3 15"

# Use xwininfo and refine
  xwininfo -root | egrep "(Width|Height)" > $file
  width=`grep Width $file | cut -c21-25`
  height=`grep Height $file | cut -c22-25`
  echo $width is the monitor width
  echo $height is the monitor height
```

findres. The **findres** script searches available resource files and displays the resource statements in effect for the specified resource. The **-c** option to **findres** lets you specify that you want the search to include an application resource file located in $HOME. Otherwise you can specify up to nine resources, so long as you enclose each one in double quotes. Here are some sample calls:

```
findres "background"
findres "background" "foreground" "scrollBar"
findres -c XTerm "background" "foreground"
```

The script handles the optional arguments by testing for their presence and then shifting them out of the shell's argument space.

```
#!/bin/sh
# getres, script to get resources
# Syntax: findres [-c] resource(s)
# Note: cmd line args must be in double quotes
# Copyright (c) Alan Southerton 1993

# Dependencies
# /usr/lib/X11/app-defaults

# Initial values
  file=/tmp/getres.$$
```

```
  usage="Usage: $0 [-c] resource(s)"

# Remove temporary file upon exit.
  trap "rm $file; exit 1 2 3 15"

# Check for valid number of arguments
  if [ "$#" = "0" ]; then
     echo $usage 1ARIGHT&2; exit 1
  fi
  if [ "$1" = "-c" -a "$2" = "" ]; then
     echo $usage 1ARIGHT&2; exit 1
  elif [ "$1" = "-c" -a "$2" != "" ]; then
     option=$1; class=$2;
     shift; shift
  fi

# Don't want to use wildcard in $HOME, so must set up
# different search locations for -c option

  if [ "$option" = "-c" ]; then
     places="$XENVIRONMENT \
            $XAPPLRESDIR/* \
            $HOME/$class \
            /usr/lib/X11/app-defaults/$class \
            $HOME/.Xdefaults \
            /usr/lib/X11/app-defaults/Xdefaults"
  else
     places="$XENVIRONMENT \
            $XAPPLRESDIR/* \
            /usr/lib/X11/app-defaults/* \
            $HOME/.Xdefaults \
            /usr/lib/X11/app-defaults/Xdefaults"
  fi

# Loop through resource locations
  for arg in $*
  do
     for place in $places
     do
       grep "$arg" $place
     done
  done
```

savedt. This script saves the current contents of the desktop in a file called .savedt in the user's home directory. Given the differences between how applications can save their geometry information, the **savedt** script does the best it can to approximate current geometry. You can execute **savedt** from the command line or include it as a Motif **.mwmrc** option. It is suggested that you execute $HOME/**.savedt** from an X startup file such as **.xinitrc** or **.xsession**.

```
#!/bin/sh
# Syntax:savedt <no options>
# Copyright (c) Alan Southerton

# Set values
  xtcheck=false; echeck=false
  file=/tmp/clone.$$

  mv $HOME/.savedt $HOME/.savedt.bak

# Generic function to get resource values
  getresvalue() {
  client=$1
  resource=$2
  resclass=$3

# This function returns a given resource value
# based on the resource with the highest precedence.
# The use of the -i option to grep pressuposes sane,
# as opposed to insane, resources.

  str=`appres XTerm $client | grep -i "$resource:"`
  if [ "$str" = "" ]; then return; fi
  set - `echo $str`

  for arg in $*
  do
    if [ "$arg" = "$client.VT100.$resource:" ]; then
       shift; value=$1; return
    fi
    if [ "$arg" = "$client.VT100*$resource:" ]; then
       shift; value=$1; return
    fi
    if [ "$arg" = "$client*$resource:" ]; then
       shift; value=$1; return
    fi
    if [ "$arg" = "$client*$resource:" ]; then
       shift; value=$1; return
    fi
```

```
    shift
  done
  set - `echo $str`
  for arg in $*
  do
    if [ "$arg" = "XTerm.VT100.$resource:" ]; then
       shift; value=$1; return
    fi
    if [ "$arg" = "XTerm.VT100*$resource:" ]; then
       shift; value=$1; return
    fi
    if [ "$arg" = "XTerm.VT100*$resclass:" ]; then
       shift; value=$1; return
    fi
    if [ "$arg" = "XTerm*VT100*$resclass:" ]; then
       shift; value=$1; return
    fi
    if [ "$arg" = "XTerm*$resclass:" ]; then
       shift; value=$1; return
    fi
  shift
  done

  value=`appres XTerm $client | \
          grep "^\*$resource" | cut -d: -f2`

  return
}

# Function to get window information
  getwininfo() {
  id=$1
      xwininfo -id $id -stats -size ARIGHT $file
      width=`sed -n "s/^.*Width: //p" $file`
      height=`sed -n "s/^.*Height: //p" $file`
      xinc=`sed -n "s/^.*x resize increment: //p" $file`
      yinc=`sed -n "s/^.*y resize increment: //p" $file`
      sbar=""; thickness=""; internal=""
      value=""; i=0;

# Get command string
  xprop -id $id ARIGHT $file
  newwindow=`sed -n \
            /WM_COMMAND/,/WM_ICON/'s/^.*{//p' $file |\
            sed s/}$//p | \
```

```
            sed s/,//gp`
  program=`echo $newwindow | cut -d' ' -f1`

# Take care of different Xterm geometry. Geometry
# does not reflect internal
# Xterm components so must factor scrollbar and
# internal border sizes. The first block of code
# begins by parsing for a default Xterm.

  xtcheck=`sed -n \
          's/WM_CLASS(STRING).*\"XTerm\"/true/p' $file`

  if [ "$xtcheck" = "true" ]; then
     name=`echo $newwindow | \
           sed -n 's/^.*\"\-name\" //p' | \
           sed -n s/\"//gp | cut -d' ' -f1`
     if [ "$name" = "" ]; then
         name=xterm
     fi

     getresvalue $name scrollBar ScrollBar
     sbar=$value; value=""
     #Clean tabs and spaces from sbar variable
     sbar=`echo $sbar | sed 's/    //gp'`

     #Check for default (no scrollbar) and for
     #turn-off option on the command line
     case $sbar in
         [Tt]rue) echo $newwindow | grep -q "\"+sb\""
                  if [ "$?" = "0" ]; then
                      sbar=false
                  else
                      sbar=true
                  fi ;;
              "") sbar=false ;;
     esac

     #Check for turn-on on the command line
     if [ "$sbar" = "" ]; then
         echo $newwindow | grep -q "\"-sb\""
         case $? in
            0) sbar=true ;;
            1) sbar=false ;;
         esac
     fi
```

```
      if [ "$sbar" = "true" ]; then
        getresvalue $name thickness Thickness
        thickness=$value; value=""
        : ${thickness:=10}
      else
        thickness=0
      fi

      #Now have to check for internal border
      getresvalue $name internalBorder InternalBorder
      internal=$value; value=""

      #Now have to check for border on command line
       echo $newwindow | grep -q "\"-b\""
       case $? in
              0) internal='echo $newwindow | \
                         sed -n 's/^.*\"\-b\" \"//p' |
\
                         sed -n s/\"//gp | cut -d' '
-f1' ;;
              1) : ${internal:=0} ;;
        esac

      # Do calculations to compensate for internal
components
        internal='expr $internal + $internal'
        width='expr \( $width - $thickness - $internal
\) / $xinc'
        height='expr \( $height - $internal \) /
$yinc'

fi

# Set new geometry for command string
echo $newwindow | egrep "(\"\-g\"|\"\-geom\"|\"\-ge-
ometry\")"
case $? in

      0) newwindow='echo $newwindow | \
         sed "s/\"\-geometry\".\"...../\"\-geometry\"
\"${width}x${height}/p" | \
         sed "s/\"\-geom\".\"...../\"\-geom\"
\"${width}x${height}/p" | \
         sed "s/\"\-g\".\"...../\"\-g\"
\"${width}x${height}/p"' ;;
```

```
     1) geometry="\"-geometry\"
\"${width}x${height}\""
        newwindow=`echo $newwindow | \
          sed -n "s/^$program/& $geometry/p"`

  esac

# Save command string to file
  echo eval $newwindow ARIGHTARIGHT $HOME/.savedt

return
}

# Main loop
  windows=`xlsclients -l | \
      sed -n 's/Window //p' | cut -d: -f1`
  for arg in $windows
  do
      getwininfo $argdone
  done
```

APPENDIX D
Xterm Escapes

ESCAPE SEQUENCES

There are numerous escape sequences that you can use with the Xterm terminal emulator. Some, as shown throughout the book, can enhance the display of Xterm windows. The majority, however, are for the specific enhancement of terminal emulation capabilities. This appendix lists the set of Xterm escape sequences.

To create an escape sequence, you must have the capacity to generate special characters such as **^H** and **^M**. Many text editors, including **vi** and **emacs**, have a mode that lets you create special characters. In **vi**, for example, you press **Esc-v** followed by **Esc** and the character associated with the escape sequence. You can also use **cat** and redirect standard input to create escape sequences (p. 84).

Table D-1 Common Symbols Defined

Symbol	Description
C	A single required character
Ps	A single, usually optional, numeric parameter composed of one or more digits
Pm	A multiple numeric parameter composed of any number of single numeric parameters, separated by one or more **;** characters
Pt	A text parameter composed of printable characters

Table D-2 Xterm Escape Sequences

Key Sequence	Description
Bel	Bell (Ctrl-G)
BS	Backspace (Ctrl-H)
Tab	Horizontal tab character (Ctrl-I)
LF	Line feed or new page (Ctrl-J)
VT	Vertical tab (Ctrl-K)
FF	Form feed or new page (Ctrl-L)
CR	Carriage return (Ctrl-M)
ESC # 8	DEC screen alignment test (DECALN)
ESC (C	Select G0 character set (SCS) C= 0 Special character and line drawing C= 1 Alternate character ROM standard set C= 2 Alternate character ROM special set C= A United Kingdom (UK) C= B United States (USASCII)
ESC 7	Save cursor (DECSC)
ESC 8	Restore cursor (DECRC)
ESC =	Application keypad (DECPAM)
ESC >	Normal keypad (DECPNM)
ESC D	Index (IND)
ESC E	Next line (NEL)
ESC H	Tab set (HTS)
ESC M	Reverse index (SCS)
ESC T Ps LF	Change window title to Ps
ESC [Ps @	Insert Ps (blank)character(s) (default=1)(ICH)
ESC [Ps A	Cursor up Ps times (default=1) (CUU)
ESC [Ps B	Cursor down Ps times (default=1) (CUD)
ESC [Ps C	Cursor forward Ps times (default=1) (CUF)
ESC [Ps D	Cursor backward Ps times (default=1) (CUB)

Table D-2 *(continued)*

Key Sequence	Description
ESC [Ps ; Ps H	Cursor position [row;column] (default=[1,1])(CUP)
ESC [Ps J	Erase in display (ED)
	Ps= 0 Clear below (default)
	Ps= 1 Clear above
	Ps= 2 Clear all
ESC [Ps K	Erase in line (EL)
	Ps= 0 Clear to right (default)
	Ps= 1 Clear left
	Ps= 2 Clear all
ESC [Ps L	Insert Ps line(s) (default = 1) (IL)
ESC [Ps M	Delete Ps line(s) (default = 1) (DL)
ESC [Ps P	Delete Ps characters(s) (default = 1) (DCH)
ESC [Ps c	Device attributes (DA1)
ESC [Ps ; Ps f	Cursor position [row;column} (default = [1,1]) (HVP)
ESC [Ps g	Tab clear
	Ps= 0 Clear current column (default)
	Ps= 3 Clear all
ESC [Ps h	Mode set (SET)
	Ps= 4 Insert mode (IRM)
	Ps= 2 0 Automatic linefeed (LNM)
ESC [Ps I	Mode Reset (RST)
	Ps= 4 Insert mode (IRM)
	Ps= 2 0 Automatic linefeed (LNM)
ESC [Ps m	Character attributes (SGR)
	Ps= 0 Normal (default)
	Ps= 1 Blink (appears as Bold)
	Ps= 4 Underscore
	Ps= 5 Bold
	Ps= 7 Inverse
ESC [3 Ps m	Set foreground color

Table D-2 *(continued)*

Key Sequence	Description
ESC [4 Ps m	Set background color Ps= 0 Black Ps= 1 Red Ps= 2 Green Ps= 3 Yellow Ps= 4 Blue Ps= 5 Magenta Ps= 6 Cyan Ps= 7 White
ESC [1 0 0 m	Set default background and foreground colors
ESC [Ps n	Device status report (DSR) Ps= 5 Status report ESC [0 n OK Ps= 6 Report cursor position (CPR) [row;column] as ESC [r ; c R
ESC [Ps ; Ps r	Set scrolling region [top;bottom] (default=full size of window) (DECSTRBM)
ESC [Ps x	Request terminal parameters (DECREQTPARM)
ESC [? Ps h	DEC private mode set (DECSET) Ps= 1 Application cursor keys (DECCKM) Ps= 4 Smooth (slow) scroll (DECSCLM) Ps= 5 Reverse video (DECSCNM) Ps= 6 Origin mode (DECOM) Ps= 7 Wraparound mode (DECAWM) Ps= 9 Send mouse row/column on button press Ps= 3 8 Enter Tektronix mode (DECTEK) Ps= 4 4 Turn on margin bell Ps= 4 5 Reverse-wraparound mode Ps= 4 6 Start logging Ps= 4 7 Use alternate screen buffer
ESC [? Ps I	DEC private mode reset (DECRST) Ps= 1 Normal cursor keys (DECCKM)

Table D-2 *(continued)*

Key Sequence	Description
ESC [? Ps I *(cont.)*	Ps= 4 Jump (fast) scroll (DECSCLM)
	Ps= 5 Normal video (DECSCNM)
	Ps= 6 Normal cursor mode (DECOM)
	Ps= 7 No wraparound mode (DECAWM)
	Ps= 9 Don't send mouse row/column on button press
	Ps= 4 4 Turn Off Margin Bell
	Ps= 4 5 No reverse-wraparound mode
	Ps= 4 6 Stop logging
	Ps= 4 7 Use normal screen buffer
ESC [? Ps r	Restore DEC Private Mode
	Ps= 1 Normal/application cursor keys (DECCKM)
	Ps= 4 Jump (fast)/smooth scroll (DECSCLM)
	Ps= 5 Normal/reverse video (DECSCNM)
	Ps= 6 Normal/origin cursor mode (DECOM)
	Ps= 7 No wraparound/wraparound mode (DECAWM)
	Ps= 9 Don't send/send mouse row/column on button press
	Ps= 4 4 Turn off/on margin bell
	Ps= 4 5 Reverse-wraparound/reverse-wraparound mode
	Ps= 4 6 Stop/start logging
	Ps= 4 7 Use normal/alternate screen buffer
ESC [? Ps s	Save DEC Private Mode
	Ps= 1 Normal/application cursor keys (DECCKM)
	Ps= 4 Jump (fast)/smooth scroll (DECSCLM)
	Ps= 5 Normal/reverse video (DECSCNM)
	Ps= 6 Normal/origin cursor mode (DECOM)
	Ps= 7 No wraparound/wraparound mode (DECAWM)
	Ps= 9 Don't send/send mouse row/column on button press
	Ps= 4 4 Turn off/on margin bell
	Ps= 4 5 Reverse-wraparound/reverse-wraparound mode
	Ps= 4 6 Stop/start logging
	Ps= 4 7 Use normal/alternate screen buffer
ESC [Ps ; Pt BEL	Set text parameters

Table D-2 *(continued)*

Key Sequence	Description
ESC [Ps ; Pt BEL	Ps= 0 Change window name and title to Pt
(cont.)	Ps= 1 Change window name to Pt Ps= 2 Change window title to Pt Ps= 4 6 Change log file to Pt
ESC c	Full reset (RIS)
ESC] 3; BEL	Disable window resizing (ignored if the **-rs** option or **cursesResize** is true)
ESC] 4; BEL	Enable window resizing

APPENDIX E

Guide to Xmenu

INSTALLING XMENU

The installation script for Xmenu is fairly well automated. It installs the Xmenu files in the proper directories (see Appendix A) and provides an opportunity for initial configuration.

The only requirement for the user is to copy the **tar** file that contains Xmenu to an appropriate directory on the machine receiving the installation. If you are not sure what directory you want to use, create a temporary directory and use that. If, however, you know where you want to install the software, change to a directory one level up in the hierarchy. For example, if you want to create **/usr/xmenu**, change to **/usr**. Then copy the **tar** file to **/usr** and run the following command:

```
tar xovf xmenu
```

This **tar** command installs and creates three subdirectories. If, for example, you selected /usr/xmenu, you would now have the following directories:

- **/usr/xmenu**—contains the scripts that service the Xmenu menus, plus subdirectories.
- **/usr/xmenu/bitmaps**—contains bitmaps for the Xmenu menus and for Xterms used with the menus.
- **/usr/xmenu/palettes**—contains alternative color resources that you can use through the Xmenu menus.
- **/usr/xmenu/misc**—contains miscellaneous scripts not used in the Xmenu menus, but useful for command line users.
- **/usr/xmenu/menus**—contains the Xmenu menus broken down into smaller units, so you can configure a smaller version of **.mwmrc** if you want.

The install script also prompts you for information on environment variables used with Xmenu. The following descriptions tell you what you need to know about these environment variables:

- $XMENU—Users can choose to use the $XMENU environment variable so that the Xmenu software knows where to look for files. This is a good weapon for anyone doing initial configuration. If you like, you can also set your system path to include the Xmenu directories. The Xmenu installation script does not set your system path. Finally, if you don't like $XMENU as a name for an environment variable, the installation script lets you specify a different variable.
- $XAPPLRESDIR—This is a standard X environment variable and one relied on heavily by Xmenu. The reason is that Xmenu stores Xterm resources in $XAPPLRESDIR/**XTerm**. If you already have an **XTerm** file in $XAPPLRESDIR, the installation script does not modify it. During normal use of the Xmenu software, however, the **XTerm** file will be modified. As a result, keyboard translations should not be edited in this file. The installation script does check for the existence of the "translations" resource keyword, and if it finds it, displays a message to the user. The message tells the user that a separate file called **XTerm.keys** should be created in the $XAPPLRESDIR.

There are a few requirements not administered by the installation script. In addition to ensuring proper file access permissions for all directories and files, the desktop administrator must make sure that the system path points to the $XMENU directory if he or she has decided not to use the $XMENU variable. If you have Xmenu diskettes, refer to the release notes in the **readme** file for additional concerns. Other definite areas of concern are:

- The **.cshrc** file must be modified for C shell users to take advantage of the *Path* Xterm.
- Installations for multiple users on the same system must be configured by the desktop administrator.

To edit the **.cshrc** file, follow the examples in the *Path Xterm—C Shell Only* section of Chapter 9.

USING XSHELL

This section of the appendix provides a quick reference to the Xmenu menus. Each menu item is listed according to the menu on which it appears, and in the order in which it appears. Only the three root windows, as initially configured, are described. This omits the default window menu, which is fairly self-evident, and special menus created by automatic configuration (see Chapter 10).

The Xmenu menus, as shipped on the distribution diskette, use a unique format for presenting menu items. On top-level menus, all items are flush right, giving the menus a distinctive appearance. See Figure E-1.

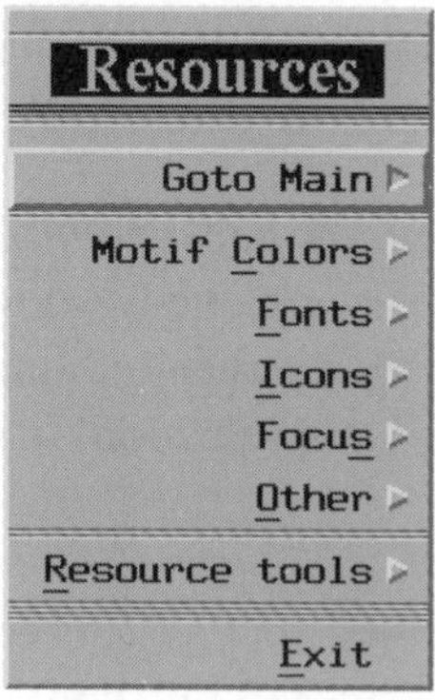

Figure E-1 The *Resources Menu*.

In cases when top-level menus group items together, the first item in the grouping provides the full menu name. For example, on the *Resources Menu*, the *Motif Colors* item is fully spelled out. The subsequent four items—*Fonts*, *Icons*, *Focus*, and *Other*—drop the word Motif. However, in referring to the menus, the full item would be used, meaning *Fonts* becomes *Motif Fonts*. This is actually a minor point, but it might help you as you read the following sections that document the menus.

Resources Menu

The *Resources Menu* focuses primarily on resources associated with the Motif window manager. Additionally, the *Resource tools* menu provides options that use X clients to manipulate resources, including **appres**, **xprop** and **xrdb**. The _Resources Menu also includes the *Exit* option, because it is traditional to place it on the root window menu associated with the left mouse button. The *Restart Motif* option has been relocated from traditional ground, however, and appears on the *Resources tools* menu.

Goto Main. For users who habitually use the left mouse button, the *Goto main* option lets you slide through the three root menus. The *Main Menu* has an identical option, which lets you slide to the *Xterm Menu.*

Motif colors. This option presents a submenu with an extensive set of choices to change colors associated with Motif resource components. Note that the *Other* option is the broadest selection you can make, but it is overridden by choices from any of the other options on the submenu.

Motif colors»Palettes. Gives you the choice of using any of several preset color schemes. The choices, which include such goodies as *Gone camping* and *Radioactive*, allow you to vary color atmosphere in one broad sweep.

Motif colors»Window background. Setting the window background color affects the frame around the window and the titlebar and optional window matte. If you set the titlebar and matte with another option, doing so overrides the effect of this selection. In other words, only the exterior frame is affected.

Motif colors»Window foreground. Setting the window foreground color affects the text displayed in windows. The foreground color is also used in establishing contrasting shadows for the frame and mattes. Note that the color of the text in the titlebar can also be controlled at the titlebar level, but no menu option is available for this. The only titlebar resource available sets the background color.

Motif colors»Window titlebar. Setting the window titlebar color sets the background color in the titlebar. This option overrides other options, such as *Motif colors»Window background.* Note that you can also set the active titlebar color with the *Motif colors» Active titlebar* option.

Motif colors»Window matte. Setting the window matte color specifies a color for the option window matte. This setting takes precedence over all other color settings that affect the matte color. To create a matte for windows, see the *Motif Other»Matte width* option.

Motif colors»Active background. Setting the active background color affects the frame around the window and the titlebar for windows with the current focus. It does not affect the color of the optional matte. You will override this option if you use the *Motif colors»Active titlebar* option.

Motif colors»Active foreground. The active foreground option affects the text displayed in the window manager components of the window with the focus. The components consist of the titlebar and the icon label.

Motif colors»Menu background. This option sets the background colors for all Motif menus. The only exception occurs if you have previously set a menu color using the menu's name in a resource statement. This is a more specific setting and therefore takes precedence over *Motif colors»Menu background*. Also note that some background colors look better than others with menus. The reason for this is the 3-D effect built into menus.

Motif colors»Menu foreground. This option sets the foreground colors for all Motif menus. As with the option to set the menu background, you can override this option for specific menus by using the menu name in a resource statement. Again, note that the colors you choose for menus can produce undesirable results given the 3-D contrast of menus.

Motif colors»Icon background. This option sets the background color for icons. In some Motif implementations, using this option enhances the appearances of icon bitmaps. If you do not set this option, the *Motif colors»Other background* is the controlling option.

Motif colors»Icon foreground. This option sets the foreground color for icons. In some Motif implementations, using this option enhances the appearances of icon bitmaps. If you do not set this option, the *Motif colors»Other foreground* is the controlling option.

Motif colors»Icon background. Using this option sets the background colors for feedback windows, which the window manager displays in several cases, such as when you restart Motif. If you do not set this option, the *Motif colors»Other background* is the controlling option.

Motif colors»Icon foreground. Using this option sets the foreground colors for feedback windows, which the window manager displays in several cases, such as when you restart Motif. If you do not set this option, the *Motif colors»Other foreground* is the controlling option.

Motif Colors»Other background. This is the most general setting for the Motif background color resource. If you were to set the background with this option—and at the same time, refrain from using any other options to set the background—all Motif components would reflect this color. For some components, such as the Motif icon box, this is the only resource option that changes the background color.

Motif Colors»Other foreground. This is the most general setting for the Motif foreground color resource. If you were to set the foreground with this option—and at the same time, refrain from using any other options to set the foreground—all Motif components would reflect this color. For some components, such as the Motif icon box, this is the only resource option that changes the foreground color.

Motif Fonts»Window frame. This option lets you set the font for the text that appears in the window titlebar. As shipped, the Xmenu menus offer the fixed, Courier, Times, Helvetica, and avant-garde fonts. Note that the larger the font size you select, the larger the resulting titlebar. Depending on your preferences, a larger titlebar can add an appealing and distinctive appearance to your windows.

Motif Fonts»Menu text. With this option, you can set the font for the text used in menus. The Xmenu software, as shipped, offers only the fixed and Courier fonts. The reason for the limited choice is proportionally spaced fonts. Other fonts, such as Times and Helvetica, often produce unacceptable spacing when used in menus.

Motif Fonts»Icon labels. Using this option lets you change the fonts for the text that appears in icon labels. The Xmenu menus, as shipped, offer fixed, Courier, Times and Helvetica fonts. For typical-size icons—50x50, or 64x64—you should use smaller fonts, such as 10- and 12-point fonts.

Motif Fonts»Feedback windows. This option sets the font for feedback windows that appear during certain operations in Motif. For example, when you restart the window manager, a feedback window appears if the appropriate resource is set (see *Motif Other»Show feedback*). The Xmenu software uses fixed, Courier, Times, Helvetica, and avant-garde fonts in sizes up to 24 points.

Motif Icons»Placement. Selecting this option lets you specify how the window manager places icons. Choosing the *Automatic* option places icons along a specified edge of the screen (see the *Motif Icons»Parking lot* option). Choosing the *User-only* option leaves icons positioned in the same area as their associated windows.

Motif Icons»Parking lot. This option informs the window manager where it should position automatically placed icons (see *Motif Icons»Placement*). The submenu that displays when you choose this option gives you eight possibilities, which are illustrated using bitmaps to represent each choice.

Motif Icons»Screen offset. This option allows you to specify the distance in pixels that icons are positioned from the screen edge. The submenu choices range from zero to five pixels.

Motif Icons»Icon box. This option leads to an extensive submenu. From the submenu you can choose whether or not to use the icon box, via the *Open* and *Close* options. If you do use the icon box, the rest of the options on the submenu let you modify its appearance and behavior. The following options are available:

Open	Activate the icon box.
Close	Terminate the icon box.
Title	Change the icon box title.
Size	Change the default size of the icon box.
Matte	Add a matte to the icon box.
Scrollbars	Add horizontal and/or vertical scrollbars.
Decorations	Add or remove icon box components.

Motif Icons»Fade icon. Selecting this option lets you specify whether or not to cause icons to be "faded" when their associated window is open. Only works with icon box icons.

Motif Icons»Decoration. With this option, you can specify the decorations for icons. Decorations are window manger components. The relevant icon decorations are image, label, image and label, and active label. The latter component expands to show the full text in an icon label whenever the icon gets the focus.

Motif Icons»Image size. Basically, this option lets you specify the size of an icon—although technically, it only increases the size of the image area in the icon. Of course, the other parts of the icon—the label and frame—also increase in size. The preset sizes on the submenu are 35x50, 50x35, 50x50, 64x64, 96x96, and 128x128.

Motif Icons»Post menu. Choosing *True* tells Motif to leave the icon menu posted when you click on the icon. Choosing the *False* submenu option removes this behavior.

Motif Focus»Explicit. Choosing this option sets the keyboard focus policy for the window manager. When set to explicit, the window manager requires that the user actually click in a window to transfer the keyboard focus to the window. At the same time, the window manager makes the window the active window and any active colors become apparent. The *Motif Focus»Explicit* submenu has the following options:

Default	Click to focus and the window rises.
Raise	Click to focus and user can set whether window rises or not, as well as the delay before the window rises.
Normalize	User can decide whether the window receives the focus when it is normalized.
Global	This option transfers focus to a globally active window when it becomes available.
Startup	This option transfers the focus to a window when it is first opened.

Motif Focus»Pointer. Choosing this option sets the keyboard focus policy for the window manager. When set to implicit, the window manager requires you to move the mouse into a window in order to transfer the focus (as well as make it active). A submenu appears when you choose *Motif Focus»Pointer.* The following items are on the submenu:

Default	Move the mouse to transfer the focus. The window does not rise.
Raise	Move the mouse to transfer the focus. Additional options let you specify whether the window rises.
Global	This option transfers focus to a globally active window when it becomes available.

Motif Focus»Colormap. This option lets you determine how the window manager transfers the colormap between applications. A colormap is simply a section of memory storing color information. Each application can have a colormap. On the *Motif Focus»Colormap* submenu, you can select *Keyboard*, which automatically transfers the colormap focus to the window with the keyboard focus; or *Explicit*, which requires a specific transfer of the focus. The way to do this in the Xmenu software is to use the *SetColormap* option, which appears on the default window menu.

Motif Other»Interactive placement. This option lets you select how you position windows when they first open. Choosing *Yes* on the submenu activates the Motif interactive placement feature, which provides you with a "tracking rectangle" to position the window. The *No* option turns off interactive placement if it is activated.

Motif Other»Resize border. This option lets you specify the width of the resize border, or outer frame, of standard Motif windows. The submenu offers preset sizes of 5, 10, 15, 20, and 25. Note that the smaller the size selected, the more difficult it becomes to actually grab the frame with the mouse pointer. When you have grabbed the frame the mouse pointer changes to a resize pointer, unless you alter this behavior with the *Motif Other»Show resize* option.

Motif Other»Matte width. With this option, you can set the matte width to any reasonable size. A matte is an inner frame in a Motif Window and resembles the matte in a mounted photograph. The *Motif Other»Matte width* option displays a text input window in which you can enter the matte size in pixels. Specifying a value of zero turns off the matte altogether.

Motif Other»Maximum client. This option lets you set the maximum size of the client areas of a Motif window. The client area is the work area of your window, including the optional matte. By default, the maximum client size is twice the size of the root window. To change the size, the *Motif Other»Maximum client* option provides a text input window. You must enter both the window width and height. For example, **1000x800** and **1024x1024** are each valid input.

Motif Other»Maximum window. With this option, you can set the maximum size of a standard Motif window. When you select the option a text input window appears. In the window, enter a value that specifies the window width and height. For example, **1000x800** and **1024x1024** are each valid input.

Motif Other»Limit resize. If you select the *True* option on the submenu, you cannot resize a window beyond the maximum size as specified in *Motif Other»Maximum* window. Selecting *False* lets you resize the window up to the default maximum, which is more than twice the size of the screen.

Motif Other»Show feedback. This option presents a submenu of feedback components in the window manager. For example, *Move* option, when set to true, will display a box containing the coordinates of a window during a move operation. You can add and subtract any of the options. Each time you select an option, it toggles its previous state.

Motif Other»Window closing. With this option, you can specify whether double clicking the mouse on the menu button (upper left-hand corner of the window frame) automatically closes the window. If you want this behavior, choose *Double-click*. Otherwise, choose *Explicit*.

Motif Other»Window menu closing. This option lets you specify whether the window menu displays when you simply click on the window menu button (upper left-hand corner of the window frame). The alternative behavior requires you to press and hold the mouse button and pull down the menu. The submenu options are *On-click* and *Pull-down*.

Motif Other»Show resize. If you don't want resize pointers to appear when you resize a window, use this option. The resize pointers assist you in establishing the direction in which you are resizing a window. Selecting *Yes* removes the resize pointers.

Motif Other»Opaque window moves. With this option, you can determine whether the full image or just an outline of a window moves when you perform a move operation. The submenu options are *Yes* for opaque moves and *No* for an outline.

Motif Other»Leave pointer at menu. Primarily for keyboard-only users, this option lets you specify whether the window pointer moves to the middle of the window when you select a move or resize operation from the window menu. The submenu offers *Yes* and *No* options. Selecting *No* maintains the default behavior, which is to leave the pointer in the area of the window menu.

Motif Other»Stipple window text. For users with monochrome systems, this option lets you turn off text stippling in the window titlebar and in feedback windows. Selecting the *Yes* option draws "clean" text. Selecting the *No* option tells the window manager to stipple the text by drawing it over the existing background. On some monochrome systems, slight blurring results from the technique.

Motif Other»3D adjustments. This option determines the shading mix between the background and foreground colors. In general, it is not necessary to make 3-D adjustments, but on monochrome systems, they might enhance window sharpness. For best results, experiment with the different values, which range from 0/100 to 100/0. The ratios adjust the amount of background to foreground color in the pixmaps from which the 3-D effect around the edges of windows is created.

Motif Other»Button bindings. This option lets you change between different sets of button bindings. Names for button bindings must correspond to defined bindings in the **.mwmrc** configuration file. The option displays a text input box, in which you supply the button bindings name. If you specify an invalid name, Motif supplies its own very limited set of button bindings.

The *Default* option lets you restore your system's default button bindings, which are defined as **DefaultButtonBindings** in **.mwmrc**.

Motif Other»Key bindings. This option lets you change between different sets of keyboard bindings. Names for key bindings must correspond to defined bindings in the **.mwmrc** configuration file. The option displays a text input box, in which you supply the key bindings name. If you specify an invalid name, Motif supplies its own very limited set of key bindings. The *Default* option lets you restore your system's default key bindings, which are defined as **DefaultKeyBindings** in **.mwmrc**.

Motif Other»Configuration file. This option lets you specify a file other than $HOME/**.mwmrc** as the window manager's configuration file. The option displays a text input window so you can supply the name of the configuration file. All in all, this is a convenient way to change between different menu systems.

Resource tools»Database load. With this option, you can update the resource manager using the contents of the **.Xdefaults** file in your home directory. Alternatively, you can specify that you want to use **.Xdefaults.bak**, or a file that you name. The submenu has three options: *.Xdefaults*, *Named file*, and *Backup file*. The *Named file* option displays a text input window.

Resource tools-Database save. This option lets you specify when changes that you make to your Motif environment are saved. The first two options on the submenu are the eponymous *Always* and *Never*. The third option lets you save changes on demand. The fourth option, *Save file*, displays a text input window so you can specify the name of a file.

Resource tools»Database query. Using this option lets you view currently set resources. On the submenu, the *All* option displays all general resources known to X resource manager. The *Diff* option uses the UNIX **diff** command to compare the currently set resources to the contents of your $HOME/**.Xdefaults** file. The resulting output displays the differences between the two sets, or issues a message saying there are no differences. The last option, *Named*, lets you query by resource name. A text input window is displayed so you can supply the name.

Resource tools»Database format. The submenu displayed by this option provides different ways to sort and clean up your default resources file, usually $HOME/**.Xdefaults**. Here is a brief explanation of each option:

Sort	Performs an alphabetical sort, treating uppercase and lowercase letters the same.
Strip spaces	Removes unnecessary spaces. Use this option repeatedly to remove multiple spaces.
Strip tabs	Removes unnecessary tabs. Use this option repeatedly to remove multiple tabs.
Strip tabs/spaces	Removes tabs and spaces. Use in conjunction with other options, or repeatedly for multiple tabs and spaces.
Trailing spaces	Removes only trailing spaces. Use repeatedly to remove multiple trailing spaces.

Resource tools»Reset behavior. This option resets the appearance and behavior of Motif to its internal defaults. If you are experimenting with different resources, this option provides a convenient way to check your work against the defaults.

Resource tools»Restart Motif. This option restarts Motif. Anyone changing Motif resources will quickly become familiar with this option, because you must select it in order for your changes to be implemented.

Exit. This option exits the window manager and your current X session. Use *Exit* when you want to return to the UNIX prompt, or to the X login screen, depending on how your system starts X.

Main Menu

In Xmenu, the *Main Menu* offers features that give you control of events at the system level. This is the menu that you should think of first when you want to display an image on the root window, recall a previous menu command, record snapshots of your worksession, or do any number of other things. Figure E-2 shows the *Main Menu* and submenus of the *ImageShow* option.

Several items on the *Main Menu* are ultimately the responsibility of the individual site to configure. These are *X clients*, *Applications*, *Desktop manager*, and *Help*. The latter item does call a simple script to display a help message, but a full help system is beyond the scope of this book. As shipped, the other menu items come with suggestions, and you may even be satisfied with the *X clients* menu.

Goto Xterm. For users who habitually use the left mouse button, the *Goto Xterm* option lets you slide to the next root menu. The *Resources Menu* has an identical option, which lets you slide to the *Main Menu*.

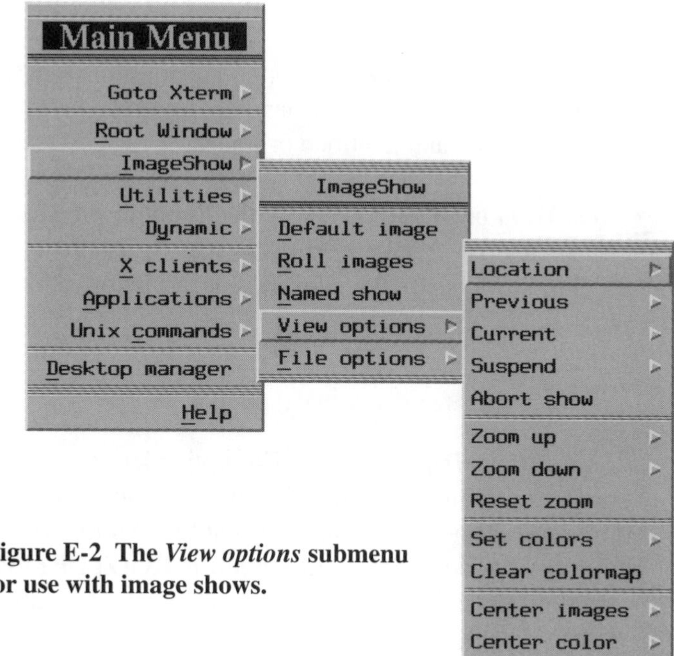

Figure E-2 The *View options* submenu for use with image shows.

Root Window»Bitmaps. Using this option, you can select one of several bitmap images to display on the root background. The Xmenu menus come with 10 images displayed in bitmap form in the menu. You simply move the menu slider to the image that you want to load.

Root Window»Patterns. This option lets you select one of several bitmap patterns to display on the root background. The patterns are derived from the standard set shipped with the X Window System. The Xmenu menus set up 14 patterns, which appear as bitmaps in the menu. To use the menu, move the menu slide to the pattern that you want to load and release the mouse.

Root Window»Colors. With this option, you can set the root window background and foreground colors. The option is designed for use with bitmaps and patterns (see *Root Window»Patterns* and *Root Window»Colors*). If you want a solid color on the root window, select the blank pattern from the *Root Window»Patterns* option.

Root Window»Pointers. This option lets you select a pointer for use on the root window. The submenu offers seven different pointers from the standard release of the X Window System. Note that the pointer you select here does not affect the pointers associated with X programs and applications.

Root Window»Default. This option restores the root window to the default gray, stippled pattern. It is a handy option if you want to clear the root window of an unwanted bitmap or image.

Root Window»Screen saver. With this option, you can specify the intervals between screen blanking. The screen saver feature is a built-in feature of the X Window System. For additional information, refer to the **xset** command in your X documentation.

ImageShow»Default image. This option lets you display a full color image on the root window. In order for this option to work, you or an administrator must specify the default image in your $HOME/**.xmenu** file. A valid example of a line to add to $HOME/**.xmenu** is **ROOTDEFIMAGE:/usr/images/stars.gif**. You can use any of several image formats, depending on your image display software. The Xmenu menus are designed to use **xloadimage**, which supports GIF, TIFF, and PostScript images, among others.

ImageShow»Roll images. This option lets you begin an image show that presents a series of images, changing the images approximately one per minute. Through other *ImageShow* options, you can specify whether the image show runs on the root window or in a standard window. It is necessary to specify a path and file specification for in $HOME/**.xmenu** for the image show. A valid example of a line to add to $HOME/**.xmenu** is **ROOTSLIDES:/usr/images/*.gif**.

ImageShow»Named show. Selecting this option presents a text input window in which you can specify a single filename for an image, or a file specification for a group of images. For example, you could specify **/usr/images/*.gif** or $MYIMAGES/***.gif**. When the image show begins, a separate window appears as an icon. You can open the icon if you want to monitor the progress of your image software. For example, **xloadimage** displays filenames and color values, among other things.

ImageShow»View options. This option displays a submenu with numerous options for modifying image shows. You can do such things as specify that the image show run in a standard window versus on the root window; change the number of colors used by the image show; and suspend and abort the show. Note that the menu is designed to work with the **xloadimage** software. The following list contains a description of each submenu option.

Location	Lets you specify whether to run the show on the root window or in a standard window.
Previous	Redisplays the previous image. Additional options let you specify the root window or a standard window.
Current	Redisplays the current image. Options let you redisplay on the root window or in a standard window. Presumably, you would use this option to view the current image after having returned to a previous image.
Suspend	Two submenu options let you either suspend the current show, or resume the show after you have previously suspended it.
Abort show	Terminates the image show and leaves the current image displayed.
Zoom up	Lets you specify the zoom level in increments of 10, ranging from 10 through 100. Choosing 100 doubles the size of the image.
Zoom down	Lets you specify the level at which you can decrease the size of an image. Increments range from 90 to 10.
Reset zoom	Resets the zoom level to normal size.
Set colors	Lets you specify the number of colors in an image show. The larger numbers—128, 160, and 192—might cause colormap conflicts in other windows.
Clear colormap	For systems that support a command to reinitialize the colormap.
Center image	Lets you specify whether the image should be centered and matted like a photograph.
Center color	Sets the color for the matte area in a centered image.

ImageShow»File options. This option displays a submenu with several options for capturing and storing parts of images to file. This feature is provided because you might display image shows and view them in a passive manner, but happen to see something that you want to retain. (The source of the images could be a remote system, or a CD disk, so you might not be able to simply note the filename and view it later.) The following submenu options are available:

Grab	Captures all or part of an image. An outline box appears when you select this option. Move the box to the image area you want to capture and press the left mouse button. The *Grab box* option lets you set different sizes.
Save	Saves the captured image to a file. A cross-hair pointer appears when you select this option. Place the pointer over the window and image is saved to a file specified by IMAGE-INBUFFER in $HOME/**.xmenu**.
Display	Lets you display the previously captured image.
Print	Lets you print the previously captured image.
Mag level	Changes the magnification at which the image is captured. A level of 1 is normal size. Other levels range from 200 to 500 percent, represented by 2, 3, 4 and 5.
Grab box	Lets you change the size of the outline box used to capture an image. Sizes range from 100x100 to 500x500.

Utilities»!!. This option lets you repeat the previous command that you executed using the Xmenu menus.

Utilities»!-1. This option lets you repeat the menu command that you executed before the previous command.

Utilities»!-2. This option lets you repeat the menu command that you executed two commands previously.

Utilities»Refresh. This option refreshes the entire screen. Use it when an unruly window or some system event has caused unwanted messages or graphics effects to appear on the screen.

Utilities»Save buffer. With this option, you can save the contents of the cut and paste buffer. By default, the buffer is saved to a file in your home directory called **cut.xsh.**

Utilities»Record. This option gives you a way to make a graphic record of your work session. The submenu supports three options—*On*, *Off*, and *In-*

terval. Selecting *Off* ends the recording session. Selecting *On* begins the recording session and the system makes a screen capture of your display at the interval you specify in minutes. The preset values are 5, 10, 15, 20, and 30.

Dynamic»Network hosts. This option presents you with a relatively current list of network hosts. Selecting the name of a host from the submenu begins a **telnet** session with that host. The list of hosts is updated when you select the *Dynamic»Configure* option and restart Motif.

Dynamic»Logged-in users. With this option, you get a relatively current list of logged in users (depending on how much time has elapsed since you last used the *Dynamic»Configure* option). Selecting a user name from the submenu begins a talk session with the user. A new window appears on your screen for the talk session.

Dynamic»Images. This option presents a list of images that is intentionally random. The list is updated each time you use the *Dynamic»Configure* option, whether or not you use it solely for the purpose of updating images, or for updating information. The option requires that the IMAGEPATH variable be set in $HOME/**.xmenu**.

X clients. This option displays a list of X clients available on your system. The list will vary from site to site. As shipped, the Xmenu menus include the **bitmap**, **ico**, **xbiff**, **xcalc**, **xclock**, **xeyes**, and **xload** clients. You can add or subtract clients by editing the **SystemClients** menu in the Xmenu version of **.mwmrc**. Clients are usually located in **/usr/bin/X11**.

Applications. This option displays a list of commercial software that you can run from your system. This is a highly site-specific option and should be configured by advanced users and system administrators.

Desktop manager. This is a site-specific menu item. If you don't use a desktop manager, remove the *Desktop manager* item from MainMenu in your **.mwmrc** file.

Help. This option presents a simple help screen that summarizes the Xmenu menu and tells you how to get further help. The help screen is also the official copyright screen and should remain as part of the software.

Xterms Menu

The *Xterms Menu* provides a selection of different Xterms, options to set colors, fonts, and other resources for Xterms, plus utilities for working with

Xterms. Most of the Xterms that you can select have a single key feature, which is appealing to some users. For example, the *Xterms»Path* option is for C shell users who like to see their prompt in the titlebar. Another example is the *DatePlus* Xterm, which is for users of any shell, and which runs a cron process that updates the time and date in the titlebar.

Unlike the two other root menus, the *Xterms Menu* does not have a slider option. If you want this option, insert the following lines at the beginning of the XtermMenus menu in your **.mwmrc** file:

```
" "                                f.nop
"       Motif Resources"      _M   f.menu ResourcesMenu
no_label                           f.separator
no_label                           f.separator
```

If you decide to use this option, Motif prevents you from popping up menus in circles. In other words, once you have displayed a menu, you cannot slide through the loop and redisplay the menu. Notice that Motif grays out the associated menu when this is a possibility.

One more word about using Xterms: If possible, don't use more than are necessary. It is easy to forget about an Xterm misplaced in a crowded icon box, or just lost on the desktop. The reason for this is you can use the *Xterm Menu* to create some memory-intensive Xterms (and you should be judicious if you do this). In the following sections, note will be made of an Xterm's memory disposition.

Xterms»Default. This Xterm uses the **8x13bold** font with a gray background and black foreground. These resources are hardcoded in the loader script and cannot be changed via the Xmenu menus. The resource name for the Xterm is **default**, although **Xmenu** appears in the titlebar. The Xmenu default Xterm uses minimum memory for an Xterm. It bears a close resemblance to the default Xterm as shipped with the X Window System.

Xterms»Date. With this Xterm, you get a display of the date and time in the titlebar. The Xterm accepts the standard output of the UNIX ***date*** command. The color, font, and other resources for the *Date* Xterm are dictated by the options you choose on other submenus on the *Xterms* menu. The *Date* Xterm has no special memory requirements.

Xterms»DatePlus. This Xterm displays a modified version of the date and time in the titlebar. In addition, it displays the hostname, user, and current ptty device for the Xterm. The *DatePlus* Xterm's resources are controlled by other submenu options. The resource name for the Xterm is Xmenu. Extra memory is used by this Xterm, because of the associated cron process.

Mainly users who don't like running a clock on their background window will appreciate the time display in the titlebar.

Xterms»Path. For C shell users only, this Xterm displays the current path in the titlebar—the GUI equivalent of displaying the path in the command prompt. You can still display the path in your command prompt, too, but if you decide to remove it, you can fill the void with the C shell's history numbering or some other command output. The resource name for the *Path* Xterm is Xmenu. Extra memory is used by this Xterm during startup, but by the time it finishes opening, memory requirements return to normal.

Xterms»Small. For variety, this Xterm displays a small window and determines its colors and other resources, including font, using a resource name of **small**. If **small** is not defined in a resource file, it will use the resources assigned to the system's default Xterm. No extra memory requirements apply to the *Small* Xterm.

Xterms»Pane. This Xterm provides a wide horizontal client area. Besides being named *Pane*, the Xterm uses resources assigned to it under the resource name of **pane**. It displays the hostname, user, and date in the titlebar. It is a convenient window to summon when you need to display very wide output. The window has no special memory requirements.

Xterms»Full. This option displays an Xterm about two-thirds the size of the root window. The Xterm uses the date and time output identical to the *Date* Xterm. The resource name for the Xterm is **full**. The window has no special memory requirements. It is mainly for users who like a large window because they like to see as much data as possible.

Xterms»Document. The *Document* Xterm is a little less than half the size of the root window. It resembles the size of a window you would find in a word processing or electronic publishing program. It displays the hostname, user, and date in the titlebar. Its resource name is **document**. Again, it is for users who prefer large amounts of data in a window, such as a page of a document. The window has no special memory requirements.

Xterms»2-3-4. This option lets you execute two, three, or four Xterms at the same time. The Xterms are almost identical to Xmenu's *Default* Xterm. The only difference is the number of the window in the titlebar. Otherwise, like the *Default* Xterm, these Xterms use the **Xmenu** resource name. No special requirements exist for this option.

Xterms»Sysadm. The *Sysadm* Xterms display information in the titlebar for doing configuration work on the system. The submenu choices are *Who*, which displays current users logged; *Console*, which starts an Xterm that displays system messages; and *Ethernet*, which displays the Ethernet address in the titlebar. The *Who* and *Ethernet* Xterms use the **Xmenu** resource name. The *Console* Xterm uses **console** as a resource name.

Xterms»Logterms. This submenu gives you a choice of four different Xterms that support log files. A log file records all activity in an Xterm session. As a result, slightly more memory is used for Xterms that create logfiles. All of the logterms use the Xmenu resource name. The available options are:

Personal	Lets you name the logfile in a text input window.
Date	Creates a logfile name with an extension consisting of the month, day, and year. For example: log.090412
Filter	Creates a logfile that records only lines of text with your user name in them. The filename is the same as if you chose the *Date* option.
Maximum	Creates two logfiles: One contains only lines of text with the user name in it; the second creates a standard logfile. Both use the same filenaming method as in the *Date* option. The standard file is **log1** plus the month, day, and year.

Xterms-Named Xterm. This option displays a text input window and lets you specify the resource name for the Xterm. If you have read about other Xterm options, you know resource names such as **Xmenu**, **full**, and **pane** can be used. You can also create your own names and define colors, fonts, and other resources in your resource files. Memory requirements for named Xterms vary.

Colors»Window background. With this option, you can set the background color of the next Xterm that you summon. Note that the option doesn't affect Xterms currently in use. The option does not increase memory requirements.

Colors»Window foreground. With this option, you can set the foreground (text) color of the next Xterm that you summon. Note that the option doesn't affect Xterms currently in use. The option does not increase memory requirements.

Colors»Scrollbar background. With this option, you can set the scrollbar background color of the next Xterm that you summon. Note that the option doesn't affect Xterms currently in use. Memory requirements are not affected.

Colors»Scrollbar foreground. With this option, you can set the scrollbar foreground color of the next Xterm that you summon. Note that the option doesn't affect Xterms currently in use. Memory requirements are not affected.

Colors»Cursor color. This option lets you set the cursor color for the next Xterm that you load. The submenu has two options: *Same as foreground*, which sets the cursor color to the text foreground color; and *Set color*, which lets you specify a color. Note that the option does not have an effect until the next Xterm is loaded. Memory requirements are not affected.

Colors»Pointer color. This option lets you set the color of the mouse pointer. The submenu has three options: *Same as foreground*, which sets the pointer to the text foreground color; *Set foreground*, which sets the foreground component of the pointer; and *Set background*, which sets the background component, or outline, of the pointer. The option does not have an effect until the Xterm is loaded. Memory requirements are not affected.

Fonts. This option displays a submenu with available monospaced fonts for Xterms, including fixed, Courier, Sony, and Schumacher. Font sizes range from 12 to 24 points. Selecting a font causes the next Xterm loaded to reflect the change. There are only minimal extra memory requirements for using larger fonts.

Scroll»Scrollbar. This option activates the Xterm scrollbar for the next Xterm loaded. The scrollbar widget uses slightly more memory, but is well worth the expense. You can also activate the scrollbar of a current Xterm by using the *Enable Scrollbar* option on the *VT Options* menu. Press Ctrl-Button 2 to display the *VT Options* menu.

Scroll»Scrollbar size. With this option, you can set the scrollbar size. The submenu offers preset sizes of 5, 10, 15, 20, 30 pixels. The changes take effect with the next Xterm you load. Slight additional memory is used for larger scrollbars.

Scroll»Buffer size. This option lets you change the buffer size associated with an Xterm's scrollbar. The submenu offers size options ranging from 100 lines to 2000 lines. Larger buffer sizes can make heavy demands on memory. The change in buffer size takes effect for the next Xterm loaded. After loading an Xterm with a large buffer, it is advisable to use this option again to reduce the buffer size for the next Xterm, if possible.

Misc»Highlight cursor. This option lets you specify that Xterm displays a highlight—solid filled—cursor as opposed to its default outline cursor. The submenu has *No* and *Yes* options. The change takes effect with the next Xterm. Memory requirements are not affected.

Misc»Internal border. This option causes Xterm to display an internal border along the left side of the window. The submenu offers border sizes of 0, 5, 10, 15 and 20 pixels. The change takes effect with the next Xterm loaded. Memory requirements are not affected.

Misc»Margin bell. With this option, you can specify whether Xterm rings a bell when you move the cursor—or advance the cursor while typing—into the right margin area. The change takes effect with the next Xterm loaded. There is no impact on memory requirements.

Misc»Visual bell. This option causes Xterm to issue a visual warning— a quick flicker of the window background—when you move the cursor into the right margin area. The change takes effect with the next Xterm loaded. There is no impact on memory requirements.

Muse. The *Muse* option loads two Xterms and opens up a channel of communication between the two. Everything that you type and display on the first Xterm is echoed on the second Xterm. The *Muse* option is useful if you are working with multiple screens, or want to share data with a co-worker on the network. Naturally, because a second Xterm is involved, memory usage increases proportionately.

Clone. The *Clone* option reproduces an existing Xterm or other X client. If you have changed resources since loading the original Xterm or X client, the cloned version does not reflect the changes. The *Clone* option is for those times that you want a window similar to an existing one, but don't want to go through all the steps it took to set up the first one. Again, because a second Xterm is involved, memory usage increases.

INDEX

N

O

P

Q

R

S

T

Z

COMPANION DISK AVAILABLE!

A High Density 3½″ Disk is available containing the *Xshell Menus* created in this book!

DISK (High Density, 3½″) Please send me _______ copy(ies) of the Companion Disk for use with the book, Southerton: *The Shell Hacker's Guide to X and Motif,* at $15.00 each, ISBN 0-471-30431-X.

BOOK Please send me _______ copy(ies) of the book, Southerton: *The Shell Hacker's Guide to X and Motif,* at $34.95 each. ISBN 0-471-59722-8.

BOOK/DISK SET Please send me _______ copy(ies) of the book/disk for Southerton: *The Shell Hacker's Guide to X and Motif,* at $49.95 each. ISBN 0-471-59723-6.

☐ Payment Enclosed ☐ Visa ☐ MasterCard ☐ American Express

Card Number_______________________________ Expiration Date____________

Signature____

NAME____

COMPANY NAME____

ADDRESS____

CITY/STATE__________________________ ZIP CODE____________

NO POSTAGE
NECESSARY
IF MAILED
IN THE
UNITED STATES

BUSINESS REPLY MAIL
FIRST CLASS PERMIT NO. 2277 NEW YORK, N.Y.

POSTAGE WILL BE PAID BY ADDRESSEE

JOHN WILEY & SONS, INC.
Attn: Continuation Department
P.O. Box 6792
Somerset, N.J. 08875-9976